The Street Names of
Bristol

Their Origins and Meanings

2nd edition

by
Veronica Smith

BROADCAST BOOKS, BRISTOL

Cover photograph and design Sally Mundy
www.angelswing.co.uk

Printed in the UK by Cromwell Press, Trowbridge, Wilts.

Dedication

I should like to dedicate this book to my dear friend Grace Cooper, whose *A-Z History of 200 Bristol Street Names* inspired this book. She unselfishly handed over her notes and encouraged me to use all the information she had acquired. She has been totally supportive throughout and, quite apart from anything else, she is a delightful person with whom to spend time.

Acknowledgements

Special thanks must go to David Harrison, editor of the *Bristol Times,* for pushing me into the project, encouraging me when I flagged, acting as a sounding board for some of my wilder ideas, and for all the helpful suggestions he made over a prolonged period.

I should like to thank in particular Mike Hooper, who has been incredibly patient. He saved my sanity at the eleventh hour by presenting me with a wealth of information he had discovered which proved to be the key to mysteries which had been puzzling me for ages. Gratitude is also extended to Tony Brake, who solved the Glendare enigma which had been giving me sleepless nights for months. I am also very grateful to the Temple Local History Group for allowing me access to their extensive archives. I must also give special thanks to Greta Barrett for her extraordinary researches into the Canowie Road connections.

Apart from Drew Marland's contribution to the illustrations in this book, his knowledge of aircraft, Anglo-Saxon, engineering, the Welsh language, English poetry and ornithology has been absolutely invaluable, and his sense of humour has lightened many a hard-working hour. Geoff Collard and Martin Cinnamond have made valuable corrections to the text. Celia Skrine has been invaluable for her proof-reading skills and musical knowledge, and any mistakes and omissions in the text are now the publisher's and mine. I have to say, too, it has been a delight working with Catherine Mason, my publisher, and Sally Mundy, my designer, who have never failed to lift my spirits on days of dark despair!

I should also like to thank the following for their interest and invaluable contributions to the first edition:

The Amenity Society, Roger Angerson, Archivist, Society of Friends, John Balmond, Anton Bantock, Malago Society, John Bartlett and John Penny - Fishponds Historians, Ray and Holly Belsher, Ian Bishop, Bitton Historian, Les Bishop, Tony Brake, Dawn and all the staff at Bristol Central Library, Reference Section, Amanda from Bristol Housing, Alan Britton, Alan Bryant, Warmley and Cadbury Heath History Group, David and Joan Caseley, Roger Coales, Michael Cory, Andre Coutances, Colin Cradock, Joan Cuff, Elizabeth Davies, Clive Denley, Mrs Norah Francis, Valerie Gearing, Margaret Green, Colin Griffin, Lynne Haynes and Rob Archer, Bristol Street Naming Dept., Mike Hooper, Martin Jubb, W.J. Kew, Builders., Kingswood and Hanham Libraries, Julian Lea-Jones, Temple Local History Group, Pat Lindegaard, Judith Lindsay-Jubb, Downend History Society, Mr and Mrs N. Lintern, Frances Long, Long Ashton and Sea Mills Libraries, The Lord Mayor's Office, Ron Martindale, Peter Moody and Tom Humphries from Charles Church Western (ex Beazer Homes), Mike Pascoe, Clifton Historian, Dave Price (DJMP@Tesco.net), Dennis Rugman, Jonathan Rowe, Brislington Conservation, Staple Hill Library, Keith Stenner, Dave Stephenson and Andy Jones, Barton Hill History Group, Roy Stone, Ethel Thomas, Barbara Tuttiett, Kingswood History Group, UWE Fishponds, Pip Walker, Maggie Wilkes, Stockwood History Group, Mr and Mrs Wiltshire, Soundwell, and Mr G.T. Wines.

The Street Names of Bristol: Second Edition

Since the publication of first edition of The Street Names of Bristol in 2001, we have had a magnificent response from the public to our invitation to provide us with new or further information. We are indebted to the following for their invaluable and good humoured corrections:

Graham Balfry, Greta Barrett, John Bartlett, Richard Bland, Richard Brereton, Lorna Brierley, James Briggs, Mark Brookes, Stephen Byrne, S.P.Casey, Mrs Joyce Cockram, Dave Cheesley, Charles Dalglish, Dorothy Davies, Alan Demster, Ivor Doney, Rosina Gingell, Alan Gray, Mrs Margaret Green, John D.A. Griffiths, Lionel Harris, David Harrison, Mike Hooper, the Rev. Jack House, Peter L. Houlton, P.R. Langfield, Julian Lea-Jones, J.M.Longbottom, R. Martindale, Bob Matthews, Harry McPhillimy, Michael Meecham, Gerry Nichols, David Osborn, Cedric Parsons, Pam Pearce, John Penny, Fred Radnedge, Stephen Rees, Miss P.M.Roberts, Jonathan Rowe, Moira Sage, Celia Skrine, Paul Smith, Carol Thorne, Ann Tooker, Lisa-Maria Wagner, Sally Watson, Mrs. Wescott, Hazel Williams, Bryan Williams, Lewis Wilshire, Mary Wright, C.A. Yeo. Thanks to Roger Mortimer of the Redland & Cotham Amenities Society for permission to use information from *Cotham Walks* by Stephen Jones. Also I am grateful to Susan Osman and producer Jenny Walmsley on the Radio Bristol morning show whose phone in brought some interesting answers to questions which puzzled me regarding street names and also to Richard Wyatt and Polly Lloyd for promoting the first edition of the book on *Let's Do Lunch* - a show which was great fun to make.

Please do not hesitate to send in any further information to:
speedwel@dialstart.net
or to my publisher at:
catherine@broadcastbooks.co.uk.

The Third edition awaits!

Picture credits

Thanks to Doug Northcott for the photographs on pages 32, 88, 94, 98, 129, 146, 152, 160, 177, 211, 274 and 291.
Thanks to Sue Bishop of *Memories*, Corn Exchange, Corn Street, Bristol, BS1 1JQ, for the photographs on pages 46, 58, 67, 74, 173, 205, 227, 269, and 240.
Thanks to Lewis Wilshire for the photographs on pages 80, 283 and 288.

Map of Bristol Districts on pages 16 and 17 by Lorna Rankin.

Introduction

Had I known that my quest to discover the origins and meanings of Bristol street names would come to dominate my entire life I might have thought twice about embarking on such an undertaking. Once I had taken the first few faltering steps, I was totally hooked on the project and I hope the end result will prove of interest to everyone who has ever wondered why a certain street was so named.

I cannot pretend to have come up with all the answers and some of my educated guesses may be way off beam, but I have investigated the names of every Close, Court, Crescent, Avenue, Road and Street, to the very best of my ability, and I welcome any corrections and comments from readers.

A Note on Sources

As I have explained in the dedication, I took Grace Cooper's *A-Z History of 200 Bristol Street Names* as my original inspiration. Grace's source was two works by a man called H.C.W. Harris, who was Housing Manager and Secretary to the City and County of Bristol during the 1950s and 1960s, and compiled a booklet rather snappily entitled *Housing Nomenclature in Bristol*. This was published by the Housing Committee in 1969 and related to the new housing estates and blocks of flats which were being built at that time.

Mr Harris had also compiled another volume, over 400 pages long, on the origin of the names of the older city streets. Two copies exist, one in the Central Reference Library and one in the Bristol Records Office. I photocopied most of the book and made notes on the rest and studied it in great detail. I soon realised nothing must be taken at face value, even the work of the esteemed Mr Harris. I found a few of his guesses to be inaccurate and was able to correct accordingly. I do so wish he were still alive. I would have endless discussions with him.

I have used the Internet extensively in my research which has been invaluable in providing details of parliamentary figures from past centuries, musicians, writers and artists. I have also been able to seek out knowledge from local sites. I have studied all the local history books I could lay my hands on, and the ones compiled by history groups throughout the city have turned up masses of information which has explained the reasoning behind the naming of many roads in the suburbs.

Books from past historians such as Braine, Elliot and Jones (details in bibliography) have revealed further meanings describing, as they do, erstwhile owners of the lands, field names and ecclesiastical figures. I have also delved into old history books from my own bookshelves, battered and bedraggled from years of handling since early childhood but informative nevertheless.

I have telephoned libraries, parish councillors and any history pundit whose name I could obtain and I am certain many will breathe a sigh of relief now my task is complete inasmuch as I will no longer be plying them with questions.

Local References

It will be noted that there are a great many references to the Forest and the King's Wood. The royal hunting grounds covered a vast area of what is now south-west Bristol from the days of the Domesday Book to the mid seventeenth century. The wooded land from which Kingswood derives its name stretched as far as Filwood in North Somerset and reached Filton in the other direction. This will explain why roads in BS13 are often named after men who had an involvement with the forest land.

A number of roads in BS13 and BS14 bear the names of residents who lived in the area long ago, according to parish records, as do several in Henbury. When the selection of these names was under debate it was decided to trawl through the old parish records, Hearth Tax exemptions and other historical documents. Other volumes which were studied for this purpose were those relating to the Enclosure Acts which came into force during the nineteenth century. Prior to this, villagers could graze their sheep and cattle on common land and collect peat and willow for basket making and hay for the stables. The Enclosure Acts allowed the fencing off of land around properties where a claim had been staked. This obviously caused dissatisfaction and hardship among those who felt they had been robbed of their rights, as indeed they had.

Bristol Castle

Many central streets still bear names reminiscent of days when Bristol Castle dominated the city. It is thought that the castle began as a wooden fort which existed to the east of the town in Saxon times, but it was the Normans who built the stone castle on the land between the Avon and the Frome. It was begun during the reign of William II, who ascended the throne in 1087, and the project was sponsored by Geoffrey Mowbray, Bishop of Coutances in Normandy. Robert of Gloucester, the Governor during the reign of Henry I, added the massive keep, and established the Priory of St. James in the Bartonin 1129.

At the outbreak of the Civil War in 1642, Bristol was held by Royalists. The castle was deemed insufficient fortification for the town, and forts were built at Hotwells, Brandon Hill, Priors Hill and Windmill Hill (later re-named St. Michael's Hill). Royal Fort House, now belonging to the University of Bristol, was built in 1761 on the site of the former Royal Fort. Bristol fell to the Parliamentarians in 1645. Cromwell was declared Lord Protector of the country in 1653, after which Royal Fort, the other Bristol forts and Bristol Castle were demolished on Cromwell's orders.

Bristol Cathedral

Several - possibly confusing - references to the church and Abbey of St. Augustines occur throughout this book. There were two St. Augustine's: the Abbey of St. Augustine's Black Canons, the church of which is now Bristol Cathedral, on College Green, was founded by Robert Fitzhardinge in 1142. The Abbey itself was demolished in the twentieth century. Nearby stood the church of St. Augustine the Less, founded by the Black Canons at least as far back as 1240. It survived the Blitz but was declared redundant and was demolished to build the Royal Hotel extension.

Explanation of some historical terms

It may also be helpful to explain some of the archaic terms that have been used in the text. In days of old, counties were divided into a hundred parishes. These were known as **Hundreds**. A **hide** was a variable unit of area of land, enough for a household. A **manor** was the district over which the court of the lord of the manor had authority. **Assizes** were periodical sittings of judges (with a jury) on a circuit throughout the English counties. This practice ended in 1972 and was superseded by Crown Courts. The **Domesday Book** was a meticulous survey of all lands and landowners in England south of the rivers Ribble and Tees, compiled by order of William the Conqueror in 1086. The name came from the OE *dom* meaning authority in judgment.

In 1662 a **Hearth Tax** of two shillings per year was imposed on every hearth in all houses, except cottages. It was a most unpopular tax, and was withdrawn in 1689. Those entitled to exemptions were persons whose houses were not of a greater value than twenty shillings, and on condition that such houses did not have more than two chimneys or firehearths in them. It was also a condition of exemption that the occupants did not have, use or occupy any lands or tenements of their own, over the value of ten pounds.

Bristol Districts

There follows a brief description of the naming of Bristol's districts, where known:

Abbots Leigh From the OE *leah,* meaning a wooded settlement or farm belonging to the Abbot. The Abbot in this case was St. Augustine.

Ashley Down This was in the manor of Asseley, which was granted to the monks of St. James's Priory by William, Earl of Gloucester in 1170.

Ashton The name means 'farm or village where ash trees grow'.

Avonmouth Self-explanatory - at the mouth of the Avon. It is a twentieth century name.

Barton Hill This name derives from OE *bere tun* meaning corn farm, outlying grange or barley farm, denoting the demesne farm of Bristol Castle.

Bedminster One suggestion is that 'Bed' was often pronounced with a long e: Bede, and 'minster' derives from monasterium, or monastery, suggesting that Bedminster was the site of a 15th century monastery founded by the monk Beda, where lepers found refuge outside the city walls. Another suggestion is that 'bed' derives from the Welsh meaning to or at and that 'minster' does not have a religious association at all but means marsh. Reference was made to the Marsh Meadows of Bedminster in *Bristol Past and Present* by Nichols and Taylor, published in 1881.

Bishopston The name means 'Bishop's Manor'. Development began in this area in the 1840s when it was still part of the parish of Horfield. When the new parish was established it was called Bishopston in honour of Bishop Monk who owned much of the land. The whole project was doomed to years of contention regarding feudal rights and other legal aspects owing to the intervention of the Rev. Henry Richards, Perpetual Curate of Horfield, who had a strong financial interest in the scheme. During the bishop's lifetime, he agreed that Bishop Monk should be patron of the development, which was to be named after Bishop Monk, but after the bishop's death, Richards reneged on this agreement. He tried to curry favour with the trustees of the Horfield estate, wanting to be made patron instead, by building the church of St. Michael and All Angels, but his efforts were in vain. He lost money in trying to establish pleasure gardens in the area and eventually had to sell land to recoup losses. Horfield prison stands on land which was once his.

Bishopsworth This literally means 'bishop's palace' from OE *woro*, enclosure or place. It was originally known as Bishport, and the present form of the name stems from the early part of the 18th century although it was, even after that period, often referred to as Bishport. The Bishop in question was Geoffrey of Coutances, great friend of William the Conqueror and interpreter as his coronation. He owned vast tracts of land in Somerset and elsewhere and took part in the baronial rising against William Rufus, but was pardoned. He died at Coutances in 1093.

Bitton At one time this was called Button although the name was derived, it is thought, from the river Boyd which runs through the village, making it Boyd-town which became corrupted into Bitton.

Brentry Two suggestions have been made as to the origin of this suburb. One is that it means 'burnt tree', while another is that it derives from the OE *beorne*, a military hero, and translating as 'tree of the warriors'. It is also possible the source was OE *brant*, meaning hill, so giving the meaning 'wooded hill'.

Brislington Brislington once lay in the Hundred of Keynsham and was formerly known as Bristleton. The name actually means Beorhthelm's farm. It is said the name originates from St. Brice, Bishop of Tours in France who died in 444AD but subsequently became a popular saint in medieval England, possibly as a result of the St. Brice's Day Massacre, 13 November 1002, when Ethelred II ordered that all Danes in England be killed in case they rose up against him. This led to a full-scale Danish invasion of England in 1003.

Broomhill The name derives from the OE for 'bramble-covered hill'.

Cadbury Heath. There was a heath here once but this had disappeared by 1827 following the Enclosure Act of 1819. The name Cadbury indicates a prehistoric settlement, *bury* meaning encampment. No trace remains but it is believed the location was near present-day Heath Rise. The name actually means 'Cada's place by the iron age fort'.

Clifton This translates in several ways - either as 'the town or farm on the cliffs', or as a town or village on the hill, or hill slope, or river bank.

Coombe Dingle This name derives from the OE *cumb* meaning 'small valley', and *dingle* is another word for dell, 'a clearing in the wood', which both aptly describe the area.

Conham The name means 'farm on the hill'.

Cotham The origin of the name is from OE - *cot* being cottage, shed, shelter or hut and *ham* covering everything from homestead to river meadow, land in a bed or enclosure. In old deeds the area is referred to as Codd (or Cod) Down, Coat Down, Coatham and Codham. The whole of Cotham in the eighteenth century was

comprised of the two estates of Cotham Lodge, the most important house in Cotham, and Redland Park. Today's Cotham Park, with the obelisks in what is known as Cotham Landscape marble at its entrance, was originally the entrance drive to Cotham Lodge. Cut and polished examples of this very rare marble, which gives the appearance of a marble landscape picture, was quarried in Cotham from rock laid down in the shallow algae-rich seas of the Jurassic period, are in the Bristol Museum and Art Gallery. It was a very popular stone for use in nineteenth century gardens. Cotham Lodge was described in 1753 as having 'a good orchard and garden, with two houses, an inn and a windmill' used for grinding snuff. The inn was particularly rowdy when executions took place at the gallows on the top of St. Michael's Hill. Cotham Church was later built over this terrible spot. In the grounds of Tower House on the Cotham Lodge estate, the tower of the old windmill was heightened to seventy feet and turned into an observatory in 1772 by the owner of Tower House, Charles Partridge. It was 250 feet above sea level. Tower House later became part of Cotham Grammar School until it moved to new buildings on Cotham Lawn Road. Both the house and the Windmill observatory were demolished by the Bristol Corporation in 1953. The Quaker Fry family, chocolate manufacturers, bought Cotham Lodge in 1845, after which it was demolished to make way for the beautiful existing Italianate buildings of Cotham Park. The elegant terraces of Cotham Brow, Cotham Road and Fremantle Road were developed a little later when part of the Redland Court estate was sold in 1865.

Downend The name has been written variously as Dowend and Downing. In the eighteenth century the only house of any significance which stood here was one belonging to a retired military man by the name of Downing so perhaps this was the origin.

Easton The word means east farmstead - the derivation of the second syllable comes from the OE *tun*.

Eastville This developed from Easton and the word is composed of east and *ville*, the French word for town. The use of the word *ville* instead of town seems to have been a fashionable late nineteenth-century affectation.

Filton There are various suggestions as to the origin of Filton. One source suggests the first syllable derives from the OE *felece*, hay, while another suggests a derivation from the OE *fealg*, newly cultivated land or filipe 'hay growing in a fallow' or hay farm. There are two further explanations offered - the Saxon *felsh* meaning rock, the OE *fille* meaning hill or field, making the most plausible explanation 'the village in a field'.

Filwood The name originates in the old Filwood Chase, part of Kingswood Forest which included the site of this estate, which is why many of the roads are named after Forest Rangers of that time.

Fishponds Self-explanatory - there were once ponds stocked with fish here.

Frenchay This was formerly known as Fromeshaw and mutated through Franshawe and Franchehay to the present spelling. The name means 'copse on the river Frome'.

Greenbank A purely descriptive name although no longer applicable.

Hanham There have been several explanations about the origin of this name, from 'the home of Haneca' to a reference to the rocks. The most probable explanation is that the land was owned by an ancient, possibly Welsh, family called *ap Hanham*.

Hartcliffe This area was once known as Dundry Slopes. Hartcliffe was the name of the hundred in which much of the land was situated. The name means a sloping ground where stags could be found.

Headley Park A field name. The OE *haepleah* translates as 'a clearing overgrown with heather', which could be the source, or it may have been the OE *heafod* - head of a valley, hilltop or headland in a field, which geographically would be more relevant to this area.

Henbury There are two possible derivations for the name of this district, which was first mentioned in historical records in 692 AD: either high fortification, or chief fortified place such as a manor house. The name may have referred to the encampment on Castle Hill near Blaise Castle on the end of the ridge overlooking Henbury. The river Hen runs through the area. Henbury was incorporated into the City of Bristol in 1935.

Hengrove Named after Hengrove House which once stood here and was described in Mathews' *Bristol Guide* as, 'a handsome seat pleasantly situated'. Apparently in a field to the west of the house there once stood a monument engraved with a poem, erected in 1536. The stone with the engraving was subsequently stolen, but the supporting stone remained on the parish boundary. When examining the bounds the Minister and Churchwarden would stop here and say a prayer, and then sing psalm 118, which begins "O give thanks unto the Lord, for He is good: because his mercy endureth for ever."

Henleaze There was an impressive residence here called Henleaze House, described as being 'pleasantly situated on the summit of extensive parklike grounds, well stocked with timber trees and embosomed in neat shrubbery'. It has been suggested alternatively that the name of the district derived from a prominent local family who lived here, the Henleys.

Highridge This is a purely descriptive name of the area.

Hillfields This estate was built on a large slope of land belonging to the Beaufort family known as the Thicket which explains the sylvan influence in the road naming.

Horfield This name comes from OE *hour* meaning dirt or filth, and pronounced 'huur'. It still means prostitute in some northern dialects and is the same word as whore. The name implies a muddy stretch of open country, which it may well have been before it was built up in the nineteenth century. Mervyn Herbert Nevil Story Maskelyne (1823 -1911). Was Lord of the Manor of Horfield and developed the area north west of the County Cricket ground with the builder James Payne around 1895. Many of the streets in this area are named after members of his family.

Hotwells. Hotwell Point was beneath St. Vincent's Cliff, where the rock juts out into the Avon just south of the Suspension Bridge. From this rock a hot spring bubbled up 'as warm as milk', pouring out up to 60 gallons a minute at a temperature of 76° F. The problem was that at low tide the spring was 10ft above river level and at high tide 26 ft below it, so access was never easy, and was primarily used by sailors as a cure for scurvy, and other skin conditions. The water was held in a brick reservoir to prevent contamination by the river, and piped down to stone basins. By 1660 it was nationally famous. Many people resorted to the well for a vast variety of ailments, from 'hot liver' to diabetes, and in 1695 it was piped to Hotwell House spa, built directly above the spring. For a

time the spa rivalled that of Bath. Bristolians had free access to the waters, and visitors had to pay. In 1775 the Hotwell turned a blood-red colour as a result of the Lisbon earthquake and even after its purity was restored, the Hotwell went slowly out of fashion after the Napoleonic Wars. Its reputation became morbid as a result of the practice of unscrupulous physicians, who would send terminally ill patients from London to eke out further payment from them. Then they generally expired in Bristol. In 1867 the Hotwell House was demolished and Hotwell point and well were dynamited to increase ease of navigation. The spring re-emerged and a pump that still exists today was erected in 1877. In the early twentieth century the water was declared unfit for public consumption. (*For further reading, see 'Holy Wells of Bath and Bristol Region' in the bibliography.*)

Kingsdown This was so named because it was royal property under the demesne of Bristol Castle. Most of the properties there were erected in the eighteenth and early nineteenth centuries, although a few may have existed from earlier times. Compulsory Purchase Orders meant the loss of many of the fine old buildings in favour of multi-storey flats.

Kingswood A very simple explanation for this naming - it was, indeed, the King's wood. Kingswood was originally known as Mireford, possibly because the roads were notoriously muddy.

Knowle This name is derived from OE *cnoll*, meaning hilltop or hillock, which is an accurate description of the terrain.

Lawrence Hill This takes its name from the old leper hospital built about 1200. Some remnants of the building could still be seen as late as 1820. A local church dedicated to St. Lawrence was demolished in the 1960s.

Lawrence Weston The Hospital of St.Lawrence in the Hundred of Barton Regis held lands here during the reign of Edward III. Weston is derived from *ton* or *tun* meaning 'farmstead to the west (of Henbury)'.

Lockleaze This district derives its name from the OE *loc*, fold, and *leaze*, pastureland.

Longwell Green This would seem to be descriptive.

Mangotsfield In the Domesday book this is referred to as Manegodesfell which derives from the OE *mane* meaning stone, *goed* which translates as wood and *felle*, a hill, which is an apt description of the area. The name could also be translated as 'Mangoda's field'.

Montpelier It has been suggested that the similarity between the hilly nature of this district and that of the French region of that name was the reason for its name, which seems to have been first used in 1830. There is a record of a Montpelier Farm here in 1840, built onto an earlier building which was used by Cromwell and Fairfax during the siege of Bristol in 1645.

Moorfields This name derives from the wealthy fishmonger Samuel Moore. He had a wholesale business in Castle Street at the beginning of the nineteenth century. He invested in land in Barton Hill, St. Philips and St. George, where he built 40 cottages and an imposing residence for himself, on what later became Barton Hill vicarage. He eventually retired to Moore's Lodge and died in 1823. The Lodge was demolished in the early 1900's and St. Luke's Mission Hall was erected in its place.

Northville A made-up name, similar to Eastville and Southville.

Oldbury Court The name is taken from the sixteenth-century mansion of this name. The land was acquired by the Bristol Corporation in the 1930s. Oldbury means old fortified place, perhaps a fortified manor house or farmstead.

Oldland At the time of the Norman Conquest this area belonged to the Bishop of Exeter, at which time it was named Aldeland. At times during its history it has been held by the same lords who held Bitton.

Patchway The Patch Way was an old local name for a road, probably Roman, which left the Old Western Trackway at Almondsbury at the point where Cribb's Causeway and the Ridgeway join. The name actually means 'the road by Paecca's home'.

Redland Many views have been put forward as to the origin of this name. One authority states it was known as Rudeland in the eleventh century, whereas another suggests it comes from the term used in Roman law to describe a property act which meant that a man's land was divided into three - one portion for his wife, one for his children and one for free disposal. In 1208 there is a reference to it being called Thriddeland with spelling variations over the years. Other deviations have been Redeloahe and Redelynton. One expert believes this means it derived from OE *rudding,* translating as 'cleared land'. In the eighteenth century the area belonged to the estates of Redland Court, a beautiful house built by John Cossins in 1732. When the estate lands were sold, after 1865, most of the houses that comprise Redland today were built.

Redcliff The spelling of this district has long been in dispute but this is, in fact, the official version without the final e. Much development took place during the Georgian era and even earlier. The self-explanatory name comes from the OE *read,* red, and *clif,* a cliff or bank. It is thought that the bank referred to is the rocky terrain of red sandstone between the Avon and the old course of the Frome, which later became known as Redcliffe Hill.

St. Anne's This district takes its name from the ancient chapel in the woods, a place of medieval pilgrimage. The religious theme is echoed in some of the roads which have been named after cathedrals.

St. George First described as a parish in 1638. Its church was pulled down in the 1970s.

St. Werburghs Named after a favourite Anglo-Saxon saint, and a place of pilgrimage to the Penny Well or Pamiwell which was situated on the border of where Conduit Road is today. Its waters were piped through the Quay Pipe, to the centre of Bristol. Heavy development of this area, to accomodate local factory workers, took place at the beginning of the twentieth century.

Sea Mills 'Sea' is not a reference to water but a corruption of 'saye', a wool and silk serge cloth woven at the mills here, which were powered by the sea tides. Before development began here in the 1920s it was a rural area and many of the roads named after fields reflect this.

Shirehampton The name is derived from the Anglo Saxon *scir,* a district or shire. Hampton is from the OE *ham-tun,* a home farm. This was a part of Gloucestershire until 1974.

Sneyd Park Sneyd derives from the OE *snaed,* which means 'a detached piece of land', in this case belonging to the bishop in Stoke Bishop. *See Stoke Bishop.*

Soundwell The derivation seems to be OE *sund*, meaning healthy, therefore 'a spring with beneficial properties'. A general-purpose healing well once stood on this spot. There were three other wells in the locality - Hopewell, Wishwell and Speedwell - all traditionally visited on May day morning.

Southmead An obvious derivation here - south meadow.

Southville A made-up name like Northville and Eastville.

Speedwell There was a Speedwell Pit but whether the district was already known by this name is uncertain. It was the name of the vessel in which local explorer Martin Pring set out from Bristol in 1603. He discovered the north part of Virginia. The name may, of course, be inspired by the flower.

Staple Hill The name seems to have been derived from OE *stapol*, post or pillar, although it has been suggested that it meant 'standing stone' in this case.

Stapleton This, too, came from the OE *stapol*, post or pillar. It has been suggested that the village grew around a collapsed Roman building.

Stoke Bishop The bishop celebrated here was the sixteenth bishop of Worcester, who had jurisdiction over this land at that time. Stoke can either mean 'a holy place', 'a meeting place', or 'a dairy farm'.

Stockwood This area was originally in the Hundred of Keynsham and the name is derived from the OE *stocc*, treetrunk or log, and wood from *wudu*, woodland. An alternative derivation for the first syllable is OE *stoc*, place or secondary settlement.

Totterdown The name is derived from the OE *tot*, a look-out post, on this high lying land which overlooked the city of Bristol.

Warmley There are two theories about this name, either that it takes its name from the Warm Lee Brook, or that derivation means either 'a forest glade infested with reptiles' or 'the place by the weir'.

Westbury-on-Trym The name means 'western fortification on the river Trym'. At the time of the Domesday Book, it was under the jurisdiction of St. Mary's Church, Worcester. It seems to have been originally known as Westminster.

Whitchurch The name means 'place with the church made of white stone.'

Whitehall Thought to have taken its name from a house which once stood here.

Withywood This was the name of one of the farms included in the Compulsory Purchase Order. The neighbourhood was originally destined to be known as Bishport, the old name for Bishopsworth, but it was thought Withywood had a better ring to it. The name is derived from OE *wioig* meaning withy, another name for willow wood.

A Note on Old English and Middle English Origins

Where the origin of a name is explained, you may find reference to OE (Old English) and ME (Middle English). A brief word of explanation may be useful.

Old English is the language spoken by the Anglo-Saxons who arrived in Britain from the fifth century onwards. It looks like this:

Wrætlic is þes wealstan; wyrde gebræcon,
Burgstede burston, brosnaþ enta geweorc

(Splendid this rampart is, though fate destroyed it,
The city buildings fell apart, the works of giants crumble…)

'The Ruin', from the *Exeter Book.*
(This poem is probably about the Roman ruins at Bath.)

By the fourteenth century, the language had evolved into what we term Middle English, which looks like this:

He sperred þe sted with þe spurez and sprong on his way,
So stif þat þe ston-fyr stroke out þerafter

(He set spurs to the horse and sprang on his way,
So vigorously that sparks were struck from the stones behind)
Sir Gawain and the Green Knight, c. 1375-1400

You will notice that there are some letters which we no longer use. These are:

þ   this makes the sound *th*, as in *thorn*

æ   this makes the sound *a*, as in *ash*

These letters were on their way out by the time that printing began, and printers tended to use the letter y in place of the þ, as it was the closest in appearance. Hence the misunderstanding about our ancestors' mode of pronunciation perpetuated by 'ye olde tea shoppe' type signs.

Pronunciation was more thorough and hard than in modern English. Thus, for example, the entry for Salthrop Road: this derives from OE *sealthearpe*, the correct pronunciation for which goes something like SAY-ALT-HAY-ARPER.

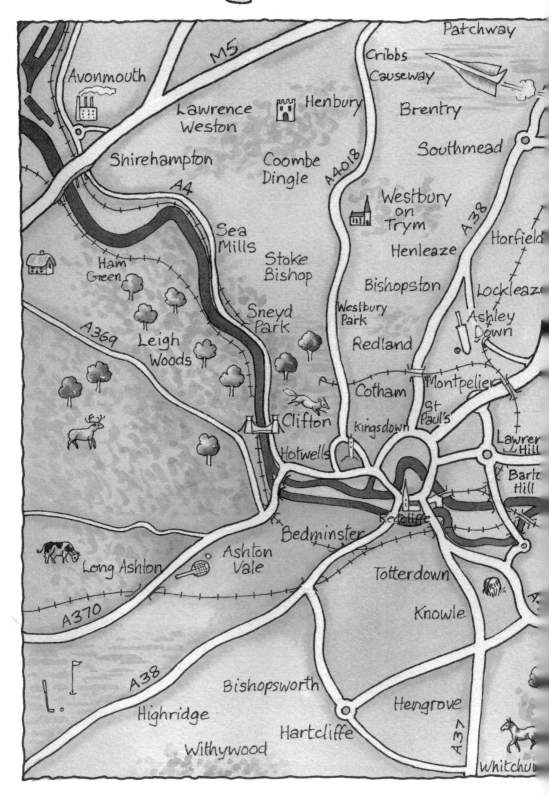

OF BRISTOL

Patchway

Bradley Stoke

Stoke Gifford

M4

Winterbourne

Brentry

Southmead

Filton

RINGROAD

M4

Westbury on Trym

A38

Horfield

Frenchay

Downend

Henleaze

M32

Mangotsfield

Bishopston

Lockleaze

Stapleton

Oldbury Court

Staple Hill

Ashley Down

Fishponds

Hillfields

Hill

edland

Montpelier

Easton

Greenbank

Soundwell

RINGROAD

otham

St Pauls

Whitehall

Speedwell

Lawrence Hill

St George

Siston Common

edcliffe

Barton Hill

A420

Kingswood

Wanmley

St Anne's

Hanham

A431

Oldland

tterdown

Knowle

Brislington

Longwell Green

Bitton

A4

Hengrove

A37

Stockwood

Whitchurch

A

ABBEY ROAD, BS9. As there is no abbey in the vicinity it has been suggested that this road was named by the developers.

ABBEYWOOD DRIVE, BS9. This appears to be a made-up name. The road was developed between the wars.

ABBOTS AVENUE / ROAD, BS15 / CLOSE, BS14. All three roads were built in the grounds of Lyons Court, a thirteenth-century house once owned by the abbots of Keynsham Abbey.

ABBOTS WAY, BS9. *See Abbey Road.*

ABBOTSFORD ROAD, BS6. This has a Sir Walter Scott connection, as do other roads in the Redland locality. Abbotsford House was the name of his home in Roxburghshire.

ABBOTSWOOD, BS15. Again an association with Keynsham Abbey. *See Abbots Close.*

ABERDEEN ROAD, BS6. It is not known whether this was called after the city of Aberdeen or in honour of George Gordon, the Earl of Aberdeen who was Foreign Secretary 1828-30 and Prime Minister of the coalition government in 1841-46.

ABINGDON ROAD, BS16. This road is perhaps named after the Oxfordshire town. Other nearby roads bear town names taken from various parts of the country. It is possible the places were of significance to the developer.

ABLETON WALK, BS9. Ableton was a field name, originally Apuldrem, on the Harford estate. It can be seen on the tithe maps of 1471.

ABRAHAM CLOSE BS5. John Abraham was Mayor of Bristol in 1865.

ACACIA AVENUE / CLOSE / MEWS / ROAD, BS16. This land, reclaimed for housing purposes from the area known as The Thicket, contains a large number of roads linked with an arboreal theme. *See Thicket Road.*

ACID ROAD, BS11. This bleak-sounding name obviously derives from the chemical industries predominating in the area. The Royal Ordnance factory was sited here until 1924. Mustard gas and picric acid (which was used in shells) were produced here for use during the First World War.

ACORN GROVE, BS13. So called because of the large oak tree growing nearby.

ACRAMANS ROAD, BS3. This is named after an important family who lived in the city and who were involved in civic duties as well as being prominent commercially. In addition to their ship building interests, they owned an iron foundry in Bedminster.

ACREBUSH CLOSE, BS13. This is the name of a field, which was originally recorded as being in the manor of Bishport and shown on a survey made in 1683 when Sir John Smyth was Lord of the Manor. The derivation is from the Old English *aecer*, a plot of arable land, and *busc*, bush.

ACTON ROAD, BS16. This is a place name in an area where random places seem to have been selected perhaps for personal reasons known only to the builder. The name, Acton, translates as 'village or homestead where the oaks grow'.

ADDISCOMBE ROAD, BS14. This is named after the military academy in Croydon where young cadets underwent training for service in the East India Company. Perhaps the builder had connections with the company.

ADDISON ROAD, BS4. Joseph Addison, statesman and poet (1672-1719) had relatives in Bedminster. He was a visitor to a house in St. Anne's and wrote some of his essays in a summerhouse there.

ADELAIDE PLACE / TERRACE, BS16. Queen Adelaide was the wife of William IV. She visited Blaise Castle in 1718.

ADELAIDE PLACE, BS5. This was probably named for the same reason as Adelaide Place in BS16.

AGATE STREET, BS3. A number of local streets around here are called after gemstones. It is possible that these names were inspired by the proximity of these streets to the old Goldstone Colliery.

AIKEN STREET, BS5. Peter Freeland Aiken was the first owner of the Great Western Cotton Mill. The factory supported hundreds of local people, and a whole community of shops, pubs and schools grew up around the place. During the early years of the twentieth century, however, it became cheaper to import cotton and eventually the plant was forced to close. The street was re-sited during the redevelopment of the area in the 1950s.

AINTREE DRIVE, BS16. An entire group of roads here are called after racecourses.

AIR BALLOON HILL, BS5. On 10th January 1784 James Dinwiddie launched an unmanned hydrogen filled air balloon from Mrs Scarce's Riding School at Bath. It travelled ten miles to descend on the high ground in the parish of St George, which was thereafter called Air Balloon Hill. On the same day Dr Parry launched an unmanned gas-filled balloon from Crescent Gardens in Bath, which came to earth just west of Wells.

AIRPORT COTTAGES / ROAD, BS14. The road led to the old Whitchurch airport, which opened on 31 May 1930 on a day of pageantry, pomp and ceremony. It closed in 1957, being replaced by Lulsgate. During the Second World War it was the base for BOAC and KLM. A wartime hangar survives as part of the sports centre.

AKEMAN WAY, BS11. This is named after an ancient Roman road, the link being the Roman remains found around this area.

ALARD ROAD, BS4. Roger Alard was permitted to cut the oaks in Kingswood Forest in the thirteenth century. The wood was used for shipbuilding. He took his timber from a wood of furches (fir trees grown to a specific shape for this purpose). They were u-shaped so that the frame of the ship could be formed without cutting the wood.

ALBANY ROAD, BS6. The Duke of Albany was a title first bestowed on a brother of Robert III of Scotland. Lord Darnley, husband of Mary Queen of Scots, also held the title, which passed to their son, James I. Queen Victoria's youngest son

Leopold was given the title. In 1882 he married Helen Frederica Augusta, Princess of Waldeck-Pyrmont, but died two years later at the age of 31. The brief marriage produced a son and a daughter. His son, Charles Edward, who succeeded his uncle as Duke of Saxe-Coburg, renounced his British title in 1914.

ALBANY STREET, BS15. Daniel Flook, owner of a shoe factory, built a large number of houses in the area for the many workers there. He strove to improve the housing for the working classes and gave his roads somewhat grandiose names. This may have been one example.

ALBANY WAY, BS15. Albany is a port in Western Australia. This road runs parallel to Mariston Way, which was the name of a ship which docked at Albany in May 1905. It may be assumed that someone from this area emigrated and travelled on the ship.

ALBEMARLE ROW / TERRACE, BS8. George Keppel was the third Earl of Albemarle and an ancestor of Mrs Keppel, mistress of Edward VII. These houses were built in the 1760s to accommodate visitors to the Hotwells Spa.

ALBERT CRESCENT, BS2 / GROVE, BS5 / PARADE, BS5 / PARK / PARK PLACE, BS6 / PLACE, BS3 / PLACE, BS9 / ROAD, BS2 / ROAD, BS16 / STREET, BS5 / TERRACE, BS16. It seems fairly certain that all these streets are named after Prince Albert, Consort to Queen Victoria, who visited the city in July 1843 to launch the SS Great Britain.

ALBERT ROAD, BS15. Another road built by Daniel Flook and given a royal name. *See Albany Street.*

ALBERTON ROAD, BS16. Before the newer houses were built here, there existed an Albert Terrace, so perhaps there is some connection here. There was, too, a Richard Alberton who was a Bailiff under a Mayor by the name of John Wickham, so there may be a local link here.

ALBION CLOSE, BS16. A branch of the Whitehall Gerrish family also ran market gardens on this land. The Close was named after one of the family probably a son bearing the traditional family forename of Albinus. *See Gerrish Avenue.*

ALBION ROAD, BS5. The Celtic name for Britain used in Roman times. The connection could be the hoard of Roman coins found nearby when the roads here were being developed for housing in the Victorian era.

ALBION STREET, BS5. Named after Albinus Gerrish, fourth son of George and Elizabeth gerrish of Cambridge House. Although his name was actually Albinus. He was the 4th son of George and Elizabeth of Cambridge House. *See Gerrish Avenue.*

ALCOVE ROAD, BS16. This was built near the site of a clay pit which stood in the middle of Shiner's fields. The pit was used as a swimming pool called the Lido until the 1970s.

ALDER DRIVE, BS5. Several roads in the area have been given tree names - perhaps a reminder of the scene before the houses were built.

ALDERCOMBE ROAD, BS9. The name means 'valley where alders grow'.

ALDERDOWN CLOSE, BS11. The development stands near a large wooded area.

ALDERMOOR WAY, BS15. The name means 'heath where the alders grow'. There is a wood near Swainswick with this name but this was an old field name in the area, too. It was part of the Barrs Court estate. *See Barrs Court Road.*

ALDERNEY AVENUE, BS4. A number of roads in the area bear the names of Channel Islands.

THE ALDERS, BS16. This is amongst a cluster of roads bearing names of trees, perhaps to underline the rural aspects of the development.

ALDERTON ROAD, BS7. This is a place name of a village in Gloucestershire which may have had family connections for the builder. The derivation of the first component is not from the tree but is a personal name, Ealdhere - thus the *tun* or homestead of Ealdhere's people.

ALDWICK AVENUE, BS13. Aldwick Court was a house belonging to S. Baker of Blagdon. He was granted land under the enclosure awards. *See Introduction.*

ALEXANDRA CLOSE / GARDENS / PLACE / PARK / ROAD, BS16 / PARK, BS6/ ROAD, BS8 / BS10. Queen Alexandra (1844-1925) was the popular and long-suffering wife of the philandering Edward VII. She was the eldest daughter of King Christian IX of Denmark and was known as the Rose of Denmark because she was considered a great beauty even into her old age. Sadly she was handicapped by deafness. The Hotwells pub 'The Rose of Denmark' was named in her honour.

ALEXANDRA ROAD, BS13. This particular Alexandra was the wife of the man whose firm built these houses, a Mr. J Kew.

ALFORD ROAD, BS4. A not unusual local surname, so this was probably named after someone connected with the development.

ALFRED HILL / PARADE / PLACE / STREET, BS2. Other personal names have been used in this and the surrounding eighteenth century streets, some of which have disappeared over the years, so perhaps the name's origin lay with the landowner or developer.

ALFRED PLACE, BS1. This was probably named for the same reason as BS2 above.

ALFRED ROAD, BS3. This is more likely to be called after a relative of the developer rather than because of any royal connection.

ALFRED STREET, BS5. This may be named after a member of the Gerrish family rather than having royal connections. *See Gerrish Avenue.*

ALFRED LOVELL GARDENS, BS15. This honours a former parish councillor who was born in the early part of the twentieth century.

ALGIERS STREET, BS3. An unlikely name for a street surrounded by others with more conventional nomenclature. This road was built by Alfred Capper Pass for members of his work force. It was possibly named to commemorate the Battle of Algiers in 1816, when a naval force under Admiral Sir Edward Pellew knocked out the city's shore batteries and freed a thousand Christian slaves.

ALL HALLOWS ROAD, BS5. This road has been variously called Burley's Lane, St. Mark's Lane, and Elmgrove Road. The present name was adopted after the church was built. At the beginning of the nineteenth century it is shown as a lane between

the brickfields and was then known as Frogmarsh. It led to a level crossing into Bloy Street. The derivation is from the OE *halga*, meaning holy.

ALL SAINTS LANE / STREET, BS1. The church was the home of the Guild of Kalendaries, men and women skilled in various crafts who kept records relating to the charities of the town, tended the sick, and said masses for the dead. They founded a library near the church to which the general public had access. All the records in it were destroyed one night when a tinker crept in to spend the night in the warm and overturned a rush light, which set fire to the building.

ALL SAINTS ROAD, BS8. This contains the church of the same name, the foundation stone of which was laid on 3 November 1864. The church was destroyed in the Second World War Blitz and was rebuilt after the war.

ALLANMEAD ROAD, BS14. This name translates as 'meadow by a stream'. Alan and Allan are pre-Saxon words meaning stream, small river, or brook. Studying the group of roads which includes this one, a picture emerges of geographical features which may have influenced the choice of name.

ALLERTON CRESCENT / GARDENS / ROAD, BS14. Allerton is a village in Somerset. The first component is a personal name. Other roads nearby were also called after locations in the West Country.

ALLFOXTON ROAD, BS7. A corruption of Allfoxden, a Manor near Holford, Somerset, which the poet William Wordsworth rented at one time for £23 per year. The first component is a personal name, *Aelfregh,* of Saxon origin, or possibly Aelfegus or Alfegus. There is no clue as to why this name was chosen.

ALLINGTON DRIVE, BS15. Built on an old orchard, all the roads in this development are called after varieties of apple. The Allington Pippin, rather uncommon these days, was raised by Thomas Laston in Lincolnshire before 1884. It has a distinctive aromatic flavour, cooks well, keeps well, and is sweet and not bland.

ALLINGTON ROAD, BS3. Allington is a small Wiltshire village near Devizes. The meaning is the homestead, farm, or village of Athelney's people.

ALLISON AVENUE / ROAD, BS4. This is possibly a surname of someone connected with the development or the land on which the roads were built.

ALMA ROAD AVENUE / ROAD BS8. These were named to commemorate the famous battle of the Crimean War on 20 September 1854 which was fought by the river Alma. It was one of the more successful campaigns as far as the British were concerned. These roads were built during that war on what had previously been a deer park.

ALMA VALE ROAD, BS8. The Crimean War is again the inspiration for this naming. The Reverend Joseph Wain formed a veterans' society in Bristol in 1892, mainly for survivors of the Crimean War, but also of other wars prior to 1860. By 1905 only 96 members remained.

ALMA CLOSE / ROAD, BS15. These were presumably also named after the battle, like the Clifton streets above.

ALMEDA ROAD, BS5. This is probably named after the Portuguese town of Almada or Almeida, besieged by the British in 1762. There is no apparent reason for the choice of name. It could also be a mis-spelling of *alameda*, a public walkway, usually a poplar grove.

ALMOND WAY, BS16. Possibly the surname of someone connected with the Gerrish family.

ALMORAH ROAD, BS3. Named, for reasons unknown, after a health resort in the Himalayas. It was the scene of a battle in the Anglo-Gurkha War, which began in 1814 when Gurkhas attacked police stations in Bhutwal. Colonels Nicholls and Gardener captured Almorah in Kumaon on 28 November 1815. The treaty of Sagulis ended hostilities in February 1816.

ALPHA ROAD, BS3. Named Alpha because it was the initial development in the area.

ALPINE ROAD, BS5. It has been suggested that this road could have been so named because of the steepness of its gradient!

ALSOP ROAD, BS15. A probable connection for this name is Uriah Alsop, owner of a steam cabinet works at the end of the nineteenth century. He lived at Bitton.

ALTON ROAD, BS7. This is a place name meaning Ella's *tun* or town. Several streets in the area are named after British towns seemingly at random, although the places may have had some significance to the developer.

ALTRINGHAM ROAD, BS5. This is one of several streets in the district named after places in Cheshire and Lancashire. This is a mis-spelling for Altrincham.

ALVERSTOKE, BS14. This is a village in Hampshire, grouped with other place names which, superficially, have nothing in common but which may have an underlying link.

ALVESTON WALK, BS9. Alveston is a Gloucestershire village, and a number of roads locally have a Gloucestershire theme. It is possible that it dates from the days when Sea Mills was linked with that county through its production of woollen cloth.

ALWINS COURT, BS1. Earl Alwin held the manors of Oldland and Upton Cheney, according to the Domesday survey.

AMBERLEY CLOSE / ROAD, BS16. Amberley is a place in Gloucestershire where, incidentally, Iron Age earthworks were excavated in 1936 by Mrs Elsie Clifford, first female president of the Bristol and Gloucestershire Archaeological Society.

AMBLE CLOSE, BS15. The Close is named after a Northumberland seaport, although the reason for this choice is unknown.

AMBLESIDE AVENUE, BS10. It was decided to call the roads in this area after places in the Lake District because of their proximity to Henleaze Lake.

AMBRA VALE, BS8. The name means 'place in the wood of the yellowhammer', in OE. Thomas Goldney bought Ambra Hill in 1747 and began to lay out the beautiful grounds of Goldney Hall on the site.

AMBROSE ROAD, BS8. Ambrose House in Hotwells was always used as the harbourmaster's residence.

AMERCOMBE WALK, BS14. In all probability this is an old field name derived from the OE *amore*, bird, and *combe*, valley.

ANCHOR LANE / ROAD, BS1. The port association is obvious.

ANCHOR ROAD, BS15. This is almost certainly named after the Anchor Boot factory which flourished in the area at the beginning of the twentieth century.

ANDEREACH CLOSE, BS14. This is another road name which seems to follow a theme of the past features of the area, with special emphasis on water. *Ann* is a Celtic word for river, and 'reach' is derived from the OE *ric* which originally meant a strip of land but has come to mean a stretch of the river. *See Allanmead Close.*

ANDOVER ROAD, BS4. Other West Country places are represented in nearby streets.

ANGEL GROUND BS4. An old field name.

ANGERS ROAD, BS4. A field name which is either derived from the OE *angr*, grassland or grazing land, or it could be the personal name of the Lords of the Manor of Angersleigh in Somerset during the reign of Edward II.

ANGLESEA PLACE, BS8. This road forms a junction with Wellington Park, and as the Marquis of Anglesey was Wellington's cavalry commander at Waterloo, this is in all likelihood a mis-spelling of his title.

ANSTEY STREET, BS5. In 1900, Anstey Littleton and Co. were accountants and auctioneers. The original road here, together with part of Lena Street, was known as Littleton Street. Later, when Anstey Street came into being in the 1890s, only the section round the corner remained as Littleton Street. It seems fairly safe to assume the company had an interest in this development.

ANSTEYS ROAD, BS15. A family of this name were prominent traders in the vicinity at the end of the nineteenth and the beginning of the twentieth century. They had premises in Jefferies Hill.

ANTHEA ROAD, BS5. It is unknown who inspired this choice of name.

ANTONA COURT / DRIVE, BS11. Antona is the Roman name for the Avon.

ANTRIM ROAD, BS9. Many roads in this area were named after locations in the UK and Eire.

ANVIL STREET, BS2. It would seem that this name was chosen because of the industrial nature of the area.

APPLEBY WALK, BS4. In keeping with other roads nearby, this is named after a town famous for its Norman castle.

APPLEDORE CLOSE, BS14. Appledore is a town in Devon: the name is derived from the OE *appuldor*, apple tree. One theory suggests that it is named after the terrain, or there is an alternative Viking connection, as Appledore in Kent was where the Vikings landed. *See Andereach Close and Allanmead Road.*

APPLEGATE, BS10. Apparently this is an old field name.

APSLEY ROAD, BS8. Apsley House was the London residence of the Duke of Wellington. Other roads in the vicinity also have connections with the Iron Duke. *See Mornington Road and Wellington Park.*

APSLEY STREET, BS5. This is named perhaps for the same reason as Apsley Road.

ARBUTUS DRIVE / WALK BS9. This is taken from the name of an ancient pathway nearby. Arbutus is a genus of tree and shrub with either bell-shaped or globular white or reddish flowers. It is sometimes known as the wild strawberry.

THE ARCADE, BS1. This is, by definition, a covered walkway lined with shops.

ARCHER COURT, BS15. A Mrs. Archer of London was sister to Sir Michael Newton of Barrs Court. In 1748 she paid for the restoration of a monument which had been erected in Bristol Cathedral to the memory of Sir Richard Newton-Cradock and his wife, also of Barrs Court. *See Barrs Court Road and Cradock Close.*

ARCHER WALK, BS14. Previously named Langdown Walk, this was renamed after an active member of the Community Council who was elected Chairman just prior to his death in 1976.

THE ARCHES, BS6. A popular name for the magnificent railway viaduct spanning the bottom of Cotham Brow and Cheltenham Road. It was built in 1874.

ARCHFIELD ROAD, BS6. This is thought to have been named after an ornamental stone arch, once part of the decorative stonework in the grounds of Cotham Park. The arch was situated at what is now the junction of Archfield Road and Cotham Grove.

ARDENTON WALK, BS10. Christian Ardenton was a widow who was resident in Westbury-on-Trym in the seventeenth century. She was buried on 4 December 1625.

ARDERN CLOSE, BS9. It is recorded in Westbury Parish records that a Sir Robert Ardern gave two houses which he owned in Lawford's Gate, worth £12 per year, for the use of the poor of Westbury Parish. This is almost certainly the same gentleman who was buried at Westbury Church on 2 March 1582. He lived at Cote, Stoke Bishop, and was a great benefactor to the poor of Westbury.

ARGUS ROAD, BS3. This is a name taken from Greek mythology, Argus being a creature with 100 eyes, only two of which slept at any one time. He was set to guard Io, whom Zeus had turned into a heifer, but he was lulled to sleep by the sweet music from the lyre of Hermes. Zeus's wife, Hera, stole his eyes and placed them on the bird sacred to her, the peacock, which is how it obtained its strange tail feathers. This road was built on the site of an old colliery of the same name.

ARGYLE AVENUE / STREET, BS5 / PLACE, BS8 / ROAD, BS16. This was the name of a noble family which has had connections with Bristol since the fifteenth century. The Dukes of Argyll were head of the Campbell clan.

ARGYLE ROAD, BS2. Parallel to Campbell Street. *See Argyle Avenue.*

ARGYLE STREET, BS3. It is assumed this is named for the same reason as above.

ARLEY COTTAGES / HILL / PARK, BS6. Originally known as Lamp Black Hill, Arley Cottages was renamed after the building of Arley Chapel. An anonymous donor provided half the capital. He was afterwards established as being John Holmes, and the chapel and hill were named after his birthplace, Arley in Worcestershire. Arley Hill should have been part of Redland Road, as was decided by the Bristol Corporation's Clarification of Street Names in 1857, but it remained known locally as Arley Hill, and the name stuck.

ARLEY TERRACE, BS5. Perhaps so named because the builder had connections with the chapel.

ARLINGHAM WAY, BS12. All the roads in this area are named after Gloucestershire villages. Arlingham is famous for the tragic murder of Amelia Phipps by a spurned admirer in 1873. Amelia was described as resembling a golden-haired china doll. She kept house for her brother, Tom, in the small farming community there. Charles Butt, a young neighbouring farmer was besotted with her but she was young and unwilling to commit herself. Things came to a head one August evening at her home, West End Farm, when Charles considered she was paying too much attention to a friend of her brother's. He persuaded her to walk with him in the lane in front of the house and a few moments later family and friends were horrified to hear the sound of a gunshot. Butt went on the run but was caught in South Wales. He was 23 years old at the time of his execution at Gloucester.

ARLINGTON ROAD, BS4 / VILLAS, BS8. Arlington is a village in Gloucestershire. The derivation is from the Anglo Saxon. The first syllable is derived from a personal name, Aelfred, and the last syllable, *tun,* means farmstead. Henry Bennett, Earl of Arlington (1618-1685) was a loyal Royalist supporter. After the restoration he was appointed Keeper of the Privy Purse and Secretary of State. He was raised to the peerage in 1663. The connection may be with the group of roads in this area named after noblemen of Charles II's court.

ARMADA PLACE, BS2. The road which used to run parallel to this was called Francis Place which led one to suppose a connection with Sir Francis Drake. However, Francis was the second name of Sir Thomas Fremantle so perhaps the wrong conclusion was drawn when the road was named. *See Fremantle Road / Square.*

ARMIDALE AVENUE, BS6. (apparently mis-spelt in Philip's Ordnance Survey A to Z) Otherwise spelt Armdale. Three Scottish villages bear this name, as does a town in New South Wales, Australia, but the reason for this choice is unknown.

ARMOURY SQUARE, BS5. An Armoury was built on this site in 1805 to hold "a stand of 20,000 arms" (muskets) to prepare for the feared French invasion. The Armoury was sold to the Corporation of the Poor in 1831 to be used as additional accommodation for the Bristol Workhouse, known as St. Peter's Hospital, but this never came into effect when it was decided to use the old Admiralty prison at Stapleton instead. The Armoury was up for sale again in 1840, and this time the purchasers demolished all but four houses within the compound, and developed the rest of the site for housing.

ARMSTRONG COURT, BS15. This is named after one of the foremost railway engineers used by Great Western Railways. Joseph Armstrong held the position of Chief Mechanical Engineer at Swindon from 1864 -77.

ARNALL DRIVE, BS10. William Arnall was Collector of the Poor Rate for Westbury-on-Trym in 1664.

ARNCLIFFE BS12. These flats are part of the Doncaster Road development and were therefore given the name of a location in the north of England.

ARNSIDE ROAD, BS10. This is one of the roads named after Lake District locations. The name means 'a hillside where eagles are found'.

ARNOS STREET, BS4. The name is taken from the mock castle built here in the 1760s, which some say - and some dispute - was built in imitation of a castle on the banks of the River Arno near Florence, Italy.

ARROWFIELD CLOSE, BS14. There is a possible historical connection here, a site on which once stood Lyons Court. The archers or arrowmen lived in the Royal Forest, which comprised part of this area at one time.

ARTHUR SKEMP CLOSE, BS5. This is named after a chairman of the University Settlement who did a great deal for the people of Barton Hill. The University Settlement was designed to provide the workers of the area with access to evening classes and the chance to develop skills of a practical, educational and sporting nature. Arthur Skemp was killed in action in France in 1917.

ARTHUR STREET, BS5. Arthur was the youngest son of George and Elizabeth Gerrish. *See Gerrish Avenue.*

ARTHURSWOOD ROAD, BS13. According to the 1683 survey, this is a field name in the Manor of Bishport. The Arthur family were Lords of the Manor of Bishopsworth in the fourteenth century.

ARUNDEL CLOSE BS13. These are named in honour of Sir Thomas Arundel, Lord of the Manor of Long Ashton. He sold the manor and accommodation for the clergy therein to John Smyth whose family lived at Ashton Court for 300 years. Long Ashton was in the Hundred of Hartcliffe.

ARUNDEL ROAD BS7. Possibly named after Arundel Castle. Nearby roads are Berkeley Road and Monmouth Road and also seem to share a castle theme.

ASCOT CLOSE, BS16. Another road in the area with a racecourse theme.

ASCOT CLOSE, BS10. There is no obvious reason for this choice of name except that it adjoins Home Close, so perhaps this was part of a farm where horses were grazed.

ASH GROVE, BS16. This is built on an area called The Thicket. *See Thicket Road.*

ASH ROAD, BS7. Among other roads with sylvan connections. *See Oak Road.*

ASH WALK, BS10. Possibly descriptive. This area was completely rural until the 1950s.

ASHBOURNE CLOSE, BS15. The name means 'the ash trees that grow by the stream', which was probably an apt description at one time.

ASHCOMBE CRESCENT, BS15. Another road with a rural flavour.

ASHCOTT, BS14. Perhaps this is a field name. The meaning is 'a dwelling by the ash trees'.

ASHCROFT ROAD, BS9. Another road with a reminder of times past - its name means 'enclosed arable land where the ash trees grow'.

ASHDENE AVENUE, BS5. This is an improvised name from the OE *aesc*, an ash tree, and *dene*, a valley.

ASHER LANE, BS2. The name comes from *aecer*, acre or arable plot. It is often used as a field name although in this case it is probably a surname, perhaps of someone who once owned property here.

ASHFIELD ROAD, BS3. Ashfield Lodge used to stand here, so the name is self - explanatory.

ASHFORD ROAD, BS12. Ashford is a town in Kent. Other roads nearby have been given similar names with no apparent link.

ASHFORD WAY, BS15. The name means 'river crossing by the ash wood' but this is not an accurate description here. Perhaps it is just a made-up name with forest undertones.

ASHGROVE AVENUE BS3 / ROAD, BS7. In both cases they are named after a house that stood on the site.

ASHGROVE ROAD, BS6. Ashgrove here is probably an amalgam of Ashley and Grove.

ASHLAND ROAD, BS13. On the 1683 survey this is the name of a field on Bishopsworth Farm. The first syllable is ME *asche* or Anglo Saxon *esce*, ash tree.

ASHLEY CLOSE, BS6. This was chosen to be in keeping with the local association with Ashley Court.

ASHLEY COURT ROAD, BS7. *See Ashley Hill.*

ASHLEY DOWN ROAD, BS7. This area was formerly in the Manor of Asseley and was granted by charter to the monks of St. James' Priory by William, Earl of Gloucester, in 1170.

ASHLEY GROVE ROAD, BS2. This was perhaps a wooded part of the grounds of Ashley Court.

ASHLEY HILL / PARADE / PARK / ROAD / STREET, BS2. These all commemorate Ashley Court, which was demolished in the 1870s. Cromwell was reputed to have slept in a farmhouse on the estate during the siege of Bristol in 1645.

ASHLEY, BS15. This may be named after R.W.Ashley and Sons, Kingswood boot manufacturers at around the turn of the nineteenth and twentieth centuries.

ASHMAN CLOSE, BS5. Queen Victoria created Sir Herbert Ashman first Lord Mayor of Bristol when she visited the city in 1899 to open a new convalescent home on the edge of the Downs which later became the Bristol Maternity Hospital. This visit was part of the celebrations to commemorate her Diamond Jubilee. The reason for the new status was that, after many years of being included in the bishopric of Gloucester, Bristol had been reinstated as a City and County with its own bishop.

ASHMEAD WAY, BS1. It is assumed this honours Frederick Dods Ashmead, Engineer to the Bristol Corporation in the early years of the twentieth century.

ASHTON AVENUE / DRIVE / ROAD, BS3 (within what was the Ashton Court estate). The name is from the OE and means 'enclosure where the ash trees grow'.

ASHTON GATE ROAD / TERRACE, BS3. These roads take their name from the village of Long Ashton.

ASHTON VALE ROAD, BS3. This name is descriptive of the geography.

ASHVILLE ROAD, BS3. This is a made-up name - the second syllable is from the Old French *ville* - country house, village, or collection of villages round a city. It was also a territorial division under the feudal system.

ASHWELL CLOSE, BS14. This is a field name taken from the 1845 tithe map of Whitchurch.

ASHWICKE, BS14. The name means 'dairy farm where the ash trees grow'. There were several dairy farms in the area at the beginning of the twentieth century.

ASSEMBLY ROOMS LANE, BS1. The Assembly Rooms, built in 1755 and demolished in 1912, had a side frontage in this lane. The glory days of the building waned when the Clifton Assembly Rooms were built in the Mall in 1811. Later it was used as a theatre for a brief period until complaints from the owners of the Theatre Royal in King Street forced it to close.

ASTRY CLOSE, BS11. Edward IV granted the Manor of Bishops Stoke and Henbury Saltmarsh by letters patent to Sir Ralph Sadlier. The Manor passed to Sir Samuel Astry in 1680. He was a barrister who died in 1704 at the age of 73. There is a fine memorial to him in Aust Church. *See Sadlier Close.*

ATCHLEY STREET, BS5. This may have some connection with Atchleys the solicitors of Clare Street. One member of the family, Edward, lived at Warmley at the end of the nineteenth century.

ATHERSTONE, BS15. The name of a Warwickshire town, but there is no obvious reason for this naming.

ATHLONE WALK, BS4. All local streets are on an Irish theme. *See Bantry Road.*

ATKINS CLOSE, BS14. John and Alice Atkins lived in the parish of Keynsham in 1670 and were exempt from the Hearth Tax.

ATLANTIC ROAD, BS11 / WALK, BS1. Possibly named to honour the Battle of the Atlantic, which kept a shipping lane open between the United Kingdom and the USA throughout the Second World War.

ATLAS CLOSE, BS16. A large property called Atlas Villa once stood in this area.

ATLAS ROAD, BS3. The Atlas Assurance Company was prominent at the time this road was built and perhaps had a vested interest. There was also an Atlas locomotive works in Foundry Lane.

ATLAS STREET, BS2. This was previously known as Atlas Terrace. There was an Atlas Bedstead Company in the vicinity at the time so perhaps the owner also had an interest in this development.

ATWOOD DRIVE, BS11. William Atwood was a rate-payer in Westbury in 1662, assessed on £10 at 2d. per £1. One of his daughters married Richard Hort, who is buried in St. Thomas' Church.

AUBREY MEADS, BS15. This commemorates Dr Aubrey, a local GP in the 1920s and 30s.

AUBREY ROAD, BS3. Aubrey was the son of the builder, W P Kingston.

AUBURN AVENUE, BS15. Named after a place in California, the scene of a gold rush during the 1840's. *See California Road.*

AUBURN ROAD, BS6. Auburn House stood on the north side of the new road in the mid-nineteenth century. It has been said the house was given this name

because of the reddish tone of the soil but another possibility has emerged. Auburn is a town in South Australia. Is there a link with Canowie Road? *See Canowie Road.*

AUDREY WALK, BS9. Obviously a woman's name, but who she was does not seem to have been recorded.

AUSTEN GROVE, BS7. All the roads in the vicinity are named after literary figures. This is after Jane Austen, the early nineteenth-century novelist who lived for part of her life in Bath. She is famous for six wittily and beautifully observed novels of the English upper-middle calss society of her times.

AVALON ROAD, BS15. A house of this name which stood on Oldland Common was owned by a family of builders called Adams, who may have been involved in this development.

AVEBURY ROAD, BS3. Named after the place of the famous stone circle in Wiltshire. The first component is a personal name, Afa, and the last syllable denotes a fort or fortified place. The theme is continued with adjoining Silbury Road.

AVENING ROAD, BS5. This is a place name, Avening being in Gloucestershire. The meaning from the OE is 'the people who dwelt by the River Avon'. The Gloucestershire connection is continued in nearby Tetbury Road.

THE AVENUE, BS8. This avenue was once lined with elms.

THE AVENUE, BS5 / BS6 / BS9. A favourite name for any straight, tree-lined street.

AVERAY ROAD, BS16. A Merchant Venturer called John Averay, who was president of the Dolphin Society, owned this land. He died in 1774.

AVON CRESCENT, BS1 / GROVE, BS9 / PARK, BS5 / STREET, BS2 / VALE, BS9 / VIEW, BS15 / WALK, BS13 / WAY, BS9. All derive their names from the local river, the name coming from the Welsh *afon*, meaning river, or the OE *abona*.

AVONDOWN CLOSE, BS10 / CLOSE, BS3. Named after the housing association responsible for these developments, now incorporated into the Guinness Trust.

AVONLEA, BS15. This is an invented name meaning 'meadow by the Avon'.

AVONLEAZE, BS9. This is a reference to the river flowing on the other side of the Portway. A pathway leads there from this street.

AVONLEIGH COURT / ROAD, BS3. This name means 'meadow by the river Avon'.

AVONMOUTH ROAD, BS11. Self-explanatory. In 1793 there was also a field under Kingsweston Hill near the river called Avon's town.

AVONSIDE ROAD / WAY, BS2. This is so called because part of the road runs parallel to the river.

AVONWOOD CLOSE, BS11. Seemingly this is purely descriptive.

AVONVALE ROAD, BS5. A made-up name. Once known as George Lane, it was renamed when the road was developed for commercial and domestic use. The name was chosen as the road dips down towards the river.

AWDLETT CLOSE, BS11. Named after Henbury Awdlett House which once stood here. The name may have derived from a family name, Audley.

AXBRIDGE ROAD, BS4. This is one of many roads named after West Country towns and villages.

AYLESBURY CRESCENT / ROAD, BS3. This is named after a town in Buckinghamshire, the first syllable of which originates from a personal noun, Aegel. There is a predominance of United Kingdom town names in the vicinity.

AYLMER CRESCENT, BS14. This was probably the surname of the owner of the land.

AYLMINGTON WALK, BS11. This is a corruption of Elmington, a manor in the Hundred of Henbury. The origin is OE - the first component is a personal name, *Athelmunds*, and thus the name means the farmstead or enclosure belonging to him.

BACK ROAD, BS3. A comparatively new development so named, it is supposed, because it runs along the back of Coronation Road.

BACKFIELDS / BACKFIELDS LANE, BS2. This was the site of the fields behind Stoke's Croft, which was developed in the middle of the nineteenth century. It is shown on Roque's 1741 map.

BACKWELL WALK, BS4. Many roads in the area are called after Somerset villages, probably because Robert de Mowbray who owned land in this area also held many manors in Somerset, including Backwell.

BADEN ROAD, BS5. It is uncertain from which source this road took its name. It may have been the region to the south west of Germany, the popular spa Baden-Baden, or maybe it was in honour of Lord Baden-Powell, founder of the Scout movement. This latter would seem the most likely as the road was built in 1903 when the gallantry he displayed in the Boer War of 1899-1902 would still have been nationally famous. Prior to development the street was known as St. James' Terrace.

BADEN ROAD, BS15. It would seem this naming was for the same reason as the road in Barton Hill, although it is sometimes used as a first name and may relate to someone connected with the area.

BADENHAM GROVE, BS11. Roger de Badenham was a descendant of John de Badenham, who landed with William the Conqueror and was granted permission to build a manor at Kingsweston in 1222.

BADGERS WALK, BS4. The name was chosen by developers for its rural connotation.

BADMINTON ROAD, BS2. This was named after Badminton House, Gloucestershire, the seat of the Dukes of Beaufort. The name is possibly derived from the 'tun of Beaumund's people' whereas other sources suggest 'the farm enclosure of Beadhu-helm'.

BADMINTON ROAD / WALK, BS16. The road leading to Badminton.

BADMINTON, BS16. This development is named after country estates.

BAGLYN AVENUE, BS16. A Mr Baglin owned a saw mill in Bett's Barton (now Buckingham Place, Downend) in the nineteenth century. This is perhaps a variant spelling of his name.

Baldwin Street, c. 1914

BAGNELL CLOSE, BS14. This is so called after Robert Bagnell, churchwarden of Keynsham Church in 1674.

BAKERSFIELD, BS15. Another of the Californian place names. *See California Road.*

BALACLAVA ROAD, BS16. This is named after the Crimean War battle on 25 October 1854, infamous for a confused order to attack which resulted in over 400 British soldiers perishing in a single charge against the enemy along a narrow valley, from which escape was almost impossible. This massacre was immortalised by Alfred, Lord Tennyson in his famous poem *The Charge of the Light Brigade.* The name Balaclava originates from the Italian *bella cala,* beautiful port.

BALDWIN STREET, BS1. This was the site of St. Baldwin's Cross, an ancient shrine; also of Baldwin's Cross Mill before the river was diverted. The present street was built in the 1880s, but the former street dated back to ancient times. One source states that a tract of land was granted to Baldwin Albis c. 1160. Henry II, when a boy, was schooled by a Mr. Matthews in letters and civic behaviour. The present street is built on the site of the old one.

BALFOUR ROAD, BS3. This is possibly named after the Rt. Hon A. J. Balfour who had a distinguished political career which began in 1874 when, at the age of 26, he entered parliament as Conservative MP for Hertford. His Bill of 1902 was significant in education, giving responsibility for primary and secondary schools to local county councils. He was leader of the Unionist party and Prime Minister from 1902-1905. He was the grandson of the 2nd Marquess of Salisbury. Other roads in the area are also named after political figures.

BALLAST LANE, BS11. There is an obvious shipping connection here.

BALMAIN STREET, BS4. It has been suggested that this is a surname, seemingly of French origin. During the Napoleonic Wars there were large numbers of French prisoners held in Bristol, 2000 at one time, (including some Spanish), and it is rumoured that some of them were put to work on the building of the New Cut between the years 1804-09. Perhaps some managed to escape and remained in the area.

BALMORAL COURT, BS17 / ROAD, BS15. Several local roads are named after royal residences.

BALMORAL ROAD, BS7. Almost certainly named after the royal residence. There is a Windsor Road in the vicinity.

BAMFIELD, BS14. This was an ancient field name. Fortunately those with a sense of continuity in the Bristol civic planning department have preserved many of these ancient field names when naming modern streets, after consultations with local history groups.

BAMPTON CLOSE, BS13. Bampton is a small town in Devon, and was the scene of a massacre in 614 when Cynegils, leader of the West Saxons, defeated the Cornish army, which lost 2000 men.

BANFIELD CLOSE, BS11. This is a field name derived from the OE *ban*, meaning bean, and *feld* meaning field or open country.

BANGOR GROVE, BS4. One of a group of roads named after cathedrals.

BANGROVE WALK, BS11. This is another field name most probably meaning a copse producing berries.

BANISTER GROVE, BS4. John Banister (1625?-1679) was violinist-in-ordinary to Charles 11. The year of his birth is given variously as 1625 or 1630.

BANK ROAD, BS11. This refers to the banks, which were built up to prevent flooding in the area.

BANKSIDE ROAD, BS4. This is a reference to the proximity of Brislington Brook.

BANKSIDE, BS16. Perhaps a reference to an embankment rather than a river bank. The area slopes on three sides from this point.

BANNER ROAD, BS6. This is named after the builder, William Banner, who was also a carpenter and undertaker and was living in the Cathay in 1872.

BANNERMAN ROAD, BS5. This was once called St. Mark's Lane. It was renamed in honour of Sir Henry Campbell-Bannerman (1836-1908) when the majority of the houses were built. Sir Henry was a Liberal M.P. who became Prime Minister when Balfour resigned in 1905. He resigned due to ill health in 1908 when Asquith succeeded to the post and died shortly afterwards. The Easton area was a Liberal stronghold in the early years of the twentieth century.

BANTOCK CLOSE, BS4. Sir Granville Bantock (1868-1948) was a composer and conductor famous for his *Scenes from the Scottish Highlands* and *Pagan Symphony*. British composers are the theme for this small area. His grandson, Anton, is a well-known local historian.

BANTRY ROAD, BS4. All surrounding roads have Irish names owing to the fact that they were built soon after the formation of what was then called the Irish Free State in 1922. The man in charge of the development was a loyal Irish nationalist and patriotically named all the roads accordingly.

BANWELL CLOSE, BS13. This is another of the roads named after Somerset villages.

BANWELL ROAD, BS3. One of the roads which seem to have a Smyth connection. Banwell was part of the Ashton Court estate. *See Arundel Close.*

BAPTIST STREET, BS2. The site of Bagpath's Mill. The area was known as Baptist Mills by 1609, which was 50 years before this religious community was recorded in East Bristol. One suggestion is that the name derives from baptiste fabric. Baptisms have been described as having taken place here, however.

BARBOUR GARDENS / ROAD, BS13. George de Barbour paid 18d. as rents of assize in 1317. The naming committee decided it would be interesting to use the surnames of past residents of the area when naming these new roads in the twentieth century.

BARCROFT CLOSE, BS5. Gilbert Barcroft (1686-1754) was an apothecary who left money, the interest from which was to be used to help the poor of St. George.

BARKER WALK, BS5. This is named after Alderman William Robert Barker, Liberal councillor for Westbury ward from 1882 to the early 1900s, when he was elected Alderman. He served as Mayor in the year 1892-3. He was associated with many religious and charitable institutions and was a strong advocate of temperance.

BARLEY CLOSE, BS17. A reminder that this was agricultural land not so long ago.

BARLEY CROFT, BS9. From the OE *Bar-leah*, boarwood or clearing, a croft being a small enclosure.

BARNABAS STREET, BS2. This is named after the church which once stood near here, and which was consecrated on 12 September 1843. A crypt was incorporated in the design to be used as a burial place, but this practice was prohibited after only one body had been interred. This attractive church with its distinctive steeple was demolished in the late 1970s.

BARNES STREET, BS5. So named after either the architect Edward William Barnes or else the Dorset dialect poet the Rev. William Barnes. The street was built c.1880. There was a Francis Kentucky Barnes who served as an alderman of the city in 1850, so it is also possible that the street was named after him.

BARNSTAPLE ROAD / WALK, BS4. All surrounding roads are called after West Country locations.

BAROSSA PLACE, BS1. This is one of the roads in Bristol named after a land battle. This battle was fought in 1811 in the Peninsular War, and was triggered by the French kidnapping of the King of Spain. Spain sent an appeal to Britain, and Sir Arthur Wellesley, later the Duke of Wellington, was placed in charge of the British forces sent to rout the French.

BARRACKS LANE, BS11. There was a barracks here where miscellaneous regiments were stationed during the middle of the nineteenth century.

BARRATT STREET, BS5. Isaac Barratt was a haulier living in Easton in 1872. Possibly this street was built on the site of his premises.

BARRINGTON CLOSE / COURT, BS15. This was one of the Gloucester hundreds at the time the Domesday Book was compiled. Many Gloucestershire names have been chosen for roads in this area.

BARRINGTON COURT, BS3. Barrington was also the name of an ancient settlement near Ilchester, so there could be a link with the Smyth family as they owned vast tracts of land in Somerset. There were also people of that name living in North Somerset in the mid nineteenth century.

BARROW HILL CRESCENT / ROAD, BS11. This is built on the site of the ancient Barrow Hill Farm.

BARROW ROAD, BS5. This was a steep, narrow lane in 1717. 'Barrow' comes from the ME *bere*, meaning lane. It is possible this was named after J. Barrow, mayor of Bristol, in 1824. He was the first old boy of Colston's School to achieve this honour.

BARROWMEAD DRIVE, BS11. This is a field name from the OE *beorg*, meaning hill, barrow or mound, - thus 'the meadow in which the barrow stands'.

THE BARROWS, BS13. This is a field name taken from the 1683 survey of the manor of Bishport.

BARRS COURT AVENUE / ROAD, BS15. These are both named after the ancient manor house which played a large part in the history of Kingswood Forest. The name comes from Lady Jane Barre who owned the land in the fifteenth century. The Newton family enlarged the court in the sixteenth century and built a large mansion there. A farm replaced this in the eighteenth century. All traces of the house have now vanished. Once known as Abbess Lane, a reference to the nuns of Laycock Abbey. The land here was owned by the church.

BARRY CLOSE, HILL / ROAD, BS15. This was always known as Cherry Orchard Hill and it has not yet been established how it transmuted into Barry Close, Hill or Road.

BARTLETT'S ROAD, BS3. This was formerly known as Bartlett Lane, indicating that someone of that name either traded or lived here in the nineteenth century, or even earlier.

BARTLEY STREET, BS3. This would appear to be a surname and, being among the roads built by Philip Clark, it is likely to be an association of his. The name itself derives from OE *beore* and *leah,* which translate as birchwood.

BARTON CLOSE, BS4. This may well have been farmland once upon a time, *barton* meaning farm.

BARTON GREEN / BARTON HILL ROAD / MANOR / ROAD / STREET / VALE, BS5 / BS2. These are built on part of the Manor of Barton Regis (Royal Farm). Barton is from the OE *beon*, part of the Manore-tun meaning corn farm, outlying grange or barley farm, denoting the demesne farm of Bristol Castle.

THE BARTON, BS15. This area was farmland at the beginning of the twentieth century.

BARTONIA GROVE, BS4. This is the name of a town in Indiana, USA, and also of a genus of plants which originated in Texas and which are propagated by seed. Some species are extremely rare. The connection with Bartonia Grove is unclear, however.

BARWOOD COURT, BS15. This is named after a district of Gloucester. Other names are connected with woods nearby so that may be have been the reason for inclusion. Alternatively it is also a place in Fife, scene of a mining disaster in 1878, which could be a possibility given the colliery connection in this district.

THE BATCHES, BS3. Batch is from *baece* or *bece*, an old name meaning stream in a valley. The more modern 'beck' derives from this.

BATES CLOSE, BS5. John Bates was Mayor from 1859-60 and a member of the City Council from 1854 to 1865. He was described as 'a big heavy man with a great deal of dignity about him'. He died in a shooting accident in July 1869.

BATH BUILDINGS, BS6. This is the site of the Grand Pleasure Gardens built in 1746 by Thomas Rennison, threadmaker. The original pool was over 400 ft in circumference. There was a smaller pool for ladies, and the Old England Tavern stood in the gardens. The place gained a reputation for debauchery and eventually closed in 1916. A part of the site was then sold to Colston's Girl's School.

BATH ROAD, BS3. This is the A4 which runs through Totterdown and Brislington to Bath.

BATH STREET, BS3. As above.

BATH STREET, BS2. As above; this would have been be the old way out of the city to Bath.

BATH STREET, BS16. As above, an alternative route to Bath.

BATHURST PARADE / TERRACE, BS3. This is named after Charles Bragge, Lord Bathurst, M.P. for Bristol in the late eighteenth century. *See Braggs Lane.*

BATHWELL ROAD, BS3. This is a made-up name - a combination of Bath and Wells, as the road is midway between Bath Road and Wells Road.

BATLEY COURT, BS15. Thomas Batley was Keeper of the Royal Forest, the King's Wood, in 1596.

BATTENBURG ROAD, BS5. Battenberg (frequently mis-spelt) is the name of the descendants of Prince Alexander of Hesse. His sons Prince Louis and Prince Henry married, respectively, a granddaughter and daughter of Queen Victoria. The family name was changed to Mountbatten because of anxiety about public anti-German attitudes during the First World War. Battenburg derives from the German *Burg*, a castle, or *Berg*, a mountain.

BATTEN'S LANE / ROAD, BS5. The road takes its name from the lane, which is listed in directories early in the twentieth century and takes its name from Batten's Quarry. Batten's Road led up to the quarry.

BATTEN ROAD, BS5. H. Cary G. Batten was sheriff of Bristol in 1894, although this road probably owes its name to Batten's Quarry. This would have been the path leading to it.

BATTERSBY WAY, BS10. Named after John Harford Battersby, a member of the famous Quaker family, who lived at Stoke House, Stoke Bishop. *See Harford Close.*

BATTERSEA ROAD, BS5. This is named after the metropolitan borough in London; other roads in the area were named on the same theme. The meaning is 'Beaduric's island'.

BATTSON ROAD, BS14. Thomas Battson was resident in the parish and tithing of Whitechurch (Whitchurch) in 1670. He was granted exemption from the Hearth Tax.

BAUGH GARDENS / ROAD, BS16. These are named after nearby Baugh Farm. A family of this name was trading in Bristol in the eighteenth century.

BAY GARDENS, BS5. All the roads in this development are named after herbs.

BAY TREE CLOSE, BS12. All surrounding roads are named after trees. Bay is a small tree with evergreen, aromatic leaves, used in cooking. It was a popular Victorian garden plant and many Bristol gardens are still graced by mature bay trees today.

BAYHAM ROAD, BS4. Bayham is near Tunbridge Wells, the site of an abbey called after a personal name Beage and *ham*, village. There is no obvious reason for this choice.

BAYLEYS DRIVE, BS15. The Bayley family owned land in South Gloucestershire in the eighteenth century.

BAYNHAM COURT, BS15. This is called after Sir Baynham Throckmorton, who was appointed Forest Ranger in 1668. *See Forest Road.*

BAYNTON ROAD, BS3. This is perhaps named after Thomas, Charles and Isaac Baynton, brewers of Ashton Gate in 1830. Maybe this was built on the site of their brewery.

BAYSWATER AVENUE, BS6. A district of London. There is no obvious reason for this choice.

BAYSWATER ROAD, BS7. Another road nearby is called after a district of London so perhaps the builder had connections there.

BEACHGROVE GARDENS / ROAD, BS16. The clue to the naming of these roads is said to be hidden in the deeds of the houses themselves, but no owners have offered an explanation yet.

BEACHLEY WALK, BS11. This is named after a village on the Welsh coast of the Severn estuary lying on a spit of land between the Wye and the Severn. Close by is the rocky island on which lie the ruins of the chapel of St. Tecla. There is no obvious reason for this choice.

BEACONLEA, BS15. This is a reference to the beacon installed on Hanham Mount in 1951 to mark the spot where John Wesley and George Whitefield preached their open- air sermons.

BEACONSFIELD ROAD / CLOSE / STREET BS8 / BS5 / BS4 / BS2 All roads thus named honour the Earl of Beaconsfield, Benjamin Disraeli (1804 -81). He was Tory Prime Minister, author, wit, and purchaser for Britain of the Suez Canal. Queen Victoria elevated him to the peerage in 1876 during his second period as Tory Prime Minister while, at the same time, he gave her the title of Empress of India. She made no secret of her preference for him over Gladstone, the Liberal leader.

BEAM STREET, BS5. A possible explanation for this name is the cotton factory which was situated nearby, a beam being the cross-piece of the weaver's loom. There was also nearby Beam Bridge Station, which was a temporary terminus of the Bristol and Exeter Railway, which ran between Wellington and Exeter, until the line was re-routed when the Whiteball Tunnel under the Blackdown Hills was completed. A coach service joined the two ends of the line.

THE BEANACRE, BS11. This would appear to be an old field name.

BEAN STREET, BS5. This may originally have been part of a smallholding where beans were grown, as there were a number of market gardens in the area. Alternatively it may have been the vegetable garden of a large house, long since gone. It is also a surname, although more common in the north of England than the south.

BEARBRIDGE ROAD, BS13. This is a field name in the Manor of Bishport (1683 Survey). The derivation is probably the OE *baer*, bare and *brycg*, which means bridge or marshy causeway. An alternative is that the first syllable could be OE *bearu* which would translate as grove or wood.

BEAUCHAMP ROAD, BS7. This is perhaps named in honour of William 7th Earl of Beauchamp (1872-38) whose family name was Lygon. He was a leading Liberal politician, and Governor of New South Wales from 1899-01. Other earldoms have been celebrated in the naming of roads in this district.

BEAUFORT CLOSE / COURT / ROAD, etc. BS3 / BS5 / BS7 / BS8 / BS16. Throughout the city and south Gloucestershire suburbs there are a great many streets all honouring the Dukes of Beaufort whose family have always played such an important role in the area. *See Badminton Road, BS2, Brinkworthy Road, BS16, Capel Road, BS11, Duchess Way, BS16, Fitzroy Road / Street, BS4, Hillfields Avenue, BS16, Lodge Drive / Hill / Drive, BS16, Raglan Lane, BS5/ Place / Road BS7, Stoke View Road, BS16, Thicket Avenue, BS16, Welton Walk BS15.*

BEAULEY ROAD, BS3. This is seemingly a mis-spelling of the Hampshire village. The name means beautiful place - from the French *beau lieu.*

BEAUMONT CLOSE, BS15. This is a town in California. *See California Road.*

BEAUMONT STREET / TERRACE, BS5. This could be a field name.

BEAZER COURT, BS16. This is named after Councillor A. S. Beazer who was instrumental in organising the building of Soundwell swimming baths. He was there at the official opening.

BECKFORD GARDENS, BS5. This road was named in honour of William Beckford (1759-44), a wealthy eccentric. He was MP for Wells and Hindon. So anxious was he to retain privacy that he bought the properties each side of his house in Lansdown Crescent, Bath. A secret pathway led from behind the crescent in which stood his house, to the tower he built to accommodate his collection of *objets d'art.* It was to this tower he would escape to write. He had always lived extravagantly and, prior to moving to Bath, he had been forced to sell the family mansion to satisfy his creditors.

BECKINGTON ROAD / WALK, BS4. This is the name of a village in Somerset; various sources suggest it means either 'the homestead, village or enclosure of

Becca's people', or that the name derives from *baec* meaning beech tree. A number of Somerset village names have been chosen for the surrounding streets.

BECKSPOOL ROAD, BS16. The Quaker Joseph Beck created a pond in the grounds of the manor house he owned from 1737. The overflow from the pond fed an additional pool, which he added to the grounds. He died in 1791.

BEDFORD CRESCENT, BS7. Presumably this is named after the town. The first syllable is a personal noun, Beda. A number of place names are used for local roads.

BEDMINSTER DOWN ROAD, BS3. *Bed* is Welsh for 'to' or 'at' and *mynster* comes from the OE for church or monastery.

BEDMINSTER PARADE / PLACE / ROAD, BS3. When Bedminster Road was first developed in 1925 it was named Butler Road after William Henry Butler, a local industrialist and magistrate, but was subsequently changed to Bedminster Road, probably because it was an extension of an existing road.

BEECH CLOSE, BS15. Probably descriptive of the terrain before development began.

BEECH ROAD, BS7. A number of local streets are named after trees.

BEECHCROFT WALK, BS7. This is near Green Close so it is probably a field name.

BEECHEN DRIVE, BS16. Beechen Cliff was the location of a conduit used by the monks of Bath Priory to carry water across the Avon to supply their fish ponds. Beechen Drive is in Fishponds so maybe that is the link.

BEECHES GROVE, BS4. This is built on the site of Hemplow House, which was demolished in 1969. Perhaps there were beeches in the grounds.

THE BEECHES, BS15. A reminder, perhaps, of past glories.

BEECHMOUNT GROVE, BS14. This may be a concocted name, as other roads nearby incorporate tree names.

BEECHWOOD AVENUE, BS15. A reminder of the days when this was all forestland.

BEECHWOOD CLOSE, BS4. This relates to the preserved beech trees growing on this site.

BEECHWOOD ROAD, BS16. A Beechwood House stood here until the 1930s, a few hundred yards from the modern health centre. The houses on the north side were built at the beginning of the 20th century.

BEGBROOK DRIVE / LANE / PARK, BS16. One authority suggests a personal name, Becca's brook; another says it was formerly Bybrook, 'from the brook', which rises on the slopes of Goreham Hill. A further suggestion is that it was from the OE *byge*, 'bend of a river' as the Frome does meander nearby. There were a house and farm of that name here once.

BEGGARSWELL COURT, BS2. The name 'Beggarswell' was first recorded in 1248. This was a spring which was one of the northern boundary markers of the city. It would now lie on the junction between Ervine Terrace and Dove Lane, St. Pauls.

BELFAST WALK, BS. Following the theme of Irish place names in the area. *See Bantry Road.*

BELFIELDS ALLEY, BS16. This is named after Captain William Belfield who lived in Malmains House, the land of which is bounded by this lane.

BELFRY AVENUE, BS 5. The name was possibly chosen because this is near Bell Hill Road.

BELFRY, BS15. This is another in the series of roads named after famous golf courses.

BELGRAVE HILL / PLACE / ROAD, BS8. Lord Belgrave subscribed to Barrett's *History of Bristol* in the eighteenth century so he seems to have had an interest in the city. Belgrave is also one of the titles of the Dukes of Westminster.

BELL BARN ROAD, BS9. This is thought to be named after the barn which stood on Haytor's farm in this area before Bell Barn Road was built.

BELL HILL ROAD, BS5. There is an inn of this name which dates from the nineteenth century, but whether the hill was called after the pub or vice versa is not certain.

BELL HILL, BS16. The Bell which gives its name to the hill was, before rebuilding, an old coaching inn. The Kingswood Enclosure Act Commissioners met here in the years 1779-84.

BELL LANE, BS1. The Bell Tavern once stood here. John Willis, a Chamberlain or Treasurer of Bristol, built it in 1579. It was here, in 1777, that John Aitken, known as Jack the Painter, attempted to set fire to the city. The Bell was destroyed and never rebuilt. Jack was hanged at Portsmouth on a gallows 67 feet high, for the benefit of the crowds that had massed to witness his execution.

BELLAMY AVENUE, BS13. Someone of this name held land here at the time of the Dundry Enclosure Award in 1815.

BELLAMY CLOSE, BS5. There was a builder of this name in St. George when this road was built, so perhaps he developed the site.

BELLAND DRIVE, BS13. Philip, 2nd Abbot of St. Augustine's Abbey in Bristol, was later appointed to Belland Abbey in Yorkshire.

BELLE VUE ROAD BS4 / BS5 / BS8 / BS9 / BS12 / BS16. There are numerous streets throughout the city and suburbs with this appellation, which has always been a popular choice of name for houses, too, meaning, as it does, beautiful view, although in many cases this scenic delight has been obscured by intervening years and developments. Bellevue Road in Brislington contained the first purpose-built houses to appear in the area. They were built in 1878.

BELLHOUSE WALK, BS11. Mr Bellhouse was one of the directors of Ladbrokes Homes who developed this site.

BELLUTON ROAD, BS4. Belluton is a village in Somerset whose name means 'homestead on the hill'. Many Somerset villages are represented in the roads throughout the area.

BELMONT ROAD, BS4. This may have been named after the scene of a Boer War battle, which took place on 23rd November 1899.

BELMONT ROAD, BS6. Belmont is both a village in Surrey and a hamlet in Somerset. A wealthy admirer of Hannah More lived at the latter location. She accepted his proposal when she was 22 but two or three times the date for the wedding was fixed, only for her fiancé to postpone it each time. Hannah felt she was being taken for a fool and broke off the engagement. Honourably he settled an annuity of £200 on her so that she was able to give up teaching and devote her time to her writing.

BELMONT STREET, BS5. William de Belemont was a prefect serving the mayor of Bristol in 1240, so it is clearly an old Bristol name, but it is not known why this road was so called.

BELOE ROAD, BS7. This is built on the site of the rugby ground used until 1918 by the Saracens and later by the Bristol Rugby Club. H.W. Beloe was at one time President of the club.

BELROYAL AVENUE, BS4. This is a made-up name, the first syllable meaning beautiful. The royal connection is obscure.

BELSHER'S COURT, BS15. The Reverend James Belsher was minister of the Hanham Road Congregational Chapel from 1884-96.

BELSTONE WALK, BS4. Named, for some reason unknown, after a town in Devon.

BELTON ROAD, BS5. The name of several villages around the country. The first syllable could be from *bael*, sacrificial fire. It is a not uncommon local name and may even have been the landowner.

BELVEDERE ROAD, BS6. This is the site of a residence called Castle Belvedere derived from the Italian, meaning viewpoint. The road commands fine views of the Forest of Dean to the north and Kelston Hill to the south.

BELVOIR ROAD, BS6. This is apparently named after the castle in Leicestershire, seat of the Dukes of Rutland. Derived from the French it means 'beautiful view' and is pronounced Beaver.

BENFORD CLOSE, BS16. A large property once stood on this land called Upper Fishponds House. It was demolished in 1935. In 1789 it was leased to a William Benford.

BENNETT ROAD, BS16. Several families of this name were living in the close vicinity at the time this road was built in 1903, so it is probably called after the owner of the land.

BENNETT WAY, BS8. J. B. Bennett was the City Engineer and Planning Officer in the 1950s and was responsible for the post war development of the city. The City Architect of that era is similarly celebrated. *See Meredith Close.*

BENSAUNT GROVE, BS10. Robert Bensaunt was Vicar of Westbury in 1458.

BENTLEY CLOSE, BS14.

BENVILLE AVENUE, BS9. This is one of a group of three roads named after Somerset villages.

BERCHEL HOUSE, BS3. Berchel was the name of a Bedminster landowner in the fifteenth century.

BERENDA DRIVE, BS15. This is one of the American-influenced names chosen by the developers, taking their theme from California Farm which was on the site of the old California Pit. Berenda Slough is the name of a dam in California. *See California Road.*

BERKELEY AVENUE / COURT / ROAD, BS7. Sometimes spelled Berkley. These are named, almost certainly, after the Berkeley family and their castle, since a favourite theme in the vicinity is earldoms and related stately homes.

BERKELEY CLOSE / GREEN / ROAD (2), BS16. The source of these namings is indisputably the Lords of Berkeley.

BERKELEY AVENUE / CRESCENT / SQUARE / PLACE / STREET, BS8. These are built on land owned by the Abbey of St. Augustine founded in 1140 by Lord Berkeley.

BERKELEY GREEN ROAD, BS5. This may possibly be the name of a local person.

BERKELEY ROAD, BS6. This is thought to be named in honour of the Hon. F.H.F. Berkeley, MP for Bristol 1835-70.

BERKELEY ROAD, BS16. This stands on a former field called The Berkleys.

BERKSHIRE ROAD, BS7. As with several other streets locally, this is named after an English county. The derivation could be forest or birch tree or, as an alternative, *barruc* meaning bare or polled oak and *scyre*, a shire. The shire-motes, or courts, were held in the shade of a polled oak in ancient times.

BERLINGTON COURT, BS1. This complex was built on the site of Mardon, Son and Hall's old factory which was known as Caxton Works. Other streets in this area are called after typefaces, possibly inspired by the Caxton name which is that of the celebrated William Caxton, who set up the first printing press in England and printed the first book in English, *Recuyell* (Compilation) *of the Historyes of Troye*, around 1475.

BERNERS CLOSE, BS4. Gerald Hugh Tyrwhitt-Wilson, Lord Berners (1883-1950), had a career in the Diplomatic Corps. He was a gifted artist and writer, but music was his first love and he composed an opera and several ballets.

BERROW WALK, BS3. This is another West Country place name.

BERRY LANE, BS7. There was a Berry Lane Farm here once, home to Reuben Rosling. The name derives from the OE *burgh*, fortification, encampment or fortified house.

BERRY CROFT, BS3. The name was taken from an old tithe map of the area.

BERWICK ROAD, BS5. This is a place name. The derivation is from the OE *bere-wic*, barley farm, outlying grange. Perhaps the builder had connections with the place, as there are no other place names used in the vicinity.

BERYL GROVE, BS4. Named after a daughter of the builder, Mr Griffee.

BERYL ROAD, BS3. This follows the theme of gemstones as in the surrounding roads. *See Agate Street.*

BETHEL ROAD, BS5. Bethel means 'house of God'. In the Old Testament it was a place 10 miles from Jerusalem, the scene of Jacob's dream. Bethel Road in Bristol, home to a large mining community, contained many Nonconformist chapels in the wake of Whitefield and Wesley.

BETJEMAN COURT, BS15. The late Poet Laureate Sir John Betjeman (1906-84) had many connections with Bristol and visited often:

Green above the flooded Avon shone the after-storm-wet-sky
Quick the struggling withy branches let the leaves of autumn fly
And a star shone over Bristol, wonderfully far and high.

Sir John Betjeman

BEVAN COURT, BS10. This is named after Aneurin Bevan, Minister for Health in Clement Attlee's postwar Labour government. He visited the city during that period.

BEVERLEY AVENUE, BS16. The theme of this and neighbouring roads is racecourses.

BEVERLEY CLOSE, BS5. The town in Yorkshire is the site of a famous minster. Other nearby roads have religious connections.

BEVERLEY GARDENS, BS9. Thomas à Becket was Provost of Beverley around 1155, and there was a priory dedicated to him at Sand Bay, Somerset, near Hutton. Another close in this group is called Hutton Close.

BEVERLEY ROAD, BS7. As with many other roads locally this called after an English town. The name means 'place or stream of the beaver'.

BEVERSTON GARDENS, BS11. Henry II, who settled this manor and that of Beverston near Tetbury on his son, granted the Lordship of Berkeley (which included Henbury) to Robert Fitzhardinge. The Lordship of Kingsweston remained in the family until 1386. Robert Fitzhardinge is best known for building the priory of St. Augustine, now Bristol Cathedral.

BEVERSTONE, BS15. As Beverston Gardens above.

BEVIN COURT, BS2. This is named in honour of Ernest Bevin, champion of the dockers and an important union figure. He served as Foreign Secretary from 1945-50 in Clement Attlee's postwar Labour government.

BEVINGTON CLOSE / WALK BS12. Named after a Gloucestershire village, as are other roads in the area.

BEXLEY ROAD, BS16. This is a town in Kent. The first syllable is the OE *byre*, box tree or thicket and the last syllable is *lea*, woodland, glade or clearing therein. This area used to be known as The Thicket. *See Thicket Road.*

BIBSTONE, BS15. This is named after a place in Gloucestershire, as are other roads close by. This may have a connection with ancient times when this area was part of the King's wood.

BIBURY CLOSE / CRESCENT, BS9. These are named after a village in Gloucestershire, the derivation being *Beages*, a fortified place. Beages was also the daughter of Earl Lippa to whom the land was granted in the eighth century by the Bishop of Worcester. This area was once in the See of Worcester.

BIBURY CLOSE, BS15. Within the Bibury estate in Gloucestershire is Oseney Abbey, which continues the religious theme of road naming in this area.

BICKERTON CLOSE, BS10. Robert de Bickerton was a landowner in this area in the early fourteenth century.

BICKFORD CLOSE, BS15. This is named after the local well-loved Dr. Bickford who died at a relatively early age, just prior to the building of this road.

BICKLEY CLOSE, BS15. The name is from nearby Bickley Farm and Bickley Wood.

BIDDESTON ROAD, BS7. This is named after a village in Wiltshire. Bieda is a personal name, so the meaning is 'Bieda's homestead or village'. A number of local roads are called after places in the British Isles.

BIDEFORD CRESCENT, BS4. A seaside town and port in north Devon. Many local roads have West Country place names.

BIDWELL CLOSE, BS10. This is a field name from the OE *bydin,* a vessel or tub and *wella,* a stream.

BIFIELD CLOSE / ROAD, BS14. Nicholas Bifield resided in Bedminster in July 1674 and was granted exemption from the Hearth Tax.

BIGWOOD LANE, BS1. This is perhaps named after J. Bigwood, a local supplier of ice houses, who had premises in Baldwin Street and Porwall Lane in the 1890s.

BILBERRY CLOSE, BS9. This follows the trend for naming streets on this development after shrubs and plants. A bilberry is a low-growing bush bearing edible blue berries.

BILBIE CLOSE, BS7. Thomas Bilbie cast the original bells of Horfield Parish Church. He was a member of the famous bell-founding family from Chew Stoke. Established before 1700, the Bilbies went out of business in 1815.

BILLAND CLOSE, BS13. This is a field name, after a field that was once part of Bishopsworth Farm, shown on the 1802 Survey. It probably derived from a personal name; Bill's land.

BINDON DRIVE, BS10. This is named after the Earl of Suffolk and Bindon who held the manor of Henbury in the eighteenth century. Bindon was a subsidiary title granted to the 6th Earl and became extinct on the death of his son the 7th Earl in 1722.

BINLEY GROVE, BS14. Binley was a field shown on the 1789 Whitchurch tithe map.

BINMEAD GARDENS, BS13. This is another field name. *Bin* is from the OE for bean, so this translates as 'beanfield'.

BIRBECK ROAD, BS9. This is seemingly a mis-spelling of Birnbeck Island at Weston-super-Mare. The name probably originated as a field name from the Old Norse *birki-bekkr,* a brook where birch grow.

BIRCH CLOSE, BS12. One of a plethora of tree names.

BIRCH CROFT, BS14. This is probably a field name. Croft is from the OE meaning a piece of enclosed land for tillage or pasture, arable land adjacent to a property.

BIRCH ROAD, BS3. There is a Lime Road nearby. Perhaps the roads were planted with these trees.

BIRCH ROAD, BS15. This adjoins Larch Road, presumably to keep alive the forest connection.

BIRCHALL ROAD, BS6. Bishop Monk's Horfield Trust once owned this site, at which time Major Sir John Birchall was church Commissioner and Trustee. He was MP for North East Leeds.

BIRCHDALE ROAD, BS14. This is an apparently made-up name.

BIRCHWOOD ROAD, BS4. Named after the nearby woodland area where birches grow.

BIRDALE CLOSE, BS10. Elizabeth Birdale was a resident of Westbury in 1668.

BIRDWOOD, BS15. Off Woodyleaze Drive, so perhaps this is named in keeping with the general woodland theme, although a family of this name lived in Pucklechurch in the mid-nineteenth century.

BIRKDALE, BS15. This is another road in a group named after famous golf courses.

BIRKIN STREET, BS2. Much of the land in this area belonged to the estate of Abraham Birkin, a soapmaker and councillor from 1662-69.

BISHOP MANOR ROAD, BS7. The Manor is that of Horfield, and the Bishop is almost certainly James Henry Monk, Bishop of Gloucester and Bristol. in the first half of the nineteenth century.

BISHOP ROAD, BS7. This refers to the above Bishop of Gloucester. The name Bishopston came into being in 1875.

BISHOP STREET, BS2. This is in keeping with local streets 'Dean' and 'Chapter'. The church owned much of the land round here.

BISHOPS CLOSE, BS9. This was so named by the developers, Bensons, because of its proximity to Bishop's Knoll.

BISHOPS COVE, BS13. A cove was an arrangement of three large stones linked with the Druid religion. There are several sites in North Somerset where remnants of the ancient faith can still be found.

BISHOPSWORTH ROAD, BS13. The district of this name was known as Bishport until the 1700s, the name being derived from bishop's palace or enclosure.

BISHOPTHORPE ROAD, BS7. The bishop in question is Bishop Monk. Thorpe can mean newly reclaimed land, a new settlement or an outlying dependent farm. *See Bishop Road.*

BISHPORT AVENUE / COURT, BS13. Bishport was the original name for Bishopsworth.

BITTLEMEAD, BS13. This was a tenement or holding mentioned in the Dundry Enclosure Award of 1815. The name may be derived from the old French *Bataille,* bloody meadow.

BLACKACRE, BS13. Developed on farm land, this was named after a field shown on the 1840 tithe map.

BLACKBERRY AVENUE / HILL, BS16. A bramble-covered hillside from times past can be imagined in this place with so many links with history. Cromwell's men marched across this land, and French prisoners in the eighteenth century were held captive at the prison on top of the hill.

BLACKBOY HILL, BS8. Thus called because the Blackboy Tavern, formerly known as the Blackamoor's Head, stood at the foot of this hill. Blackamoor was a name popularised at the time of the Crusades when it was used as a description for north African Muslims specifically, and many inns were given this name

complete with a suitably illustrated sign - a necessary refinement in days when the majority were unable to read or write. Charles II was also known as the Black Boy because of his swarthy complexion. Another theory is that the name derived from the dead malefactors, preserved with a coating of tar, hanging from the nearby gibbet on the Downs. *See Blackmoors Lane.*

BLACKDOWN CLOSE, BS14. Another instance where a field name has been used.

BLACKFRIARS, BS1. Robert Fitzhardinge introduced Benedictine monks, called Blackfriars because of their habit, to Bristol. *See Blackswarth Road.*

BLACKHORSE LANE / PLACE / ROAD, BS16. Black Horse Farm once stood nearby.

BLACKHORSE ROAD, BS15. This is named after the pub of the same name at the beginning of the road.

BLACKMOORS LANE, BS3. Probably a very old name. It is not unremarkable that it should appear in this area, close by the stronghold of the Knights Templar who provided food and lodging for the Crusaders, whose aim was to convert the Muslim 'infidels' in the eastern Mediterranean to Christianity. Their rivals were the knights of St. John of Jerusalem who had similar aims. *See Blackboy Hill.*

BLACKSWARTH ROAD, BS5. This land was owned in medieval times by the Benedictine monks of St. Augustine (the Blackfriars). The soil here was also black because of the surrounding coal pits. The word swarth or swart means very dark. This street was originally known as Fire Engine Lane, so called because of the pumping engine used to raise the coal. Power was generated by water by means of fire. A suggestion has been made that Blacen's enclosure is the origin of the name, but black seems more probable.

BLACKTHORN CLOSE / ROAD / WALK, BS13. This is a field name derived from the OE *blaec-porn*, blackthorn or sloe.

BLAGDON CLOSE, BS3. This is among other roads with West Country village names.

BLAGROVE CLOSE / CRESCENT, BS13. This is the name of an individual who held land in the Dundry Enclosure Award 1815.

BLAISDON COURT, BS10. This was named in error. Blaisdon was a manor parish and village in the Hundred of Westbury but it was in that of Westbury-on-Severn, not Westbury-on-Trym.

BLAISE WALK, BS9. St. Blaise was a fourth-century bishop in Armenia who performed a miraculous cure on a boy who was choking to death because of a fishbone in his throat. He was subsequently tortured - some say with iron combs - and martyred by the Romans. He became a popular medieval saint, venerated by the ill and those suffering from sore throats in particular. St. Blaise is also the patron saint of wool combers, possibly because of the manner of his death. A chapel was built and dedicated to St. Blaise in the thirteenth century on the site of a former Roman temple, where even before that time there had been an Iron Age fort. The eighteenth-century folly of Blaise Castle (from which Blaise Walk derives its name) was built on the site in 1766.

Blackboy Hill, c. 1910

BLAKE ROAD, BS7. Following the fashion locally for artists' names this road is named after William Blake (1757-27). As well as being a painter he was also an engraver, poet and mystic. Blake was the author of the immortal hymn 'Jerusalem'.

BLAKENEY ROAD, BS7. Most probably named after the town in Gloucestershire.

BLANDFORD CLOSE, BS9. The connection here is that it runs off Dorset Road. Perhaps the builder had links with that part of the country.

BLENHEIM DRIVE, BS12. Another aircraft connection here, in Filton. The Bristol Blenheim was a twin-engined medium bomber which entered service with the RAF in 1937 and served with distinction in the Second World War.

BLENHEIM ROAD, BS6. Perhaps named after the palace, as there are other streets in the close vicinity on a royalty theme.

BLENHEIM STREET, BS5. Possibly named after the Battle of Blenheim on 13 August 1704 when Marlborough's troops, together with the Austrian army, defeated the French and their allies the Bavarians. It subsequently became celebrated more than any other battle in song, verse, and general popular memory. The village in Bavaria where the battle took place was actually called Blindheim, which somehow transmuted to Blenheim.

BLENMAN CLOSE, BS16. The name of a former landowner in the early nineteenth century.

BLETHWIN CLOSE, BS10. John Blethwin was resident in Westbury parish in 1699. He married Mary Gainor in Westbury Church on 13 February 1699.

BLOOMFIELD ROAD, BS4. This was built on the site of the former Bloomfield market garden, run by the Ford family.

BLOY STREET, BS5. This is an OE field name from *blaw* meaning cheerless, windswept.

BODEY CLOSE, BS15. This honours a headmaster of Cadbury Heath School, Edgar Bodey. He held the post from 1901 to 1929.

BODMIN WALK, BS4. Another road with a West Country town name.

BOILING WELLS LANE, BS2. This name is taken from a spring on the hillside, which fed the stream upon which stood Lower Ashley House. This was the country residence from 1732 to 1762 of Sir Michael Foster, Recorder of Bristol. The house was demolished in the 1820s. The water was very gaseous and gave the appearance of boiling. This lane was not given its name until 1989, when the St. Werburgh's Local History Group requested that the Council name the lane after this ancient local spring. *See Pennywell Road.*

BOLTON ROAD, BS7. This could be a place name or the name of someone connected with the development. The first syllable's derivation is from bole or trunk of a tree.

BOND STREET, BS1. Probably named after Frederick Blight Bond, a local architect responsible for many building schemes in the city. Alternatively it could be called after the famous London street. Another Bond was Richard, Bailiff of Bristol in 1478.

BONNINGTON WALK, BS7. This is a mis-spelling of Richard Parkes Bonington (1801-27), an artist who lived in France and died on a visit to England.

BONVILLE ROAD, BS4. An Elizabeth Bonville married into the well-known Brislington Fox family, and male members of the family, even up to the present day, have taken the name as a first name.

BOOT LANE, BS3. This is from the OE *botl*, a dwelling, so this would indicate an inhabited lane.

BOOTH ROAD, BS3. This is named after General William Booth (1829-12) founder of the Salvation Army. There is a citadel nearby. He began his work among the impoverished slum dwellers of London and later worked in the United States.

BORDESLEY ROAD, BS14. A town in Warwickshire. The meaning from the OE is 'wood from whence boards were obtained'.

BORLEYTON WALK, BS13. This is a field name, in the Manor of Bishport as shown on the 1683 survey. The derivation is uncertain but it is possibly from the OE *baer*, bare, *leah*, woodland, glade or clearing and *tun*, enclosure, farmstead or village.

BORVER GROVE, BS13. This was the name of the local landowner in 1815.

BOSCOMBE CRESCENT, BS16. Among other roads with West Country place names. There is no apparent reason for this choice.

BOSTON ROAD, BS7. The town in Lincolnshire whose name derived from the stone cross from which St. Botolph preached Christianity in the ninth century.

BOSWELL STREET, BS5. This is built on the site of Boswell House.

BOTHAM DRIVE, BS4. This is named in honour of Ian Botham, who played for Somerset and captained the English Test cricket team in the 1980s.

BOUCHER PLACE, BS2. A Mrs. Mary Boucher presented a valuable silver tankard to the Bristol Corporation in 1709 in memory of her late husband.

BOULTERS ROAD, BS13. The name of a landowner listed in the Dundry Enclosure Award 1815.

BOULTON'S LANE / ROAD, BS15. There was a Samuel Boulton, carpenter and undertaker, in business here in 1899.

BOUNDARY ROAD BS11. Self-explanatory.

BOURCHIER GARDENS, BS13. Henry Bourchier was the second Earl of Essex and was granted the Manor of Bedminster in 1522 by Henry VIII, whom he served as Captain of the Bodyguard and Chief Captain of the King's Forces. He died following a fall from his horse in March 1539 and, as he had no heirs, the land reverted to the Crown.

BOURNE CLOSE / LANE / ROAD, BS5. These roads commemorate Hugh Bourne (1772 -52), founder of the Primitive Methodists.

BOURNEVILLE ROAD, BS5. This used to be known as Madhouse Lane, as Whitehall House was a lunatic asylum in the 1850s. Bourneville was the name of the garden suburb in Birmingham founded by George Cadbury of the chocolate company of the same name, so perhaps the connection here is the confectionery factory in nearby Greenbank, which has been owned by Packers, Carsons, Cavenham Foods, Elizabeth Shaw, Famous Names and Leaf Industries.

BOURTON WALK, BS3. Many roads in the area are called after Somerset villages.

BOUVERIE STREET, BS5. This is the family name of the Earls of Radnor. It was also the name of the owner of Longford Castle in Wiltshire: he possessed quarries at Pucklechurch, the black marble from which was used for fireplaces and gravestones, so he may have had business interests in this part of the city. (It occurs as a London street name as well. Easton had a Piccadilly which was demolished in 1872.)

BOVERTON ROAD, BS12. After the death of the last of the Gayner family, his trustees sold the land here to N.D. Reyne of Boverton House, Chepstow, and T. R. Jenkins, a Bristol builder.

BOWDEN CLOSE, BS9. This is a field name from Bowden's fields. A farm of this name was once on this land.

BOWDEN PLACE, BS16. This is perhaps named after the original landowner.

BOWDEN ROAD, BS5. This is a mis-spelling of a town in Cheshire which derives from the OE *bog dun* meaning an arched or rounded hill.

BOWER ROAD / WALK, BS3. The name is derived from the OE for cottage.

BOWERLEAZE, BS9. Most probably this is a field name, meaning 'field where a cottage stood'.

BOWOOD, BS16. The theme here is stately homes. Bowood is the seat of the Marquis of Lansdowne and it is situated in Wiltshire, near Calne. It houses a fine art collection.

BOWRING CLOSE, BS13. Robert Bowring married the daughter of William, son and heir of Sir John Inyn of Inns Court.

BOYCE DRIVE, BS2. This was the name of the vicar who came to the parish when the church was rebuilt in St. Werburgh's, having formerly stood in the city centre, in 1878. He had been the city vicar before the church was moved, and his congregation were so devoted to him that they travelled to St. Werburgh's every Sunday to hear him preach. It is said that Mina Road was filled with horse-drawn carriages bringing them to his new location before every service.

BOYCE'S AVENUE, BS8. In 1763, Thomas Boyce, a wig-maker, kept lodging houses here for visitors to the Spa. Within ten years he was bankrupt.

BRABAZON ROAD, BS12. The Bristol Brabazon was named after the Minister of Transport in the 1945 Labour Government, Lord Brabazon of Tara. It was a monstrously huge aeroplane for 1949; indeed, at 230 feet its wingspan was 37 feet greater than a modern jumbo jet's. It is thanks to this aircraft that Bristol has one of the longest runways in the world; to accommodate it, Filton's runway was doubled in length to 2750 yards, and the village of Charlton was demolished to make way for it. It was powered by eight Bristol Centaurus engines coupled to four pairs of contra-rotating props, and could lumber along for 5,500 miles at a stately 250 MPH. It epitomised post-war British thinking about the future of air travel: a continuation of the pre-war luxury of the Empire flying boats for the privileged few. But meanwhile, the Americans had huge fleets of big machines left over from the recent conflict, and more in the pipeline. No-one wanted the Brabazon, the project was abandoned in 1953 and it was eventually broken up. Meanwhile, the village of Charlton had been demolished for nothing. *See Charlton Road.*

BRACEWELL GARDENS, BS10. David Bracewell was appointed Dean of Westbury College in 1391.

BRACEY DRIVE, BS16. Richard Bracey was a landowner here in the 1840s.

BRACTON DRIVE, BS14. Henry de Bracton (sometimes referred to as Bratton) was a friend of Henry III and an itinerant judge. The choice here is clearly the Forest connection. *See Introduction and Forest Road.*

BRADESTON GROVE, BS16. Sir Thomas de Bradeston was Lord of the Manor of Winterbourne during the reign of Edward III and Keeper of Kingswood Forest. He died c. 1374. Another member of the family, William, was appointed Abbot of Bristol in 1234. There are memorials to the family in Winterbourne Church.

BRADHURST STREET, BS5. This is thought to be an old field name deriving from the OE *brad*, broad and *hyrst*, a hill, often wooded.

BRADLEY CRESCENT / ROAD, BS11. A common place name all over the country although these roads were probably called after the village in Gloucestershire. The meaning is 'broad pasture'.

BRADWELL GROVE, BS10. This is named after a place in the Peak District, in keeping with the general theme of the area.

BRAEMAR AVENUE / CRESCENT, BS7. All the roads in this development are on a Scottish theme.

BRAGG'S LANE, BS2. Prior to 1850 this street was known as Limekiln Lane. Bragg is probably Charles Bragge, Lord Bathurst. But since the County Regiment (the Gloucesters) used to be known as the Old Braggs in honour of Col. Philip Bragg who was appointed in 1734, this could be the origin, particularly as it leads into Gloucester Lane.

BRAIKENRIDGE ROAD, BS4. This is named in honour of a benefactor who made his fortune in the West Indies. His name was George Weare Braikenridge (1775-1856) and he was a collector and antiquarian who lived at Broomwell House. During the 1820s he collected watercolours and drawings of Bristol's dock area, and of the back streets of the city and panoramic views. He also amassed a fine collection of botanical plates. The collection is now held at the Bristol Art Gallery.

BRAINSFIELD, BS9. This is almost certainly an old field name.

BRAKE CLOSE, BS15. This is probably a field name. Brake is an old name for thicket.

BRAKEWELL GARDENS, BS14. This is a field name shown on the 1840 tithe map.

BRAMBLE DRIVE / LANE, BS9. Within the type of environs where such plants would have a natural habitat.

BRAMBLING WALK, BS16. This follows the trend of using bird names in the locality.

BRAMLEY COURT, BS15. This was built on the site of an orchard; all the streets in this little section are named after varieties of apple.

BRANCHE GROVE, BS13. This is named after a tenement or holding mentioned in the Dundry Enclosure Award of 1815.

BRANDON STREET / STEEP, BS8. This comes from the Irish St. Brendan (490-573). A chapel to this saint was erected on the summit of Brandon Hill and attached was a hermitage where dwelt an anchorite, Lucy de Newchurch. A later inhabitant in the fourteenth century, Reginald Taylor, bequeathed money for the building of Temple Church. The chapel was demolished, not surprisingly, in the reign of Henry VIII and a windmill was built there in its place. This vanished at some stage, before 1673. The Cabot Tower on top of Brandon Hill was built in 1897 to commemorate Cabot's voyage to America in 1497.

BRANGWYN GROVE, BS7. Another artist honoured in this development. Sir Frank Brangwyn was particularly noted for his murals (1867-1956).

BRANKSOME CRESCENT / DRIVE, BS12. Branksome is a suburb of Bournemouth. The first syllable is from a personal name, Brunac.

BRANKSOME ROAD, BS6. Other place names used nearby are of significance to the builder alone.

BRANSCOMBE ROAD, BS9. This is a village in Devon. The meaning is 'Branco's valley', from the Welsh for raven.

BRANWHITE CLOSE, BS7. Named after the Bristol-born landscape artist Charles Branwhite (1817-80). His father, Nathan, who lived at No. 1 College Green, was a well-known painter of miniatures.

BRATTON ROAD, BS4. This is probably named after the Wiltshire village of this name or it could be another Henry Bratton connection *See Bracton.*

BRAUNTON ROAD, BS3. This is a seaside resort and nature reserve in Devon, famed for its miles of sand dunes. It means 'village where the broom grows'.

BRAYNE COURT, BS15. Henry Braine, or Brayne, was Keeper of the Forest in the sixteenth century. Later members of the family mined coal in the area.

BREACH ROAD, BS3. There is a Breach Hill near Chew Stoke. The derivation is from the OE *brec,* land broken up for cultivation. Other place names have been used for nearby streets.

BREAN DOWN AVENUE, BS9. This is a peninsula in Somerset where traces of an ancient encampment still linger. It has been suggested that the ancient names of Brean Down and Brandon actually refer to the same tract of land.

BRECKNOCK ROAD, BS4. This relates to a place in Wales now more usually referred to as Brecon (the Welsh principality of Brycheiniog). The name comes from Brychan, a mythical king of Wales.

BRECON ROAD, BS9. This follows the trend in this area for the use of place names.

BREDON NOOK ROAD, BS10

> *In summertime in Bredon*
> *The bells they sound so clear;*
> *Round both the shires they ring them*
> *In steeples far and near,*
> *A happy noise to hear.*
>
> A.E. Housman, A Shropshire Lad

Bredon is in Worcestershire and was immortalised by the poet A.E. Housman, but 'nook' has no obvious connection. This is a cul-de-sac, however, so it may be implying seclusion.

BREDON CLOSE, BS15. This is named after a town near Tewkesbury. There were many links between these two places in earlier times.

BRENDON CLOSE, BS15. All local roads are named after ranges of hills.

BRENDON ROAD, BS3. The Brendon Hills are in Somerset. Many streets round here are named after ranges of hills perhaps because of the geography of the area. Brendon means 'Broom hill'.

BRENNER STREET, BS5. This is perhaps named after the Brenner Pass connecting Austria with Italy but there seems no reason for this choice (though there is an Alpine Road in the area).

BRENT ROAD, BS7. This is a place name. 'Brent' is an old name for hill from the OE *brant.*

BRENTRY AVENUE, BS5. There is no obvious reason for this choice of place name.

BRENTRY HILL / LANE / ROAD, BS10. One authority suggests the meaning is 'burnt tree' while another suggests 'tree of the warriors' from OE *beorna,* military hero.

BRERETON WAY, BS15. Possibly named in connection with Stanley Hall which still stands at the top of the hill, but which was known locally as Brereton's House after a Mr Brereton, who was also known locally as "The Irishman". A Captain Brereton failed to quell the Bristol riots in 1831 and later shot himself in shame, but it is therefore unlikely that he would be commemorated in this way.

BREWERTON CLOSE, BS10. Henry Brewerton was a resident of Westbury in 1668.

BRIAR WAY / WALK, BS16. *See Thicket Road.*

BRIARSIDE ROAD, BS10. This is named after a house that once stood in the area.

BRIARWOOD, BS9. This is a field name from the OE *brer*, briar, and *wudu*, wood or woodland. Until development took place it was a favourite place for children to build dens and cycle down the stony track.

BRIAVELS GROVE, BS6. This is a place in the Forest of Dean named after an obscure Welsh saint. All that is known of him is his feast day, 17 June, at which time the waters of St. Briavel's Well at Clearwell are reputed to take on a curious sheen.

BRICK STREET, BS2. This is almost certainly indicative of the trade which used to be carried on there.

BRIDEWELL STREET, BS1. The name is taken from the London Police HQ, which, in turn, derived its name from nearby St. Bride's (Bridget's) Well.

BRIDGE FARM CLOSE, BS14. This is named after the farm which stood there.

BRIDGE ROAD, BS5. This is adjacent to the old railway bridge, now demolished.

BRIDGE ROAD, BS17. Again this refers to an old railway bridge.

BRIDGE STREET, BS5. A massive viaduct crosses the main road near here.

BRIDGE ROAD, BS8. The road which leads from the Suspension Bridge to the village of Failand.

BRIDGE VALLEY ROAD, BS8. This leads from the valley towards the Clifton Suspension Bridge.

BRIDGE WALK, BS7. Not far from the railway line.

BRIDGE LEAP ROAD, BS16. This is situated by the Leap Stream.

BRIDGES DRIVE, BS16. John Bridges was a prominent local resident (1725 -76) who lived at Upper Fishponds House prior to William Benford. *See Benford Close.*

BRIDGMAN GROVE, BS12. Charles Bridgman farmed the land on which this road was built.

BRIDGWATER ROAD, BS3. The road leads to that town.

BRIERCLIFFE ROAD, BS9. This name was chosen to evoke the picturesque quality of the surrounding landscape.

BRIERY LEAZE ROAD, BS14. This is a field name meaning 'meadow where briars abound'. This is shown on the 1840 Whitchurch tithe map. It lay near Thistle Ground.

BRIGHT STREET, BS5. This is named after one of the directors of the cotton factory. *See Aitken Street.*

BRIGHT STREET, BS15. At the beginning of the twentieth century a family called Bright owned market gardens in the area and perhaps owned the land on which this street was built. Alternatively, a Sir John Newton of Barrs Court married Susanna, widow of Sir John Bright in the eighteenth century.

BRIGHTON CRESCENT / TERRACE, BS3. These are sited among other roads called after British towns.

BRIGHTON MEWS, BS8. Many roads in the area have a connection with George IV and Brighton was, of course, his favourite resort.

BRIGHTON PARK, BS5. There was a trend in the area at the time these houses were built to name roads after fashionable places.

BRIGHTON PLACE BS15. This is near London Road, which leads into Regent Street, so it would appear to be the royal connection here as in BS8, George IV being the Prince Regent before the death of his father George III.

BRIGHTON ROAD, BS6. There are a number of roads in the area with royal and aristocratic connections.

BRIGHTON STREET, BS2. No obvious reason for this choice as it does not link in any way to surrounding streets. Perhaps it was a resort dear to the builder's heart.

BRIGSTOCKE ROAD, BS2. The owner of the land in the eighteenth century was John Brigstock and he was responsible for the development of many streets in the area, which was known as the Brigstock estate, lying between Stokes Croft and Grosvenor Place. He had several daughters who all married well and whose husbands gave their names to roads he built. William Henry Temple Brigstocke inherited the estate from his father in 1833 and it was he who added the final "e" when his social position improved. He died childless and the estate passed to his three sisters. The land was sold by auction at the Full Moon hotel in July 1867 and the market gardens which existed there were built over by local developers, who retained memories of the family in their choice of names for the new roads. *See Campbell Street and Dalrymple, Drummond and Hepburn Roads.*

BRIMBLES, BS7. Brimbles and Great Brimbles were arable fields on the land being farmed by Benjamin Bridgman in 1830.

BRINKWORTHY ROAD, BS16. This road was once called Brinkworth, which suggests a connection with the small town near Wootton Bassett. Perhaps the link is the Dukedom of Beaufort; in all probability the family owned land there.

BRINMEAD WALK, BS13. This is a field name which could be derived from the Celtic *bryn,* a hill, and *mead,* of course, means meadow.

BRISCOES AVENUE, BS13. This is another tenement or holding mentioned in the Dundry Enclosures Award 1815.

BRISLINGTON HILL, BS4. The name originated from St. Brice who died in 444 AD, *lien* a tied or feudal estate, and *tun* a farm enclosure or village.

BRISTOL AND EXETER MEWS, BS1. In 1835 Bristol merchants agitated for an extension of the Great Western Railway line to be extended to Exeter. Permission was granted in 1836 and Brunel was commissioned to undertake the work, which was completed in 1844.

BRISTOL HILL, BS4. There have been many explanations put forward as to the origin of the name Bristol, e.g. the site of the bridge, assembly place by the bridge, Brightric (*see Brislington*). There is a school of thought which dates the bridge as being built before the town so the town takes its name from the bridge. This would concur with the first theory.

BRISTOL ROAD, BS16. *See Bristol Hill.*

BRISTOWE HOUSE, BS16. This is a variation once used for Bristol.

BRITANNIA ROAD, BS5. This began life as Berlin Road and was hastily altered with the advent of the First World War. Britannia seems to have been of Roman origin. The Romans portrayed Britain as a woman seated on a rock. There are other roads nearby called Roman Road and Albion Road. The familiar figure of Britannia which appeared on the old penny was modelled on Frances Stewart, an object of Charles II's desire for many years, though she refused to succumb to him, eloping with the Duke of Richmond instead. Charles banished them from court but relented eventually. Rumour has it that once she was married her high moral values disappeared and she was happy to become his mistress.

BRITANNIA ROAD BS12 Another Filton aircraft. The Britannia was built in response to a BOAC requirement of 1946 for a medium-range transport aircraft. Problems with the development of its Proteus turboprop engines delayed its advent until 1952, and, though a popular machine, familiarly known as the 'whispering giant', it was rapidly superseded by the first jet airliners.

BRITANNIA ROAD, BS15. Might this have been one of Daniel Flook's roads with imposing names? *See Albany Street, Albert Road and Regent Street.*

BRITISH ROAD, BS3. This was originally called Victoria Road. It was changed to its present name, as there were many Victoria Roads in the city, causing some confusion before the advent of the postcode. The later naming of British Road was after the British School, which was demolished in the late 1990s.

BRITTEN COURT, BS15. This has long been a well-known name in the area but the usual spelling is with an o.

BRIXHAM ROAD, BS3. Other, apparently random, places are represented in the roads in the area.

BRIXTON ROAD, BS5. This is a district of London. There are several London influenced names in the area. The first syllable is a personal name Beorhtric.

BROAD OAK ROAD, BS13. This is a field name taken from the 1683 survey of the manor of Bishport.

BROAD PLAIN, BS1. A descriptive name of a street which was once part of St. Philips Plain.

BROAD QUAY, BS1. This is a reminder of the days when the masts of ships could be seen in the middle of the city, before Broad Quay was filled in to make the street and square it is today. The development has always been controversial.

BROAD STREET, BS1 / STREET / ROAD, BS15. These roads were so named because they were broad in comparison to the surrounding streets.

BROAD WALK, BS4. A straightforward descriptive name of the street.

BROAD WEIR, BS1. This is named after the weir which feeds water from the River Frome into the moat that used to surround Bristol Castle. There are very few remains of the Norman Castle, but the moat is still intact and filled with water, although it is now covered with culverts. Broad weir is directly over the moat, which then runs around the east of Castle Park before flowing into the Floating Harbour.

BROADBURY ROAD, BS4. This may have been the name of a farm.

BROADFIELD AVENUE / ROAD, BS4. This is apparently an old field name.

BROADLANDS DRIVE, BS11. This is a field name which is self-explanatory.

BROADLEAS, BS13. Another field name, taken from the 1840 tithe map.

BROADLEYS AVENUE, BS9. A field name meaning 'wide meadows'.

BROADMEAD, BS1. There could be the obvious explanation of this name - broad meadow - but another suggestion has been made. Pryce in his *History of Bristol* suggests that it was named for the material *brodemedes*, a woollen cloth which was permitted to be woven only in Bristol. It was called Brodemede as far back as 1383.

BROADOAK HILL, BS13. This would have been a landmark years ago.

BROADOAK WALK, BS16. This continues the sylvan theme on this land which was once called The Thicket. *See Thicket Road.*

BROADSTONE WALK, BS13. The site of another tenement or holding mentioned in the Dundry Enclosure Award 1815.

BROADWAY AVENUE, BS9. The name is from Broadway Farm, which used to stand on this ground. Peregrine Rosling owned it in the late nineteenth century.

BROADWAY ROAD, BS6. This may be named after the town in Worcestershire.

BROADWAY ROAD, BS7. An old field name from the Horfield parish map of 1843.

BROADWAY ROAD, BS13. This may have been a field name.

BROADWAYS DRIVE, BS16. This is a field name shown on 1845 tithe map.

BROCKHURST GARDENS / ROAD, BS15 This sounds like an old field name meaning 'badger's wood'.

BROCKLEY WALK BS13. This is named after the Somerset village.

BROCKS ROAD, BS13. This is a private road listed in Dundry Enclosure Award 1815.

BROCKWORTH CRESCENT, BS16. The name is taken from the Anglo-Saxon meaning 'homestead by a brook'. This road runs near the river Frome.

BROMLEY HEATH AVENUE / ROAD, BS16. This is an ancient name for this area which translates as 'fields where broom grows'.

BROMLEY ROAD, BS7. This is named after the Reverend W. H. Bromley Way, Rector of Stapleton 1869-79. It is suggested that these houses were originally built for use by the Army Officers stationed at the newly built Horfield Barracks, although the siting of the houses so far away from the barracks is hard to explain.

BROMPTON COURT, BS15. So named because it was built on an old orchard. Peaches, apricots and nectarines are often grafted on to a Brompton rootstock.

BRONCKSEA ROAD, BS7. Among a group of Scottish place names but a location of this name does not appear on the map. The similar-sounding bonxie, however, is the Scottish name for the Great Skua, a seabird, and derives from this bird's unappealing habit of attacking people's heads and vomiting upon them.

BROOK GATE, BS3. This crosses Colliter's Brook.

BROOK HILL / LANE / ROAD, BS6. This must refer to the tributary of the river Frome which provided the water for the cress beds further downstream.

BROOK LANE, BS16. This is close to the water flowing through Snuff Mills.

BROOK LINTONS, BS4. This must have been an old field name. It is close to Brislington Brook.

BROOK ROAD, BS3. This refers to the Bedminster Brook.

BROOK ROAD, BS5. The brook here would be the Coombe Brook.

BROOK ROAD, BS16. This Fishponds Road is named after the Bully brook, which has only been culverted in recent times. The brook was mentioned in the surveys of Kingswood Chase. The brook fed the local 'Fish Ponds', which have long been filled in.

BROOK ROAD, BS15. This is close to Warmley Brook.

BROOK STREET, BS5. This might be a surname rather than a stream.

BROOKDALE ROAD, BS13. Perhaps a field name.

BROOKFIELD AVENUE, BS7. This is a made-up name, possibly relating to geographical features.

BROOKFIELD ROAD, BS6. A house called Brookfield Lodge used to stand here.

BROOKFIELD WALK, BS15. This is apparently an old field name.

BROOKLAND ROAD, BS6. Many local roads are called after sporting venues. This one celebrates motor racing.

BROOKLEA, BS15. This would seem to be a field name - 'meadow by the river'.

BROOKLEAZE, BS9. Almost certainly a field name.

BROOKLYN ROAD, BS3. One theory has it that this road was named after the borough of New York. However as part of the road was built before World War II, there must have been a longer-standing association with Brooklyn on the part of the builders or developers. After the war rubble from the bombed Bedminster streets was shipped to New York to be used as hardcore for a road in Brooklyn, which was opened by the Bristol-born Hollywood star, Cary Grant.

BROOKSIDE ROAD, BS4. Self-explanatory.

BROOKTHORPE AVENUE, BS11. This is a field name denoting an outlying farmstead near a brook.

BROOK VIEW WALK, BS13. It overlooks the Malago stream.

BROOM HILL, BS13. Field name. Broom is from the OE *brom*, bramble.

BROOMHILL ROAD, BS4. This road was built along the ancient pathway called Broomhill Lane and Broomhill House also stood on this land. It is said that the hillside was a blaze of yellow where the broom grew before development took place.

BROWNING COURT, BS7. This is among other roads dedicated to poets and novelists. Robert Browning (1812-99) is perhaps best known today for his ode *O to be in England now that April's there*, and the narrative poem, *The Pied Piper of Hamelin*. His wife, Elizabeth Barrett (1806-61), whom he married in 1846, was also a poet, her best-known work being *Sonnets from the Portuguese*. They lived in Florence, as the Italian sun was beneficial to Elizabeth who was in delicate health. She died in 1861. They had one son, the sculptor Robert Barrett Browning (1849-1912).

BRUCE AVENUE / ROAD, BS5. Bruce Cole was a director of nearby Packer's Chocolate factory. He was a well-known benefactor who died young.

BRUNEL LOCK ROAD, BS1. The lock designed by Brunel lies alongside this road; the previous lock was getting too small for the job and in 1844 Brunel was invited by the Dock Company to produce an estimate for the work. However, they were reluctant to pay for it. Meanwhile the inadequacy of the old lock was demonstrated when the coping stones had to be removed to allow the SS Great Britain to pass through. The Dock Company came to their senses and the new lock was finally completed in 1849. Brunel also built the hydraulically-operated swing bridge which passes over the lock. The bridge uses tubular wrought iron strength members, a mode of construction subsequently and more dramatically used by Brunel on the bridge over the River Tamar at Saltash.

BRUNEL WAY, BS1. Isambard Kingdom Brunel (1806-59) packed a lot of engineering into a short life, and quite a lot of that in Bristol. In 1828, to prevent the Floating Harbour from silting up, he built a special dredger, which acted rather like a bulldozer; this pushed the sediment into the flow to the Underfall which he also built, whose sluices are still periodically opened to flush out the mud. From 1835 he engineered the GWR rail link from London to Bristol. The Box Tunnel, near Bath, is reputed to be lit by the rising sun on 9 April, Brunel's birthday. Brunel's paddle steamer, the Great Western, was launched in Bristol in 1837, and the Great Britain, the first iron-built, screw-driven ship in the world, in 1843. The difficulty that the latter ship experienced on leaving the Floating Harbour (*see Brunel Lock Road*) led Brunel to devise a plan to dam the Avon at Avonmouth; although the plan was not adopted, it pointed the way to the eventual eclipse of Bristol by Avonmouth as a major port. Brunel also submitted a design for the Clifton Suspension Bridge which was adopted in 1831 but not completed until 1864. Brunel made the news again in October 1998, when the SS Great Britain Project removed his beloved cigar from the photograph used in their publicity material. A spokesperson said that it was 'inappropriate for a potential role model to be seen smoking'. *See Great Western Road.*

BRUNSWICK PLACE, BS1 / SQUARE / STREET, BS2. The building of the square began in 1769 and was finished in 1788, during the lifetime of Charles William Ferdinand, Duke of Brunswick. Five houses on the east side were built in 1786 by a Tontine, a type of co-operative insurance organisation, at a cost of 5000 guineas each. The Tontine expired in 1860 when residents who were original subscribers were reduced to five, and a draw was held to determine who should have which house. The chapel was built in 1836 and the first Nonconformist marriage was solemnised there.

BRUNSWICK STREET, BS5. This is in a group of roads called after royal dynasties.

BRYANSONS CLOSE, BS16. In view of the field names used in adjacent roads perhaps this was a land agent on the Beaufort estate.

Isambard Kingdom Brunel

BRYANT'S HILL, BS5. A man of this name was underground manager at Cork Pit, Deep Pit and Starveall Pit, so there may be a connection here.

BRYANTS CLOSE, BS16. A part of the Riverwood House estate, this portion being developed by Jack Bryant. *See Riverwood Road.*

BRYNLAND AVENUE, BS7. This thoroughfare was developed from two closes - Brynlands and Horsehill. The area towards St. Michael's Church was once known as Russell's Fields.

BUCKINGHAM GARDENS / PLACE, BS16. Royal residences are favoured for street naming in this locality. Buckingham Place used to be known as Bett's Barton before the present houses were built.

BUCKINGHAM PLACE / STREET / VALE, BS8. Honouring Richard Grenville, Duke of Buckingham and Chandos (1823-89). He visited Bristol in 1867. The first component is a personal name, *Bucca.*

BUCKINGHAM ROAD, BS4. This is named after Edward, Duke of Buckingham, of Thornbury Castle who was a frequent visitor to the nearby St. Anne's Chapel from 1508 until his death in 1521.

BUDD HOUSE, BS2. William Budd was born in Devon in 1811 and came to Bristol in 1841 to become physician at St. Peter's Hospital for the Sick and Needy. He realised that the cause of the frequent cholera epidemics in the city was unsanitary conditions, and lack of drainage. Through his efforts the disease was virtually stamped out in Bristol by 1866.

BUDE AVENUE, BS5 / ROAD, BS12. This is a seaside resort in Cornwall, and named after the stream Bude. There is no obvious reason for this choice of name.

BULL LANE, BS2. There was once a public house of this name in Great George Street.

BULLER ROAD, BS4. This is perhaps named after Sir Redvers Buller (1839-1908) who was awarded the Victoria Cross for bravery in the Zulu War of 1879. He had seen action in China, Canada, Ashanti, South Africa, Egypt and the Sudan prior to his participation in the Zulu War. In 1899 he travelled to South Africa again at the outbreak of the Boer War in command of an army of 70,000. He suffered losses at Colenso and Spion Cop but managed to relieve Ladysmith. In 1900 he was passed over for promotion and despatched to the backwater of Aldershot. The following year, as a result of an indiscreet speech he made, he was relieved of his command. *See Ladysmith Road.*

BURBANK CLOSE, BS15. This choice by the developers was influenced by the fact that the California Pit was formerly on this site. Burbank is a district of Hollywood immortalised in Rowan and Martin's cult TV show 'Laugh-In' as beautiful downtown Burbank. The Californian Burbank was called after a nineteenth-century dentist, Dr. David Burbank. *See California Road.*

BURCHELLS AVENUE / GREEN / CLOSE / ROAD, BS15. The Burchells were a family who owned a great deal of land in St. George and Kingswood. Burchell is spelt as Burshall on the 1845 tithe map.

BURCOTT ROAD, BS11. Burcott is a hamlet in Somerset.

BURFOOTE GARDENS / ROAD, BS4. Anne Burfoote was resident in Brislington in July 1670 and was granted exemption from the Hearth Tax.

BURFORD GROVE, BS11. This is a town in Oxfordshire among other Cotswold place names.

BURGESS GREEN CLOSE, BS4. This was an old field name, but misspelt. It should have been Burges. Many high-ranking citizens made pilgrimages to this area in past times to visit the holy well here. *See St. Anne's Road, Park Road, etc.*

BURGHILL ROAD, BS10. This name was selected erroneously. Burghill was a hamlet in the Hundred of Westbury-on-Severn, not Westbury-on-Trym. *Burg* means fort - thus 'fort on the hill'.

BURGHLEY ROAD, BS6. Together with Walsingham and Effingham roads, this is named after a Tudor statesman, William Cecil, Lord Burghley, who was Secretary of State and Lord Treasurer during Elizabeth I's reign.

BURGIS ROAD, BS14. Edward Burgis was a resident in the parish of Brislington and Burnett in 1670 and was granted exemption from the Hearth Tax.

BURLEY AVENUE / CREST / GROVE, BS16. George and William Burley were seedsmen living in Barton Hill in the mid nineteenth century. They may have had connections with the Gerrishes, whose market gardens covered all this land at one time.

BURLINGTON ROAD, BS6. This commemorates Richard Boyle, Earl of Burlington (1695-1753) a patron of the arts. He built the original Burlington

House in Piccadilly, London, later restyled into an outstanding example of Regency architecture. The present gallery was built in the grounds of the original house where it houses the books, manuscripts, paintings and relics belonging to the Royal Society, and is home to several other learned societies. The Royal Academy of Arts holds its annual exhibition there.

BURNBUSH CLOSE, BS14. A field name taken from the 1840 tithe map. There were two fields - Little Burnbush and Great Burnbush.

BURNELL DRIVE CLOSE, BS10. Refers to a local benefactor.

BURNEY WAY, BS15. Another of the California place names. *See California Road.*

BURNHAM CLOSE / DRIVE, BS15. This is named after Thomas Burnham, a District Councillor in the 1920s.

BURNHAM ROAD, BS11. A number of roads nearby have been named after Somerset villages.

BURNSIDE CLOSE, BS10. Continuing the theme of using Lake District locations for naming local roads.

BURRINGTON WALK, BS3. Another of the roads named after Somerset villages in this area.

BURTON CLOSE, BS5. Possibly named after the Dorset village of Burton.

BURTON CLOSE, BS1. Simon de Burton was Mayor of Bristol on five occasions. In 1305 he began the building of St. Mary Redcliffe Church and also built almshouses for 16 women in Long Row, St. Thomas Street.

BURTON COURT, BS8. Possibly named after a person connected with the development of the road, or with Queen Elizabeth's Hospital.

BURYCOURT CLOSE, BS11. Richard de Bury was Prebend of Lawrence Weston in 1331. He became Dean of Wells and Bishop of Durham in 1333 and subsequently Lord Chancellor and Lord High Treasurer under Edward III, who employed him on various diplomatic missions. He was a patron of learning and a collector of books. He wrote *Philobiblion*, a handbook to his own library at Durham, which was reprinted in the nineteenth century. He was born at Bury St. Edmunds in Suffolk.

BUSHY PARK, BS4. This is from either the OE *byse*, bush or thicket, or the Old French *boisserie*, place covered with wood.

BUTCOMBE WALK, BS4. This is a village in Somerset, owned by Bishop Gregory, who had custody of Bristol Castle in 1084. He held 280 manors which passed, on his death, to his nephew, Robert de Mowbray.

BUTTERFIELD CLOSE / ROAD, BS7. The medieval church upon which the present structure of Horfield Church was developed was unsafe and almost completely rebuilt in 1831, apart from the 15th century tower. The road is named after the architect of the rebuilt church, William Butterfield, who enlarged the building in 1847. He designed many locally famous buildings, including Highbury Chapel and Coalpit Heath Church.

BUTTERWORTH COURT, BS4. Sited among other roads called after British composers, this celebrates the short life of George Butterworth (1885-1916)

whose main works were orchestral pieces influenced by old folksongs. He wrote settings for Housman's *A Shropshire Lad*. He served with distinction in the First World War and fought in the Battle of the Somme. He was awarded the Military Cross there in July 1916 and killed by a sniper a month later.

BUTTON CLOSE, BS14. This follows the trend for local developments to be named after those associated with Kingswood Forest. This road is named after Matthew de Button, who was convicted of trespassing in the Forest and killing four deer in 1370.

BUXTON WALK, BS7. This is a road in an area where a number of English place names have been used. Buxton is a spa town in the Peak District.

BYRON PLACE, BS8 / STREET BS5, BS2. It is most likely that all the Byron appellations refer to Lady Noel Byron, widow of the poet, who was a great benefactress and bought the Red Lodge for Mary Carpenter to open Britain's first reform school for girls.

CABOT GREEN, BS5. No obvious reason for this choice. Perhaps just celebrating a Bristol hero. *See John Cabot Court.*

CABOT WAY, BS1. A famous name with a Bristol connection is the theme of these roads.

CADBURY HEATH ROAD, BS15. Probably the oldest name in the district. *See Districts section in the introduction.*

CADDICK CLOSE BS15 In 1939 A company of commercial artists of this name had their premises in the area and W. Caddick was secretary of the Rechabite Society.

CADE CLOSE, BS 15. This was called after Rev. Cade, a Methodist Minister involved with the Cock Road school. The Methodists were untiring in their efforts to promote the importance of education and opened a number of schools. The clergy and church members worked as unpaid teachers.

CADOGAN ROAD, BS14. A local surname but it is not known whether it was the builder or the owner of the land. It was also the name of one of the first surgeons appointed by the Bristol Royal Infirmary.

CAEN ROAD, BS3. William the Conqueror and his wife were buried in Caen, Normandy, but there is no obvious reason for the naming of this street.

CAINE ROAD, BS7. Adjoining roads have a Manx connection so this road was clearly named for Sir Hall Caine (1853-1931), once famous author of *The Manxman, The Deemster* and other novels with an Isle of Man background. He was a member of the House of Keys 1901-1908. He was an associate of Dante Gabriel Rossetti, the Pre-Raphaelite painter.

CAINS CLOSE, BS15. A boot factory owned by people of this name flourished late nineteenth/early twentieth century though the opinion is held that the Cain family in question were those members of the Cock Road gang and their descendants who were often convicted, of robbery, murder and many other crimes, on reputation rather than hard evidence.

CAIRNS CRESCENT, BS2. In some old street directories this was written as Cairn's Crescent suggesting it was the name of someone who lived here. Another theory is that there was a pyramid of rough stones here marking a boundary. This would, in fact, be close to the boundary set out in the 1373 charter.

CAIRNS ROAD BS6. It seems likely this was named after Hugh McCalmont, lst Earl Cairns, Lord Chancellor in 1868 and 1874-80, as a nearby road is named after another Lord Chancellor.

CALCOTT ROAD, BS4. Could be a place name. The first syllable means cold - 'a cold dwelling'. It appears as a surname in local directories so this, too, is a possibility.

CALDBECK CLOSE, BS10. Roads on a Lake District theme predominate here.

CALDICOT CLOSE, BS11. Nicholas Caldicot was granted the manor of Lawrence Weston in the reign of Edward II.

CALDICOT CLOSE, BS15. All roads in this group are called after famous castles.

CALEDONIA MEWS / PLACE, BS8. The Roman name for the northern part of Britain, now just Scotland. It comes from two Celtic words, *cael,* Gaul or Celt and *don* (or *dun*}, a hill.

CALIFORNIA ROAD, BS15. A farm of this name used to exist before the development took place, built on the site of a pit of the same name. The road used to be known variously as Dodds Lane and Pit Lane. The unusual name inspired the developers to use Californian place names for all the surrounding roads

CALLICROFT ROAD, BS12. There was a farm of this name run by the Barton family at the beginning of the twentieth century.

CALLINGTON ROAD, BS4. A village in Cornwall, the name of which derives from OE *calo,* 'bare' or 'bald', and *tun,* 'farm'; so translating as 'farm on the bare hill'. *Calo* originally meant bare and unfledged (as in a young bird); hence the modern 'callow', as in the term 'callow youth'. The geographical aspects of the area continue to unfold with the names. *See Allanmead Close.* Another possible theme is that the Vikings were routed at Callington by King Alfred. *See Ravenhead Road.*

CALLOWHILL COURT, BS1. Hannah, the daughter of Thomas Callowhill, a member of the Society of Friends, became the wife of William Penn, the founder of Pennsylvania. The land on which Penn Street and the now defunct Callowhill and Philadelphia Streets were built was once an orchard belonging to Dennis Hollister, Hannah's grandfather.

CAMBERLEY ROAD, BS4. Probably named after Camberley in Surrey, in keeping with other local streets named after towns, but the connection is not clear.

CAMBORNE ROAD, BS7. Sited among other streets called after British towns. No obvious pattern emerges.

CAMBRIDGE CRESCENT, BS9. This stands on the site of Cambridge House, a Georgian building which was demolished in order for these houses to be built.

CAMBRIDGE PARK, BS6. Probably named after George, Duke of Cambridge (1819-1904). He was a Field Marshal and Commander-in-Chief of the British Army from 1856 when he saw active service in the Crimea. He was an extremely popular officer.

CAMBRIDGE ROAD, BS7. There were two terraces on Gloucester Road, one between Longmead Avenue and Radnor Road known as Oxford Terrace, and one between Bishop Road and Cambridge Road which was called Cambridge Terrace.

CAMBRIDGE STREET, BS5. All surrounding streets are named after royal houses and noble families so almost certainly after the Duke of Cambridge. *See Cambridge Park.*

CAMBRIDGE STREET, BS3. Perhaps after the Duke as there is a Richmond Street nearby.

CAMDEN ROAD, BS3. Probably after the London district, called after the Marquis of Camden who was a freeman of the Society of Merchant Venturers in 1789.

CAMDEN TERRACE, BS1. Most probably called after Charles Pratt, lst Earl Camden (1714-94), Lord Chancellor in 1766 under Pitt.

CAMELFORD ROAD, BS5. A market town in Cornwall whose name means 'ford over the River Camel'. No obvious reason for this name selection.

CAMERON WALK, BS7. Named after Sir David Cameron (1865-1945), Scottish painter, etcher and book illustrator.

CAMERTON ROAD, BS5. Named after a mining village near Radstock, Somerset. Perhaps so named because of its proximity to the Whitehall Pit.

CAMP ROAD, BS8. Named after Camp House, the residence of Bristol mayor Charles Pinney at the time of the Bristol riots in 1831, when the house was used by the military. Camp House itself was named after the Iron Age hill fort on Observatory Hill which, at the time, was called the Roman camp.

CAMPBELL STREET, BS2. Named after Francis Campbell, the first husband of Georgina Bristocke. He died in 1851. *See Dalrymple Road and Brigstocke Road.*

CAMPBELL FARM DRIVE, BS11. Campbells Farm once stood on this land.

CAMPION WALK, BS4. After Thomas Campion, a physician, poet and musician (1567-1620), who set his own poetry to music. All nearby streets are named after British composers.

CAMWAL ROAD, BS2. Named after a company which had its premises here from the 1920s until the 1960s, producing lemonade.

CANADA WAY, BS1. Bristol's seafaring connection is emphasised here.

CANBERRA GROVE, BS12. Following the pattern of naming roads in the area after aircraft. The English Electric Canberra was the RAF's first jet bomber. It first flew in 1949, and was a great success; the RAF still has some.

CANFORD LANE / ROAD, BS9. There once stood on this site Canford House and farm. In Morgan's Guide of 1871 the house is described as being surrounded by rich meadow fields and arable land. A likely derivation is an OE personal name - thus 'Cana's ford'.

CANNON STREET, BS3. Prior to 1870 the spelling was 'canon' suggesting an ecclesiastical origin.

CANON'S ROAD, BS1. Site of the marsh belonging to the Augustine canons of the Abbey church.

CANON'S WALK, BS15. This is named in honour of Canon Dandy, one time vicar of Kingswood.

CANOWIE ROAD, BS6. Built on the site of Canowie House, which was occupied in 1871 by Richard Boucher James, his wife Mary and their three children. Richard James was a farmer from South Australia and Canowie, north of Adelaide, was his sheep station. It seems likely that he named his house after his Australian property. Not far from here is Auburn Road. Auburn is also an Australian town in the same region as Canowie, but no link has been established

CANTELL GROVE, BS14. Elinor Cantell is recorded as living in the tithing of Keynsham in January 1670. She was exempt from paying Hearth Tax.

CANTERBURY STREET, BS5. Probably named after the Kent city, the meaning being fort or town of the Cantwere i.e. people of Kent. An alternative suggestion is that it was a tribute to Viscount Canterbury (1814-77), MP for Cambridge and Governor of Trinidad.

CANTOCK'S CLOSE, BS8. This has also been spelt Quantock's Close and Cantoke's Close. It was in existence in 1378 and probably was derived from a person living there. A Roger Cantocke held a civic post in the city in 1237 so perhaps it was his family home.

CANVEY CLOSE, BS10. Canvey Island is in the Thames estuary, in the county of Essex. Perhaps the owners of the land on which these houses were built had connections with Essex.

CANYNGE ROAD / SQUARE, BS8 / STREET, BS1. Named in honour of William Canynges the younger, whose mansion stood in nearby Redcliffe Street. He is buried in St. Mary Redcliffe Church which he helped remodel. On his tomb he is depicted as a priest because he retired in 1417 to Westbury College, where he became Dean. He is described on his tomb as being 'ye richest merchant in ye towne of Bristowe'. He was five times Mayor of the city. Much of his fortune came from his immense shipping fleet and he provided work for a large percentage of the population of Bristol.

CAPEL ROAD, BS11. The Capels held the Manor of Aust until 1642 when it passed to Sir Samuel Astry *(see Astry Close)*. Arthur, Lord Capel was beheaded in 1649 for giving allegiance to Charles 1. His daughter married the first Duke of Beaufort. Edward Capel held the manor of Henbury (from Ralph Sadlier) from 1653 to 1681. He died June 1681 and was buried at Henbury.

CAPEL COURT, BS15. Named after Bert Capel, who farmed this land before it was given over to housing. There were farmers of that name in the area since the mid-nineteenth century.

CAPGRAVE CLOSE / CRESCENT BS4. John Capgrave (1394-1464) was a theologian and historian who wrote a Life of St. Keyna, after whom Keynsham was named. He was an Augustinian friar and spent most of his life at the friary at Lynn.

CARAWAY GARDENS, BS5. All roads in the development called after herbs.

CARDIGAN ROAD, BS9. Many roads locally named after peers of the realm. The Earldom of Cardigan has been borne by the Brudenell family since 1661. The 7th earl, inventor of the garment which bears his name, led the Light Brigade at Balaclava. *See Balaclava Road.*

CARDILL CLOSE, BS13. As with several other local roads, named after a castle.

CARISBROOKE ROAD, BS4. All roads in the direct vicinity are named after castles; this one is on the Isle of Wight.

CARLTON PARK, BS5. A place name - there are many of this name around the country. It has been suggested it is a corruption of Charlton and comes from the OE *ceorl-* a freeman of the lowest rank, a free peasant, *tun* being 'homestead', 'village' or merely 'enclosure'. It has been suggested there may have been a house of this name here prior to development.

CARLTON COURT, BS9. The Carlton cinema once stood here.

CARLOW ROAD, BS4. An Irish theme to the roads here. *See Bantry Road.*

CARLYLE ROAD, BS5. Perhaps named after Thomas Carlyle, the historian and essayist; but a local directory, published at the time the road was built, listed a person of that name living close by and also a local firm similarly named, so perhaps this was the origin.

CARMARTHEN ROAD, BS9. Many streets in the district are named after Welsh towns and counties for no apparent reason.

CARNARVON ROAD, BS6. Many local roads are named after the nobility - this one after the Earls of Carnarvon, whose family name is Herbert. The title dates from 1793. The fifth earl worked with Howard Carter in excavating Tutankhamen's tomb. He died in Cairo in April 1923, five months afterwards, aged 57.

CARR HOUSE BS2. John Carr was a sixteenth century philanthropist who made a fortune from the manufacture of soap. He founded Queen Elizabeth's Hospital. *See John Carr's Terrace.*

CARRINGTON ROAD, BS3. Either a place name or after Sir Frederick Carrington, a cavalry leader in the Boer War. There is, too, another possibility: there was a noble family of this name who had connections with the Smyth family, who owned much of the land in this area.

CARTER'S BUILDINGS, BS8. This section of Portland Street has been known by this name since time immemorial. Perhaps a man called Carter had these houses built. There were maltsters of this name at Stone Buildings, Clifton Hill, in 1830.

CARTLEDGE ROAD, BS5. Named in honour of Arthur Cartledge, Bristol Rovers' Goalkeeper before the First World War. He went on to play for First Division Aston Villa.

CARY COURT, BS2. John Cary was a seventeenth century merchant with advanced ideas on free trade and a determination to help the poor and needy.

CASHMORE HOUSE, BS5. Miss Hilda Cashmore was the Warden of the University Settlement in Barton Hill from 1911 to 1937. *See Arthur Skemp Close.*

Castle Street in the 1920s

CASSELL ROAD, BS16. Perhaps the name of the builder or landowner.

CASSEY BOTTOM LANE, BS5. Cassey is a corruption of 'causeway' which, in turn, is derived from the old Norman French *caucie* - an embankment or raised way in marshy land.

CASTLE CLOSE, BS10. After Blaise Castle.

CASTLE FARM ROAD, BS15. There was a Castle Inn Farm nearby.

CASTLE ROAD, BS15. The site of the old mock castle demolished when the Water Board bought the land.

CASTLE STREET, BS1. Site of the Inner Ward of Bristol Castle which stood for nearly six centuries. An octagonal tower survived here until rebuilding took place in the 1920s.

CATBRAIN HILL / LANE, BS10. From the Middle English *cattes-brazen,* a description of the local soil - rough clay mixed with stones.

CATER ROAD, BS13. Seemingly a surname, maybe the owner of the land. It is thought that there was some connection with the wholesale grocers, Cater, Stoffel and Forte. Perhaps Gateway took them over and then established their depot here in the late 1960s.

CATHAY, BS1 Being close to the river this street was possibly named in connection with trading routes to China.

CATHERINE MEAD STREET, BS3 The street was built on land belonging to the house described as 'St. Catherine at Brightbow without Bristol', in the parish of Bedminster. Founded by Lord Robert de Berkeley c. 1200 for a Warden and seven poor brethren, the charitable house was used as a hostel for pilgrims and other travellers later in his lifetime. The house was demolished in the 1880s, and Wills' tobacco factory erected in its place.

CATHERINE STREET, BS11. St. Catherine is the patron saint of wheelwrights, and was martyred on a wheel. The Catherine after whom this street is named, though, is said to be a connection of the Jefferies, ship repairers.

CATO STREET, BS5. Probably named after the Cato Street Conspiracy of 1820, which was almost as notorious in its day as the Gun Powder Plot. A group of militant political radicals, headed by Arthur Thistlewood, planned to incite revolution in England by blowing up Lord Harrowby's house in Grosvenor Square, by which they hoped to destroy the entire Cabinet who were dining there. The plan was developed in an attic lodging in nearby Cato Street and had been incited by the recent Peterloo Massacre in Manchester. However, government spies had been following the conspirators, who were intercepted in Cato Street on 23rd February 1820, where one of them was stabbed to death during the arrests. Thistlewood and several of his co-conspirators were later hung. Thousands of high-ranking persons subsequently visited the little attic in Cato Street on tours conducted by the police officers, and were especially thrilled by the blood stains still on the floor. *The Sunday Observer* of 3rd March 1820 reported: *"Among others attracted to the spot, we remarked several of the fair sex, who braved the inconvenience of the difficult ascent to the loft for the gratification of their curiosity."*

CATTISTOCK DRIVE, BS5. Cattistock is a town in Dorset. Perhaps the owner of this land had connections there.

CATTLE MARKET ROAD, BS1. The cattle market was established here in 1830. In 1874 the Great Western and Midland Railways boards reconstructed it.

CATTYBROOK STREET, BS5. Named after the hamlet in Gloucestershire. There is some doubt about the origin of the first component. It may be a personal name, Cada of Celtic root, or 'Catta's brook' or 'the cat's brook'.

CAUSLEY DRIVE, BS15.

> *In blue Bristol city at tall-tide I wandered*
> *Down where the sea-masts their signals were shining,*
> *I heard a proud seaman on the poop-deck reclining*
> *Shout to the stars that about the ship blundered…*
>
> Charles Causley, *Ballad of the Five Continents*

Named after the poet Charles Causley, b.1917. He served in the Royal Navy during the war, and many of his poems have a nautical flavour. He was prevailed upon to declare this road open by Councillor Colin Cradock, whose choice of naming it was.

CAVAN WALK BS4. All Irish names in this area. *See Bantry Road.*

CAVE COURT / STREET, BS2. Stephen Cave resided in Brunswick Square in 1793. John Cave and Co. are listed in the Mathews Directory of that year as being Colour Manufacturers. Daniel Cave, a partner in the Castle Bank and Lord Mayor owned an elegant residence in Stokes Croft at the beginning of the nineteenth century.

CAVE DRIVE, BS16. This was named after Sir Charles Cave, a major landowner in the area.

CAVENDISH GARDENS, BS9. Takes its name from Cavendish Square in London where Margot Asquith famously rode her horse up the Grand Staircase. Cavendish is the family name of the Dukes of Devonshire.

CAVENDISH ROAD, BS9. Almost certainly for the same reason as Cavendish Gardens.

CAVENDISH ROAD, BS12. In view of the naming of nearby streets (Durban and Pretoria), perhaps called after the navigator Thomas Cavendish (1555-92), who circumnavigated the globe, stopping off at South Africa.

CECIL AVENUE, BS5. This could be a surname or a first name or it may even commemorate Lord Robert Cecil, M.P. and Colonial Secretary, and President of the League of Nations Union 1923-45. He was awarded the Nobel Peace Prize in 1937. Another possibility is an earlier Lord Cecil, either David, who held a high position at the court of Henry VIII, or his son Robert, one of the trusted courtiers of Elizabeth I.

CECIL ROAD, BS8. A field name - from 'Cecil's Littlefields'. *See under Litfield.*

CECIL ROAD, BS15. Sir Robert Cecil, Earl of Salisbury, was the first to grants leases for coal mining in Kingswood. There was a great deal of dissatisfaction in the area at the time because the Player family held the monopoly, and this was an attempt to rectify the situation.

CEDAR CLOSE, BS15 There was a house called The Cedars not far from here.

CEDAR CLOSE, BS12. Amongst other roads with tree names.

CEDAR GROVE / PARK, BS9. Perhaps cedars grew here before the development took place.

CEDAR HALL, BS16. After the property, called Cedar House prior to 1802, which was rebuilt as flats in the 1970s.

CEDAR ROW, BS11. On the edge of the golf course, so probably a reflection of the rural scene.

CEMETERY ROAD, BS4. A one-way street leading, appropriately, to the rear entrance of Arnos Vale cemetery.

CENNICK AVENUE, BS15. John Cennick was the first to preach a sermon when the Moravian church held its meetings in a private house, before the chapel was built. He composed a number of hymns. *See Tippett's Road, BS15.*

CENTAURUS ROAD, BS12. Amidst other roads named after mythical creatures which gave their names to aircraft engines produced by the Bristol Aeroplane Company. The Bristol Centaurus was the last of the Bristol piston aero-engines.

CENTRAL AVENUE, BS15. A literal naming.

CENTRAL AVENUE, BS11. Typical of the area's brevity in street naming.

CERES CLOSE, BS15. After the carved figure of Sally-on-the-Barn which is rumoured to have come from Lacock Abbey. Ceres was the Roman goddess of agriculture. The carving can be seen over the gateway to Court Farm.

CERNEY LANE, BS11. Another on the Cotswold village theme.

CHADLEIGH GROVE, BS4. The name of a village in Devon.

CHAKESHILL CLOSE / DRIVE, BS10. Taken from Chaxhill or Chakeshill which was erroneously assumed to be in the Hundred of Westbury-on-Trym. It was, in fact, part of the Hundred of Westbury-on-Severn.

CHALCROFT WALK, BS13. Field belonging to Bishopsworth Farm in 1802. Derived from OE *cealc*, chalk, and *croft* - a small enclosure.

THE CHALET, BS11. Name of a house on this site which was demolished in 1965.

CHALKS ROAD, BS5. In 1733 this was known as The Footpath It was the site of Strachan and Henshaw's coalpit. It is an old field name from the OE *cealc* - 'chalk' or limestone.

CHALLENDER AVENUE, BS10. The name of Deborah Challender appears in the Westbury Poor Book. She received relief to the extent of 4 shillings per week. She lived in the Stoke Bishop area in 1689.

CHALLONER COURT, BS1. A corruption of the name Chandler. William Chandler was a Bristol merchant of the mid seventeenth century.

CHAMPION ROAD, BS15. Named after William Champion, owner of a zinc manufacturing plant at Warmley Towers. The zinc was manufactured from calamine or black-jack and it was the first works of its kind to be established in Europe. He also owned copper mills here.

CHAMPNEYS AVENUE, BS10. The Champneys were Bristol merchants in the seventeenth century, Richard Champneys was the warden of the Society of Merchant Venturers 1687-8. The family are recorded as living in Bristol as early as 1383.

CHANCERY STREET, BS5. In 1275 Robert Burnell, the wealthy and influential Bishop of Bath and Wells, transferred the Chancery court to Bristol.

CHANDOS ROAD, BS6. The last Duke of Chandos (1823-89) visited Bristol in 1867 and was presented with the Freedom of the Merchant Venturers' Society.

CHANNEL'S HILL, BS9. The reason for this naming has not been discovered.

CHANNON'S HILL, BS16. This name exists in numerous variants. In 1610 it was Chennell Hill, in 1777 it was Shannaways Hill, in 1830, Channis Hill and in 1842 Channel's Hill. By 1863 it was spelt with an extra l. It is thought the derivation is Old French *chanel*, watercourse, though some have suggested *Charnells* - from the OE *cyrran* meaning 'to turn'.

CHANTRY GROVE, BS11. The influential Inskip family had a house of this name in Abbot's Leigh. Sir Thomas Walter Hobart Inskip, son of a solicitor, was a prominent lawyer. He was born in Bristol in 1876 and in 1918 was elected MP for Central Bristol. He served as secretary-general under the Unionist ministry and in 1928 was appointed Attorney-General. He lost his seat in the 1929 election but stood for Fareham in 1931 and won. He had previously resigned his position as attorney-general but was later persuaded to take up the post again.

CHANTRY GROVE, BS16. In keeping with the religious namings nearby.

CHANTRY ROAD, BS8. Either so named because of the proximity of St. John's Church or after the village near Frome in Somerset.

CHAPEL BARTON, BS3. West Street Baptist chapel was at the corner of this road.

CHAPEL CLOSE, BS15. Self-explanatory.

CHAPEL GARDENS, BS10. There is a Methodist chapel nearby.

CHAPEL GREEN LANE, BS6. The lane that runs to Redland Chapel Green. The Green has always been known as Redland Green, and the naming of this road is Victorian or later.

CHAPEL LANE, BS16. The small chapel still standing in Chapel Lane (at 724 Fishponds Road) was originally a Baptist Meeting House, and has been used by various denominations over the years. It became a store for Beacon Motors in 1969.

CHAPEL LANE, BS11. The Methodist chapel was incorporated into the building of this road.

CHAPEL LANE, BS5. This refers to Croft End chapel.

CHAPEL ROAD, BS13. Adjacent to chapel.

CHAPEL ROAD, BS5. Fairly near St. Mark's Baptist chapel.

CHAPEL ROAD, BS15. The chapel in question was demolished for road widening in the 1960s

CHAPEL STREET, BS2. The Mission chapel stood in adjoining Victoria Street.

CHAPLIN ROAD, BS5. This may have been called after Henry, 1st Viscount Chaplin (1840-1923), politician and sportsman, whose horse, Hermit, won the Derby in 1867. Or it may have more local connections, as the name was not uncommon in the area.

CHAPTER STREET, BS2. All the nearby streets have an ecclesiastical theme.

CHARBOROUGH ROAD, BS10. Named after a location in Dorset.

CHARBURY WALK, BS11. All other nearby roads are called after locations in Gloucestershire so perhaps this is a mis-spelling of Charlbury.

CHARD HOUSE, BS14. Continuing the theme of Somerset villages.

CHARDSTOCK AVENUE, BS9. Village in Dorset. The name derives from Cerdic, King of the West Saxons and OE *stoc*, a secondary settlement. It lies among other roads with West Country place names.

CHARFIELD ROAD, BS10. Amidst other roads bearing place names with no discernible link.

CHARFIELD, BS15. There is a little cluster of roads here called after locations in Gloucestershire which may have been on land owned by the Lords of the Manor of Siston in past times.

CHARGROVE, BS15. A village near Cheltenham, Gloucestershire.

CHARIS AVENUE, BS10. Charis was the wife of Vulcan, God of Fire. There is no obvious reason for this choice though Harris suggests that she is associated

with places, graces and delights which the builder may have thought the development offered.

CHARLECOMBE COURT / ROAD, BS9. Named after a Somerset village

CHARLES PLACE, BS8. It is not known who this road is named after.

CHARLES ROAD, BS12. After Charles Bridgeman, the last owner of Church Farm.

CHARLES STREET, BS1. Named in honour of Charles 11 as the area was developed shortly after the Restoration.

CHARLOTTE STREET, BS1. Queen Charlotte (1744-1818) was the wife of George III. She was of German descent.

CHARLTON AVENUE, BS12 / GARDENS / LANE / PLACE / ROAD, BS10. These names refer to the village wiped out to clear the way for the Brabazon runway. The name is derived from OE *ceorl*, a low class freeman and *tun*, meaning 'farmstead' or 'village'.

CHARLTON MEAD COURT / DRIVE, BS10. *See Charlton Avenue.*

CHARLTON ROAD, BS15. Site of Charleton Pin Works. Robert Charleton, a Quaker, invented a pin machine and, in partnership with a man called Lambert, mechanised the pin industry.

CHARLTON STREET, BS5. Near Robert Street, so perhaps named for the same reason as BS15.

CHARMINSTER ROAD, BS16. Village in Dorset. Derivation is church or minster on the River Cerne, though it has been suggested that 'minster' could mean marshland, thus perhaps indicating a village prone to flooding. A number of random place names are used in this area.

CHARNELL ROAD, BS16. The Charnell Brook used to power the Charnell Mill in ancient times. According to Roman authority Thomas Codrington this may have been the site of a Roman causeway. There was once a Charnell's Wood here, by Rodway Hill. When the Charnell Down was dug up, bones were discovered there, leading to the belief that there had been, at one time, a charnel house on the site.

CHARNHILL BROW / CRESCENT / DRIVE / RIDGE / VALE, BS17. Charn Hill is a section of the common.

CHARNWOOD, BS17. This takes its name from a wooded spot on the common.

CHARTER WALK, BS4. The Charter referred to is that granted by Edward III defining the boundaries of Bristol. The surrounding roads echo this theme.

CHARTERHOUSE ROAD, BS5. Captain Foxcroft owned this land until 1927. He resided at Hinton Charterhouse near Bath.

CHASE ROAD / THE CHASE, BS16. Both refer to the Chase which remained after deforestation of much of Kingswood Forest. *See Forest Road.*

CHATSWORTH ROAD, BS4. Chatsworth House in Derbyshire is the magnificent seat of the Dukes of Devonshire. Standing in 11 square miles of grounds, the house was built in the Ionic style, between 1687 and 1706. The north wing was added in 1820.

CHATSWORTH ROAD, BS16. Among other seemingly random place names.

CHATTERTON GREEN, BS14 / SQUARE / STREET, BS1.

> *Clifton, sweet village! Now demands the lay,*
> *The loved retreat of all the rich and gay…*

> Thomas Chatterton, *Clifton*

Celebrating the brief life of the poet Thomas Chatterton, whose suicide on 25 August 1770 raised him to cult status. He managed to fool experts with his writings which included the 'Rowley Poems' which were attributed to a fifteenth century monk. He was born in Redcliffe in 1752. The front wall of his birth house is still preserved, opposite St. Mary Redcliffe church. The rest of the house was sacrificed when Redcliffe Way was constructed in 1938.

CHAUCER WALK, BS7. In keeping with the choice of literary names for local streets this street celebrates Geoffrey Chaucer (1340-1400). His most famous work was the *Canterbury Tales*, written in about 1387. Printed by Caxton in 1475, it was one of the first printed books in the English language.

CHAUNDEY GROVE, BS13. This was a landowner at the beginning of the nineteenth century.

CHAVENAGE, BS15. Named after a place in Gloucestershire, with a large manor house.

CHEAPSIDE STREET, BS3. Cheapside is a district of London where the mercers, saddlers and other craftsmen had their halls. The name derives from 'cheap' meaning shop. No obvious reason for this road to be called thus.

CHEAPSIDE, BS2. This road borders St. Paul's churchyard as does London's Cheapside, so this may be the reason for the choice in this case. *See Cheapside Street.*

CHEDDAR GROVE, BS3. Many local roads named after places in Somerset.

CHEDWORTH ROAD, BS7. When the Domesday Book was in the process of compilation Chedworth was in the Rapsgate hundred and was held by Wulfward. There was a toll here on salt at that time.

CHEDWORTH, BS15. There was a Roman Villa at Chedworth in Gloucestershire.

CHEESE LANE, BS2. A very old street, still known by its medieval name, as is nearby Bread Street.

CHELMSFORD WALK, BS4. Following the religious association here, this road is called after a city with a noted cathedral.

CHELSEA PARK / ROAD, BS5. This area of Easton was formerly known as Frogmarsh and comprised mainly market gardens. When building began in the second half of the nineteenth century many local streets were called after fashionable London districts.

CHELSTON ROAD, BS4. There is a small town in Somerset which may have some long-distant link with this area.

CHELTENHAM LANE / ROAD, BS6. Leads to Gloucester Road, and thus eventually to both Gloucester and Cheltenham. Part of the road was originally called Catherine Terrace.

Cheltenham Road c. 1907

CHELVEY CLOSE, BS13. A hamlet in the Hundred of Hartcliffe and Bedminster.

CHELWOOD ROAD, BS11. Named after a Somerset village, as is a road nearby, but the reason is not apparent.

CHEPSTOW PARK, BS16. Following the theme of race-courses in the naming of all the roads in this group.

CHEPSTOW ROAD, BS4. Among a group of roads called after castles.

CHEQUERS CLOSE, BS15. An inn of this name once stood here.

CHERINGTON, BS15. Named after a Gloucestershire village where an ancient statue representing a hunter god was found.

CHERITON PLACE, BS9. There is a place in Hampshire with this name. Dorset Road is nearby, so there may be a connection with the South of England.

CHERITON PLACE, BS15. John de Cheriton was Edward II's steward in 1316.

CHERRY GARDEN LANE / ROAD / CHERRY GARDENS, BS15. Named after Cherry Garden Hill.

CHERRY GROVE, BS17. There used to be a large number of market gardens in the area.

CHERRY LANE, BS2. Built on the site of a cherry orchard.

CHERRY ORCHARD LANE, BS5. An inn of this name once stood here attached to Pocock's, a large and celebrated grammar school.

CHERRY TREE CLOSE / CRESCENT, BS16. Another section of housing built on The Thicket. that has been given the names of trees or shrubs. In the case of The Crescent, cherry trees were planted on the grass verge in front of the houses so that each house had at least one. *See Thicket Road.*

CHERRY WOOD, BS15. Market gardens dominated the landscape here before development took place.

CHERRYTREE ROAD, BS16 *See Cherry Tree Close.*

CHERTSEY ROAD, BS6. This was named after a town in Surrey, the site of a Benedictine Abbey, but it is not known why.

CHESHAM WAY, BS15. Named after a market town in Buckinghamshire, but it is not known why.

CHESSEL STREET, BS3. From the Anglo Saxon *ceastel* meaning a heap of stones or a collapsed building according to one authority, although another explanation could be that the word is a variation of *chester*, deriving from the Latin *castra*, a military camp.

CHESSINGTON AVENUE, BS14. Part of the estate developed by the Swiss millionaire Leonard Nidditch and named after the town where he had inaugurated a similar scheme. *See Gilda Close.*

CHESTER PARK ROAD, BS16. The Chester family were prominent landowners during the reign of Elizabeth I.

CHESTER ROAD, BS5. This road would seem to be named after the town as roads nearby follow this trend.

CHESTER STREET, BS5. This was probably named after a person as a number of surnames have been employed as street names in this area.

CHESTERFIELD AVENUE / ROAD, BS6. Probably after Philip Dormer Stanhope, Fourth Earl of Chesterfield, who had links with this city. Born in 1694, he sat in the House of Commons as a Whig until he succeeded to the title in 1726. He was Ambassador at The Hague 1728-30 and Lord Lieutenant of Ireland 1745-46. He died in 1773.

CHESTERFIELD ROAD, BS16. There are a number of roads in the area called after aristocratic families, this style of nomenclature being in vogue at the time these properties were built.

CHESTERS, BS15. This is another old field name, many of which have been used for modern streets in the area.

CHESTNUT CLOSE, BS14. There seems to have been no houses of this name in the area so perhaps these trees grew on the hill where later the houses were built.

CHESTNUT WALK, BS13. A house called 'Chestnut Court' once stood near here.

CHESTNUT COURT, BS17. There was a house here in the 1920s called 'The Chestnuts', home to a man called Joseph Legg.

CHESTNUT ROAD, BS16. In 1900 there was a house nearby called 'The Chestnuts', the residence of Mr. J. Cunningham.

CHESTNUT WAY, BS15. Not named after a house but rather describing the topography of the area.

CHETWOODE CLOSE, BS10. Named after a house which once stood in the area

CHEVIOT WAY, BS15. Among a group of roads named after ranges of hills.

CHEWTON CLOSE, BS16. Place name - the first syllable may refer to the River Chew. Among other roads with place names which seem to form no particular pattern.

CHEYNE ROAD, BS9. From Cheyne Walk in Chelsea, home of Thomas Carlyle. There was a Lord Cheyne who sold his manor to Sir Hans Sloan, the celebrated physician and botanist (1660-1753).

CHICHESTER HOUSE, BS4. Following a local theme of famous cathedrals.

CHILTERN CLOSE, BS15. All the roads in this development are called after ranges of hills.

CHILTON ROAD, BS4. William de Chilton was a civic dignitary in Bristol during the reign of Henry III.

THE CHINE, BS16. A chine is a fissure or ravine, the term deriving from the OE *cinu*. So called because of its proximity to Wickham Glen.

CHINE VIEW, BS16. *See The Chine.*

CHIPHOUSE ROAD, BS15. So called because this was the place where the wood was cut and shaped like pencils for the pit props used at Soundwell Colliery. A row of colliery workers' cottages here was known as Chiphouse Rank.

CHIPPERFIELD DRIVE, BS15. A town in Hertfordshire and also a surname, but the reason for this naming is unknown.

THE CHIPPINGS, BS16. The name means place where merchants store their goods but there is no apparent reason why this name should be used here. It may have been a field name.

CHISBURY STREET, BS5. A hamlet in Wiltshire. The first syllable is from a name, Cussa, and the last syllable derives from OE *byrig* meaning 'fort' or 'town'. There is an ancient camp near the village.

CHITTENING ROAD, BS11. This name derived from a field name, Chitning Warth, a warth being a piece of reclaimed marsh land. This dates from medieval times.

CHOCK LANE, BS9. Originally Chalk Lane as this was the site of a lime-burning and clay pipe industry. Alleged to be Westbury's oldest house, although a claim has been made that this honour falls to Elsie Briggs' house just outside the churchyard gates.

CHRISTCHURCH AVENUE / LANE, BS16. Called after the nearby church.

CHRISTCHURCH ROAD, BS8. After the impressive church which dominates the area.

CHRISTMAS STREET / STEPS, BS1. Until 1775 Christmas Steps was known as Queen Street and led to Christmas Street, originally called Knifesmith Street as the armourers and cutlers had their premises here. The 1385 will of Robert Gradely refers to Knyzt-mass Street, possibly a combination of Knight and Mass as the Eucharist processions on holy days once took place here. Throughout the ages the street appears on maps as Cultellare, Knightsmith, Christsmith, Cutlersmass and Christmas.

CHUBB CLOSE, BS15. This is named after Alan Chubb, the council surveyor at the time this road was built.

CHURCH AVENUE / ROAD, BS9. The church here is St. Mary Magdalene's. J. S. Harford of Blaise Castle laid the foundation stone in 1858.

CHURCH AVENUE / STREET, BS5. Pertaining to St. Mark's Church, which is now deconsecrated.

CHURCH CLOSE / LANE, BS10. Henbury church dates from the beginning of the thirteenth century.

CHURCH DRIVE, BS5. Land belonging to St. George's Church.

CHURCH HILL / PARADE, BS4. The church here is St. Luke's.

CHURCH LANE / ROAD, BS3. This was near to St. John's Church.

CHURCH LANE, BS8. St. Peter's was the parish church of Cliftonwood.

CHURCH LANE / STREET, BS1. The church here is the Temple church with its famous leaning spire.

CHURCH LANE, BS16. Leads eventually to Winterbourne Down church

CHURCH LEAZE, BS11. Situated between two churches, St. Mary's and St. Bernard's.

CHURCH ROAD, BS5. Until 1733 this was known as the Turnpike Road. Afterwards it was called St. George's Road when the district became known as Easton St. George.

CHURCH ROAD, BS7 This leads up to Horfield church.

CHURCH ROAD, BS9. Leads to Westbury parish church.

CHURCH ROAD, BS13. The Congregational church stands in this road.

CHURCH ROAD, BS15. This road joins High Street, Kingswood directly opposite Holy Trinity church. Years ago this was known as Poorhouse Lane as it led to a building serving this purpose.

CHURCH ROAD, BS16. The road which passes the very pretty parish church of Frenchay.

CHURCH ROAD, BS16. The church here is St. Stephen's with its adjoining school.

CHURCH ROAD / VIEW, BS12. This refers to St. Peter's Church, Filton.

CHURCH STREET, BS5. The church here is St. Luke's opened 19 September 1843.

CHURCH VIEW, BS16. The church in view is St. James's.

CHURCHDOWN WALK, BS11. All roads in the area named after locations in Gloucestershire.

CHURCHILL DRIVE, BS9. Near roads called Hutton and Hammond so perhaps a cricketing connection.

CHURCHILL ROAD, BS4. No obvious link with surrounding roads. Perhaps the builder had links with this Somerset village or does it honour Sir Winston Churchill and his impressive political career?

CHURCHILL CLOSE, BS15. This was the name of a farmer upon whose land modern houses were built, mostly those that form the Grange estate.

CHURCHLANDS ROAD, BS3. It must be assumed that the church owned the land on which this road was built.

CHURCHSIDE, BS16. Literally beside Frenchay church.

CHURCHWARD CLOSE, BS15. Named after George Churchward, Chief Mechanical Engineer based at GWR HQ, Swindon. He held the post from 1902-21. Born in Stoke Gabriel in Devon, he was a brilliant mathematician at school, but left at sixteen to work for the South Devon Railway. He standardised and improved boiler design, creating the 'city' and then 'Star' class engines, the fastest and most efficient in their day. He died in 1933, knocked down by a steam locomotive close to the Swindon works, and is buried in the churchyard of Christchurch, Swindon.

CHURCHWAYS AVENUE / CRESCENT, BS7. This is an old field name.

CHURSTON CLOSE, BS14. Perhaps after Churston Ferrars near Brixham. Several place names with no discernible link have been used in these roads.

CIRCULAR ROAD, BS8. This circles part of Durdham Down.

CITY ROAD, BS2. Built in 1871 as a way to the city from Ashley Road. The first house on the left coming from Stokes Croft bore an inscription to this effect.

THE CLAMP, BS15. Thought to be an old field name.

CLANAGE ROAD, BS3. Derivation is OE *clæne*, 'field free of weeds'. The area was always known as 'The Clanage' or 'Kenn's Clanage'.

CLARE AVENUE, BS7. This leads off Claremont Avenue and may be just an abbreviation of that name.

CLARE ROAD, BS6. As this is close to Nugent Hill the obvious reason for the naming is Robert Nugent, Viscount Clare. *See Clare Street BS1.*

CLARE ROAD, BS5. This could well be a surname. People by this name have lived in the area over the years and may have owned the land.

CLARE ROAD, BS15. Gilbert de Clare was the Earl of Gloucester in 1218.

CLARE STREET, BS1. Built in 1771 and named as a tribute to Robert Nugent, Viscount Clare, a Whig MP who donated £580 towards the rebuilding of Bristol Bridge in 1766.

CLARE STREET, BS5. Perhaps another member of the Gerrish family. *See Gerrish Avenue.*

CLAREMONT AVENUE / ROAD, BS7 / STREET, BS5. The origin of the name is Claremont Park in Surrey, built by the renowned Sir John Vanbrugh, who designed Kingsweston House. There were two houses of this name in Bristol at one time, one in Bishopston and one in Stapleton Road, and it is likely the roads were built on the sites of these properties. The last syllable is from the French *mont* meaning 'mount'. The first syllable is derived from the Earl of Clare who owned the Surrey residence.

CLAREMONT TERRACE, BS5. There was a Claremont Villa on Church Road so perhaps the name was taken from there.

CLARENCE AVENUE / GARDENS / ROAD, BS16 / PLACE, BS2 / ROAD, BS1, BS5. It is believed all owe their origins to William, Duke of Clarence (1765-1837) third son of George III. He was crowned William IV in 1830 and was known as the Sailor King because of his illustrious naval career.

CLARENDON ROAD, BS6. Named after the Earldom of Clarendon (family name Villiers). The first Earl of Clarendon was Edward Hyde, after whom the London park was named. He was advisor to Charles II while in exile and married the King's niece. He wrote one of England's greatest historical accounts, *The History of the Great Rebellion.*

CLARK STREET, BS5. Named in honour of Mr G. B. Clark of Manchester, the founder, in 1837, of Clark, Acramans, Maze and Co, later to become the Great Western Cotton Company. *See Aitken Street.*

CLARK DRIVE, BS16. Named after the couple who ran Begbrook Farm for forty-six years. Mrs Clark, when widowed, sold the land, which was used to develop this housing estate.

CLARKE STREET, BS3. Philip Percy Doveton Clarke built a number of roads here in the 1860s.

CLATWORTHY DRIVE, BS14. A village in Somerset. The name is derived from the OE *clate* 'burdock', and *worpig* meaning 'enclosure': the place where the burdock grows.

CLAVELL ROAD, BS10. Samuel Clavell was overseer of the poor in 1686.

CLAVERHAM ROAD, BS16. Village near Yatton, Somerset. First syllable is from OE *clæfre* meaning 'clover'. A few other place names have been used in the vicinity but there is no apparent link.

CLAY BOTTOM, BS5. Descriptive of location and soil type.

CLAY HILL, BS5. Once the site of Alfred Bennett's Clay Hill Brick Works.

CLAY PIT ROAD, BS6. Obviously the site of a clay pit but no details available.

CLAYDON GREEN, BS13. It is possible this was an old field name.

CLAYFIELD ROAD, BS4. From the Clayfield-Ireland family, once important landowners in the area. They lived at Brislington Hall, where a DIY centre was later built.

CLAYMORE CRESCENT, BS16. So named because the road is built on the site of an old brick works.

CLAYPIECE ROAD, BS13. This was a field belonging to Filwood Farm which was owned by the Hall family for five hundred years. It was acquired by Bristol Corporation in the 1930s. Derivation: OE *clæg* 'clay' and Old French or Middle English *pece* 'plot of land'.

CLAYPOOL ROAD, BS15. Seemingly an old descriptive name for this small area.

CLAYTON STREET, BS5. There are a number of towns of this name scattered across the country but none seems to have connection with this road.

*The **British Lion** pub in the 1940s, on the corner of Clement Street and Elton Street, BS2*

CLAYTON STREET, BS11. Descriptive: it used to be called Clayfield Street.

CLEAVE STREET, BS2. The daughter of the owner of the Mina Road Brick Works, Richard Mogg Bryant, became Mrs Cleave when she married. There was a bricklayer called Henry William Cleave living in the area, so perhaps this was the family into which she was married.

CLEEVE AVENUE / GARDENS / HILL / LAWNS / ROAD, BS16. The name, taken from Cleeve Lodge, predominates in this area.

CLEEVE LODGE CLOSE / ROAD, BS16. As Cleeve Avenue.

CLEEVE PARK ROAD, BS 16. As Cleeve Avenue.

CLEEVE ROAD, BS4. Seemingly after the village in Somerset.

CLEEVEWOOD ROAD BS16. A continuation of the Cleeve theme.

CLEMENT STREET, BS2. There was a church here of this name which was bombed in the Second World War.

CLEVE ROAD, BS12. This road was known as Victoria Road until comparatively recently.

CLEVEDALE, BS16. Apparently a made-up name.

CLEVEDON ROAD / TERRACE, BS6. Called after the seaside resort in Somerset; the name means 'hill with cliffs'.

CLIFF COURT DRIVE, BS16. A house of this name used to stand nearby. The lodge still remains. It was once the home of C. H. Elliot, who recorded a history of the area.

CLIFFORD GARDENS, BS11. The barony of de Clifford was created in 1299 and the family inherited the Kings Weston estate from the Southwell family in 1775.

CLIFT HOUSE ROAD / SPUR, BS3. Dower House of Ashton Court. Lady Smyth (widow of Sir John Hugh) lived there 1802-25. It was purchased by the Corporation and demolished. It was used a diphtheria hospital in the early 1900s.

CLIFT PLACE, BS1. A variation of cliff.

CLIFT ROAD, BS3. As Clift House Road.

CLIFTON COURT / DOWN ROAD / HILL / PARK ROAD / ROAD / VALE / VALE CLOSE, BS8. All named after the district in which they are located. The area was developed largely in the eighteenth century, when prosperous merchants desired to live away from the noisome smells of the docks and overcrowded alleys of the centre of the city. When the fashion for taking the waters at the Hotwells Spa was at its height speculators cashed in by building properties for the visitors to lease.

CLIFTON WOOD ROAD / CRESCENT / TERRACE, BS8. Built upon what were the wooded slopes descending from Clifton to Hotwells.

CLINTON ROAD, BS3. This could be a surname of someone connected with the development although there was no-one of the name living locally at the time the road was built. It is the family name of the Dukes of Newcastle.

CLIVE ROAD, BS14. It would seem this choice was influenced by Robert Clive (1725-74), one of the founders of British rule in India. He first went to India in the service of the East India Company at a time when hostilities between the French and English there were just beginning so he joined the army and received his commission as ensign in 1747. After a spectacular routing of the French forces at Arcot he returned to England for two years before returning to India as a lieutenant-colonel in 1775. He avenged the outrage of the Black Hole of Calcutta by his victory over the Nawab of Bengal at Plassey. He returned to England in 1760 and was elected MP for Shrewsbury. He was made an Irish peer in 1762 and was knighted in 1764. He returned for one more year in India. An opium addict, he committed suicide following a parliamentary enquiry during his absence.

CLONMEL ROAD, BS4. *See Bantry Road.*

THE CLOSE, BS10. Seemingly an old field name.

CLOTHIER ROAD, BS4. This may have been named in honour of Alderman P. F. 'Frank' Clothier, member of the City Council, trade union leader and JP, famous for his phrase 'Do your best and leave the rest'. He was renowned for his sense of humour. He died in the 1950s when in his nineties. Another school of thought believes the naming to be in honour of Mr R. Clothier of Scotland House Farm, Stockwood Lane, who founded the Hungerford Christian Fellowship.

CLOUDS HILL AVENUE / ROAD, BS5. Name derived from OE *clud* meaning 'rock'.

CLOVELLY CLOSE / ROAD, BS5. After the North Devon village. The name means 'woodland glade' or 'clearing by the ravine'. No obvious reason for this choice.

CLOVER GROUND, BS9. Field name taken from the 1825 Westbury-on-Trym Survey.

CLOVERDALE DRIVE, BS15. Another in the series of California inspired names. *See California Road.*

CLOVERLEA ROAD, BS15. One of the old field names which have been retained in the area. Its old name was Gipsy Lane because the old Romany families used to return here year after year.

CLYDE GARDENS, BS5. One of the developers apparently lived in Clyde Gardens, Bath, and so suggested this name.

CLYDE GROVE, BS10. Among other names with a Scottish flavour.

CLYDE LANE / PARK / ROAD, BS6. Seemingly all called after the river in Scotland. Scottish names were popular in the era when these houses were built.

CLYDE ROAD / TERRACE, BS4. Perhaps after the first Baron Clyde, a distinguished military man who died in 1863.

CLYDE TERRACE, BS3. Probably for the same reason as that in BS4.

CLYDESDALE CLOSE, BS4. Perhaps from the horses used to plough the fields here in former times. A Clydesdale is a breed of draught horse.

COALEY ROAD, BS11. Called after the village near Dursley, Gloucestershire. The meaning is from the OE *cofa* meaning 'recess in a hillside' or 'cave' and *leah* meaning 'wood, woodland or clearing'. The names of a number of Gloucestershire towns have been used for streets in this area.

COAPE ROAD, BS14. William Coape was living in the parish and tithing of Whitechurch in 1670 and was granted exemption from the Hearth Tax.

COATES WALK, BS4. Continuing the theme of British composers, this celebrates the life of Eric Coates (1886-1957), famous for his lively orchestral suites, ballets and marches. He wrote the theme music for 'The Dambusters' and composed 'Sleepy Lagoon', the introductory music to the radio programme 'Desert Island Discs'.

COBBE HOUSE, BS2. Frances Power Cobbe was one of the first to endeavour to improve women's standing within the law. She was instrumental in bringing about the Married Women's Property Act.

COBBLESTONE MEWS, BS8. A converted stable yard.

COBDEN STREET, BS5. Called after Richard Cobden (1804-65), the Victorian statesman and free trader. Prominent in the Anti-Corn Law League.

COBHORN DRIVE, BS13. This is a field name from when Bishopsworth was the estate of Earl Temple of Stowe. The name derives from the OE *cobb* meaning 'lump' or 'summit' and *horn*, a projecting nook of land or bend.

COBOURG ROAD, BS6. Named in honour of Prince Leopold of Saxe-Coburg, nephew of Queen Victoria's consort and husband of Princess Charlotte (d.1817); he visited the city in 1830.

COCK ROAD, BS15. The name derives from the old practice of trapping forest birds by driving them into nets spread across the paths.

CODRINGTON PLACE, BS8 / ROAD, BS7. Probably from the Gloucestershire family of this name. Sir John Codrington was standard-bearer to Henry V at the Battle of Agincourt. Sir Christopher Codrington, who was M.P. for East Gloucestershire, was commanding Officer of the Codrington troop of Gloucestershire Yeomanry which was called upon to help quell the Bristol Riots of 1831. The uprising was against Sir Charles Wetherell, the Recorder of Bristol, because he opposed the Reform Bill. A crowd gathered outside his house in Queen Square. The Riot Act was read but the mob was increasing by the minute and Sir Charles had to make his escape over the roofs of adjoining houses. Captain Gage, under Col. Brereton's command, tried to pacify the rioters but to no avail. The Mansion House was attacked and looted and Lawford's Gate prison and the Bishop's Palace were burnt down. Four of the rioters were hanged and Brereton killed himself. Insurance claims filed totalled nearly £150,000. Sir Christopher died in 1863 aged 59. Another of the family, Admiral Sir Edward Codrington, was involved in the defeat of the Turkish fleet at Navarino in 1827. The painter W.J. Müller recorded the riots in a set of vivid paintings now housed in the City Art Gallery.

CODY COURT, BS15. The name of the pilot who landed a plane in Hanham in 1921 during an air display and carnival.

COGAN ROAD, BS15. A Welsh surname and place name, perhaps the owner of the land before development. It is also the name of a locomotive in the Hall series designed by Collett for GWR. This road is near where the old railway line ran so perhaps this is the reason for the naming. *See Collett Close.*

COGSALL ROAD, BS14. Thomas Cogsall resided in the parish and tithing of Keynsham in January 1670. He was exempt from Hearth Tax.

COLCHESTER CRESCENT, BS4. Viscount Cowdray was Liberal M.P. for Colchester from 1895-1910. He was also the head of the contracting firm S. Pearson and Son the developers of this estate.

COLDHARBOUR LANE / ROAD, BS6. From the French 'col' meaning ridge and 'd'arbres', of trees. Col in modern Englishmeans the low saddle part of a ridge. It has been disputed that there was once a Roman villa here, although Coldhaorbour Lane forms part of the Roman Road from Bath to Sea Mills.

COLDPARK GARDENS / ROAD, BS13. Field name from OE *cald* meaning 'cold and cheerless' or 'exposed' i.e. bleak parkland.

COLDRICK CLOSE, BS4. Another rather desolate-sounding field name.

COLE ROAD, BS2. Named after the Cole family who ran a fertilizer business (known locally as Cole's Boneyard) in Feeder Road. Arthur Cole lived in Brislington at Oakleigh on Bath Road from 1911-1958.

COLEBROOK ROAD, BS5. Joseph Colebrook, who died in 1729, was a benefactor who left money to assist the poor of St. George.

COLEFORD ROAD, BS10. This road runs parallel to Lydney Road so is clearly called after the Forest of Dean town.

COLE MEAD, BS13. Field name taken from 1902 survey of the Manor of Bishport. Name derived from OE *col* meaning 'coal' or 'charcoal'.

COLERIDGE ROAD, BS5. Samuel Taylor Coleridge (1772-1834), author of the famous 'Rime of the Ancient Mariner', was a frequent visitor to Bristol. He was an opium addict and wrote most of his poem 'Kubla Khan' while in an opium trance until interrupted by a 'person from Porlock'. The epitaph on his tomb describes him as 'a truly great and good man with a sweet and angelic disposition'.

COLESHILL DRIVE, BS13. Coleshill was the birthplace in 1332 of John Randolph, Master of St. Catherine's Hospital, Bedminster.

COLLEGE AVENUE / COURT / ROAD, BS16. Surrounding what was St. Matthias College, now the University of the West of England.

COLLEGE FIELDS / ROAD, BS8. So named because of nearby Clifton College, a prestigious boys' public school.

COLLEGE GREEN, BS1. In 1200s this was used as a cemetery by the monks of St. Augustine's and by Gaunt's hospital. Referred to as Viridis Place (the green place). In 1865 Roman coins were found by workmen lowering the ground on the north side of the Cathedral.

COLLEGE ROAD, BS9. So named after Westbury College founded by Bishop John Carpenter in 1447 to take the place of an earlier building which was believed to date from soon after the arrival of Christianity in this country, near the end of the sixth century AD. William Canynges the Younger retired to Westbury College and became Dean. He died there in 1474.

COLLEGE SQUARE, BS1. This is the area behind the Deanery. The original Deanery stood at right angles to the Norman gateway, and was demolished to construct Deanery Road and the Central Library. The Deanery is now in Charlotte Street.

COLLEGE STREET, BS1. Name taken from the Dean and Chapter of the Cathedral church, who owned the land on which this was built in 1771. It was home to the poets Robert Southey and Samuel Taylor Coleridge.

COLLETT CLOSE, BS15. Named after Charles Benjamin Collett (1871-1952), chief mechanical engineer of the great Western Railway from 1922-41. He designed the new Castle express passenger locomotive, and then the King express locos of 1927-30, the heaviest and most powerful in Britain. *See Churchward Drive and Armstrong Close.*

COLLIN ROAD, BS4. One of the early secretaries of the Sutton Dwellings Trust, a philanthropic body set up following the death of W. R. Sutton, who left a million pounds to provide houses for the working classes. The houses and flats in this and the adjoining roads were erected by the trustees in 1924 with a subsidy from the local authority.

COLLINGWOOD AVENUE, BS15. Probably named for the same reason as the road in BS6. This road is sited near Southey Avenue, and the Bristol-born poet Robert Southey included Nelson in his *Lives of the British Admirals (1833).*

COLLINGWOOD ROAD, BS6. Named in honour of Cuthbert, 1st Baron Collingwood who took control at the Battle of Trafalgar on Nelson's death.

COLLINS STREET, BS11. George Collins was sub-manager of the Cold Stores on the Docks and was a local councillor who lived in Shirehampton. He was organist at his local church.

COLLINSON ROAD, BS13. The Rev. John Collinson was a Vicar of Long Ashton in the Hundred of Hartcliffe from 1787-93. In 1791 he published his monumental *History of Somerset* in three volumes, which is still acclaimed today. He died in 1793.

COLLITER CRESCENT, BS3. After Colliter's Brook, a natural feature. Colliter was thought to have been a personal name. Perhaps he owned the land here.

THE COLONNADE, BS8. The word derives from the Italian *colonnato* meaning supported on columns. These elegant dwellings were built when the area was at its most fashionable and one of the early tenants was Ann Yearsley, the Milkwoman Poetess, protégée of Hannah More. Hannah promoted Ann's work, amazed that such work could be produced without formal education, but Hannah's controlling of the proceeds from the sale of Ann's *Poems on Various Occasions,* published in 1785, brought resentment on Ann's part. Ann finally managed to obtain what she considered rightfully hers and published a further anthology and a play, but the promised fame and fortune eluded her and she died in obscurity in Melksham in 1806 aged 54.

COLSTON AVENUE / COURT / DALE / HILL / PARADE / ROAD / STREET, BS1/ BS16 / BS2 / BS5. All named in honour of one of Bristol's most famous benefactors, Edward Colston, who died in 1721. He made his fortune as a merchant trading in, among other commodities, slaves. This has diminished his memory as a philanthropist in recent years. He founded a boys' school which still exists, although at a different location. A girls' school was founded in the nineteenth century, and a preparatory school and various societies were formed in his memory including the Dolphin and the Anchor Societies, all charitable foundations.

COLTHURST DRIVE, BS15. Edward Colthurst owned Oldland Manor in the seventeenth century

COLWYN ROAD, BS5. A seaside resort in North Wales. The name means white or fair camp. One of several seaside towns represented in neighbouring streets.

COMB PADDOCK, BS9. A field name listed in the 1825 Westbury-on-Trym survey.

COMBFACTORY LANE, BS5. This once led to the local comb factory.

COMMERCIAL ROAD, BS3. Once the commercial centre of the area but now mainly residential with high-rise flats.

COMMON ROAD, BS15. Self-explanatory.

THE COMMON, BS12. Self-explanatory.

COMMONFIELD ROAD, BS11. Self-explanatory field name.

COMPTON DRIVE, BS9. Perhaps named after John Compton, Marquis of Northamptonshire, who laid the foundation stone of the Clifton Suspension Bridge.

COMPTON STREET, BS5. The name of many villages throughout the country. Derived from OE *cumb,* 'valley,' and *tun* 'enclosure', 'farmstead' or 'village'.

COMYN WALK, BS16. Mrs Mary Comyn lived in the middle of the eighteenth century and had associations with Rodway Manor house at Mangotsfield (still standing), through Sophia Colston, wife of Alexander. She was the great-niece and heiress of philanthropist Edward Colston.

CONCORDE DRIVE / ROAD, BS12. Named in honour of the famous Bristol-built supersonic aircraft, a joint engineering triumph by engineers from Bristol and Toulouse, France.

CONDER HOUSE, BS7. Charles Conder (1868-1909) was an Australian painter of the Heidelberg School greatly influenced by the French Impressionists.

CONDOVER ROAD, BS4. A village in Shropshire. The first syllable is from the river Cound and the last two syllables OE *ofer*, 'bank'. It is not known why this name was chosen.

CONDUIT PLACE / ROAD, BS2. A conduit is a channel for conveying water, and medieval Bristol was criss-crossed with these pipes which led from springs around the city to provide water for the inhabitants through many fountainheads. Conduit Road runs along part of the course of the Key Pipe. This was the main Bristol conduit that piped the spring water from the Pennywell or Pamiwell Spring (*see Pennywell Road*) in St. Werburgh's, down to the city. The head of the Key Pipe was by the side of the city docks, and its waters were thought to cure rheumatism. Visitors would come from miles around to bathe their legs in the water as it gushed out. The Key Pipe connected with the Redcliffe Pipe, and there is now an annual Pipe Walk along part of the route of the Redcliffe Pipe, from St. Mary Redcliffe church to the Huge Well at Knowle.

CONGLETON ROAD, BS5. A place name - all the roads in the area are called after towns and villages in Cheshire and Lancashire. Derivation uncertain - could be old Norman *kengr* 'a bend' or perhaps *kengull* 'a cluster' - the Cheshire town is actually on a bend of the River Dane.

CONHAM HILL / ROAD / VALE / VALE ROAD, BS15. Derives from OE name - Cana.

CONIFER CLOSE, BS16. Named after one of the houses in Crescent School, Conifer House which once stood on this site.

CONISTON AVENUE / ROAD, BS9. The name of the village and lake in the Lake District which Arthur Ransome used as the setting for his children's novel *Swallows and Amazons*. Donald Campbell died there while attempting to break his water speed record in 1967. One authority gives the derivation as meaning 'King's Manor'. No obvious reason for this choice.

CONISTON CLOSE, BS15. All streets in this group called after locations in the Lake District. *See Coniston Avenue.*

CONNAUGHT ROAD, BS4. Among a host of roads with Irish names.

CONSTABLE ROAD, BS7. Another road in the 'British painters' series. John Constable (1776-1837), celebrated for his Suffolk landscapes.

CONSTITUTION HILL, BS8. Named in imitation of the London street.

CONWAY ROAD, BS4. All the roads surrounding the mock Gothic castle of Arno's Court have been given the names of famous castles.

CONYGRE GROVE / ROAD, BS12. From the old Manor House which stood here originally called Cunigar House in 1678. Leased to Jacob Millett, feltmaker, sugarmaker, grocer and M.P.

COOK CLOSE, BS15. A mix-up on locations here when the council named this road. The Mr Cook after whom this was named was Warmley RDC's (Rural District Council) only lorry driver in the 1930s. He lived in a cottage between what is now The Happy Shopper and Neads Drive, North Common.

COOK STREET, BS11. Named after William Cook, a Shirehampton councillor who lived at Hallen.

COOK'S FOLLY ROAD, BS9. Cook's Folly was a crenellated tower built in 1693 and demolished in 1932. A mansion was added in the 1870s.

COOKSLEY ROAD, BS5. This was named after the solicitor to the Gerrish family who would probably have organised the sale of all these parcels of land for housing. He managed their affairs for many years. *See Gerrish Avenue.*

COOKWORTHY CLOSE, BS5. Named after William Cookworthy, who established a china works in Castle Green in 1768 in partnership with Richard Champion making imitation Dresden porcelain. The business could not survive the competition from Josiah Wedgwood.

COOMBE BRIDGE AVENUE / DALE / LANE, BS9. Coombe is the general theme of many roads in the area. The name derives from the OE *cumb*, meaning 'small valley' or 'hollow'. The Saxons in turn got the word from Welsh, in which *cwm* still means valley.

COOMBE ROAD, BS5. A fairly common surname locally, so perhaps that of the landowner.

COOMBE WAY, BS10. Near Coombe Hill.

COOMBES WAY, BS15. There is no obvious reason for this choice.

COOPER ROAD, BS9. A farmer by the name of Cooper owned land in Westbury-on-Trym in 1872 and a descendant built houses on the land.

COOPERAGE LANE / ROAD, BS5. Casks and barrels used to be made at a factory here.

COOPERATION ROAD, BS5. The Co-operative movement was established in Bristol in the 1880s and the branch office was in this area.

THE COOTS, BS14. Area name taken from the 1840 Whitchurch tithe map.

COPELAND DRIVE, BS14. Land developed by a Midlands company who named the road after pottery and china manufacturers.

COPLEY COURT, BS16. In 1656 Captain Copley obtained a patent from Cromwell for making iron from pit coal and set up a works in the Forest. Sadly his venture failed in spite of expert advice from one Dud Dudley. *See Dudley Court.*

COPLEY GARDENS, BS7. John Singleton Copley was a portrait painter who worked in oils and pastels. He was born in Boston, Massachusetts in 1737, but settled in London in 1776. His son was the famous Lord Lyndhurst, the barrister who made his name by defending one of the Luddites. In 1824 he became Attorney-General.

THE COPPICE, BS13. Field name taken from the 1683 survey. It was in the Manor of Bishport and was derived from the Old French *copeiz* - an area overgrown with trees or bushes.

COPSE ROAD, BS4. Self-explanatory. Again the old French *copeiz* is the source.

COPTHORNE ROAD, BS7. Copthorne is a town in Surrey. Other local roads are named after various locations in the British Isles.

CORBET CLOSE, BS11. Robert Corbet possessed the Henbury Hundred in the reign of Edward I.

CORDWELL WALK, BS7. Thomas Cordwell was a parishioner who worked zealously for the church in the 1890s.

COREY CLOSE, BS2. Probably named after a nineteenth-century parochial benefactor. There were two medical men in the area whose name was spelt without the 'e'; or it was possibly named after Thomas Corey, a merchant in the city in 1830.

CORFE PLACE, BS15. All streets in this group called after castles.

CORFE ROAD, BS4. Another group of roads named after famous castles.

CORIANDER WALK, BS5. Following the theme for bestowing the names of herbs on all the streets on this small estate.

CORINTHIAN COURT, BS1. There are some curious names in this development which initially caused difficulty in making links. 'Corinthian' is a style of architecture; a frequenter of brothels (an old name for bordellos was corinths); an aristocratic follower of fist-fighting and horse racing; and a kind of brass alloyed from gold, silver and copper. Nearby are Tiffany Court and Raphael Court and the only connection between the three is a church in South Carolina which has Corinthian arches, a Tiffany window and a painting by Raphael. In fact it would appear that this particular Corinthian is a typeface style inspired by the proximity of Caxton Gate.

CORKER'S HILL, BS5. Probably called after someone who lived here years ago.

CORN STREET, BS1. There are three views on this name, firstly the obvious - site of a corn market - secondly a John Corn of Shropshire used to own land in the area, and thirdly it may have been named after Coernicus who succeeded Ella as Warden of Bristol Castle. Corn Street is the site of 'The Nails', four brass topped round tables, upon which bargains were struck by eighteenth century businessmen, and of a clock on the front of the Corn Exchange whose extra hand shows Bristol time, eight minutes behind GMT. Bristol time was abandoned with the advent of the railways and their timetables.

CORNHILL DRIVE, BS14. The Cornhill family were landowners in the city during the reign of Henry 111. The charter of William Rufus mentions an Edward Hupcornhill.

CORNISH GROVE / ROAD / WALK, BS14. Named after a resident, William Cornish, who lived in the area in 1670 and was exempt from Hearth Tax.

CORNLEAZE, BS13. This was a field at Pigeon House farm on Earl Temple's estate. Leaze derives from OE *læs* 'pasture'.

ANCIENT MONEY TABLES, OR NAILS
CORN ST. BRISTOL. FRED LITTLE
COPYRIGHT

The Corn Street Nails, or money tables, photographed in the early twentieth century looking much as they did when financial bargains were struck on them by eighteenth century traders.

CORNWALL ROAD, BS7. Presumably named after Cornwall, which in turn derives its name from the Welsh tribal name *Cornovic.*

CORNWALLIS AVENUE / CRESCENT / GROVE, BS8. These streets took their name from Cornwallis House, described as 'a beautiful double house with shrubbery and pasture land at the western side and surrounded by a lofty stone wall coated with ivy'. It was built by Henry Hobhouse (1714/1773), member of a well-known West Country family. One of his descendants, Sir Charles Hobhouse, was MP for East Bristol.

CORONATION AVENUE / ROAD, BS16. The coronation referred to here is that of Edward VII in 1902.

CORONATION ROAD, BS3. This road dates from the coronation of George IV, in 1820.

CORONATION CLOSE / ROAD, BS15. Site of the old Coronation Pit.

CORONATION ROAD, BS16. Celebrating the coronation of George V1, in 1936.

CORSLEY WALK, BS4. Named after Corsley Heath in Wiltshire.

CORSTON WALK, BS11. Next to another road named after a Somerset village.

COSSHAM ROAD / WALK, BS5 / STREET, BS16. Handel Cossham was born in Thornbury in 1824. He made a fortune from coal mining in Speedwell, Whitehall, Yate and Parkfield and was elected Mayor of Bath in 1882. After his death in 1890 the collieries were sold and the money was used to build the hospital which bears his name.

COSSINGTON ROAD, BS4. Named after a village in Somerset. Other local roads are named after West Country locations.

COSSINS ROAD, BS6. John Cossins was a London grocer who married Martha Innys and bought the manor of Redland from her uncle, George Martin. He was responsible for the building of Redland Green Chapel in 1743. He died in 1759 aged 76. The road was built on land sold by the Redland Chapel Trust. The Trust had been established by John Cossins to provide an income for the maintenance of the building and ministry of the Chapel.

COSTILAND DRIVE, BS13. A field shown on the 1794 survey as being part of Long Ashton Manor - probably derived from Old Norman French *castel* meaning 'castle, fortification, ancient encampment, residence'.

COTE DRIVE / ROAD / LANE / PADDOCK, BS9. *See Cote House Lane.*

COTE HOUSE LANE, BS9. Cote House was where Thomas and Josiah Wedgwood entertained such celebrities as Wordsworth, Coleridge, Southey and the inventor Humphrey Davy. The lodge still remains. St. Monica's Home was built on the site of the old house as a memorial to the wife of H. H. Wills, Bristol's tobacco magnate and public benefactor. A cote would seem to make reference to the site of somewhere dove cotes were once in evidence.

COTE LEA PARK, BS9. Another variation on the Cote theme.

COTHAM BROW / GARDENS / GROVE / HILL / ROAD / SIDE / PARK / VALE / LAWN ROAD, BS6. Cotham Road was constructed in 1829 as a traffic bypass of St. Michael's Hill for traffic to and from Clifton, and the remainder of the area developed between then and 1880. The earliest mention of the place seems to be in 1754 when William Hulme, a snuffmaker of Maryleport Street leased a windmill there but he went bankrupt three years later. However, the first three houses of Cotham Vale, surrounded by fields, appear as part of the Cotham House Estate on a map of 1743, and the remains of an old stone gateway are built into the walls of No. 1 Cotham Vale. The entrance pillars to the drive of Cotham House can still be seen at the beginning of Cotham Park. Cotham Lawn Road was named after Richard Fry's house, Cotham Lawn. Its boundary walls remain across Hartfield Avenue on Cotham Road. Cotham Lawn Road was built through the old Gallows Field. The actual site of the gallows is said to be the apse of Cotham Church. It was here that Bristol's Marian martyrs were burnt to death between 1555 and 1557, their suffering extended by the malicious intervention of those "who went to Redland for green wood for the execution of those blessed saints…when near at home on the Back or Quay he might have had dry." In the wall of Cotham Church is a fragment of Bewells or Bueols Cross, which was one of the boundary markers of the city of Bristol in the twelfth century.

COTMAN WALK, BS7. Following the artistic theme, John Sell Cotman (1782-1842) was a landscape painter of the Norwich School who worked mainly in watercolours.

COTRITH ROAD, BS10. Richard Cotrith was given land in the Saltmarsh area of the Hundred of Henbury in the fourteenth century. Nicholas Cotrith and his wife Alice rented Tide Grove in Saltmarsh from the Bishop of Worcester in 1275 for 20 shillings per year.

COTSWOLD ROAD / VIEW, BS3. The derivation is from OE *cod*, a holy man who settled by a spring, and *wald*, a tract of high woodland, hill or down. Many of the roads in this area are named after ranges of hills.

COTSWOLD VIEW, BS15. Perhaps named for its high, hillside position.

COTTAGE PLACE, BS2. Descriptive of this remnant of old Kingsdown now swamped by hospital buildings.

COTTINGTON COURT, BS15. Lord Cottington held land in the area during the reign of Charles II.

COTTISFORD ROAD, BS5. This is the name of a small town in Oxfordshire near Tackley. *See Tackley Road.*

COTTLE GARDENS / ROAD, BS14. Cottle is a famous Bristol family name: Joseph Cottle published the *Lyrical Ballads,* by Wordsworth and Coleridge, 1798.

COTTONWOOD DRIVE, BS15. A town in California. *See California Road.*

COTTRELL AVENUE / ROAD, BS5. From the Cottrell-Dormer family, who owned much of the land in the area.

COULSON WALK, BS15. A mixture of the developers' names Couldridge and Gibson.

COULSON'S CLOSE / ROAD, BS14. This would seem to be the name of someone who owned land here prior to development. A number of people with the surname are listed as living in the Bristol area over the years including Alfred Coulson, a schools inspector in the 1920s.

COUNTERPOOL ROAD, BS15. This naming remains a mystery.

COUNTERSLIP, BS2. Seemingly a corruption of 'Countess slip'. The Countess in question was the wife of Robert, Earl of Gloucester, the man responsible for the building of Bristol Castle. A slip is a stone slope serving as a landing place by the river, and Counterslip is on the site of the watergate to the Castle, where boats would have been boarded.

COUNTERSLIP GARDENS, BS14. The chapel was moved here from St. Philips.

COUNTESS WALK, BS16. Several local roads have been given female titles because of their proximity to Duchess's Park.

COUNTY STREET, BS3. This is near the county boundary.

COURT CLOSE, BS7. Leading off Manor Court Drive.

COURT FARM ROAD, BS15. From the ancient farm sold by John Britton to John Dennys in 1643.

COURT ROAD, BS7. Named after Horfield Court. In 1843 the government bought part of Horfield Court Farm to build the barracks which were pulled down in the 1960s.

COURT ROAD, BS15. There are two roads thus named in the area, one in Kingswood, one in Oldland. That in Kingswood takes its name from a house called Mounthill Court, that in Oldland perhaps from Barr's Court.

COURTENEY CRESCENT, BS4. Until 1900 there was a road in Keynsham of this name which probably honoured a renowned person of the parish in days gone by.

COURTFIELD GROVE, BS16. Probably a made-up-name from Oldbury Court and the fields which would have once surrounded it.

COURTLANDS LANE, BS3. A made-up name from the fact that the lane was on land belonging to the Ashton Court estate.

COURTNEY ROAD / WAY, BS15. Probably a made-up name influenced by nearby Court Road.

COURTSIDE MEWS, BS6. This perhaps takes its name from nearby Redland Court Road.

COUSINS LANE, BS5. Probably the occupant of a dwelling here long ago.

COUSINS MEWS, BS4. Named after Samuel Cousins, a nineteenth-century landowner.

COVENTRY WALK, BS4. Named after the famous cathedral city. Other nearby roads are named on the same theme.

COWDRAY ROAD, BS4. Possibly named after the ruined Tudor mansion Cowdray Park in Sussex, continuing the theme of castles in the area. *See Colchester Crescent.*

COWLER WALK, BS13. Cowlers Paddock was a field belonging to Bishopsworth Farm shown on the 1802 survey. Cowler is most likely to be a personal name.

COWLING DRIVE / ROAD, BS14. Commemorates Stephen Cowling, church-warden of Brislington 1674.

COWPER ROAD, BS6. Judging by the names of adjoining roads this must take its inspiration from Earl Cowper, the statesman (1834-1905) and member of Gladstone's Cabinet.

COWPER STREET, BS5. Following the trend in nearby streets the Cowper in question must be the poet William Cowper (1731-1800)

COX COURT, BS15. Built on the site of an orchard, this group of roads have been called after different varieties of apple.

CRABTREE WALK, BS5. Field name. Crabtree Ground was a field of approximately six acres in Whitehall where George Whitefield preached to congregations of more than 20 000 people in the 1730s.

CRADOCK CLOSE, BS15. The Cradock family used to own Barr's Court.

CRANBERRY WALK, BS9. In keeping with the shrub names used in this locality.

CRANBOURNE ROAD, BS12. Aylward Sneaw, governor of Bristol Castle in 980, founded a small monastery at Cranbourne.

CRANBROOK ROAD, BS6. From the Cran brook which flows through the district.

CRANDELL CLOSE, BS10. Origin uncertain but could be a field name from OE *cran* meaning 'heron' or 'crane' and dell meaning 'hollow'.

CRANE CLOSE, BS15. Crane's firework factory once stood near here.

CRANHAM CLOSE, BS15. Named after a place in Gloucestershire, as are several roads in this area.

CRANHAM ROAD, BS7. Near Tuffley Road, so perhaps the builder had connections with Gloucestershire.

CRANLEIGH GARDENS / ROAD, BS9. A town in Surrey but no clue as to why this name was chosen.

CRANMORE CRESCENT, BS10. A small town on the Isle of Wight. Several Hampshire and Dorset locations have been used in road-naming in this area.

CRANSIDE AVENUE, BS6. Located beside the Cran brook.

CRANSLEY CRESCENT, BS6. Perhaps an improvised name based on 'meadow by the Cran'.

CRANTOCK AVENUE, BS13. Named after a seaside village near Newquay, but no obvious reason for this choice.

CRANWELL GROVE, BS14. Close to the site of the old Whitchurch Airport. Cranwell in Lincolnshire is home to the RAF College, so the name was presumably chosen for its aeronautical association.

CRATES COURT, BS15. The name of the owners of a boot factory here in the late nineteenth century.

CRAVEN WAY, BS15. This name was chosen by developers who were not from this area so this was a name of significance only to them.

CRAYDON GROVE / ROAD / WALK, BS14. Jeffery Craydon was resident in the parish and tithing of Whitchurch in 1670 and was exempt from Hearth Tax.

CREDITON CRESCENT, BS4. A road named, like the others in the locality, after a West Country town.

CRESCENT ROAD, BS16. The Crescent School used to stand on this site.

THE CRESCENT BS9, BS16. Descriptive of the layout in both cases.

THE CREST, BS4. Situated at the top of a hill.

CRESWICKE AVENUE, BS15 / ROAD, BS4. Francis Creswicke leased Kingswood Chase in 1689. He died in 1732. His family lived at Hanham Hall while another branch lived at the Great House in Small Street, later the site of the General Post Office. It was here the family entertained Charles I and his sons.

CREW'S HOLE ROAD, BS5. The origin of this name is Scruizehole, a family who occupied the land many years ago. It was the Victorians who invented the legend of the hole in which men hid to avoid the press gangs.

CRIBB'S CAUSEWAY, BS10. Legend has it that the place owed its name to Tom Cribb, the fabled bare-fist fighter, but that was quashed by the discovery that the

name had appeared on a map four years before the boxer was born. The name Crybe could have been a personal name - Crybe's dwelling - or it could have derived from *Crib* - a manger or hovel.

CRICKLADE ROAD, BS7. Mervyn Herbert Nevil Storey-Maskelyne (1823-1911) was a local landowner and benefactor, and also M.P. for Cricklade. *See Maskelyne Avenue.*

CRIPPS ROAD, BS3. After Sir Stafford Cripps, MP for Bristol East then later South East from 1931-50.

CRISPIN WAY, BS15. St. Crispin was the patron saint of leatherworkers, which was apt in an area in which bootmakers predominated, although it may celebrate Miles Crispin, whose lands in Gloucestershire are recorded in the Domesday book.

CROFT AVENUE, BS16. Perhaps after Herbert Croft, who collected and preserved Chatteron's correspondence and used them as the basis for a novel. Chatterton's mother came from Stapleton.

THE CROFT, BS15. This occurs twice. In both cases this is an old field name.

CROFT VIEW, BS9. Runs off South Croft.

CROFTON AVENUE, BS7. Named after a Wiltshire village. Other West Country names have been used for surrounding roads.

CROFTS END ROAD, BS5. This takes its name from the farm which once stood here.

CROKESWOOD WALK, BS11. A field name most probably derived from the family name of William and Peter Croc or Crook who held land here in the thirteenth century.

CROME ROAD, BS7. John Crome (1768-1821) was a landscape painter who founded the Norwich School of Painters. *See Cotman Walk, BS7.*

CROMER ROAD, BS5. A few roads in the area are called after seaside resorts.

CROMWELL COURT, BS15. The area had a number of connections with Oliver Cromwell and that period in history.

CROMWELL ROAD, BS6, BS5 / STREET, BS3. All the streets bearing Cromwell's name mark places where his troops marched.

CROMWELLS HIDE, BS16. Near Wickham Court, where Cromwell stayed before his attack on the city in 1645.

CROOMES HILL, BS16. John Croome owned a house here in the nineteenth century.

CROPTHORNE ROAD, BS7. The name of a town in Worcestershire, near Throckmorton. Baron Throckmorton was a forest ranger in the seventeenth century.

CROSBY ROW, BS1. Either a place name or a surname. The 1850 Bristol Directory lists a Thomas Crosby who may have had associations with the development.

CROSCOMBE DRIVE / WALK, BS13. Benjamin James of Croscombe was granted lands under the Dundry Enclosure Award 1815.

CROSS ELMS LANE, BS9. This originated as a field name.

CROSS STREET, BS16. This is reputed to be the site of the old Wyfe's Cross, once located at the centre of the old forest at a crossroads.

Oliver Cromwell

CROSS WALK, BS14. This adjoins Charter Walk and alludes to the marking out of the boundary in 1373 when Bristol became a city and county, uniquely in England.

CROSSFIELD ROAD, BS15. One of the many field names used in this area.

CROSSLEAZE ROAD, BS15. A name taken from the 1840 Whitchurch tithe map.

CROSSWAYS ROAD, BS4. Perhaps so named because it is a straight road which cuts across a number of other streets.

CROW LANE, BS1, BS10. The Henbury Crow Lane takes its name from an old hostelry, and the same could well apply to the Crow Lane in the city.

CROWN GARDENS / HILL / ROAD BS15. There was a pit here with this name.

CROWN HILL / CROWN HILL ROAD / CROWN HILL WALK, BS5. Another pit site belonging to Handel Cossham, so this may be the link.

CROWN LANE / ROAD BS16. Another area connected with the mining industry.

CROWNDALE ROAD, BS4. This would seem to be a made-up name.

CROWTHER PARK / ROAD / STREET, BS7. Not a place name and no-one with that surname seems to have any connection with any of these developments.

CROYDON STREET, BS5. Named after John Croydon, a currier, who lived in nearby Easton Road in 1872.

CUFFINGTON AVENUE, BS4. The builder of these houses was called Cuff and the name was developed from this.

CULVER STREET, BS1. Apparently there was always some confusion about the naming of this road as it has, in the past, been known as Culvert Street. It is true there was a culvert running beneath the street. Another suggestion is that it was built on the site of the culver, or dovecote, of Gaunt's Hospital, although this has never been conclusively proved. *Culfre* is an OE word meaning 'dove'.

CULVERWELL ROAD, BS13. Culverwell Close was one of the fields belonging to the Home Farm.

CUMBERLAND BASIN ROAD, BS8. Possibly named as for Cumberland Street, BS2. Between 1800 and 1810 an ambitious plan was carried out which created a vastly extended quayside. A floating harbour was formed from the old river bed where ships could lie at anchor without being grounded in the Avon mud. The main flow of the river was diverted into the New Cut. Brunel was responsible for a great deal of this work, designing the lock on the Cumberland Basin and new efficient dredging systems. *See Brunel Lock Road, BS1.*

CUMBERLAND CLOSE / PLACE, BS8 / GROVE, BS6 / ROAD, BS1. Named for the same reason as Cumberland Street, BS2. The ruined gatehouse portals of the old Bristol prison, which was burnt in the riots of 1831, still stand in Cumberland Road. The actual gaol was used until Horfield prison opened in 1886. The footbridge crossing the New Cut from Coronation Road is called Gaol Ferry Bridge.

CUMBERLAND STREET, BS2. Building began here around 1770 and took its name from William Augustus, Duke of Cumberland (1721-65), son of George II. He was known as The Butcher - a reference to his harsh treatment of the rebels after the Battle Culloden.

CUNNINGHAM GARDENS, BS16. Named after Alderman Robert George Cunningham, a much respected member of the City Council and Chairman of the Libraries Committee who died in 1965.

CURLAND GROVE, BS14. A village near Corfe, following the theme of West Country villages.

CURLEW CLOSE, BS16. All roads called after British birds in this area.

CUSTOM CLOSE, BS14. There are two fields shown on the 1840 Whitchurch tithe map - Great Custom and Little Custom.

CUTLER ROAD, BS13. A field name in the Manor of Bishport shown on the survey of 1683. Probably a personal name, suggesting that the field was rented from Sir John Smyth by a man called Cutler.

CYPRESS COURT / GROVE, BS9. Perhaps emphasising the green elegance of the suburb.

DAISY ROAD, BS5. Probably after a relative of the builder.

DAKOTA DRIVE BS14. Not far from the old Whitchurch airport, so perhaps this road is called after the aircraft which was in service in the 1950s. BOAC operated Dakotas from here. One, G-AGJU, was written off when it ground-looped while landing on 3 January 1947. The crew of three survived.

DALBY AVENUE, BS3. Named after Councillor Kenelm Antony Philip Dalby, who was Lord Mayor of Bristol from 1964 -5.

DALE STREET, BS5. This runs parallel to Hill Street.

DALE STREET, BS2. There was once a Hill Street adjoining Dale Street, which was an odd choice as both streets were on the level.

DALKEITH AVENUE, BS15. Probably named after the Scottish town.

DALRYMPLE ROAD, BS2. A nineteenth century Brigstocke family connection. Georgina Campbell (nee Brigstocke) married General John Hamilton Elphinstone Dalrymple, who succeeded to the Earldom of Stair in the1860s. *See Brigstocke Road.*

DALSTON ROAD, BS3. A place name of uncertain derivation. It could be OE *dael,* meaning 'share of land' and the familiar *tun* meaning farmstead, town.

DALTON SQUARE, BS2. Named after John Dalton, a brickmaker and owner of the land in 1740 when he leased the land to William Lawrence, a house carpenter who was almost certainly the developer of the square.

DAMPIER ROAD, BS3. Named after William Dampier (1652-1715), a privateer, explorer and hydrographer who came from Somerset. Dampier published his *Voyage round the World* in 1687 after expeditions to Northern Australia and New Guinea. He became acquainted with Alexander Selkirk, the real-life shipwrecked sailor who was rescued and subsequently became famous after a possible meeting between Selkirk and Defoe in The Star inn, Cock and Bottle Lane, off Castle Street. Defoe was inspired by his tale to write *Robinson Crusoe.* Curiously, Dampier was the pilot of the ship which picked up Selkirk after two years on his island, and was able to vouch for his identity.

DANBURY CRESCENT / WALK BS10. This road, called after a town near Chelmsford, is among other roads seemingly named at random after English towns.

DANCEY MEAD, BS13. One of the fields belonging to Bishopsworth Farm in the Manor of Bedminster listed in the survey of 1798. The source may be OE *denu,* valley.

DANGERFIELD AVENUE, BS13. A field name taken from the 1794 survey belonging to Home Farm, Manor of Long Ashton.

DARLEY CLOSE, BS11. There is a Darley Abbey in Derbyshire dating from 1140. The connection may be that the land in this area was owned by the church at one time.

DARNLEY AVENUE, BS7. Either named after the town of Darnley in Renfrewshire, or Lord Darnley, second husband of Mary, Queen of Scots. No known connection with the area.

DARTMOOR STREET, BS3. A place name, the first syllable denoting the River Dart in Devon. Local place names feature strongly in street naming in this area.

DAUBENY CLOSE, BS16. Giles Daubeny was a Constable of Bristol and Custodian of Kingswood Forest in the reign of Henry VII.

DAVENTRY ROAD, BS4. Place names predominate in the area, Daventry being a town in Northamptonshire. Its claim to fame as far as Bristol is concerned is that a certain John Beale was arrested in Daventry for the murder of Charlotte

Pugsley in Leigh Woods in 1857. He was hanged in January 1858. Afterwards a crime reporter named Austin published a confession that Beale was alleged to have made.

DAVEY STREET, BS2. Mr Davey was a J.P. and partner in the tobacco firm of Franklin, Davey, Morgan and Co-President (in 1884) of the Grateful Society, a charitable organisation.

DAVID STREET, BS2. Perhaps after a thirteenth-century Abbot of St. Augustine's Abbey, named David. The Abbey of St. Augustine's Black Canons, the church of which now forms the Cathedral, was founded by Robert Fitzhardinge in 1142. Nearby was the church of St. Augustine the Less, founded by the Abbots around 1240. *See Belland Drive, Kilkenny Street, Pipe Lane, and St. Augustine's Parade.*

DAVID'S ROAD, BS14. Possibly named after a relative of the developer.

DAVIS CLOSE, BS15. Named after Sidney Davis, a local landowner and benefactor who lived at Earlstone House.

DAVIS STREET, BS11. Named in honour of local councillor George Davis, who lived at Burlington House, Shirehampton.

DAWES CLOSE, BS16. Built on land where Miss Dawes' cottage used to stand. She was an ex-schoolteacher.

DAWLISH ROAD, BS3. a seaside village in South Devon. Many roads in the area are called after West Country towns.

DAWN RISE, BS15. This resulted from a competition for schoolchildren to devise a street name based on the local coat of arms.

DAY'S ROAD, BS5. Dr Day was an immensely popular local doctor whose large house and surgery stood on the land where, in later years, a row of shops including the post office and the Co-op was built.

DE CLIFFORD ROAD, BS11. Lord de Clifford inherited Kingsweston House and the estate from the Southwell family in 1775. The de Clifford barony was created in 1299, making it one of the oldest in the UK. The estate was sold to Mr Philip Miles in 1837 and the family lived at Kingsweston House until the end of the Second World War. Some of the de Clifford family are buried in Henbury church.

DE VEROSE COURT, BS15. After Sir John de Verose (or Deverose) who held the Manor of Oldland in the fifteenth century.

DEAN CLOSE, BS15. Another railway connection here. William Dean held the post of chief mechanical engineer for GWR at Swindon from 1877-1902. *See Armstrong Close.*

DEAN CRESCENT / LANE / STREET, BS3. Ecclesiastical-sounding street names figure quite strongly in the area.

DEAN STREET, BS2. This lies near Bishop Street.

DEAN ROAD, BS11. A name chosen by the developer, so perhaps it was the name of someone associated with the company.

DEAN'S DRIVE, BS5. The Dean and Chapter owned lands in the Chase, of which this area was once part.

DEANERY CLOSE / ROAD, BS15. The Bristol Cathedral Deanery House once stood nearby. *See College Square.*

Davis Street, Avonmouth

DEANERY ROAD, BS1. The location of the Cathedral deanery.

DEANS MEAD, BS11. A field name. *Dean* in this case would seem to be derived from OE for valley, i.e. 'the valley meadow'.

DEEP COOMBE ROAD, BS3. This seems to be a field name.

DEEP PIT ROAD, BS5. The name is a relic of the days when this was a coal-mining area. The main shaft of Easton Colliery was at least 1,464 ft deep, some say 2,000 feet. To this day nobody seems to know exactly where the old mine workings run beneath Bristol, which is a blessing in disguise for property values, as it has not been unknown for some Bristol gardens to develop sudden large sink holes after heavy rain. *See **Secret Underground Bristol** in the Bibliography.*

DEERHURST, BS15 The site, in Gloucestershire, of Odda's chapel, which is now a listed building. The place is mentioned in the Domesday Book as being a hundred whose land was owned by St. Peter's, Westminster and St. Denis, Paris.

DEERING CLOSE, BS11. Sir Robert Southwell (1635-1702) was a distinguished diplomat and owner of the Kingsweston estate. He married Elizabeth, daughter of Sir Edward Deering. History relates that William of Orange (William III) was once rowed up the river as far as the Lamplighters in 1690, accompanied by Sir Robert Southwell, and that the King spent the night at Kingsweston House.

DEERSWOOD, BS15. Thought to be an improvised name recalling the days when this was part of the forest.

DELABERE AVENUE, BS16. John Delabere held one yard of land in payment for carrying the King's writs from Gloucester Castle to Bristol in the fifth year of the reign of Henry III (1221). The Delaberes were a well-known Gloucestershire and Hereford family.

DELIUS GROVE, BS4. One among a cluster of streets bearing the names of famous composers. Frederick Delius was born in Bradford to German parents in 1862. He wrote works for chorus and orchestra, as well as piano and violin concertos. He was an English Romantic with a highly individual style. He died in 1932.

THE DELL, BS9. A rustic name was chosen here in keeping with the scenery.

THE DELL, BS15. again, presumably descriptive of the location.

DELVIN ROAD, BS10. From the field name Delvine. The derivation may be from OE *dael* meaning 'share of land or valley', although one expert supports the theory that *del* means quarry. The last syllable could mean 'beautiful' which would be more in keeping with the first interpretation.

DENBIGH STREET, BS2. This would seem to be named after the place in North Wales or the Earldom of that name - probably the latter, as noble names figure in the choice of street names in the area.

DENHAM HOUSE, BS13. A widow called Mrs Denham lived in one of the tithings of the Hartcliffe Hundred in 1670. She was among those exempt from Hearth Tax.

DENLEIGH CLOSE, BS14. Probably a field name meaning 'field in the valley'.

DENMARK AVENUE / STREET, BS1. As Denmark Place is next to prince Street, this street name probably refers to Princess Alexandra of Denmark who married Prince Edward, who subsequently became King Edward V.

DENMARK PLACE, BS7. As this is next to Prince Street, it appears to be honouring Queen Anne's husband. *See Denmark Street above.*

DENNOR PARK, BS14. Dennor means 'the sloping side of a valley', derived from OE *denu, dene* and *ora*, slope or hillside, continuing the geographical features theme in the area. *See Allanmead Close.*

DENSTON WALK, BS3. Perhaps from the village in Suffolk. The name derives from the OE *denu* - a valley.

DENTWOOD GROVE, BS9. Seemingly a made-up name.

DERBY ROAD, BS6. One of many roads in the vicinity of the Gloucestershire County Ground, named after cricketing counties.

DERBY STREET, BS5. Probably named after the fourteenth Earl of Derby, as his family name is Stanley and there is a road of this name close by. This man was a distinguished Victorian statesman and held important government offices under Canning, Peel and Disraeli. He was also a classical scholar and translated Homer's *Iliad.* The Earl of Derby was three times Prime Minister, in 1852, 1858 and 1866-68.

DERHAM ROAD, BS13. Perhaps after Walter Derham, the archaeologist.

DERMOT STREET,BS2. This surname appears in a contemporary local directory so it is possible this street was named after the owner of the land.

DERRICK ROAD, BS15. This may be named after Eli Derrick, a local coal dealer in the 1930s.

DERRICKE ROAD, BS14. John and William Derricke resided in the Parish and tithing of Whitchurch in 1670 and were exempt from paying Hearth Tax.

DERRY ROAD, BS3. A place name, the derivation being *deru* meaning 'oak'.

DERWENT CLOSE / ROAD, BS5. Situated amongst other place names.

DEVON GROVE / ROAD, BS5. Named after the county. The derivation is from the Denas tribe (men of Devon) who inhabited the area in Roman times, according to one source.

DEVONSHIRE ROAD, BS6. The origin of this name would seem to be confirmed by nearby Cavendish Road, as this is the family name of the Dukes of Devonshire. The Duke in question here is most probably the Eighth (1833-1908), a noted statesman in a family tradition of politicians, who refused the premiership on more than one occasion. He founded the Liberal Unionist Party which broke with Gladstone on the matter of Home Rule for Ireland and set the course of Anglo-Irish politics for decades to come. The fourth Duke had been Prime Minister from 1756-57.

DIAL LANE, BS16. A very old name for a lane on what was Mark's riding (i.e. portion).

DIAMOND STREET, BS3. Celebrating Queen Victoria's Diamond Jubilee in 1897.

DIBDEN CLOSE / LANE / ROAD, BS16. The name means low, deep, wooded valley and is a very old name for what must have been the boggiest part of the parish.

DICKENS CLOSE, BS7. In keeping with the local literary theme this close was named after the great nineteenth-century novelist Charles Dickens (1812-70).

DIDSBURY CLOSE, BS10. The ecclesiastical connection here is Didsbury College, which moved to this location from Didsbury, Manchester.

DIGHTON STREET, BS2. The name of an influential Bristol family.

DILLON COURT, BS5. This honours the memory of Monsignor William Dillon who was responsible for the building of St. Patrick's Roman Catholic church in 1923. He died in 1955.

DIMOND ROAD, BS5. Possibly named after William Wyatt Dimond, actor and manager of the Theatre Royal for many years.

DINGLE CLOSE / ROAD / VIEW / THE DINGLE, BS9. A reference to nearby Coombe Dingle.

DINGLEWOOD CLOSE, BS9. Name chosen by the developer in keeping with the other names in the district.

DINGSWALK, BS2. One authority states this is from the OE word meaning dingle while another asserts it was a dialect word. This small area has always been known as 'The Dings' and it has been suggested it was a reference to the industries here and the striking noise of metal hammers. Another theory suggests a derivation from the seventeenth century name of the district, *Bengs*, which meant 'a grazing meadow', or 'place where withies grow'. Withies are used in basket making.

DIXON ROAD, BS4. This could be named after Charles Dixon, a Relieving Officer for the Public Assistance Board in the 1940's. He lived in nearby Harrowdene Road.

DOCK GATE LANE, BS8. This is self-explanatory. It led to Pooles Wharf, from where, until recently, dredgers operated. A possibly apocryphal story relates that the occupants of the prestigious recent Cumberland Basin residential development across the harbour, annoyed by the sounds of the dredgers discharging at all hours, organised a petition requesting that the times of the tides be changed.

DODISHAM WALK, BS16. William Dodisham was Lord of the Manor of Oldbury Court in 1430.

DOLMAN CLOSE, BS10. There are several possibilities for the origin of this name. There is a shield in the name of Dolman in Henbury church. There was also an Alexander Dolman who was a member of Bristol City Council in 1688. Alternatively, a John Dolman leased the well at Hotwells in 1750. He was a preacher at two Dissenting chapels as well as being a basket maker and dispenser of spa water. In the twentieth century there was Sir Harry Dolman, businessman and director of Bristol City Football Club.

DOLPHIN STREET, BS1. Site of Dolphin Tavern.

DOMINION ROAD, BS16. Might this road commemorate a shipping connection?

DONALD ROAD, BS3. Named after Donald Griffin, cousin of the builder, W. J. Kew.

DONCASTER ROAD, BS10. Place names have been the choice for many of the roads in this area.

DONEGAL ROAD, BS4. Irish names predominate in this vicinity. *See Bantry Road.*

DONGOLA ROAD, BS7. This and surrounding streets are named after famous battles. Dongola is the name of a town in the Sudan, on the left bank of the Nile six hundred miles north of Khartoum, and scene of a decisive battle in 1896 in Lord Kitchener's campaign to stamp out the Mahdi's rebellion against British control of the region. This road was developed in 1898.

DOONE ROAD, BS7. Called after a glen on the Isle of Man, as are all the rest of the roads in this group. Several roads nearby have a Manx connection. In this case it may be due to an anglicised spelling of *dhoon*, picturesque. Dhoon Glen was a favourite halt on the Manx Electric Railway. The island was a popular holiday destination for Victorians and Edwardians.

DORCHESTER ROAD. BS7. Among a number of roads called after British towns.

DORESTER CLOSE, BS10. John Dorester was resident in Westbury Parish in 1564.

DORIAN CLOSE / ROAD, BS7. As the road was built on ex-War Department ground this follows the local trend for roads named after battles and could be a mis-spelling of Doiran, a battle of the First World War fought in Mesopotamia.

DORMER ROAD, BS5. From the Cottrell-Dormer family who owned much land hereabouts. *See Cottrell Road.*

DORSET GROVE, BS2. Among other roads in the area called after English counties.

DORSET ROAD, BS9. Near Cheriton Road, which was named after a place in Hampshire. Possibly, in this case, the builder had links with Dorset.

DORSET ROAD, BS16. Among a collection of roads called, apparently randomly, after different parts of the British Isles.

DORSET STREET, BS3. Possibly named after Thomas Sackville, First Earl of Dorset, who was a distinguished statesman in the seventeenth century. The name Dorset is derived from the Celtic *Dwr* 'water' and Anglo Saxon *set* meaning a settlement. The tribe who lived there styled themselves 'the water dwellers'.

DOUGLAS ROAD, BS7. Continuing the theme of Isle of Man names in the area.

DOUGLAS ROAD, BS15. After the well-known motor cycle company, which traded here for years before becoming part of the Westinghouse group.

DOULTON WAY, BS14. The developers from the Midlands opted for names of famous potteries on this development site.

DOVE LANE, BS5. Perhaps this was once the site of a dovecote in the grounds of a long-vanished house, maybe even the one belonging to Solomon Moore from whom Moorfields took its name. He was a wholesale fishmonger trading in Castle Street, and he owned all the fields in this area. He was responsible for building forty of the houses there. When he retired in 1808, he moved to a house in what is now Avonvale Road, where he died in 1823.

DOVE STREET, BS2. Possibly named for the same reason as Dove Lane. Near the junction of Dove Street and Hillgrove Street were once buried the bodies of Captain Pugsley and his wife. The Captain was a Royalist officer who died defending the fort on Prior's Hill during the English Civil War, and was buried where he fell "under the turf marked with his blood" where the hill sloped down to Stoke's Croft. The place was marked with a monumental tablet. His widow never remarried and had a hut built in the field where Fremantle Road now runs, and gave sweets, cakes and toys to the children who played there. It became a favourite children's playing area. A spring in the field became known as Mother Pugsley's Well, and the field, Mother Pugsley's Wellfield. When she died in 1705, well into her eighties, she was buried according to her instructions in her wedding shift, without a coffin, her bier carried to the ground commonly known as Nine Trees. A Fiddler and two maids strewing herbs went before her corpse, while the bells of St. Nicholas Church tolled. This was witnessed by ten thousand admiring spectators.

DOVERCOURT ROAD, BS7. A seaside resort in Essex. There is no obvious reason for this choice.

DOVEY COURT, BS15. J.C. Dovey and Co. owned the nearby Golden Valley Mills in the 1930s.

DOWDESWELL CLOSE, BS10. Dowdeswell was an estate near Cheltenham which, after the suppression of the Knights Templar who owned it, was granted by Edward III to Westbury College.

DOWLAND CLOSE, BS4. John Dowland (1562-1626) was a composer of secular and sacred music mainly for the lute, and spent much of his adult life as court lutist to the Queen of Sweden. He was said to be the finest lute player of his time but his tunes were so mournful that the Latin motto was coined 'semper Dowland semper dolens'. (Always Dowland, always miserable.)

DOWLING ROAD, BS13. J. Dowling held land here in 1815.

DOWN VIEW, BS7. This block of flats replaced a Victorian house of the same name. It overlooks Purdown.

DOWNEND PARK / ROAD, BS7. Downend Farm once stood near this site.

DOWNEND PARK / PARK ROAD / ROAD, BS16. Leading into Downend.

DOWNEND ROAD, BS15 / BS16. The Downend Road in Downend itself used to be known as Skelton's Hill, after a Dr. Skelton who used to live in the big house on the hill. It was later demolished and a Mormon church was built on the site.

DOWNFIELD ROAD, BS8. Before development these were fields leading on from the Downs.

DOWNLEAZE, BS9. A made-up name, perhaps taken from Down House with the OE second syllable *laes* meaning pasture, meadowland or possibly *lesan*, to glean or gather.

DOWNLEAZE, BS16. Almost certainly a field name. The derivation is as above.

DOWNMAN ROAD, BS7. After John Downman (1750-1824), a portrait and subject painter.

DOWNS COTE AVENUE / DRIVE / GARDENS / PARK / VIEW, BS9. An indication of proximity to the Downs. All the roads in this group are named after the Cote estate on the edge of the Downs, on which they were built. Cote House was once home to Douglas Robinson, a member of a prominent local family which built up a vast paper and packaging empire based in Bristol. In *Some Notes About Cote*, Elizabeth Robinson recalled one of the duties of the owner of Cote House was to keep the White Tree on the Downs whitewashed to act as a beacon in the dark. This task was performed annually by the gardener.

DOWNS PARK East / West, BS6. Self-explanatory.

DOWNSIDE CLOSE, BS15. Amongst other roads in the area called after abbeys. Downside Abbey in the Mendips was built by the Benedictines, in a fusion of Early English and Perpendicular styles. Work began in 1872 and continued well into the twentieth century. As Pevsner says, 'it is Pugin's dream of the future of English Catholicism come true.' *(The Buildings of England - North Somerset and Bristol)*

DOWNSIDE ROAD, BS8. Descriptive.

DOWNTON ROAD, BS4. Named after a village in Wiltshire.

DOWRY ROAD / SQUARE, BS8. All the land here was once known as the Dowry, probably referring to an unknown woman's marriage portion.

DR. WHITE'S CLOSE, BS1. After the benefactor who built the almshouses in 1613.

DRAGON WALK, BS5. This road was so named because of the association of this mythical creature with the equally mythical (some think) St. George.

DRAGONSWELL ROAD, BS10. Derived from OE *draca* meaning 'dragon'. It was the name of a field on the now-vanished Westmoreland Farm, where there was a pond which never froze over because of a warm spring which fed it. However the legend arose that the source of the pond s warmth was really a dragon warming it with his hot breath.

DRAKE ROAD, BS3. One of a number of roads in the area named after famous sea captains of Elizabethan and Jacobean times.

DRAYCOT PLACE, BS1. John Draycot was a Bristol merchant in the fourteenth century.

DRAYCOTT ROAD, BS7. Draycott is a village near Cheddar. As the road is near Uphill Road it suggests the builder may have had Somerset connections. The meaning of the name is 'a shed for drays'.

DRAYDON ROAD, BS4. The name of a village on Exmoor. It is taken from a surname - Richard Draydon held lands in Somerset in the fourteenth century. Draydon is also the name of a wood near Dulverton in Somerset, where silver and lead mining once took place.

DRAYTON CLOSE, BS14. Drayton is a village in Somerset. The meaning of the word is 'a farmstead with a slope for dragging down loads'. *See Allanmead Close.*

DRAYTON ROAD, BS9. There is a whole group of roads here called after locations in Somerset suggesting that the landowner or builder may have had interests in that county.

THE DRIVE, BS14. This may have been the site of the driveway to Whitecross Court Farm.

THE DRIVE, BS9. Possibly named after the drive to one of the fine old houses which once graced this area beyond the Downs.

DRUETTS CLOSE, BS7. This is a surname, possibly of someone connected with the development, although there is no trace of the name in local directories.

DRUID HILL / ROAD / STOKE AVENUE / WOODS, BS9. Clearly this place had pagan origins.

DRUMMOND COURT, BS15. Archibald Drummond inherited a manor house in the area called Highfield, which he had pulled down. A farm was subsequently built on the land. *See Drummond Road BS16.*

DRUMMOND ROAD, BS2. Another Brigstocke family connection. Agnes Brigstocke, was married to a man called Francis Drummond. *See Brigstocke Road.*

DRUMMOND ROAD, BS16. After Archibald Drummond, M.D., who lived at Ridgeway House.

DRYLEAZE ROAD, BS16. This would appear to be a field name.

DUBBERS LANE, BS5. Dubbin is a preparation of grease for the treatment of leather. Perhaps there were folk here employed in that capacity. 'Dub' can also mean a puddle or a muddy patch, which could well have been applicable before the road was made up. Otherwise it is possible it was the name of someone who traded or lived in the lane. A John Dubber lived in Stapleton in the late nineteenth century, and possibly he held property here.

DUBLIN CRESCENT, BS9. There seems to be some Irish link here, possibly connected with St. Ursula's School. This leads off Antrim Road.

DUCHESS ROAD, BS8. This leads off Beaufort Road, so the Duchess must have been the Duchess of Beaufort. *See Duchess Way.*

DUCHESS WAY, BS16. Although this continues a regional theme of female titles, the inspiration for this name is the nearby land on which the Dowager Duchess Elizabeth of Beaufort was killed in a riding accident on 7 May, 1760. There is an obelisk to her memory in the grounds of Stoke Park House.

DUCIE ROAD, BS5. Once known as Pack Horse Lane, the road was later renamed in honour of H.J.R. Moreton, the Earl of Ducie (1827-1911) who was Lord Lieutenant of the city in the latter part of the nineteenth century. A Sir Robert Ducie is recorded as having purchased the Tortworth estate in Gloucestershire in the fifteenth century. The family retained Gloucestershire connections and founded Alexander Hosea's school at Wickwar in 1860. *See Moreton Street.*

DUCIE ROAD, BS16. Possibly named for the same reason as Ducie Road, BS5.

DUCKMOOR ROAD, BS3. This name may be a corruption of Doucemoor, the first vicar of the church of St. Francis in Ashton.

DUDLEY COURT, BS15. Named after Dud Dudley, born 1599, son of the Earl of Dudley, of Dudley Castle, Worcestershire. After leaving Oxford University he managed an iron furnace and began to experiment with smelting iron. A series of disasters, including the destruction of his works by persecutors who were jealous of his closely-guarded secret iron-smelting formula, resulted in his being thrown into a debtors' prison. He was bailed out by Charles I and in gratitude fought with the royalists in the Civil War. He was captured after the siege of Gloucester and was imprisoned in London, where he was sentenced to be shot. He somehow managed to escape and fled to Bristol on crutches. It was there that that he encountered Captain Copley. *See Copley Court.*

DUDLEY GROVE, BS7. This is the family name of the Earls of Leicester, but there is no clear reason for this choice.

DUGAR WALK, BS6. This was the name of the wood which occupied the site on which were built Cranbrook Road and Elton Road.

DULVERTON ROAD, BS7. A town in Somerset. Other streets nearby are named after West Country places but no clear link has been discovered.

DUNCOMBE LANE / ROAD, BS15. Originally Dencombe Lane, named after the house of that name which stood near here.

DUNDAS CLOSE, BS10. The link here is the Harford family who owned the Blaise estate. Abraham Gray Harford-Battersby married Elizabeth Dundas Gray, daughter of Major General Thomas Gray, on 11 May 1816. She died on 23 January 1828.

DUNDONALD ROAD, BS6. Scottish title borne by the family of Cochrane. Many roads in the area are named after aristocratic families, as was the fashion when these houses were built.

DUNDRIDGE GARDENS / LANE, BS5. There was a house of this name which once stood here, although on the 1610 map of Kingswood, Dundridge was actually the name of the district.

DUNDRY VIEW, BS4 / CLOSE, BS15. So named because of the view which is afforded here of Dundry and Dundry church, which was built in 1482.

DUNKELD AVENUE, BS12. Site of an abbey in Scotland. In the eleventh century the hereditary lay abbot was Ethelred, son of Queen Margaret of Scotland. The West Country connection is that Ethelred's father, Malcolm Canmore, was slain by Morel of Bamborough, a kinsman of Robert de Mowbray who owned scores of manors in Somerset and Gloucester.

DUNKERRY ROAD, BS3. Perhaps a mis-spelling of Dunkery, after Dunkery Beacon on Exmoor. All other roads nearby are named after West Country hills.

DUNKIRK ROAD, BS16. Named after a village in Gloucestershire. This road is situated near Drummond Road. Dr. Drummond married an heiress from Rudgeway; they owned lands around Dunkirk in the early nineteenth century.

DUNMAIL ROAD, BS10. Dunmail Raise is in the Lake District. This is sited amidst other roads named after similar locations.

DUNMORE STREET, BS3. Prince Edward fled to the Hills of Dunmoore in 1265 to escape being slain by Simon de Montfort, Earl of Leicester.

DUNSTER GARDENS, BS15. Following the castles theme of roads nearby, Dunster is a famous castle in Somerset, built in the twelfth century.

DUNSTER ROAD, BS4. *See Dunster Gardens.*

DURBAN ROAD, BS12. Near to Pretoria Road, so part of a South African connection.

DURBIN WALK, BS5. After John Durbin, Mayor of Bristol 1760. John Durbin Junior became Mayor in 1777.

DURDHAM PARK BS6. Named after the adjoining Durdham Down.

DURDHAM ROAD, BS2. Probably named after the city's Durdham Down.

DURLEIGH CLOSE, BS3. Place name taken from the OE *deer* and *leah*, meaning 'woodland or clearing where deer graze'.

DURNFORD AVENUE / ROAD / STREET, BS3. It is most likely that local Bedminster builders J. Durnford and Sons built these roads.

DURSLEY ROAD, BS11. The names of Gloucestershire towns have been chosen for many roads in this area.

DURVILLE ROAD, BS3. A town in Gloucestershire. The first syllable derives from a name, Deorsige, the second is from the French *ville*, town.

DURWESTON WALK, BS14. Named after a Dorset village, in keeping with neighbouring Sturminster Road.

DUTTON CLOSE / ROAD / WALK, BS14. William Dutton lived in the parish and tithing of Brislington in 1670. He was exempt from Hearth Tax.

DYERS CLOSE, BS13. Dyers Road was a private road mentioned in the Dundry Enclosure Award 1815, probably a road leading to the Dyers House which once stood in nearby Eagle Drive, BS12.

DYLAN THOMAS COURT, BS15. Among a group of roads named after modern poets. The Welsh poet Dylan Thomas (1914-53) is probably most famous for his radio drama, *Under Milk Wood.*

DYRHAM CLOSE, BS9. Dyrham is a place in Gloucestershire, which is believed to have been the site of a battle in 577 AD when the West Saxons conquered the Britons and three kings fell in battle. The name means enclosure for deer. Dyrham Park is a beautiful seventeenth-century mansion set in a deer park, and now belongs to the National Trust. The close was probably named after the house.

DYRHAM ROAD, BS15 / DYRHAM, BS16. Sir William Dennys, the local landowner, founded a guild at Dyrham, near Pucklechurch, in 1520. He had enclosed a park there in 1512.

EAGLE ROAD, BS4. Eagle House, built in 1769, once stood here. It was described by Morgan, who compiled a book describing Bristol's important houses in the nineteenth century, as 'a beautiful spot with a fine lawn surrounding it and abundantly stocked with shrubs of the choicest kind.' The house was built in 1769 and demolished in 1934 to build this road.

EARL RUSSELL WAY, BS5. Named after the inn of the same name which, in turn, honours Lord John Russell (1792-1878), who served as Prime Minister from 1846-1851. He was instrumental in formulating the 1832 Reform Bill and his government was responsible for the Free Trade movement and the reduction in working hours for women.

EARL STREET, BS2. This street was established here as long ago as 1737. The Earl would seem to be Leofwine, Governor of Bristol Castle in 1049, although there is a possibility the origin is William Earl who endowed the adjoining priory of St. James with several manors in Somerset. The Rev. Henry J. Foster believed the Earl to be Sir Thomas Earle, one time Mayor of the city.

EARLSMEAD, BS2. Again there is dispute as to the Earl involved. One source states Robert, Earl of Gloucester and builder of Bristol Castle as this area would have been with the demesne; others opt for Leowine, while one authority asserts it was the son of Henry I.

EARLSTONE CLOSE / CRESCENT, BS15. Called after a house of the same name which stood here.

EASEDALE CLOSE, BS10. Another Lake District name. Easedale Tarn lies near Grasmere and was a favourite spot of the Wordsworths.

EASTCROFT, BS9. Perhaps a field name from long ago. West Croft is nearby.

EAST DUNDRY ROAD, BS14. Self-explanatory. *See Dundry Close.*

EAST GROVE, BS6. A mirror image of West Grove on the opposite side of Brook Road.

EAST HILL, BS9. Adjoins Eastfield Road.

EAST PARADE, BS9. Runs in the opposite direction from West Parade.

EAST PARK / EAST PARK DRIVE, BS5. The central road in a development which lies in East Bristol and is quite near Eastville Park.

EAST PRIORY CLOSE, BS9. In a group of roads celebrating the area's religious connections in the past.

EAST RIDGE DRIVE, BS13. East Ridge was a field name used at Whitehouse Farm in the Manor of Long Ashton recorded on the 1794 survey, the name being self-explanatory.

EAST SHRUBBERY, BS6. Built in the grounds of a demolished house.

EAST STREET, BS3. The arrangement of the roads in Bedminster has led to speculation that it was once a Roman settlement.

EAST STREET, BS11. A purely geographical name.

EAST VIEW, BS17. Self-explanatory.

EASTBOURNE ROAD, BS5. After the Sussex seaside town. The last syllable is OE *burna* meaning 'stream'. Many roads in this locality are called after seaside resorts.

EASTBURY ROAD, BS16. This is the name of a village in Dorset. The last component is the OE *byrig*, 'fort' or 'town'.

EASTCOTE PARK, BS4. Probably made up. The first syllable is a personal name Eadwine and the last syllable ME *cot*, 'cottage or shelter for sheep and wayfarers'.

EASTCOURT GARDENS, BS16. As this is sited by Wickham Court in the eastern part of the city it must be a contrived name.

EASTFIELD ROAD BS6, BS9 / TERRACE, BS9 / EASTFIELD, BS9. In all instances, Cotham and Westbury-on-Trym, the name is taken from a nearby house.

EASTGATE ROAD, BS5. East because it is in Eastville and gate as it is the gateway to the city's east side. There was never a city gate here, although the site on which the Eastgate centre is built covers land once owned by the Gas Board. A house called Wide Gates stood here prior to development.

EASTLAKE CLOSE, BS7. Sir Charles Eastlake was President of the Royal Academy 1850-65.

EASTLEIGH CLOSE / ROAD, BS16. Probably a field name rather than a reference to the Hampshire town in this instance.

EASTLEIGH ROAD, BS10. Place name. The last syllable means 'meadowland'.

EASTLYN ROAD, BS3. Thought to be a made-up name. *East Lynne* was a popular Victorian melodrama written by Mrs Henry Wood (1861).

EASTMEAD LANE, BS9. This must surely be an old field name.

EASTNOR ROAD, BS14. Named after a place on the Gloucestershire/ Worcestershire border. Another place in that area is represented in the surrounding roads but no link can be made.

EASTON ROAD / WAY, BS5. The name means East farmstead or village. The Eyston family once owned land and property here so there is a slight possibility the name is derived from them although the geographical position is the more likely.

EASTOVER CLOSE, BS9. The OE *ofer* means 'shoreline' or 'river bank' which is hardly applicable here. Perhaps just a made-up name. Many roads in the area bear the first syllable East. Also nearby are three other roads completing the entire compass. Over in this instance may be a reference to the village near Almondsbury.

EASTWOOD CRESCENT / ROAD, BS4. From Eastwood Farm, a seventeenth century building which is still standing in Wyndham Crescent.

EATON CLOSE BS14, BS16 / CRESCENT, BS8 / STREET, BS3. Joseph Eaton, a Quaker, was a wholesale ironmonger. He helped finance the building of the General Hospital in 1851. He lived in Redcliffe Parade, and flags on shipping and on the shot tower flew at half-mast on the day of his funeral in 1858.

EBENEZER LANE, BS9. At the top of this lane in the mid 1850's stood Ebenezer House, about a mile from where the lane starts today.

EBENEZER STREET, BS5. From the Methodist church nearby. The Hebrew word meant 'stone of help' and is taken from the story of Samuel.

EDEN GROVE, BS7. Perhaps after the Reverend John Eden who campaigned for better education in the 1820s.

EDGECOMBE CLOSE, BS15. This is situated near the old mining area so the name could be that of a son of Annie Braine who owned the Golden Valley pit. She was previously married to Edgecombe Lavers.

EDGECUMBE ROAD, BS6. In common with many roads in this locality, this road is named after a member of the aristocracy, in this case the Earl of Mount Edgecumbe, created 1789.

EDGEFIELD CLOSE / ROAD, BS14. Built on farmland.

EDGEWARE ROAD, BS3. Edgware is a town in Middlesex. The first syllable is a personal name Edge and the last syllable means weir. Place names figure largely in the roads round here.

EDGEWARE ROAD, BS16. Nearby is Kensington Road so perhaps the builder had London connections.

EDGEWOOD CLOSE, BS14. Continuing the theme of description in the area. Hengrove itself translates as 'a clearing in the forest on the hillside'. *See Allanmead Close.*

EDGEWOOD ROAD, BS15. Another in the California place name group. *See California Road.*

EDINGTON GROVE, BS10. William Edington was Dean of Westbury College 1323-35 and subsequently became Bishop of Winchester 1356.

EDMUND CLOSE, BS16. King Edmund I, called the Grand, was murdered at Pucklechurch on 26 May 946.

EDNA AVENUE, BS4. Named after a daughter of the builder, Mr Griffee.

EDWARD ROAD, BS4. Almost certainly in honour of the Prince of Wales, born 9 November 1841, eldest son and second child of Queen Victoria. Later he became Edward VII. Died May 6 1910.

EDWARD ROAD, BS15. Possibly a personal name of someone of significance who lived in the area. No clue is provided by the names of the surrounding streets.

EDWARD STREET, BS5. First name of a member of the market-gardening Gerrish family. *See Gerrish Avenue.*

EDWARD STREET, BS5. There is a Herbert Street close by so perhaps they were relatives of the builder.

EDWARD BIRD HOUSE, BS7. Continuing the local district theme, Edward Bird was an historical and landscape artist who moved to Bristol and is buried in the Cathedral. He opened the first evening Art School for Young Gentlemen in 1797.

EFFINGHAM ROAD, BS6. Most probably dedicated to the Earl of Effingham. Lord Howard of Effingham was instrumental in defeating the Spanish Armada in 1588.

EGERTON BROW / ROAD, BS6. This land was developed between 1870 and 1900. Egerton is the family name of the Dukes of Bridgwater. Francis Egerton (1736-1803) was responsible for building the first canal in England. It ran from the Worsley coalmine, which he owned, to Manchester. The canal was later extended to Runcorn and the Mersey and became the Manchester Ship Canal. Francis Egerton never married and the earldom became extinct upon his death.

EIGHTH AVENUE, BS7. Another of the American-style roads in the area.

ELBERTON ROAD, BS9. Elberton is a village near Thornbury. Perhaps the owners of this land had links with this part of Gloucestershire.

ELBERTON, BS15. Among a clutch of roads named after Gloucestershire villages listed in the Domesday book.

ELBURY AVENUE, BS15. Thought to be a made-up name.

ELDERBERRY WALK, BS10. This is marked on some maps as Elderbury but it seems to have been called after the tree.

ELDERWOOD DRIVE, BS15. A cluster of sylvan names on this development.

ELDERWOOD ROAD, BS14. Almost certainly a field name as these are favoured for roads in this locality.

ELDON TERRACE, BS3. Possibly a first name or surname to judge by surrounding roads.

ELDON WAY, BS4. Either named after one of two villages - one in Hampshire, one in Durham - or after the Earl of Eldon, Lord Chancellor in 1801. The name is derived from 'Ella's hill'.

ELEVENTH AVENUE, BS7. Continuing the USA theme.

ELFIN ROAD, BS16. Elfin House once stood on this land.

ELGAR CLOSE, BS4. Sir Edward Elgar (1857-1934), born in Worcestershire, was a pre-eminent Edwardian English composer, the most important since Purcell. He was professor of music at Birmingham University and was knighted in 1904. His music enjoyed a revival recently after his best known piece, the *Pomp and Circumstance*, was included in the music for the wedding of the Prince and Princess of Wales on 29 July 1981. Other famous works include *The Enigma Variations* and *The Dream of Gerontius.*

ELGIN AVENUE, BS7. Named together with others in this development after Scottish locations.

ELGIN CROFT, BS13. Perhaps after Charles Bruce, son of the Earl of Aylesbury and Elgin, who owned land in Somerset.

ELGIN PARK, BS6. The Earl of Elgin was Governor-General of Canada in 1847 and Viceroy of India in 1862.

ELGIN ROAD, BS16. Probably named for the same reason as Elgin Park.

ELKSTONE WALK, BS15. Elkstone is a place near Cirencester. It was in the Rapsgate Hundred, according to the Domesday book, at the time of which it was held by Ansfrid of Cormeilles. Previously two Leofwins had held it as two manors.

ELLACOMBE ROAD, BS15. After Rev H. T. Ellacombe of St. Mary's, Bitton, who wrote the famous history of the parish.

ELLBRIDGE CLOSE, BS9. Thomas Ellbridge gave the Parish of Westbury the interest of £100 for good purposes: 20 shillings for the sermon on 3rd January and the rest for the distribution of bread to the poor It is thought he was the son of John Ellbridge, founder of the Bristol Royal Infirmary.

ELLESMERE ROAD, BS4. Shropshire town. The first syllable is a personal name, Ellie, while the last syllable is OE for lake. No obvious reason for this choice.

ELLESMERE ROAD, BS15. Among other roads given Lake District names.

ELLFIELD CLOSE, BS13. A field name recorded in surveys of 1780 and 1794 in the Manor of Long Ashton. First syllable derived from OE *elle* or *ellern*, 'elder tree'.

ELLINGHURST CLOSE, BS10. This was once a farm in the Hundred of Henbury the name meaning 'wooded hillock where elders grow'.

ELLICOTT ROAD, BS7. Thought to be named after Charles John Ellicott (1819-1905). He was Dean of Exeter before being appointed as Bishop of Gloucester and Bristol in 1863. He wrote a number of theological works and was reputedly held in great esteem.

ELLIOT AVENUE, BS16. This was built on the Riverwood estate and was named after the builder. *See Riverwood Road.*

ELLIS AVENUE, BS3. The middle name of the builder's son. *See Garth Road.*

ELLISTON LANE / ROAD, BS6. In all likelihood someone who either owned or developed the site.

ELLSWORTH ROAD, BS10. Anthony Ellsworth was churchwarden of Westbury-on-Trym church in 1684.

ELM LANE / ROAD, BS6. Self-explanatory.

ELM PARK, BS12. Built on land which included a field called Horn Croft where elm trees may well have grown.

ELM ROAD, BS7. *See Oak Road.*

ELM ROAD / WAY, BS15. Probably from the rows of huge elms which once covered Honey Hill.

ELM TREE AVENUE, BS16. Probably descriptive.

ELMCROFT CRESCENT, BS7. Probably a made-up name.

ELMDALE GARDENS, BS16. Named after the Housing Association which erected these properties.

ELMDALE ROAD, BS3. Thought to be an improvised name.

ELMDALE ROAD, BS8. Elms were probably a feature of the grounds in which this road was built.

ELMFIELD / ELMFIELD CLOSE, BS15. Almost certainly a field name.

ELMFIELD ROAD, BS9. The road was called after a nearby school.

ELMGROVE AVENUE, BS5. All Hallows Road used to be known as Elmgrove Road, and this was a turning off it.

ELMGROVE ROAD, BS16. The 1903 Ordinance Survey map shows an Elmgrove House standing on the east side of the road, leading to the Grove.

ELMGROVE ROAD / PARK, BS6. These roads are close to Redland Green, which was part of the Redland Court Estate. Many magnificent trees, especially copper beeches, still grace the gardens of the Victorian houses built in this area, and it is probable that the estate also boasted fine groves of elms, after which these roads were originally named.

ELMHURST AVENUE, BS5. Near the park where these trees once grew in abundance.

ELMLEA AVENUE, BS9. Emphasis here is on the rural aspect of the locality.

ELMLEIGH AVENUE / CLOSE / ROAD, BS17. Built on farm land. 'Leigh' derives from OE *leah*, 'meadow'.

ELMORE ROAD, BS7. A place near Gloucester. The next road is also called after a Gloucestershire village so perhaps there is a link with the builder or landowner.

ELMORE, BS15. Other Gloucestershire place names have been used for roads in this area.

THE ELMS, BS16. The emphasis is on tree names in this development.

ELMTREE CLOSE / WAY, BS15. Probably descriptive of the land before development.

ELMTREE DRIVE, BS13. There used to be an Elm Tree Farm near here.

ELSBERT DRIVE, BS13. This sounds like a made-up name, possibly deriving from Elsie and Bert.

ELSTREE ROAD, BS5. Built during the period when cinema-going was at its most popular, this road appears to be have named after the Hertfordshire film studios. It is near Embassy Road, Embassy being the name of a popular cinema at that time.

ELTON LANE / ROAD, BS7, STREET, BS2. The Elton family played a large part in the history of Bristol. They held the baronetcy of Clevedon and two were Members of Parliament, five were Mayors, and five were Sheriffs.

ELTON ROAD, BS8. Presumably from the same source as BS7.

ELTON ROAD, BS15. The Elton family also owned land on this side of town. *See BS7.*

ELVARD COURT / ROAD, BS13. Elvard was a tenant of Sir John Smyth when the survey of Bishport Manor was made in 1683.

ELVASTON ROAD, BS3. A village in Derbyshire. The first component is a personal name. Many place names were used in road naming in this locality.

ELY GROVE, BS9. A few ecclesiastical names are scattered throughout local roads. The cathedral at Ely in Cambridgeshire was begun in 1083 and is famous for its exquisite Lady Chapel.

EMBASSY ROAD / WALK BS5. The only explanation can be that the builder was a big cinema fan. *See Elstree Road.*

EMBLETON ROAD, BS10. The name of a Lake District location in keeping with neighbouring roads.

EMERSON SQUARE, BS7. Named after Ralph Waldo Emerson (1803-82), an American poet, philosopher and essayist.

EMERY ROAD, BS4. From Emery's Farm, demolished in 1967. Now the site of Condover Road.

EMLYN ROAD, BS5. Lord Emlyn (1855-1905) was chairman of Great Western Railways and this land may have belonged to GWR at one time.

EMMETT WOOD, BS14. From OE *æmette* meaning 'ant'. The word survives in West Country dialect, where it is used to describe both ants and, more usually, tourists.

EMRA CLOSE, BS5. John Emra was the Vicar of St. George parish from 1809-42. He was well known as a painter of local scenes. He and his daughter Frances did a great deal to help the poor of the area.

ENFIELD ROAD, BS16. A town in Middlesex; the first syllable is a personal name. Quite a few place names are used in this area.

ENGLISHCOMBE ROAD, BS13. Named after the estate of James Hassell near Bath, which was granted land under the Dundry Enclosure Award in 1815.

ENNERDALE ROAD, BS10. Named after a lake in Cumberland as are many of the roads nearby.

EPNEY CLOSE, BS12. Many roads nearby have Gloucestershire village names.

EPSOM CLOSE, BS16. All the roads in this development are called after racecourses.

EPWORTH ROAD, BS10. Epsworth Manor, Gainsborough, Lincs was the birthplace of John Wesley. Henbury Methodist church, standing nearby, requested this choice of name.

ERIN WALK, BS4. Irish names seem a popular choice for the streets in this locality. *See Bantry Road.*

ERMINE WAY, BS9. The Roman influence is shown here in this choice of name. Ermine Street was one of the main roads across the country during the Roman occupation.

ERMLETT ROAD, BS6. Thought to be a made-up name.

ERNEST BARKER CLOSE, BS5. Sir Ernest Barker was a distinguished author and professor. He was President of the University Settlement.

ERNESTVILLE ROAD, BS16. Made-up name probably combining the builder's name with the French ville meaning 'town'.

ERVINE TERRACE, BS2. Unknown derivation. It could be a surname, but nobody of that name was listed in the directory when the street was built in the early part of the nineteenth century.

ESSERY ROAD, BS5. Named after Albert Essery, solicitor and clerk to the St. George Highway Board. He was active in local politics. The houses were built on land owned by Sir J.Greville Smyth.

ESSEX STREET, BS3. Called after the county. The name means the East Saxons.

ESSON ROAD, BS5. Probably a corruption of Easton, which was originally Eston.

ETLOE ROAD, BS6. Place name from a parish in West Gloucestershire. The first syllable is a personal name and the last syllable from OE *hlæw*, 'low hill' or 'mound' - thus 'Eata's (or Etta's) hill'; possibly his burial mound. In the Domesday Book it is shown as being held by Roger de Berkeley.

ETON ROAD, BS4. Several roads built around here at this time were called after public schools.

ETTRICKE DRIVE, BS16. The name of a family who lived at Overn Lodge, Cleeve Hill, Downend in 1676. The three brothers William, Andrew and Anthony were associated with William Player in the development of the coal industry in Kingswood Forest.

EUGENE STREET, BS2. After Prince Eugene of Savoy (1663-1736), an Austrian military hero who defeated the French at Blenheim, Oudenarde and Malplaquet. He was also successful in the campaign against the Turks at Peterwardein in 1716. Prince Eugene was jointly in command with the Duke of Marlborough in this latter campaign, and there was formerly another Eugene Street which ran parallel with marlborough Street.

EVANS ROAD, BS6. Believed to be named in honour of P. F. Sparke Evans, the local benefactor who gave a large portion of land in St. Philips Marsh to be used as a park.

EVE ROAD, BS5. *See Lawrence Avenue.*

EVELYN ROAD, BS10. The person for whom the road was named, and whether this was a man or woman, is unknown.

EVENLODE GARDENS, BS9. Called after a village near Moreton-in-Marsh. Other roads locally have been named after places in the Cotswolds, the link appearing to be cloth manufacture.

EVERCREECH ROAD, BS14. Somerset place names here are interspersed with other themes. Perhaps the original owner of the land possessed other estates in Somerset.

EVEREST AVENUE / ROAD, BS16. Built on land which was known as Snowden from the field names Great and Little Snowden, so the choice of name is apt. The mountain was named after Sir George Everest (1790-1866), Surveyor-General of India 1830-43.

EXCHANGE AVENUE, BS1. The Exchange, designed by John Wood of Bath and completed in 1743, has a side frontage to this avenue.

EXETER BUILDINGS, BS6. The Marquess of Exeter, John Brownlow Cecil, accompanied the Prince Consort to Bristol in 1843 for the launching of the SS Great Britain. He married a lady with a famous local surname, Poyntz. *See Poyntz Court.*

EXETER ROAD, BS3. West Country towns seem a favourite choice when naming roads in this area.

EXLEY CLOSE, BS15. The name of the owners of Swinford Mill, where flock manufacture was carried out prior to the Second World War.

EXMOOR STREET, BS3. Place name derived from the River Exe.

EXMOUTH ROAD, BS4. The theme here is seaside resorts.

EXTON CLOSE, BS14. The name of a village in Somerset, in keeping with the general theme in this area.

EYER'S LANE, BS2. It would seem this lane owes its name to the eminent Sir Robert Eyres (1666-1735) who was Recorder of Bristol from 1704-8, Judge from 1709-23, Lord Chief Justice of the Common Pleas from 1725-35, MP for Salisbury 1698-1710, and Solicitor General in 1708.

FABER GROVE, BS13. Walter Faber paid 2 shillings rent of assize to Redcliff in 1317 when it was part of the Hundred of Hartcliffe.

FAILAND CRESCENT / WALK BS9. Several roads nearby are named after local villages.

FAIR FURLONG, BS13. A descriptive field name in the Manor of Bishport, shown on the 1683 survey.

FAIR LAWN, BS15. Again, this seems to be an old field name.

FAIR VIEW DRIVE, BS6. Descriptive.

FAIRACRE CLOSE, BS7. This was the name of a field before the area was developed.

FAIRFAX STREET, BS1. Named after Baron Thomas Fairfax, commander-in-chief of the Roundhead troops during the Civil War, who captured nearby Bristol Castle in 1645. He approved of the trial and deposition of Charles I but tried to prevent his execution. Five years later he was one of the deputation that went to The Hague to invite Charles II back to England, but, disgusted with the rioting and immorality of the Dutch court, he retired to his estates in Yorkshire on a vast pension and spent the rest of his life writing his Memorials, Psalms and poems.

FAIRFIELD PLACE/ROAD, BS3. Named after a house which once stood nearby.

FAIRFIELD ROAD, BS6. Some sources suggest that there was once a house here of this name, but no trace has been found of such a building. It is more likely to derive from a field name.

FAIRFOOT ROAD, BS3. No obvious reason for this name. Might this have been the surname of the landowner, perhaps?

FAIRFORD CLOSE, BS15. At the time of the Domesday Book, Fairford was included in the Hundred of Brightwells Barrow, held by Britric. It was subsequently held by Queen Matilda (1102-67)

FAIRFORD ROAD, BS11. In common with many other roads in the area, this is named after a Gloucestershire village.

FAIRHAVEN ROAD, BS6. This is the name of a port in Massachusetts but there is no obvious reason for its inclusion here.

FAIRLAWN AVENUE, BS12. A made-up name. The avenue now lies within the B.Ae. security area.

FAIRLAWN ROAD, BS6. Named after Fairlawn House, built in 1874 by T.H.W. Hall, a Bristol cheese manufacturer. Later this became the home of George White, founder of the British and Colonial Aeroplane Company.

FAIRLYN DRIVE, BS15. Lyn from OE *hlynn*, a torrent, while the Irish and Welsh versions *linn* and *llyn* mean pool. The only water nearby is the brook which flows in the Warmley Valley.

FAIROAKS, BS15. A Californian place name. *See California Road.*

FAIRVIEW ROAD, BS15. Named after the house belonging to the Fussell family, who owned a boot factory in the area. They also owned a colliery at Oldland. This house housed a fine art collection amassed by Philip Fussell.

FAIRWAY CLOSE, BS15. A field name.

FAIRWAY, BS4. A reference to the proximity of the golf course.

FALCON CLOSE, BS9. Thought to be so named because of its proximity to Falcondale Road.

FALCON CLOSE / DRIVE / WALK, BS12. Among a host of other nearby roads with bird names.

FALCONDALE ROAD / WALK, BS9. This was the name of MP John Harford's house in Lampeter. *See Lampeter Road.*

FALFIELD ROAD, BS4. There is no obvious reason for naming this road after a place in Gloucestershire.

FALFIELD WALK, BS10. Among a group of roads called after Gloucestershire villages.

FALKLAND ROAD, BS6. A village in Somerset, also a town in Fife, but the road was most probably named in keeping with neighbouring roads with the same initial letter.

FALLODON CLOSE / WAY, BS9. There is a village named Falloden in Northumberland, but the development was probably named after Viscount Grey of Fallodon (1862-1933). He was Foreign Secretary at the outbreak of the First World War and famous for the words 'The lamps are going out all over Europe; we shall not see them lit again in our lifetime'. The road was built at the time of his death.

FALLOWFIELD, BS15. Almost certainly a field name.

FALMOUTH ROAD, BS7. Named after a Cornish seaside resort standing on the River Fal.

FANE CLOSE, BS10. Named after Sir Francis Fane who died in 1689, whose family were patrons of the living in Westbury-on-Trym for 150 years.

FANSHAWE ROAD, BS14. This could be a place name or surname. The meaning is 'high wood'.

FAR HANDSTONES, BS15. This was one of the old field names.

FARADAY ROAD, BS8. Most probably named after Sir Michael Faraday (1791-1867). He was the son of a Westmorland blacksmith who came to London at the invitation of Sir Humphry Davy to become his assistant. Davy is also honoured in a local road. Faraday made many important discoveries in chemistry and electro-magnetism and the farad, a unit of electrical capacitance, is named after him. Faraday's Law, which is also named after him, states that an electrical current may be measured in terms of the quantity of an electrolyte which it decomposes. Faraday was also famous for his popular Christmas lectures, which he gave to the public every year from 1829 onwards, a tradition which is continued by the Royal Institution in London to this day.

FARINGTON ROAD, BS10. A surname or place name - the meaning being 'village or town where the ferns grow'. Perhaps named after James Farington (1747-1821), the notable British artist.

FARLEIGH WALK, BS3. Many local streets are called after Somerset villages.

FARM COURT / ROAD, BS16. This led to Downend Farm, which existed as early as the 1600s. It was demolished in 1958.

FARMER ROAD, BS13. The surname of a tenant of Sir John Smyth at the time of the survey of Bishport Manor in 1683.

FARMWELL CLOSE, BS13. This probably derives from a field name from the Anglo Saxon *waella*, a stream. Farm derives from the Old French *ferm*, meaning 'land held on lease', a farm.

FARNABY CLOSE, BS14. Another in the British composers series, this development celebrates Giles Farnaby (1566-1640), a composer of madrigals and short pieces for virginals.

FARNDALE, BS5. Possibly a made-up name.

FARNE CLOSE, BS9. This runs off Fallodon Way and the link is Northumberland. The Farne Islands are a group of seventeen rocky islets off the coast of that county, populated mainly by seabirds and seals. The largest island is Lindisfarne, the seventh-century retreat of St. Cuthbert, and nearby is Holy

Island, joined to the mainland at low tide by a meandering sand causeway, but surrounded by treacherous quicksands as well.

FARR STREET, BS11. After James Farr of Barrow Hill Farm, who ran an omnibus service to Bristol and was a local councillor at the time this road was built. James Farr lived late nineteenth/early twentieth century and the houses were built in the early years of the twentieth century.

FARR'S LANE, BS1. Probably after Richard Farr, an eighteenth century merchant whose office address was 'On the Quay'.

FARRANT CLOSE, BS4. Richard Farrant (1530-81) was organist to Elizabeth I at St. George's Chapel, Windsor. He wrote church music and the anthems 'Call to Remembrance' and 'Hide not thy Face', which are still sung today.

FAWKES CLOSE, BS15. These houses were built on the site of Crane's firework factory.

FEATHERSTONE ROAD, BS16. Possibly named after a town in Yorkshire with an interesting derivation, as it stems from tetralith or cromech, meaning three upright stones and a headstone. It could also have been the surname of the owner of the land. The builder of the road was J.T. Adams.

FEEDER ROAD, BS2. This road runs alongside the Feeder canal, which connects the upper Avon with the Floating Harbour.

FELIX ROAD, BS5. Unknown origin, although it could have been either the forename or surname of the builder or the owner of the land.

FELSTEAD ROAD, BS10. This might be a mis-spelling of Felsted, a village in Essex.

FELTON GROVE, BS3. Many local roads are named after Somerset villages.

FENBROOK CLOSE, BS16. Thought to be an old field name.

FENNELL GROVE, BS10. Robert Fennell was overseer of the poor for the Westbury tithing in 1683. He died in August 1712 and was buried at Westbury church.

FENTON ROAD, BS7. A place name meaning 'village or farmstead by the fen'. It was also the name of the firm of Leeds locomotion engineers who built the Great Western Railway engines.

FERMAINE AVENUE, BS4. In keeping with nearby roads with a Channel Islands theme, this is the name of a Guernsey bay.

FERN CLOSE, BS10. All roads in the area have a woodland theme.

FERN ROAD, BS16. This leads off Shrubbery Road.

FERNBANK ROAD, BS6. From Fernbank House, named after a school for young gentlemen in the mid 1800s which stood on this site.

FERNDALE AVENUE, BS4. A favourite name for any road in a dip near woodland.

FERNDALE AVENUE, BS15. Another Californian place name. *See California Road.*

FERNDALE ROAD, BS7. A section of this road runs across what was known as the Far Home Ground before the area was developed. Perhaps this name was chosen because of its rural connotations.

FERNDOWN CLOSE, BS11. Named after the nearby woodland.

FERNHURST ROAD, BS5. *Hurst* is an old name for the deepest part of the wood where, of course, ferns would be most likely to be found. There was a wooded area nearby at one time.

FERNSTEED ROAD, BS13. A field name derived from the OE *fearne,* fern, and *stede* or *styde*, a place or site.

FERRY ROAD, BS15. The site of the old ferry at Hanham Court.

FERRY STREET, BS1. The site of the old Redcliffe ferry.

FIDDES ROAD, BS6. This was built on land owned by Bishop Monk's Trust, and Fiddes was the name of one of the Trustee's Scottish relatives.

FIELD LANE, BS15. Once a lane leading to Mount Pleasant Farm.

FIELD ROAD, BS5. Undoubtedly this once was a field.

FIELD VIEW, BS5. This commands a view of the playing field of the rebuilt Easton School.

FIELDVIEW DRIVE, BS16. This was the name of one of the houses at Crescent School, demolished to make way for housing.

FIENNES CLOSE, BS15. Perhaps named after Nathaniel Fiennes, who was the Roundhead Governor of the captured Bristol castle throughout the Civil War. He later surrendered the castle to Prince Rupert to save the Bristol people being massacred by the avenging Royalist forces.

FIFTH AVENUE, BS7. Another of the transatlantic namings.

FIFTH WAY, BS11. Another of Avonmouth's succinct namings.

FILTON AVENUE / GROVE / LANE / ROAD, BS7 / BS16. At least part of Filton Avenue used to be known as Red Lane. *See under* **Filton** *in the introduction.*

FILWOOD BROADWAY, BS4. It was thought suitable that this highway should have an important-sounding name, leading as it did through an area with a population equivalent to a county town such as Taunton.

FILWOOD DRIVE, BS15. Derived from Filwood Chase, part of the King's forest.

FILWOOD ROAD, BS16. Named after Filwood House which once stood here.

FIR TREE CLOSE, BS12. Self-explanatory.

FIR TREE LANE, BS5. Self-explanatory.

FIRECLAY ROAD, BS5. Fireclay works in the area are shown on the 1918 Ordnance Survey map. Fireclay is a heat-resistant clay used to line furnaces and in the making of firebricks.

FIREWORK CLOSE, BS15. Built on the site of Crane's firework factory. *See Crane Close.*

THE FIRS, BS16. Many roads in Downend are endowed with tree names.

FIRST AVENUE, BS4. The initial development in the area.

FIRST WAY, BS11. Self-explanatory.

FISHER AVENUE / ROAD, BS15. This may refer to the old name of this street, which was Fishing Lane.

FISHPONDS ROAD, BS16. This was the old road which led to the New Pools in Kingswood Forest. In the 1600-1700s the area was inhabited by colliers and quarrymen living in mud huts they had constructed. Land owners encouraged them to convert these into stone built dwellings and allocated half an acre to each inhabitant. The name Fishponds seems to have been first used in the early eighteenth century.

FISHPOOL HILL, BS10. This leads to the site of an old farm. Perhaps there were fishpools there.

FITCHETT WALK, BS10. Sir Thomas Fitchett was a local landowner. His son John married Isobell, daughter of Robert Hill. Sir Thomas's arms are on the memorial to Sir Richard Hill in Westbury church. Sir Thomas died in 1396 and his son in 1434. The name is sometimes spelt Fichett.

FITZGERALD ROAD, BS3. The name of the owner of the land, a farmer.

FITZROY ROAD, BS16. This was the first name of Lord Raglan of Somerset, Commander-in-Chief in the Crimean War and blamed by posterity for much of that débâcle. He died of cholera at the Crimea in 1855, and his body was brought to Bristol for burial at the family seat of Badminton. However, a more likely source for the name is from Fitzroy Somerset, the family name of the Dukes of Beaufort.

FITZROY STREET, BS4. Almost certainly named after the Dukes of Beaufort.

FITZROY TERRACE, BS6. As above.

FIVE ACRE DRIVE, BS16. A field name taken from a tithe map.

FLAXMAN CLOSE, BS7. John Flaxman (1755-1826) was a Yorkshire-born draughtsman and sculptor of some eminence, admired at home and abroad, especially in Italy, and was called by Thomas Wedgwood 'A genius of sculpture'. He designed the monument in honour of the boy poet, Thomas Chatterton, in St. Mary Redcliffe church, and a monument to a Mrs Morley in Gloucester Cathedral.

FLORENCE PARK, BS6. Perhaps named after the Italian city.

FLORENCE PLACE BS3 / ROAD, BS16. In both cases thought to be named after the wife of the builder.

FLOWERS HILL / CLOSE, BS4. A farm of this name once stood here. It was demolished to build the Hungerford Community Centre in 1964. Flowers Hill itself is now part of Knowle Golf Course.

FLOWERWELL ROAD, BS13. A field belonging to Down Farm in the Manor of Bedminster shown on the 1798 survey.

FOLLIOT CLOSE, BS16. Someone of this name possessed lands near Frenchay during the reign of Edward V1 in the sixteenth century. A Henry Folliott, possibly an ancestor, was Abbot of Gloucester in the thirteenth century.

FOLLY LANE, BS2. This used to be a very common name for roads, farms and houses, especially for public land held by those paying rent to the king. The derivation is said to come from 'folk land'. This area would have been part of the castle property.

THE FOLLY, BS16. After the Folly brook which runs nearby.

FONTANA CLOSE, BS15. An American influenced name deriving its inspiration from the old California pit. Fontana is a Californian town.

FONTHILL ROAD, BS10. Thought to be named after Fonthill Gifford in Wiltshire. The Gifford family owned large portions of land in this part of the country.

FONTHILL WAY, BS15. Font Hill was an ancient street here.

FONTMELL COURT, BS14. Named after a Dorset village, following the trend set by Sturminster Road.

FONTWELL DRIVE, BS16. A West Sussex racecourse among other roads on the same theme.

FOOTSHILL CLOSE / DRIVE / ROAD, BS15. Presumably descriptive.

FORD STREET, BS5. This could be a place name, after the village in Wiltshire, but it is more likely to be named after a surname of someone connected to the district, possibly James Ford, who was an alderman and prominent public figure. He died in 1889, just prior to the building of this street.

FORDE CLOSE, BS15. A religious theme in naming roads here. Forde Abbey at Forde, near Chard in Somerset, is now a National Trust property.

FORDELL PLACE, BS3. This seems to be a made-up name.

FOREST AVENUE / ROAD / WALK BS16. An obvious choice of name, as this was the entrance to the King's Forest.

FOREST DRIVE BS10. Built in a wooded area.

FOREST EDGE, BS15. Descriptive of the locale.

FOREST ROAD, BS15. Again, a reminder of past times when this was all part of the King's forest.

FORTFIELD ROAD, BS14. Field name from the ME *forthay* - an island of dry ground in marsh land.

FOSSEDALE AVENUE, BS14. An improvisation stemming from New Fosseway Road.

THE FOSSEWAY, BS8. After the Roman road running from Lincoln to Exeter. The derivation is from the Latin *fossa* - a ditch.

FOSTER STREET, BS5. Either named after the builders - there was a Foster family who were well known building contractors at the time - or after the Reverend John Foster (1770-1843), Minister of Stapleton Baptist church and essayist.

FOUNDRY LANE, BS5. Self-explanatory. There were several foundries in the area in the early part of the nineteenth century.

FOUNTAINE COURT, BS5 The Rev. James Fountaine was the chaplain at the Fishponds Asylum from 1850-1921. The Fishponds Asylum was a workhouse. The building, in later years, became known as '100 Fishponds Road' and was used to accommodate elderly people on a short-term or long-term basis. It was demolished for the building of the housing estate.

FOUNTAINS DRIVE, BS15. All roads in this development are named after famous abbeys. The ruins of Fountains Abbey, which was founded in 1132 for the Cistercians by Archbishop Thurston of York, and later dissolved by Henry VIII, are three miles south-west of Ripon in Yorkshire.

FOUR ACRE AVENUE / CRESCENT / ROAD, BS16. Almost certainly built on a field of this name.

FOUR ACRES, / FOUR ACRES CLOSE, BS13. A field name taken from the 1840 Whitchurch tithe map, when Bishopsworth was part of the Earl Temple's estate. The Planning Department attempted to name all the streets in this area after the old sites on which they were built.

FOURTH AVENUE, BS7. Named after a street in New York. There is a definite transatlantic influence in the street namings of this area.

FOURTH WAY, BS11. No explanation for this name, other than it being possibly the fourth street the builder had constructed.

FOX CLOSE, BS4. Named after Samuel Fox, a nineteenth-century landowner.

FOX COURT, BS15. There seems to be a number of roads in this little group with old-time forest connections. Perhaps this was named after John Fox, who is listed as a taxpayer in the Hanham Abbots and Oldland area in medieval times.

FOX HOUSE, BS4. Named after the Fox family, who ran Brislington Asylum for many years. Dr Edward Long Fox first opened his asylum in 1804 specifically for the treatment of mental illnesses, using several private houses which were linked together. In the grounds were cottages for the use of patients of social standing. All the windows had metal frames to minimise the fire risk, an innovation at the time.

FOX ROAD, BS5. From the Old Fox, a pub which was in existence as early as 1752 and is still standing today.

FOXCOMBE ROAD, BS14. Almost certainly an old field name.

FOXCOTE ROAD, BS3. Named after a hamlet in Gloucestershire. It also means 'fox cover', but the connection is not clear.

FOXCOTE, BS15. In the Domesday Book, Foxcote is described as being owned by the See of Worcester, this village of three hides being in the manor of Wattlescomb leased by Morin. A hide was a variable unit of area of land, large enough for a household.

FOXCROFT ROAD, BS5. Named after Captain C.T. Foxcroft, M.P. for Bath and original owner of the land which was sold to Bristol Housing Ltd. In 1927 the land was eventually purchased by the Bristol City Corporation.

FOXGLOVE CLOSE, BS16. Developers used names of wild flowers in this area.

FRALEY ROAD, BS9. Perhaps the name of the builder or landowner.

FRAMPTON CRESCENT, BS16. Many of the roads in this development are named after villages around Bristol.

FRAMPTON COURT, BS15. In the Domesday Book, Frampton was one hide in Greston Hundred, the land belonging to the church of Winchcombe.

FRANCIS PLACE, BS15. There is no obvious reason for this name.

FRANCIS ROAD, BS3. Possibly the owner of the land. There were several people bearing this surname living in the area at the beginning of the twentieth century.

FRANCIS ROAD, BS10. Among other roads which seem to be first names, so perhaps Francis was a relative of the builder.

FRANCOMBE GROVE, BS7. Thomas Francombe was a bell-ringer at Horfield Parish church in 1773.

FRANKLIN COURT, BS1. Another of the roads named after typefaces. Franklin was named after its inventor, Benjamin Franklin, who was sent to London from America in 1724, aged 18, to buy type fonts for the printing business to which he was apprenticed. However his American letters of introduction were lost and he was forced to remain in Islington for two years until he could earn enough to pay his passage home. He became friends with William Caslon and used the Caslon typeface when printing the American Declaration of Human Rights. *See Berlington Court.*

FRANKLYN LANE / STREET, BS2. George Franklyn was a partner in the tobacco firm Franklyn, Davey and Morgan. He was Mayor of Bristol from 1841-2, Master of the Society of Merchant Venturers 1847-48 and President of the Dolphin Society. He died in 1875.

FRASER STREET, BS3. Alfred Capper Pass, son of the founder of the Mill Lane Engineering Company, bought most of Windmill Hill. He built streets of houses for his workers, this being one of them. Fraser was his mother's maiden name and also the name of one of his sons.

FRAYNE ROAD, BS3. After William Frayne, a benefactor who died in 1893 at the age of 73. He was President of the Colston Society in 1873 and gave many monetary gifts to St. Mary Redcliffe church where there is a stone to his memory. In his will he left £2,000 towards the restoration of the tower of St.Thomas's church. He and his brother were in business together in Carlton Place, North Street, Bedminster.

FREDERICK PLACE, BS8. After Frederick Augustus (1763 -1827), Duke of York and Albany. He was the second son of George II and married the eldest daughter of Frederick William of Prussia. His army career was marred by a scandal involving his mistress Mary Ann Clarke and bribery.

FREDERICK STREET, BS3. The inspiration behind this naming is likely to be Vicky (1840-1901) eldest and favourite daughter of Queen Victoria, who became Empress Frederick on marrying the German emperor in 1858. She was a much-loved figure in England where she often came on visits. Her son was the popularly loathed Kaiser Wilhelm who was on the German throne during the period 1914-18 when Germany and England were at war.

FREELAND BUILDINGS, BS5 / PLACE, BS8. Referring to the ownership of the land

FREEMANTLE GARDENS / ROAD, BS5. The street is on the site of part of the extensive Kingswood Forest. At least one authority believes the name is borrowed from the Old French *froid mantel,* meaning cold cloak, and the Swedes have a saying which translates as 'the forest is the poor man's jacket'.

FREESTONE ROAD, BS2. From the building material frequently used in the past for house building and facing. It comes from the Old French *franchpere* meaning a stone of excellent quality.

FREMANTLE LANE / ROAD / SQUARE, BS6. Most of the land in this area was owned by Sir Thomas Francis Fremantle (1798-1890) who was M.P. for Buckingham and Chief Secretary for Ireland from 1845-46. He was married to the daughter of Sir George Nugent, and she was grand daughter to Robert, Earl Nugent, Viscount Clare. The road was built around 1839 on a field containing Mother Pugsley's Well. There was a public outcry as the land had long been used as a children's playing field, but protests were in vain and the development that we see today was started immediately. Captain Pugsley's burial tablet was incorporated into the buildings of Fremantle Road. *See Dove Street, Hillgrove Street, Nine Trees Hill, Nugent Hill.*

FRENCHAY CLOSE / HILL / ROAD / PARK ROAD, BS16. Frenchay has appeared on maps through the ages as Fromshaw (1248) Fromescaw (1257) Framshaw (1397) Franshaw (1608) and Frenchaw (1675). Frenchay Park Road led to Frenchay Park, now the site of Frenchay Hospital.

FRESHLAND WAY, BS5. Mr. T. Humphries, Development Co-Ordinator for Beazer Homes, was asked to supply a name for this cul-de-sac. He says he chose the name because it was a fresh development, and because no other road in Bristol had this name.

FRIARY ROAD, BS7. A reference to St. Bonaventure's Roman Catholic friary which was sited in this road. The school and club still remain, although the entrance is now in Egerton Road.

FRIENDSHIP ROAD, BS4. A public house of this name stands on the corner of the road.

FRIEZEWOOD ROAD, BS3. Derived from OE *fyrs*, furze. Perhaps an old field name.

FRIPP CLOSE, BS5. C. B. Fripp was another of the backers of the Great Western Railway company on its opening in 1833, together with Bright and Maze, after whom other streets in the area were named. *See Freshland Way.*

FROBISHER ROAD, BS3. One of Queen Elizabeth I's 'seadogs', Sir Martin Frobisher(1535-94) was the first Englishman to attempt to find a North West Passage through Canada to China, sailing from Bristol harbour. He tried for fifteen years but was unsuccessful, although he named the Frobisher Strait where he discovered iron ore. In 1585 he sailed with Sir Francis Drake to the West Indies, and in 1588 distinguished himself against the Spanish Armada. He died at Plymouth of wounds he received when on an expedition to relieve Brest against the Spanish.

FROG LANE, BS1. A reminder of far-off days before development began. There was also a Cow Lane which was under the present Park Street viaduct.

FROGMORE STREET, BS1. From the OE *mere* meaning pool. Apparently frogs abounded here in the distant past.

FROME PLACE, BS16 / STREET, BS2 / TERRACE, BS16. All lie beside the river of this name.

FROME VALLEY ROAD, BS16. Built in the valley of the Frome.

FROMESIDE PARK, BS16. Self-explanatory.

FROOMSHAW ROAD, BS16. One of the ancient names for Frenchay. Shaw means a wood, therefore 'a wood near the River Froom', which underwent several spellings.

FRY'S CLOSE, BS16. Perhaps a tribute to Joseph Storrs Fry who lived at Frenchay. He owned Frenchay Grove and 35 acres of land around it. It may be, however, named after Zephaniah Fry who, it is noted in the Kingswood enclosure awards of 1779-84, owned land in Frenchay and Stapleton.

FRYS HILL, BS4. : This originates from William Fry, first owner of The Grove.

FULFORD ROAD / BS13 / WALK, BS3. An old name for the area.

FURBER COURT / ROAD / RIDGE / VALE, BS5. Robert Furber was a Wesleyan Methodist who built Bryants Hill church. Furber Road was formerly known as Grouty's Lane.

FURNWOOD, BS5. Seemingly a made-up name.

FURZE ROAD, BS16. The name was chosen because it runs off Gorse Hill. *See Thicket Road.*

FURZEWOOD ROAD, BS15. Descriptive of how the area used to look.

FUSSELL COURT, BS15. Abraham Fussell was a Warmley man who made a fortune in the boot trade with his revolutionary methods of manufacture. He donated a great deal of money towards the building of the Congregational chapel in Hanham Lane. *See Fairview Road.*

FYLTON CROFT, BS14. This is the old spelling of Filton. There was a link-up between Fylton and Filton, as they were both within the King's Forest. Aircraft are another connection: Filton has always been recognised as the aircraft construction area of Bristol, while the city's first airport was at Whitchurch, near the old Fylton site. This was later superseded by the one at Lulsgate.

G

GABLE ROAD, BS5. A reference to the style of the houses.

GADSHILL ROAD, BS5. As this street was completed soon after the death of Charles Dickens it may well be an allusion to his home, Gad's Hill House in Kent.

GAGES CLOSE / ROAD, BS15. They were both old streets dating back to 1841. There may be a connection with John Gage and his involvement in the Bristol Riots. *See Codrington Place.*

GAINSBOROUGH SQUARE, BS7. Thomas Gainsborough (1727-88) was one of England's greatest landscape and portrait painters.

GALWAY ROAD, BS4. Amidst many other roads named after places in Ireland. *See Bantry Road.*

GANDER CLOSE, BS13. Field name from OE *gandra*, 'gander' or 'goose'. Perhaps a poultry farm was here in days gone by.

GARDEN CLOSE, BS9. Built in the grounds of Sea Mills Farm - the kitchen garden perhaps?

THE GARDENS, BS16. Market gardens covered these slopes before the houses were built.

GARDNER AVENUE, BS13. Apparently this was the surname of the man who owned the land upon which this road was built.

GARFIELD ROAD, BS5. No obvious reason for this choice of name unless it was the surname of the developer.

GARNET STREET, BS3. Many of the local roads are called after gemstones. *See Beryl Road.*

GARNETT PLACE, BS16. Seemingly a surname but it is not known who is being honoured. Perhaps a parish councillor?

GARTH ROAD, BS3. Named after Garth Kew, the builder's son.

GAS LANE, BS2. Site of the old gas works.

GASFERRY ROAD, BS1. This led to the ferry which carried workers over the harbour to the gasworks on the north side.

THE GASKINS, BS7. The name appears on an old Horfield tithe map. The word is actually an abbreviation of 'galligaskins', a sixteenth century word for wide hose or breeches. Perhaps this refers to the shape of the field.

THE GASTONS, BS11. Field name from the Anglo-Saxon *gærs-tun*, a grass enclosure or enclosed yard for the rearing of cattle.

GATCOMBE ROAD, BS13. Thomas de Gatcombe held land in the Hartcliffe Hundred in 1321.

GATEHOUSE AVENUE / CLOSE, BS13. Gatehouse Lees was a field name at Bishopsworth, Earl Temple's estate.

GATHORNE ROAD, BS3. Second forename of a member of the Hill family prominent in south Bristol in the nineteenth century. One was MP for Bristol South. Another theory is that is was an old field name meaning 'gap on a projecting piece of land'.

GATTON ROAD, BS2. This is a place in Surrey, the meaning being 'place where goats are kept'.

GAUNT'S LANE, BS1. Gaunt's Hospital once stood here. Maurice de Gaunt, grandson of the 1st Earl of Berkeley, founded it. He married Alice de Gaunt and took her name.

GAY ELMS ROAD, BS13. A field name on Crox Bottom Farm. This was one of the farms purchased from the Ashton Court Estate in 1928-9 when the estates of Knowle and Bedminster were extended. Gay is from the (Old) French *gai* - brightly coloured.

GAYNER ROAD, BS7. The Gayner family once lived at Church Farm.

GAYS ROAD, BS15. The Gay family were horse dealers in the St. George area.

GEE MOORS, BS15. This was an old manor owned by the Weston family. In 1238 one of the Westons was Mayor of Bristol.

GELFE CLOSE, BS1. Named after Gelfe Wharf, which was itself named after the Swedish port. Cargoes of timber were sent from Bristol to Sweden.

GEOFFREY CLOSE, BS13. Geoffrey, Bishop of Coutances in Normandy, is believed to have been the Bishop in Bishopsworth. He owned much land in this area following the Norman Conquest, including the Manor of Bishport. He was the interpreter at Williams coronation and took part in the baronial rising against William Rufus, holding Bristol Castle. Known as 'the fighting bishop' he held the post of constable of Bristol Castle. It was said he was a man of wonderful talents and great bravery but proved himself more fitted for the army than the church. He died on 2 February 1093.

GEORGE AND DRAGON LANE, BS5. Name taken from a nearby public house.

GEORGE STREET, BS5. The name of one of the Gerrish family. *See Gerrish Avenue.*

GEORGE WHITEFIELD COURT, BS1. After the preacher who did so much good work among the Kingswood colliers and who was responsible for the building of the Tabernacle there.

GERALD ROAD, BS3. This may have been a member of the Smyth family.

GERRISH AVENUE, BS5. The Gerrish family owned a great deal of property in the St. George area. George and Elizabeth Gerrish lived in Cambridge House which later became 91 Gilbert Road. It was their grandson who lived at Belle Vue, which was demolished in 1925.

GERRISH AVENUE, BS16. Built on the site of Albinis Gerrish's market garden.

GIBBSFOLD ROAD, BS13. Gibbs Fold was a tenement or holding listed in the Dundry Enclosure Award of 1815. 'Fold' is from OE *fald*, enclosure.

GIBSON ROAD, BS6. Derived from Gibson's Court at the back of Sydenham Road. Gibson was probably the owner of the land as there were a number of

Gibsons living in this area just prior to the construction of the road. A Thomas Gibson resided in Cotham Road and was a member of the City Council from 1870 until his death in 1885.

GIFFORD ROAD, BS10. Godfrey Gifford (1235-1302), Bishop of Worcester, founded the College of Westbury for secular priests in what was originally a monastery in 1290. He was politically motivated, negotiating with Llewelyn, Prince of Wales, in 1272 and the Scots in 1289. He was in constant dispute with his Chapter at Worcester; he was, however, a considerable benefactor to the Cathedral.

GILBERT ROAD, BS15. Gilbert de Clare, Earl of Gloucester, held the honour of Frankpledge in the early thirteenth century in Oldland and Upton. From the 15th century onwards rural communities were often administratively divided into thithings, or groups of ten households. Each household in a thithing was bound to the other by frankpledge, by which all members were answerable for the good conduct of, or any damage done by, each other.

GILBERT ROAD, BS5. This could well have been another member of the Gerrish family. *See Gerrish Avenue.*

GILDA CLOSE / CRESCENT / PARADE, BS14. Named after Gilda, wife of the Swiss millionaire Leonard Nidditch who designed the area as a private garden estate built around a village green. Tenants for this estate were carefully vetted. Streets were named after his family or towns with his family's connections. The estate, once called Gildaville, was taken over by the council during the war and a POW camp was built on the village green. It was planned that Gilda Parade would have its own cinema and restaurant but this never came to fruition. *See Valentine Close and Chessington Avenue.*

GILL AVENUE, BS16. Alderman Charles Richard Gill (1870-1956) was a member of the Housing Committee from 1922 to 1956 and Chairman for nineteen years. He was Lord Mayor 1947-8 and a J.P. He was an outstanding civic figure and miners' leader.

GILLARD CLOSE / ROAD, BS5. A man called Gillard in the 1930s purchased the land on which this road was built. He experienced a great deal of difficulty gaining permission to develop the site.

GILLEBANK CLOSE, BS14. Probably an old field name; the name suggests a slope covered in fragrant flowers. Gillyflower is an old name for stocks or wallflowers.

GILLINGHAM HILL, BS5. In the 1960s Lionel Gillingham was listed as living in Dundridge Lane, probably where these houses were developed, so presumably he owned the land.

GILLRAY CLOSE, BS7. James Gilray (or Gillray) was a political caricaturist noted for his savage and coarse portrayals of contemporary high life. He became an imbecile in 1811.

GILPIN CLOSE, BS15. The Gilpin brothers were leather factors and importers in Kingswood in the 1930s.

GILROY CLOSE, BS15. Californian town. *See California Road.*

GILSLAKE AVENUE, BS10. This was a farm in the Hundred of Henbury. In 1777 it was recorded as Jills Lake.

GILTON HOUSE, BS3. This was a field name taken from the Brislington tithe map.

GINGELL'S GREEN, BS5. Built in 1968 and named after George Gingell, a straw and hay dealer who was born in the 1880s who traded from this site, which was then known as Gingell 's Barton. Three generations of the Gingell family later traded as butchers in Lawrence Hill, from 1915 to the 1980s. The shop was run by three generations of the family between 1915 and the 1980s.

THE GLADES, BS5. Clearly descriptive.

GLADSTONE DRIVE, BS15 / ROAD, BS14, BS16 / STREET, BS3, BS5. All named in honour of William Ewart Gladstone (1809-98). He served four separate terms as Prime Minister and was, in addition, a classical scholar of some eminence who wrote much on religious topics.

GLAISDALE ROAD, BS16. A place in Yorkshire. The name means 'valley of the River Glas'. There are other local roads with British place names.

GLANVILLE GARDENS, BS16. After Rev John Glanville, whose efforts resulted in the building of the Whitefield Tabernacle.

GLASS HOUSE LANE, BS2. Self-explanatory.

GLASTONBURY CLOSE, BS15. All the roads in this group are named after abbeys.

GLEBE ROAD, BS5. This road was developed on glebe land belonging to the nearby church of St. George. A glebe is quoted as being a portion of land assigned to a parson as part of his benefice.

GLEBELANDS ROAD, BS12. The glebe lands covered a large area and were rented out to various people in the eighteenth century.

GLEN DRIVE, BS9 / LANE, BS4 / PARK and PARK GARDENS BS5. Descriptive, of the valley around which these roads were built.

THE GLEN BS6, BS15. Another descriptive name.

GLENA AVENUE, BS4. The name of an Irish lake. Many Irish places names are used here. *See Bantry Road.*

GLENARM ROAD / WALK, BS4 Village in Northern Ireland. There is no obvious reason for this choice.

GLENAVON PARK, BS9. Derived from *glen*, valley and Avon, the nearby river.

GLENBURN ROAD, BS5. Amidst a section of roads incorporating the word Glen.

GLENCOYNE SQUARE, BS10. The name of both a park and a bay in the Lake District, near Ullswater.

GLENDALE BS8, BS16 (2). A popular name for any low-lying street.

GLENDARE STREET, BS5. Glendare was the name of the house in St. Michaels Hill which was the residence of Miss Herapath, daughter of the eminent forensic scientist. The family owned land in Barton Hill sold by Miss Herapath when development of the area began in the 1860s. *See Herapath Street.*

GLENDEVON ROAD, BS14. Seems to be a made-up name.

Gloucester Road, Bishopston in the days of the trolley buses in the early twentieth century

GLENEAGLES DRIVE, BS11. Named after a famous golf course.

GLENEAGLES ROAD, BS15. Amidst a collection of roads called after golf courses.

GLENFROME ROAD, BS5. This was known as Wee Lane until the houses began to spring up in the 1920s/30s. The road is in the glen by the Frome.

GLENROY AVENUE, BS5. Among a host of streets with the first syllable 'glen'.

GLENSIDE CLOSE, BS16. Descriptive of location.

GLENSIDE PARK, BS16. Among other rustic names.

GLENTWORTH ROAD, BS8, BS6. Viscount Glentworth, son and heir of the 2nd Earl of Limerick, was Major Commandant of the 1st Gloucestershire Artillery Corps stationed in Whiteladies Road. He died in 1896 at the age of 56.

GLENVIEW ROAD, BS4. Near Glen Lane.

GLENWOOD DRIVE, BS15. It is low-lying and comparatively wooded here.

GLENWOOD ROAD, BS10. Probably once a field as it lies among others similarly named.

GLENWOOD, BS16. Following on the Thicket theme of surrounding roads.

GLOSTER AVENUE, BS5. A popular shortening for Gloucester, and Gloster Avenue is also short. Possibly named after the regiment.

GLOUCESTER LANE, BS2. The reason for this naming is unknown.

GLOUCESTER ROAD / ROAD NORTH, BS7. Sections of the A38, which runs to Gloucester.

GLOUCESTER STREET, BS2, BS5, BS8. A number of streets bear this name, probably because a large percentage of Bristol was formerly included in the county of Gloucestershire at one time.

GLYN VALE, BS3. A John Glyn owned lands in the seventeenth century, which eventually came to be included in the Smyth estate.

GODFREY COURT, BS15. Perhaps named after Bishop Godfrey, the first Constable of Bristol Castle and nephew of William I, for whom he held the wardship of Kingswood Forest (for his uncle William I).

GOFFENTON DRIVE, BS16. Roger de Goffenton (sometimes written Gossington), was granted lands for guarding the King's forest in 1287.

GOLDNEY AVENUE / ROAD, BS8. The Goldney family lived here, in a house which is still standing and famed for its eighteenth century orangery, beautiful gardens and extraordinary underground fountain and grotto, built by William Goldney and decorated by a statue of Neptune and thousands of polished shells. Now a hall of Residence for students of the University of Bristol, the Goldney gardens and grotto can be visited on certain Open Days.

GOLDSBURY WALK, BS11. Field name. An encampment where gold was found.

GOLF COURSE LANE, BS10. Self-explanatory.

GOOD SHEPHERD CLOSE, BS7. The name of a nearby church.

GOODEVE PARK / ROAD, BS9. Captain Goodeve built a fine mansion adjoining Cook's Folly in the 1850s and was a well-known medical practitioner. He had the unusual forename of 'Hurry', His face was badly scarred through an injury he received while hunting tigers in India.

GOODHIND STREET, BS5. It has been said the land on which this street was built was owned by the Whitchurch family of this name but in 1849 Samuel Goodhind, an attorney of Small Street died and one of his descendants claims the street was named after him, being built in the same year. He lived at Penstone Lodge, Stapleton Road, and owned an estate in the area.

GOODNESTON ROAD, BS16. A village in Kent. The name means Godwin's village, town or farmstead. No apparent reason for this choice.

GOODRING HILL, BS11. The reason for this naming is unknown.

GOODWIN DRIVE, BS14. This may be a surname belonging to someone connected with Court Farm, which once stood nearby.

GOODWOOD GARDENS, BS16. Amongst other roads named after racecourses.

GOOLDEN STREET, BS3. The man who gave the land on which Holy Nativity church was built was thought to be Daniel Haythorn Goolden, a solicitor of Small Street Court, in the middle of the nineteenth century.

GOOSELAND CLOSE, BS14. An old field name.

GORDON AVENUE / CLOSE / ROAD, BS5. All these roads were named for 'Chinese Gordon', Charles George Gordon (1833-85), who fought in the Crimea War, the Chinese War and in the Sudan. He was killed in 1885, by which time he held the rank Major General. Gordon Road was once known as Johnny Crow's Lane.

GORDON ROAD, BS8 Named in honour of the Duke of Richmond and Gordon.

GORE ROAD / GORE'S MARSH, BS3. There are two speculations as to the origin of this name: it could either derive from the Anglo Saxon *gor* meaning 'dirt', 'filth' or 'muddy stream' or the Celtic *grywe*, marsh. 'Gore' later came to mean a triangular piece of ploughed land. There was, too, at one time a coalmine owner in Ashton called Gore and it has been suggested he was the owner of this land. The family was related by marriage to the Smyths of Ashton Court.

GORHAM CLOSE, BS11. There were two rocks in the Avon Gorge known as Goram's Chair or the Giant's Chair; folk legend has it that Goram and his brother Vincent set out to create the Gorge. Goram partook rather too liberally of the wine and nodded off leaving Vincent to do the job on his own. In completing the task he won the hand of the lovely Avona. Some say Goram was so brokenhearted that he threw himself into the Bristol Channel where his head and shoulders still protrude in the shape of Steepholm and Flatholm. It is said a giant footprint can be found in Blaise Wood where the trench he was building peters out.

GORLANGTON CLOSE, BS14. Edward Gore-Langton was an important landowner in the area.

GORSE HILL / LANE, BS5. Built on land formerly known as The Thicket. *See Thicket Road.*

GOSFORTH ROAD, BS10. Continuing the theme of Lake District names in this area.

GOSLET ROAD, BS10. Named after Edward Goslet, Overseer at Keynsham Workhouse in 1674.

GOTLEY ROAD, BS4. After Gotley Lodge, which is still standing. The road was built on the site of Woodbine Farm, demolished in 1938.

GOTT DRIVE, BS4. From Gotley Lodge.

GOULSTON ROAD, BS13. Goulston was churchwarden in Bedminster and gave the bell to Bishopsworth church (St Peter's) built in 1843.

GOULTER STREET, BS5. A. W. W. Goulter, a Land Surveyor, made an offer for an area known as the Turkey Field. The road that bears his name covers part of the field.

GOURNEY CLOSE, BS11. Robert de Gourney succeeded Maurice de Gaunt in 1222 as Lord of the Manor of Redwick in the Hundred of Henbury. The Gourneys (or Gurneys) wielded a great deal of influence in the West Country in medieval times and gave their name to such places as Gurney Slade, Barrow Gurney and Farrington Gurney. Gournay is a place in Normandy. The family appears to have died out in the sixteenth century. There is an effigy of Robert de Gournay in the Lord Mayor's Chapel in Lower Park Street.

GRACE COURT, BS16. After the legendary cricketer Dr. W.G. Grace.

GRACE DRIVE, BS15. Named after Dr Henry Grace, brother of the famous cricketer W.G.Grace. The nameplate on the house reads: "Were loved by the sick poor they served." The street was named in the later 1950's.

GRACE PARK ROAD, BS4. Built on a former cricket ground so the famous cricketing name of Grace seemed an obvious choice.

GRACE ROAD, BS16. Again, after Dr. W. G. Grace, whose family home was nearby.

GRAEME CLOSE, BS16. The Graeme family owned and lived in Oldbury Court from the mid-eighteenth century to the early part of the nineteenth prior to the occupation of the Vassall family.

GRAHAM ROAD, BS3. Major Oliver Graham owned this land on which W.J. Kingston built these houses.

GRAHAM ROAD, BS5. The most likely person inspiring this choice is Robert George Graham, J.P., member of the Lawford's Gate Highway District Board.

GRAHAM ROAD, BS16. This may be named after Sir Gerald Graham (1831-99), a Lieutenant General who fought in the Sudan.

GRAINGER COURT, BS11. A number of people in the locality bear this name.

GRAMPIAN CLOSE, BS15. The theme in this area is hill and mountain ranges.

GRANBY HILL, BS8. John Manners, Marquis of Granby, was a frequent visitor to the area when it was at the height of its popularity. He was also a subscriber to Dowry Chapel.

GRANGE AVENUE / COURT, BS15. Charles Bragge owned the original house of this name. The next owner, Samuel Whittucks, demolished it.

GRANGE CLOSE NORTH / GRANGE COURT ROAD, BS9. A Grange Dairy and a Court Farm existed here at the end of the nineteenth century.

GRANGE DRIVE / PARK, BS16. This is a small cul-de-sac built in the 1950s on what was part of the grounds of Fromeshawe House. There seems to be no special reason for the naming.

THE GRANGE, BS11. This may be named after a house owned by the Cave family which stood on this land.

GRANGEVILLE CLOSE, BS15. Town in California. *See California Road.*

GRANGEWOOD CLOSE, BS16. Near Grange Drive.

GRANNY'S LANE, BS15. An old name but no one seems to remember who Granny was.

GRANTHAM LANE / ROAD, BS15. Perhaps called after the town in Lincolnshire although there is a possibility it was the surname of the landowner.

GRANSTON CLOSE, BS4. Welsh place name, which may have held some meaning for the developer.

GRANVILLE CLOSE, BS15. Sir Beville Granville was killed at the Battle of Lansdown, near Bath, in 1643.

GRANVILLE STREET, BS5. Perhaps as Close BS15.

GRASMERE CLOSE, BS10. Another Lake District name amongst any number on that theme in this area.

GRASS MEERS DRIVE, BS14. A field name from the 1840 tithe map. Mary Colston owned this land then.

GRASSMERE GARDENS, BS15 Among other roads called after locations in the Lake District although this is a mis-spelling for Grasmere.

GRATITUDE ROAD, BS5. It has been said that this road was named by the builder, who was grateful for the opportunities he had been given in life!

GRAVENEY CLOSE, BS4. It seemed appropriate to name this road in honour of Tom Graveney OBE, a former England cricketer and Gloucestershire captain, as a cricket ground once stood here.

GRAY'S CLOSE, BS10. There is a Harford family connection here. John Scandrett, who lived in the late eighteenth century, married Mary, the daughter of Abraham Gray. The Harfords owned Blaise Castle.

GRAYLE ROAD, BS10. Mary Grayle was a resident of Westbury Parish in 1600.

GRAYLING HOUSE, BS9. The original landscaping included a fountain and a pool, in which grayling, a species of fish, may be presumed to have lived.

GREAT ANN STREET, BS2. Named after Queen Anne, this area was once one of the roughest in the city, many residents living in appaling conditions. The worst slums were cleared in the 1930s.

GREAT BROCKERIDGE, BS9. Apparently an old field name.

GREAT DOWLES, BS15. A field name.

GREAT GEORGE STREET, BS1. This street was named after George III, who reigned from 1760-1818. He was a popular monarch in spite of his temporary derangement during the years 1788-1804. He was also a pioneer of sea-bathing.

GREAT HAYLES ROAD, BS14. This road takes its name from one of the ancient boundaries creating Bristol as a county by charter of Edward III in 1373.

GREAT LEAZE, BS15. This is an old field name.

GREAT WESTERN LANE, BS5. Here stood the Great Western Cotton Factory, which provided work for so many of the Barton Hill folk. Many of the employees were brought in from the north of England including the Manager, whose daughter, Eva Turner, was a well-known opera singer. An underground school for the children of the employees ran the length of the building.

GREAT WESTERN WAY, BS1. The original western terminus of the Great Western Railway from London to Bristol was built on the southern edge of this site, and the original passenger terminus survives as the Commonwealth Exhibition Centre. The area to the north of the passenger station was the Goods Station, and was extensively rebuilt in the 1920s into what was the largest covered goods yard in Europe - and probably, the world. *See Brunel Way.*

GREEN CLOSE, BS7. An old field name.

GREEN CROFT, BS5. Undoubtedly a field name as it leads off Meadow Vale.

GREEN LANE, BS11. A reminder of how it once looked.

GREEN SIDE, BS16. Emphasising the rural aspect of the surrounding area.

GREEN STREET, BS3. This is most likely to be the builder's name.

THE GREEN, BS15. There was a field near here called Green's Moor so this name probably derives from that.

GREEN WALK, BS4. Off Greenwood Road.

GREENACRE ROAD, BS14. Off Longacre Road so presumably these were fields on a long vanished farm estate.

GREENACRES, BS9. Without doubt a field name.

GREENBANK AVENUE / ROAD / VIEW, BS5. Derivation is OE *grene* meaning 'grassy spot', 'village green'. The building of Greenhaven altered the road line of Greenbank Avenue and some houses were lost. Greenbank Avenue is now two separate roads - East and West.

GREENBANK ROAD, BS15. It may be assumed this is descriptive.

GREENDALE ROAD, BS3. Probably an apt description when this road was built at the beginning of the twentieth century.

GREENDALE ROAD, BS6. Probably a made-up name. It was built on a field where blackberries grew.

GREENDITCH AVENUE, BS13. A tenement or holding referred to in the Dundry Enclosure Award 1815. From OE *grene* meaning 'grassy spot' and *dic*, a dike or ditch.

GREENDOWN, BS5. Most probably descriptive of what was wasteland leading to the quarry.

GREENFIELD AVENUE / ROAD, BS10. Self-explanatory.

GREENFINCH LODGE, BS16. Birds' names have been used throughout this development.

GREENHAVEN, BS5. A made-up name evoking a peaceful place in Greenbank for senior citizens. A Ward Councillor suggested the name.

GREENHILL GROVE / LANE, BS3. This was the name of the builder responsible for these houses.

GREENLANDS WAY, BS10. Evoking past scenes, this road runs parallel to Meadowland Road.

GREENLEAZE AVENUE / CLOSE, BS16. Almost certainly an old field name.

GREENLEAZE, BS4. A simple name meaning green fields.

GREENMORE ROAD, BS4. A made-up name from the surnames of the building partnership that built the road - Green and More.

GREENORE, BS15. Named, for some reason unknown, after an Irish seaport.

GREENPARK ROAD, BS10. A made-up name.

GREENRIDGE CLOSE, BS13. A field name.

GREENSIDE CLOSE, BS10. Illuminating the rural aspects of the area.

GREENVIEW, BS15. Seemingly descriptive.

GREENWAY BUSH LANE, BS3. A popular road name. There is a hamlet so called in Gloucestershire. Derivation obvious.

GREENWAY DRIVE / PARK, BS10. Pointing up the rural aspect.

GREENWAY ROAD, BS6. Possibly named after Francis Greenway (1777-1837), the Clifton architect who was to become the greatest influence on Australian architecture. In his mid-thirties he was found guilty of forging a financial document and was sentenced to death. This was commuted to 14 years deportation. He arrived in Sydney as a "gentleman convict" in 1814 and impressed Governor McQuarie, who allowed him to set up an architectural practice. He was granted a full pardon and went on to design some of Sydney's most famous buildings.

THE GREENWAY, BS16. Part of the area once called The Thicket. *See Thicket Road.*

GREENWAYS, BS15. Among a group of rural names,

GREENWOOD CLOSE, BS10. A reference to the surrounding countryside.

GREENWOOD ROAD, BS4. In honour of the Rt. Hon. Arthur Greenwood, M.P., Minister of Health under the Labour government of 1929-31. He initiated the Housing Act of 1930 that dealt with slum clearance and came to be known as the Greenwood Act.

GREGORY COURT, BS15. There was a forester of this name in the seventeenth century whose walk was from Siston Common to Mangotsfield mill; or was this named after J. Gregory, owner of an iron foundry in the district in the 1890s?

GRENVILLE CLOSE, BS4 Perhaps after George Grenville, Prime Minister in 1763.

GRENVILLE PLACE, BS8. William Wyndham Grenville, 1st Baron Grenville (1759-1834) was Lord High Steward of Bristol from 1810 to 1834. He was a respected statesman, acting as Speaker of the House of Commons in 1789 and Foreign Secretary in 1791-1801. He was a cousin of William Pitt.

GRENVILLE ROAD, BS6. It has been suggested that this road owes its name to Sir Richard Grenville, subject of Tennyson's poem 'The Revenge'. He was an Elizabethan sailor who was killed when his ship fought alone against a Spanish fleet in the Azores in 1591.

GREVE COURT, BS15. Built on a former orchard, this is probably named after a variety of cooking apple, James Grieve, although mis-spelt.

GREVILLE ROAD / STREET, BS3. Named after Sir J. H. Greville Smyth, whose family owned the land on which these roads were built.

GREYLANDS ROAD, BS7. Self-explanatory.

GREYSTOKE AVENUE / GARDENS, BS10. Named after a location in the Lake District because of its proximity to Henleaze Lake.

GREYSTONES, BS16. This is near the old Quaker burial ground so perhaps that is the reason for this choice of name.

GRIGGFIELD WALK, BS14. Thomas Grigg was a significant landowner in this area.

GRIMSBURY ROAD, BS15. Called after an old house of this name belonging to the Weston family.

GRINDELL ROAD, BS5. The name of the family who owned the field on which these houses were built between the wars. They were well-known horse dealers.

GRINFIELD AVENUE / CLOSE / COURT, BS13. The Grinfield family settled in Bedminster during the reign of Edward I, according to a flat stone monument in St. John's church, Bedminster, since demolished.

GRITTLETON ROAD, BS7. A village in Wiltshire. It has been suggested Grittle is from the Old English *grect-hline*, 'gravel hill'. Place names are frequently given to roads in this district.

GROSVENOR ROAD, BS2. This is the family name of the Dukes of Westminster. It seems the family may have had long-standing interests in Bristol.

GROVE AVENUE / ROAD, BS9. There was a house here called The Grove, home to the Tothill family. William Tothill was M.P. for Bristol in 1848-52.

GROVE AVENUE / THE GROVE, BS1. Prior to the building of Queen Square there was a grove of trees here that was a popular walk in what was then called the Town Marsh.

GROVE BANK, BS16. This road was part of the development built on the grounds of Riverwood House and refers to the property's earlier name. *See Riverwood Road.*

GROVE LEAZE, BS9. An old field name.

GROVE PARK AVENUE / PARK ROAD / PARK, BS4. So named because of nearby Grove House.

GROVE PARK, BS6. Descriptive. It led to Lovers' Walk.

GROVE AVENUE / ROAD / PARK / TERRACE, BS16. This road was built on a field known as Grove Close. This was owned by Archibald Drummond, M.D. who lived at Ridgeway House (previously known as Rudgway House).

GROVE ROAD, BS6. Near Elm Lane.

THE GROVE, BS15. This would have been near Earlstone House so probably there was a grove in the grounds.

GROVE VIEW, BS16. The view commanded here is that of the tall trees of Snuff Mills.

GUERNSEY AVENUE, BS4. Following the local trend for Channel Island names.

GUILDFORD ROAD, BS4. All the roads nearby are called after cathedral cities.

GUINEA LANE, BS16. There was a Guinea Lane here as long ago as 1779, when it was mentioned in the Kingswood Enclosure Award. This was a short word for guinea fowl so perhaps they were kept here. The birds were first imported from China in the seventeenth century.

GUINEA STREET, BS1. This is thought to have slavery connections, as Guinea in Africa was a target for the slave traders.

GULLIMORE GARDENS, BS13. Probably a field name; 'gully' derives from the French *goulet*, 'gullet' and describes a drain; and more from OE *mor*, 'moor' or 'marsh'.

GULLON WALK, BS13. Gullons was the name of a field on Bishopsworth farm shown on the 1802 survey. It is thought to be a personal name.

GULLONS CLOSE, BS13. This is the oldest recorded name of the site.

GULLYBROOK LANE, BS5. A field name taken from the St. George tithe map.

GUNTER'S HILL, BS15. Several families bearing this name lived in the area over the years.

GUTHRIE ROAD, BS8. Named after the great benefactor of Clifton College, Canon John Guthrie, who was, by all accounts, a handsome and popular man.

GWILLIAM STREET, BS3. These roads were built by the son of the founder of the Capper Pass works and related to a family member.

GWYN STREET, BS2. Again, probably the name of the developer or owner of the site. There was, at the time the street was built, a Mr Humphrey Gwyn, Chairman of the Bristol and District Land Company who may have been responsible for the construction.

HADLEY COURT, BS15. Amongst other roads called after golf courses.

HADRIAN CLOSE, BS11. Celebrating the area's Roman connections, this road was named after the famous Emperor who built the wall between Newcastle and Bowness-on-Solway. He lived 76-138 AD.

HAIG CLOSE, BS9. Named in honour of Field-Marshal Earl Haig, a member of the famous whisky family and ex-pupil of Clifton College. These houses were built at a public cost of £500,000 for the purpose of providing accommodation at reasonable rents for disabled veterans of the First World War. Many of these re-homed veterans were survivors among the slaughtered thousands who died at the 1916 Battle of the Somme and successive indecisive battles of 1917, for which Haig has since been held largely responsible.

HALBROW CRESCENT, BS16. Daniel Halbrow resided in the area in the eighteenth century.

HALDON CLOSE, BS3. Among other roads nearby called after places in Devon.

HALFACRE CLOSE / LANE, BS14. An old field name.

HALL STREET, BS3. The island was once part of the grounds of a mansion called Percy Hall. *See Percy Street.*

HALLARDS CLOSE, BS11. A field name, Hallard probably being a personal name.

HALLEN COURT / DRIVE / ROAD BS9/ BS10. All pertain to the village of this name.

HALLS ROAD, BS15. This may have been named after Robert Halls, a Baptist preacher.

HALSBURY ROAD, BS6. Called after Hardinge Stanley Giffard, 1st Earl of Halsbury, who visited Bristol in 1892. As well as serving three terms as Lord Chancellor, he was an authority in jurisprudence and edited *The Encyclopedia of the Laws of England* when already over eighty. Perhaps his most famous case was his defence of Arthur Orton, the Tichborne claimant. This was a sensational affair. In 1854 Roger Charles Tichborne, heir to a Hampshire baronetcy, disappeared on a trip to Valparaiso in Chile. 11 years later a man purporting to be him left Wagga Wagga in Australia where he had been living under the name Tom Castro, and sailed for England. He arrived on Christmas Day 1866 and convinced many people, including Roger's mother, that he was the missing heir. He was finally unmasked as an impostor, tried for perjury and sentenced to fourteen years' hard labour. What became of the real Roger Tichborne was never known.

HALSTOCK AVENUE, BS16. A village in Somerset. One authority gives the meaning as 'holy place'. No obvious reason for this choice of name.

HALSTON DRIVE, BS2. Named after a nineteenth-century parochial benefactor.

HALSWELL GARDENS, BS13. Thomas Halswell inherited the Manor of Ashton from his father Hugh and sold it in 1600 to Sir Hugh Smyth of Ashton Court.

HALWYN CLOSE, BS9. Near Newlyn Walk, so given the name of a Cornish village.

HAM LANE, BS16. From the OE *ham* meaning homestead.

HAMBROOK LANE, BS16. Leading to the village of this name.

HAMMERSMITH ROAD, BS5. A district of London. Near Sloan (sic) Street so perhaps the builder had London connections.

HAMILTON ROAD, BS5/ BS3. In both cases there were a number of people living in the area at the time the houses were built, so landowners seem to be the most probable origin of the namings.

HAMMOND CLOSE, BS4. One suggestion is that this road is named after the cricketer Greg Hammond, while others suggest Walter Hammond (1903-65), the great batsman and captain of England and Gloucestershire.

HAMMOND GARDENS, BS9. Named after a village in Somerset.

HAMPDEN ROAD, BS4. A village in Buckinghamshire, birthplace of John Hampden (1594-1643), who led the protest against King Charles I's demand for ship money - a tax levied on British ports to maintain the fleet, and obviously most unpopular in Bristol. Hampden was tried before the Court of Exchequer and judgement was given against him, but the sympathy of the country - and of Bristol - was with him, and in 1640 the Long Parliament reversed the judgement. When the Civil War broke out three years later Hampden raised troops against the King, and he was killed in a skirmish at Chalgrove Field in 1643.

HAMPSTEAD ROAD, BS4. Suburb of London. The name means manor or homestead.

HAMPTON CLOSE, BS15. The Hampton family were owners of Barrs Court.

HAMPTON CORNER, BS11. Perhaps derived from the name Shirehampton.

HAMPTON LANE / PARK / ROAD, BS6. Possibly named after a Wiltshire village on land held by Earl Roger of Hereford.

HAMPTON STREET, BS15. Possibly after the Hamptons of Barr Court.

HANBURY CLOSE, BS15. St. Werburgh (d. 700) was a princess of Kent who decided to become a nun at an early age, her mother being Saint Ermenhild and her father, Wulfhere, the newly converted Christian prince of Mercia. She became Abbess of Minster-in-Thanet, then of Ely, and was later asked to take charge of the convents in Weedon (Northamptonshire), Hanbury (Staffordshire) and Threckingham (Lincolnshire). She was a very popular saint in the Middle Ages, famously banishing geese for good from Weedon, where they had been damaging crops. Her venerated relics rested at Hanbury until 875 AD, when they were moved to Chester to protect them against marauding Danes. Hanbury Close is named in her honour. *See Trentham Close and Weedon Close.*

HANBURY ROAD, BS8. This road was built c. 1860 on a field owned by the Society of Merchant Venturers known as Road Close. It may have been called after Hanbury Villa which stood in Whiteladies Road, or else after the village in Worcestershire or the town in Staffordshire. The name means 'high fort'.

HANDEL AVENUE, BS5. In honour of Handel Cossham, M.P. for Bristol East.

HANDFORD WAY, BS15. The Handford Device was an instrument used on California Speedway car racing at Fontana, California. This is part of the California Road development with its associated American namings.

HANFORD COURT, BS14. This follows the tradition of local streets being named after Dorset towns and villages.

HANHAM ROAD, BS15. One source gives the derivation of Hanham as meaning 'the home of Haneca'. More probable is that the road is named after the old Bristol family of Hanham who once owned this land.

HANOVER COURT / PLACE / STREET, BS1. Named after the House of Hanover which ruled Britain for 100 years. The street was completed in 1716 and was named in honour of George I.

HANOVER STREET, BS5. as above.

HARBOUR WALL / WAY, BS9. Descriptive.

HARBURY ROAD, BS9. A village in Warwickshire. The first syllable means hoary or grey. It could also be from Hereburgh, a woman's name of the Saxon period.

HARCOURT AVENUE / HILL / ROAD, BS6. The origin here would seem to have been Sir William Vernon Harcourt (1827-1904} the eminent Liberal M.P for Oxford in 1868. He was also Chancellor of the Exchequer from 1892-95, and leader of the House of Commons in 1894. Sir William was considered to be one of the finest orators in the House.

HARDEN ROAD, BS14. Mrs Harden, a widow, lived in Brislington in 1670 and was exempted from paying Hearth Tax.

HARDENHUISH ROAD, BS4. A village in Wiltshire, birthplace of the Rev. Francis Kilvert (1840-79). He was a village curate in Clyro, Wales, and Langley Burrell in Wiltshire. He kept an astounding series of diaries, hailed as 'the finest in the English language, after Pepys' describing the lives of all strata of society that he encountered in his parishes, but with particular reference to his affection for young girls. Most of his diaries were destroyed by relatives after his death, but the three that survived caused a sensation upon publication in 1939.

HARDWICK CLOSE, BS4. There was a Hardwicke family which once farmed in the Brislington area, and may well have owned the land on which these houses were built.

HARDWICK CLOSE, BS15. The Hardwicke family owned a farm at nearby Lees Lane.

HARDY AVENUE, BS3. It seems probable that this avenue was named in honour of Thomas Hardy, the great nineteenth-century poet and novelist, who died in 1928. These houses were built two years later.

HARDY CLOSE, BS15. Among a complex of roads named after poets and writers. Thomas Hardy (1840-1928) is one of England's greatest novelists, and his works, among which the most famous are probably *Tess of the D'Urbervilles*, *Far from the Madding Crowd* and *Jude the Obscure*, were influenced by Greek tragedy and set in Wessex in south-west England, centring on Dorset. Hardy was also a fine poet.

HARDY ROAD, BS3. Nearby roads are called Nelson and Trafalgar, leading to the supposition that the Hardy in question here is Vice-Admiral Sir Thomas Masterman Hardy, Bart (1769-1839), Flag-Captain on the 'Victory', Nelson's flagship at the battle of Trafalgar in 1805.

HARECLIVE ROAD, BS13. This was the Saxon name for Hartcliffe. *Hare* meant army in OE, and *clive* is a steep rugged rock or cliff. Many battles were believed to have been once fought in this area.

HAREFIELD CLOSE, BS15. There was once a Harefield Hall at Warmley.

HAREWOOD ROAD, BS5. After Henry Charles George Lascelles, Earl of Harewood (1880-1947). He married Mary, the Princess Royal, daughter of George V.

HARFORD COURT, BS9. Named, as the Frenchay road, after the Harford family who were bankers and ironfounders. One branch of the family owned the Blaise estate.

HARFORD DRIVE, BS16. *See Harford Court.*

HARLECH WAY, BS15. Among a group of roads named after castles.

HARLESTON STREET, BS5. A village in Suffolk. The first component is a personal name.

HARMER CLOSE, BS10. John Harmer was a merchant who owned Pen Park Villa, one mile north of Westbury. He married Anne, only daughter and heiress of William Jefferies in 1752. The joint names appear on a shield in Westbury church.

HARNHILL CLOSE, BS13. A field name which could be from the OE *haeren*, 'the rocky hill' or perhaps from the Anglo-Saxon *Har*, hoary, grey or hare's hill. Harnhill was a village in the Garsdon Hundred.

HAROLDS WAY, BS15. Named after the local Hanham councillor to Kingswood, Harold Mealing, who was a milkman in the area for many years. He was nicknamed The Midnight Milkman, as his deliveries were so early that they took place late at night. The road was named for him on his retirement.

HARPTREE COURT, BS15. Sir John Newton of Barrs Court, BS15, had the Harptree quarterings incorporated into his coat of arms.

HARPTREE GROVE, BS3. From the twin villages East and West Harptree in Somerset. The first syllable is derived from the OE *hearpe*, harp. The names of many other Somerset villages are used for local roads.

HARRINGTON AVENUE / GROVE / ROAD / WALK, BS14. John Harrington was one of the officials responsible for granting exemption from the Hearth Tax in 1670 and 1674 in the Hundred of Keynsham.

HARRIS COURT, BS15. Possibly named after Benjamin Harris, a local boot manufacturer.

HARROW ROAD, BS4. One of several roads in the area named after public schools.

HARROWDENE ROAD, BS4. a made-up name. The inappropriate last syllable is from the OE *denu*, valley.

HARTCLIFFE ROAD / WALK / WAY, BS13. The estate was built on land that was once part of the Hundred of Hartcliffe (or Hareclive) and Bedminster. The district was originally to have been called Dundry Slopes.

HARTFIELD AVENUE, BS6. Named after a village in Sussex, but the reason for this is unknown.

HARTGILL CLOSE, BS13. William Hartgill was one of the commissioners appointed by Edward VI in the second year of his reign to survey all the churches and charities in this part of Somerset, including Bedminster.

HARTINGTON PARK, BS6. Another street name pertaining to the peerage, the Marquis of Hartington being the title of the eldest son of the Duke of Devonshire. The Eighth Duke (Spencer Compton Cavendish1833-1908) founded the Liberal Unionist party. He was Secretary of State for Ireland from 1870-74 and bitterly opposed Gladstone's policy of Home Rule for Ireland.

HARVEY'S LANE, BS5. Clearly an old name denoting that this was the path to Harvey's dwelling.

HASKINS COURT, BS15. Named after Haskins Pottery, a significant production company in the area.

HASSELL DRIVE, BS5. Thomas Hassell was Mayor of Bristol in 1824.

HASTINGS CLOSE / DRIVE, BS3. Among other roads called after English towns.

HATHERLEY ROAD, BS7. Named after William Page Wood, Baron Hatherley (1801-81). He was a trustee of the Bishop Monk's Horfield Trust. The name derives from the OE for hawthorn wood, or else 'pasture by or on the heather'.

HATHWAY WALK, BS5. After William Hathway, who was Mayor in 1872. He died in 1895 aged 87.

THE HAVEN, BS15. It was built in the early 1960s and was given this name because it was exactly that: a group of specially-built bungalows, being a haven for elderly persons.

HAVERSTOCK ROAD, BS3. A suburb of London. The name derives from the OE *stoc* meaning place or secondary settlement, or *stoec*, which is a log, or tree trunk.

HAWBURN CLOSE, BS4. This road was built where Hemplow House stood until 1969, so perhaps there was a hawthorn hedge by a stream in the grounds.

HAWESWATER BS10 / HAWESWATER CLOSE, BS15. In both cases other roads in the vicinity are called after locations in the Lake District.

HAWKESBURY ROAD, BS16. There is a Gloucestershire village named Hawkesbury Upton. A lofty monument stands there dedicated to Lord Robert Edward Henry Somerset (1776-1842), a distinguished general who fought in the Peninsular Wars and was present at the Battle of Waterloo. The word Hawkesbury is derived from the OE personal name, *Hafoc*, Hawk and OE *burh*, a fortification or encampment.

HAWKFIELD CLOSE / ROAD / WAY, BS13. The area was known locally as Hawkfield Meadow and there was once a hamlet of that name.

HAWKINS CLOSE, BS15. Many local roads have been named after former residents. Perhaps this honours Alfred Samuel Hawkins, owner of Church Farm in the 1930s.

HAWKINS STREET, BS2. Named after Sir John Hawkins, who owned a brewery here in the seventeenth century. The brewery is supposed to have supplied the ale for the royal party when Queen Anne visited the city. Sir John Hawkins also served a term as Mayor of Bristol.

HAWKSMOOR CLOSE, BS14. Almost certainly an old field name.

HAWKSWORTH DRIVE, BS15. Another road named after an important Great Western railway engineer, Frederick Hawksworth, who was born in 1875 in Swindon. He designed the elegant 'county class' locomotive in 1947, which had great strength on curves and steeply inclined track. After the nationalisation of the railways in 1949 Hawksworth had to resign from the post of Chief Mechanical

Engineer, which had served the GWR for over a century, as the work became spread over different departments. The last locomotives rolled out of Swindon just over a decade later, the end of the great steam era. *See Collett Close.*

HAWLYN CLOSE, BS11. This would appear to be a made-up name.

HAWTHORN AVENUE, BS15. Among other nearby roads with sylvan connotations.

HAWTHORN CLOSE, BS12. Again, a woodland theme.

HAWTHORNE GARDENS / THE HAWTHORNES, BS16. Possibly named after a house which stood here.

HAWTHORNE STREET, BS3. The American novelist Nathaniel Hawthorne (1804-64) had ancestral connections with the West Country, which he mentions in *The Scarlet Letter* and other works. His ancestors are buried in Dundry church.

HAYCOMBE, BS14. Possibly an old field name.

HAYCROFT ROAD, BS12. The name originated as a field on Meadowsweet Farm. Later a house called Haycroft was built on the land.

HAYDOCK CLOSE, BS16. All roads in this development called after famous race courses.

HAYDON GARDENS, BS7. Plymouth-born Benjamin Robert Haydon (1786-1846) was a talented painter of biblical subjects, and was also well known for his autobiography and diary. His life was a long struggle against debt - he was imprisoned four times - and family misfortune, as five of his children died. He lived, according to his biographers, on the verge of insanity, but had an unshakeable self confidence - some called it egotism - which caused him to quarrel with all of his patrons. He committed suicide in 1846.

HAYES CLOSE, BS5. C.A. Hayes was Lord Mayor of Bristol, 1909-11.

HAYLEIGH HOUSE, BS13. Probably taken from an old field name.

THE HAYMARKET / HAYMARKET WALK, BS1. The hay market was established here in 1786. It was the venue for the annual St. James Fair, but the resultant public disorder and other scandals caused the fairs to be banned in 1837. When the land was developed as a shopping centre in the 1950s the excavations revealed the Haymarket having been built over part of the burial ground for St. James' Priory on College Green.

HAYNES LANE, BS16. Named after the family who owned Pendennis Farm, which stood in the lane.

HAYTHORN COURT, BS16. This was the surname of one of the owners of Hill House, upon the site of which Haythorn Court was built.

HAYTOR PARK, BS9. From the Devon hamlet of the same name. The OE derivation is 'ivy-clad rock or hill'. There was a farm of that name here, before development took place.

HAYWARD ROAD, BS5. There is some dispute about the origin of this street name. Either it is named after Rowland Hayward, who owned the Manor of Hanham, which included this area in the sixteenth century, or, as mentioned in Saniger's *Leaves from a Barton Hill Notebook*, the Barton Regis Hundred which included this district was divided into tithings, each of which had its own Hayward and Road Surveyor. A hayward was one who had responsibility for ensuring that the fences and enclosures erected to prevent cattle straying were secure.

HAYWARD ROAD, BS16. The Grange Manor was granted to Rowland Hayward in 1553.

HAZEL AVENUE, BS6. Perhaps nut trees did grow here when the scene was more rural.

HAZEL GROVE, BS7. Again, possibly descriptive.

HAZELBURY DRIVE BS15. Probably derived from an old field name.

HAZELBURY ROAD, BS14. Thought to be a made-up name.

HAZELCOTE ROAD, BS14. Almost certainly a field name.

HAZELDENE ROAD, BS12. This is thought to be a made-up name.

HAZELTON ROAD, BS7. This road was built upon land belonging to the long since demolished Hazelton Farm.

HAZELWOOD COURT / ROAD, BS9. From the mansion of that name upon whose grounds this road was developed.

HEADFORD AVENUE, BS5. People of this name owned a boot factory in St. Paul's before the First World War, so there might there be a connection.

HEADFORD ROAD, BS4. This may be the surname of someone connected with the construction of the road.

HEADLEY LANE / ROAD / WALK / PARK AVENUE / ROAD, BS13. A field name. *See Districts section in the introduction.*

HEART MEERS, BS14. A field here of this name is shown on the 1840 tithe map.

HEATH COURT / GARDENS/ WALK, BS16. The word heath figures largely in local nomenclature and is descriptive of the scrubland characteristic of this area before development took place.

HEATH ROAD / STREET, BS5. Both refer to the proximity of Heath House. It was the Dower House of the Smyth family of Ashton Court.

HEATH ROAD / RISE, BS15. As with Mangotsfield, descriptive of the terrain before development.

HEATHCOTE ROAD / WALK, BS16 / DRIVE, BS 17. These would appear to be field names.

HEATHER CLOSE, BS5. Self-explanatory.

HEATHERDENE, BS14. This appears to be a field name.

HEATHFIELD CRESCENT, BS14. Most probably named after the Somerset village.

HEBER STREET, BS5. Cheshire-born Reginald Heber (1783-1826), Bishop of Calcutta, was a deacon at twenty-nine and created bishop at thirty-nine. His greatest achievement was the establishment of Bishop's College in Calcutta. He wrote several hymns, the most well-known today being probably 'From Greenland's Icy Mountains" as well as sermons and poems, but apart from a general popularity his connection with Bristol is not clear.

HEBRON ROAD, BS3. Named after the Hebron Methodist Chapel which was built in 1854 at a cost of £6,000. The name was often used for Nonconformist places of worship. Hebron is today a West-bank town on the borders of Jordan and Israel, now riven with dissent and warfare but one of the oldest cities in the world and the burial place of Abraham, his wife and their two sons and daughters-in-law.

HEDGEMEAD CLOSE / VIEW, BS16. Built in 1968, these roads owe their name to the owner and developer of the site, Mr Frederick Hedges of Winterbourne.

HEDWICK AVENUE / STREET, BS5. Probably a made-up name.

HEGGARD CLOSE, BS13. A field name in the Manor of Bishport shown on the 1683 survey. Probably from the OE *heg* meaning hay and *geard* meaning enclosure or yard.

HELLIER WALK, BS13. Named after Henry Hellier (1662 -97) Doctor of Divinity and Fellow of Corpus Christi College, Oxford. He was born at Dundry and achieved prominence by preaching a sermon in Oxford in 1697 accusing James II of breaking his Coronation Oath. He committed suicide later that year.

HEMMINGS PARADE, BS5. John Hemmings owned this land and sold it in 1868 to the Primitive Methodists for the construction of the Hebron Chapel.

HEMPLOW CLOSE, BS4. Hemplow House was a large and ancient house that once stood in Brislington. It was demolished in 1969.

HENACRE ROAD, BS11. A field name. The river Hen runs through the area.

HENBURY GARDENS / HILL / ROAD, BS9, BS10. Henbury means 'high or chief fortification'. This could have been a reference to the ancient encampment on Castle Hill near Blaise Castle.

HENBURY ROAD, BS15. Built on what was known as The Patch, but it is not known why the name Henbury was chosen.

HENCLIFFE ROAD, BS14. Field name from OE *henn*, hen or water hen and *clif,* cliff or bank. There was a Hencliff Wood in the Hanham area.

HENCLIFFE WAY, BS15. *See Hencliffe Road.*

HENDERSON ROAD, BS15. After Dr W.D. Henderson, a physician and surgeon, who had a practice in the area in the late eighteenth and early nineteenth century.

HENDRE ROAD, BS3. A village near Bridgend in Wales, but there is no obvious connection with this road.

HENFIELD CRESCENT, BS15. This road was most probably built on a field that belonged to a poultry farm.

HENGASTON STREET, BS3. Possibly a field name. The derivation is from the OE *henges* meaning horse, although one authority suggests that it may derive from the personal name Hengest or Horsa, often found in Somerset, a reminder of the Danish influence dating from 449. One authority interprets the meaning as a grass enclosure.

HENGROVE AVENUE / LANE / ROAD / WAY, BS4 / BS14. From Hengrove House which once stood here. *See Districts section in the introduction.*

HENLEAZE AVENUE / GARDENS / PARK / DRIVE / ROAD / TERRACE, BS9. From Henleaze House described as being 'pleasantly situated on the summit of extensive park like grounds, well stocked with timber trees and embosomed in neat shrubbery'. One theory was that Henleaze was a corruption of Henleys, a once-prominent family in the area.

HENLEY GROVE, BS9. The Henley family lived at Henley Grove Villa, demolished long ago. Robert Henley was a parliamentary candidate for Bristol in 1679, in the place of Sir Robert Cann, who had been expelled from the House of Commons in 1680 for expressing disbelief in the Popish Plot. Robert Henley petitioned unsuccessfully against the return of the successful member of parliament, Sir Robert Cann, and had to forfeit his seat. He died in 1719 aged 38.

HENNESSY CLOSE, BS14. Alderman Walter Hennessy died in 1965 after many years as a councillor. A one-minute silence was observed at the planning meeting following his death as a mark of respect, as is the custom when aldermen die.

HENRIETTA STREET, BS2/ BS5. There are various theories regarding the origin of these street names. One is that the name was chosen in honour of Henrietta Maria, wife of Charles 1, another that the honour goes to Henrietta Howard, mistress of George II, or even called after the London street named after Henrietta Cavendish, daughter of John Holles, Duke of Newcastle. It could equally well have been called after someone connected with the land on which the houses were built. A closer Bristol connection is that 'Henrietta Maria' was also the name of a ship financed by the Merchant Venturers' Society, captained by Thomas James, who was trying to establish a trade route through the North West Passage. Also involved in this venture was a Captain Foxe. In the case of the Easton street this might be the most likely connection as there is a Fox Road a few hundred yards away.

HENRY STREET, BS3. Built by W.H. Green. Henry was his second name.

HENRY WILLIAMSON COURT, BS15. Among a host of roads called after twentieth-century writers. Henry Williamson (1895-1977) is best known for his nature writings, such as *Tarka the Otter* and *Salar the Salmon*, which chronicle the wildlife year centring on the Taw and Torridge rivers in North Devon.

HENSHAW CLOSE / ROAD / WALK, BS16. Possibly named after John Henshaw, who was secretary of the Kingswood and Parkfield Collieries.

HENSMAN'S HILL, BS8. Named after the Rev. John Hensman (1780-1864), curate in charge of the Dowry Chapel from 1810 and vicar of Clifton from 1847 to 1864. He was a very popular clergyman. A Chapel of Ease was erected in Victoria Square to his memory.

HEPBURN ROAD, BS2. Another nineteenth century Brigstocke family connection. Emily Brigstocke, the youngest of the three Brigstocke sisters, married Henry Poole Hepburn, a colonel in the Scottish Fusiliers. *See Brigstocke Road.*

HERALD CLOSE, BS9. Earl Herald held leased land from Bishop Laud in this hundred at the time of the Domesday Book. Laud Close is nearby.

HERAPATH STREET, BS5. William Herapath (1796-1868)was the owner of this land in Barton Hill. His father owned the Packhorse Inn where William was born. He was a skillful analytical chemist, and as such one of the first forensic scientists, his reputation being made when he gave evidence for the prosecution during the 1835 trial of Mary Ann Burdoch, who was eventually convicted of poisoning her wealthy lodger, Mrs Smith, after the dead woman's relatives became suspicious and had her body disinterred. Mary Ann Burdoch was publicly hanged at the old gaol in Cumberland Road. Herapath was once a political radical, and after the passing of Bristol's Municipal Reform Act after the 1831 riots he became a member of the town council. However, his radicalism cooled and he lost his place on the new town council, subsequently becoming a J.P. Herapath was also one of the founders of the Bristol Medical School. His eldest son, William Bird Herapath, was also a distinguished toxicologist, but died in the same year as his father.

HERBERT CRESCENT, BS5. Thought to be the name of the builder.

HERBERT STREET, BS5. Named after one of the numerous members of the Gerrish family, who owned a great deal of property in this area. *See Gerrish Avenue.*

HERBERT STREET, BS3. Probably Sidney Herbert (1810-61), 1st Baron Herbert of Lea, a member of the family of the Earls of Pembroke who have had associations with this city for many years, serving as Lord Lieutenants and Stewards.

HEREFORD ROAD, BS2. Named after the cathedral city of Hereford in the Welsh marches. The meaning is 'a ford where a marching column could pass'. A number of streets in the area are called after nearby towns.

HEREFORD STREET, BS3. As above. The Bishop of Hereford once held land in the Bristol area.

HERKOMER CLOSE, BS7. Sir Hubert von Herkomer (1849-1914) was born in Bavaria but came to England in 1857 and became a naturalised Englishman. He was a popular portrait and subject painter, famous for works such as 'Chelsea Pensioners', 'Tennyson', and 'Herbert Spencer'. He was knighted in 1907. This is another in the British artists series.

HERMITAGE CLOSE, BS11. From the house of that name. A Mrs Wright was the occupant in 1899.

HERMITAGE ROAD, BS16. After a house that once stood here, described by the Rev. Emlyn Jones in his *History of Mangotsfield* as being 'the prettiest homestead in the Parish'. One occupant was a Mr Lanaway, after whom a road in Downend is named, followed by a Mr Vining in 1870. In 1882 a Mr Ronayne was living there and the house was demolished before 1905.

HERON ROAD, BS5. Either arbitrarily named after the bird, or possibly after Caroline Heron, who lived in the area in 1872. However, her connection with this road is unknown.

HERRIDGE CLOSE / ROAD. BS13. Herridge Farm appears on the Dundry Enclosure Award of 1815. The name is derived from OE *haeg*, enclosure, or fenced-in part of a forest.

HERSEY GARDENS, BS13. Hersey was a tenant of Sir John Smyth, according to the survey of the Manor of Bishport of 1683.

HESDING CLOSE, BS15. Earnhulf de Hesding held Hanham at the time of the Norman Conquest in 1066.

HESTERCOMBE ROAD, BS13. This may be a field name, with the first component being a personal name.

HEYFORD AVENUE, BS5. A place name in Oxfordshire. It means 'ford used at the time of the hay harvest'. The Cottrell-Dormer family, who owned the land upon which Heyford Avenue was built, had family connections with Heyford in Oxfordshire.

HEYRON WALK, BS13. Adam de Heyron owned a great deal of land in the Long Ashton area during the reign of Henry I.

HICKS COURT, BS15. There was an Ernest Hicks, insurance agent, living in Watsons Road in the 1920s. Many of these recently-named local roads are named after previous inhabitants.

HIGH ELM, BS15. Thought to be a field name.

HIGH GROVE, BS9. This road is built on high ground and is a splendid example of well-designed early council houses built in the 1920s. All too soon, resources were cut and economies were made in style, space and materials.

HIGH PARK, BS14. Descriptive.

Bristol High Street, looking towards Wine Street, with Sir Samuel Morley's statue in the foreground

HIGH STREET, various. In all cases 'high' refers to the local importance of the street, rather than its geographical location.

HIGHAM STREET, BS3. A Kentish place name. Translates from the OE as 'high homestead'.

HIGHBURY ROAD, BS3 / BS7. A place name that translates as 'fortified place on a hill'.

HIGHBURY VILLAS, BS2. Named after Highbury Chapel and Highbury House nearby. The ecclesiastical architect William Butterfield, whose other work included Horfield Parish church and Coalpit Heath church, designed Highbury Chapel.

HIGHCROFT, BS15. Probably after an old field name.

HIGHDALE CLOSE, BS14. An odd choice of name as it seems to be a contradiction in terms. no obvious reason for this naming.

HIGHETT DRIVE, BS5. Named in honour of Charles Highett, Mayor of Bristol in 1891.

HIGHFIELD AVENUE / GARDENS, BS15. Highfield was an estate here in the reign of Henry VIII.

HIGHFIELD GROVE, BS7. This appears to be a made-up name.

HIGHGROVE STREET, BS3. Named after the house of that name in Wells Road, Knowle.

HIGHLAND CRESCENT / SQUARE, BS8. One source cites Chilcott's map of 1853 on which 'Island Place' is shown in this vicinity, Highland being perhaps a corruption of this. Another authority suggests that the naming was influenced by the many Scotsmen who came to the area seeking work at the quarry.

HIGHLEAZE ROAD, BS15. Probably a field name.

HIGHMEAD GARDENS, BS13. A field name from the Manor of Bishport, in the survey of 1683. It means 'high meadow'.

HIGHMORE COURT / GARDENS, BS7. Named after Joseph Highmore, a portrait and subject painter who lived from 1692-1780. His work was generally rapidly executed at one sitting, achieving good likenesses but sacrificing some elegance and style. It is similar in style to that of Hogarth.

HIGHRIDGE CRESCENT / GREEN / PARK / ROAD / WALK, BS3/ BS13. Named for their geographic features.

HIGHVIEW ROAD, BS15. Descriptive.

HIGHWOOD LANE / ROAD, BS12. Descriptive.

HIGHWORTH ROAD, BS4. A village in Wiltshire. One source suggests that the last syllable is from the OE *worp* that originally meant enclosure but later came to mean 'open place in the village'. Another suggests *wyrth*, an estate or manor, usually well watered.

HILHOUSE, BS11. George Hilhouse owned a large amount of land in the area in the early nineteenth century.

HILL AVENUE / STREET, (2) BS3 / BURN, BS9 / CREST, BS4 / END DRIVE / GROVE, BS9, STREET, BS5 / BS1 / BS15 / VIEW CLOSE, BS15 / VIEW ROAD, BS13 / VIEW, BS12 / BS8 / BS16 / BS9. In all cases appropriately named by location. Hill End House once stood on the site of Hill End Grove BS9.

HILL HOUSE ROAD, BS16. Named after the imposing house of that name which was home to many prominent people including Alderman Page, who donated some land to the council in order that a park might be built for the local people. The last private owners were the Punters, organ makers, who occupied the house until the late 1970s.

HILL LAWN, BS4. This takes its name from Charles Hill, the Bristol merchant who lived at Wick House from c.1792 until his death in 1836. It is also shown as a field name on the 1846 tithe map.

HILLBURN ROAD, BS5. Possibly descriptive of the former landscape. It leads into Hillside Road.

HILLFIELDS AVENUE, BS16. This was the land owned by the Duke of Beaufort and called The Thicket. It was developed in the 1920s as a leafy estate. *See Thicket Road.*

HILLGROVE STREET, BS2. The last syllable indicates the original appearance of the land upon which this very steep street was built. Nearby Nine Tree Hill seems to bear out the picture of wooded slopes. *See Dove Street.*

HILLSBOROUGH ROAD, BS4. Given the proximity of Arno's Vale Castle, this may have been named after the castle of this name in Northern Ireland owned by the Marquises of Downshire.

HILLSBOROUGH, BS8. Perhaps the landowner had Yorkshire connections, as this is a village not far from Sheffield.

HILLSDON ROAD, BS9. A made-up name, although someone connected with this development may have been called Hill, as there were people of that name living in the area, both landowners and builders.

HILLSIDE AVENUE, BS15. Descriptive.

HILLSIDE ROAD, BS5. Formerly known as Cuckoo Lane before the houses were built here.

HILLSIDE, BS8 / BS16 / BS6. Self-explanatory.

HILLSIDE STREET, BS4. There was a house here of that name before development took place.

HILLTOP GARDENS / ROAD, BS16. Descriptive of the site.

HILLTOP GARDENS / VIEW, BS5. Certainly an apt name.

HILLYFIELD ROAD, BS13. A field name. There were numerous fields in the area incorporating the word Hill, such as Hill Piece, Hilly Close.

HILTON COURT, BS5. Many Bristol Mayors are celebrated in roads in the area. This is named in honour of John Hilton, whose term of office was from 1524-25.

HINTON DRIVE, BS15. There was a Hinton Green farm at Oldland. Hinton was originally a field on the Barrs Court Estate.

HINTON ROAD (2), BS5/ BS16. Common place name. There are two alternatives as to its derivation, both OE, *hea-tun*, 'situated on high ground' and *higna-tun* - the monks' or nuns' homestead. Bristol Corporation owned the manor of Hinton.

HOBB'S LANE, BS1. Possibly named after Thomas Hobbs, a victualler who traded on the Quay in the eighteenth century.

HOBHOUSE CLOSE, BS9. Charles Hobhouse was MP for Bristol East in 1900.

HOCKEY'S LANE, BS16. Perhaps the landowner. A number of people bearing this surname were listed in local directories from 1850-1903.

HOGARTH WALK, BS7. William Hogarth (1697-1764) was a painter, engraver and perhaps England's most famous social satirist, probably best known for paintings such as 'The Rake's Progress', and 'Marriage à la Mode'.

HOGUES WALK, BS13. Hogues Road was a private road listed in the 1815 Dundry Enclosure Award. It perhaps led to the dwelling of a person of that name.

HOLBEACH WAY, BS14. Edith, the daughter of one of the Lyons family of Lyons Court, which once stood nearby, married a man called Holbeach.

HOLBROOK CRESCENT, BS13. Holbrook's was a tenement or holding mentioned in the Dundry Enclosure Award 1815.

HOLCOMBE, BS14. A small town near Shepton Mallet where the main industry is quarrying. Perhaps a one-time landowner also had estates in Somerset.

HOLDENHURST ROAD, BS16. A village in Dorset; the name translates as 'holly wood'.

HOLFORD COURT, BS14. A Somerset town. Other such West Country place names have been used in this section.

HOLLAND STREET, BS2. Tradition has it that the Dutch basket weavers lived and worked here many years ago, so perhaps that is the reason for the naming of this street.

HOLLIDGE GARDENS, BS13. James Hollidge was Sherrif of Bristol in 1699, Mayor of Bristol in 1708-09, Chamberlain in 1710-39 and Master of the Society of Merchant Venturers.

HOLLISTER'S DRIVE, BS13. This was a tenement or holding mentioned in the Dundry Enclosure Act of 1815.

HOLLOW ROAD, BS15. Descriptive naming.

HOLLWAY CLOSE / ROAD, BS14. Ann Hollway lived in the tithing of Chewton in the parish of Keynsham in 1670. Although she had two chimneys in her house she was exempt from Hearth Tax.

HOLLY CLOSE, BS5. Near Holly Lodge Road.

HOLLY CRESCENT / HOLLY HILL ROAD, BS15. Possibly evoking the landscape as it once was.

HOLLY GROVE, BS16. Continuing the thicket theme here. *See Thicket Road.*

HOLLY LODGE ROAD, BS5. A house of this name once stood here, home to the Ballard family.

HOLLYBUSH LANE, BS9. Describes the locale.

HOLLYGUEST ROAD, BS15. An old field name. This used to be known as Dodd's Lane.

HOLLYLEIGH AVENUE, BS12. A field name translating as 'meadow where the holly grows'. This was built on land belonging to Church Farm.

HOLLYMEAD LANE, BS9. Near Hollybush Lane, so possibly this was a feature of the terrain.

HOLLYRIDGE, BS14. Thought to be a field name.

HOLLYWOOD ROAD, BS4. Possibly a corruption of holy wood, a place of pilgrimage in the past for the hordes of people, including royalty, who came to nearby St. Anne's Well to benefit from the curative powers of its waters. St. Anne's Well still exists, but it is in a bad state of repair due to vandalism. However, on the 1841 census this road is marked as King's Arms Lane. It was called Grove Road until 1929, when it became Hollywood Road, so the link may also be due to the new fashion for American talking pictures which was sweeping the country by the end of the twenties.

HOLMDALE ROAD, BS12. This would appear to be a made-up name.

HOLMES GROVE, BS9. Possibly named after Sir Robert Holmes (1622-92), the seventeenth-century naval commander of semi-piratical British squadrons. He fought against the Dutch under Prince Rupert of the Rhine, captured New York, reduced the Dutch settlements in Africa and burned Dutch shipping off the coast of the Netherlands.

HOLMES HILL ROAD, BS5. One theory is that the street is named after George Holmes and that his family lived here. Marcus, another member of the family, was a local artist who exhibited during the 1830s. His work can be seen in the Bristol Art Gallery. He married the daughter of Parson Emra of St. George. However 'The Holmes' was an old name for this part of St. George, appearing on the 1610 map as 'The Holims'. The name means 'low pasture near water'.

HOLMES STREET, BS5. Almost certainly this was named in honour of a member of the Holmes family, most probably Marcus. *See Holmes Hill Road.*

HOLMESDALE ROAD, BS3. A made-up name, perhaps from the surname of someone connected with the development or the site.

HOLMWOOD, BS15. A forest-influenced naming.

HOLSON CLOSE / ROAD, BS14. Richard Holson was resident in Keynsham in 1674. He was exempt from paying Hearth Tax and had one chimney in his house.

HOLST GARDENS, BS4. All the roads in the area are named after British composers. Gustav Holst (1874-1934) who was born in Cheltenham of German parents, is probably most famous for his orchestral suite 'The Planets'.

HOLTON ROAD, BS7. Named after a village in Somerset, deriving its name from the OE *hol*, hollow or *holt* meaning wood or thicket or spur of land.

HOLY WELL CLOSE, BS4. Near to the location of the famous St. Anne's well.

HOME CLOSE, BS10. An old field name.

HOME GROUND, BS9. A field name shown on the 1825 survey of Westbury-on-Trym.

HOMEFIELD DRIVE, BS16. An existing building, which was converted and integrated into this development, was known as Homefield.

HOMELEAZE ROAD, BS10. A field name.

HOME MEAD, BS14. The name is taken from the 1843 Bedminster tithe map. Creswicke Road covers the ground today.

HOMEMEAD DRIVE, BS4. The name of a field taken from the 1846 tithe map. Later it was the sports ground for Robertson's jam factory. The road was named by the Brislington Conservation and Amenity Society.

HOMESTEAD GARDENS, BS16. A cosy name, probably given by the developer.

HOMESTEAD ROAD, BS12. After a house called 'The Homestead' which was used as a branch of Lloyds Bank before its final demolition. It is now inside the B.Ae. security area.

HONEY GARSTON CLOSE / ROAD, BS13. A field name from the OE *hunig*, sweet or honey, and *gaers-tun*, a paddock or grass enclosure.

HONEY HILL ROAD, BS15. This was the ancient name for this hill, which was once covered with primulas, wild hyacinth and wood anemones, so the OE *hunig* would have been appropriate for this sweet-smelling place.

HONEY WAY, BS15. *See Honey Hill Road.*

HONEYMEAD, BS14. This would seem to be an old field name. There was a Honey Splott field on the land belonging to Brook Farm.

HONEYSUCKLE LANE, BS16. The theme chosen for this development was wild flowers.

HONITON ROAD, BS16. Named after Honiton in South Devon.

HOOPER ROAD, BS14. James Hooper resided in the tithing and parish of Keynsham in 1670. He had two chimneys but was exempt from Hearth Tax.

HOPE COURT / ROAD / SQUARE, BS8. Named after Lady Henrietta Hope who, together with Viscountess Glenarchy, provided funds for the building of the chapel.

HOPE CHAPEL HILL, BS8 *See above.*

HOPETOUN ROAD, BS2. Named after John Henry Louis Hope (1860-1908), 7th Earl of Hopetoun, first Governor General of Australia.

HOPEWELL GARDENS, BS11. A field name from the Anglo-Saxon *hop* meaning an enclosed plot in marshland, a small enclosed valley and well- spring.

HOPKINS COURT, BS6. John Hopkins was Mayor of Bristol in 1600.

HOPLAND CLOSE, BS15. Following an American theme for local street namings, this is a town in California. *See California Road.*

The wide expanse of the Horsefair in the early twentieth century.

HOPP'S ROAD, BS15. Clearly a personal name, but there seems no record of this inhabitant's identity.

HORESHAM GROVE, BS13. An ancient cross known as Horesham Cross once stood on Horesham Green near the intersection of roads leading from Bedminster to Long Ashton, Pill and Portbury.

HORFIELD ROAD, BS2. The way to Horfield. The view has been expressed that the name is derived from Horu, a Saxon chief who fought the Romano-Britons, the thinking being that he owned this land (i.e.Horu's field}, but history does not bear this out as the area was called Langelei in the 1000s and later Harfelle, Horefelle and Horsfield.

HORLEY ROAD, BS2. A place name, the meaning being 'tongue of land formed by two streams'.

THE HORNBEAMS, BS16. Among other local roads called after trees.

HORSECROFT GARDENS, BS15. The name of a field on the estate of Barrs Court.

THE HORSEFAIR, BS1. Descriptive of its past use. In later years it was the site of a fairground, but the crowds became too riotous to control and the practice ceased. The area was completely rebuilt after the Second World War, when the new Broadmead shopping centre was built in the 1950s.

HORSEPOOL ROAD, BS13. 'The Horsepools' was a field name from the 1683 survey of Bishport Manor. The first syllable could actually mean horse, but the OE *horsc*, foul or dirty - is also evocative.

HORSESHOE DRIVE, BS11. Overlooks the horseshoe bend in the river Avon.

HORWOOD COURT, BS15. Possibly named after the Horwoods of Pucklechurch, who ran a farm in the area in the 1890s.

HOSEY WALK, BS13. Hosey's Tyning was a field name in Bishopsworth (Earl Temple's estate) It probably derived from a personal name.

HOST STREET, BS1. Varying interpretations have been put forward as to the origin of this name, as it has also been referred to in the past as Horse Street and Hore Street. The name Hore could derive from William Hore, who was Mayor of Bristol in 1312. It has also been suggested that the holy sacrament, or Host, might have been carried this way in processions on holy days in pre-Reformation times. This was one of the first streets in the city to be paved.

HOT WATER LANE, BS15. This denotes where a spring was situated. It flowed into Charnell's brook. The stream was, in fact, icy cold, but as it bubbled up it gave the impression of boiling water.

HOTTOM GARDENS, BS7. The name of a wood once in existence to the east of where the old barracks stood. It was sometimes spelt Hotham Wood.

HOTWELL ROAD, BS8. The hot wells were noted for their medicinal properties as far back as the fifteenth century, but the practice of taking the waters only became fashionable among aristocratic society after the pump room was erected in 1695. One of its most most famous visitors was the composer, Joseph Haydn. *See Hotwells in the introduction.*

HOULTON STREET, BS2. In 1748 Mr and Mrs Joseph Houlton conveyed earl's Mead, a parcel of land in the outlying parish of St. James, to the Corporation of Bristol. This was the same James Houlton who owned Farleigh Hungerford Castle and Grittleton House in Wiltshire. Earl's Mead is shown on an1840 map of Bristol, lying just to the south of Houlton Street. The street was therefore probably named in his honour.

HOWARD AVENUE, BS5. There were a number of traders in the area in the late nineteenth century so it would seem that the name comes from the owner of the land.

HOWARD ROAD, BS6. Apparently the builder of this road was William Howard who lived near the Downs.

HOWARD ROAD / STREET, BS5. Again possibly named after the landowner.

HOWECROFT GARDENS, BS9. A Howcroft House is listed in the 1872 directory, so perhaps this road was built on the site of the house.

HOWES CLOSE, BS15. Named after a manager of Haskins pottery, which stood near here.

HOWETT ROAD, BS5. This could be a surname, but no one of that name appears in the local directories in the late nineteenth and early twentieth centuries, when this road was built.

HOWSMOOR LANE, BS17. An ancient name, preserved throughout the years, deriving from the Norse *haugr,* low, and the OE *heah*, moor.

HOYLAKE DRIVE, BS15. The name of a golf course, situated among other roads bearing similar names.

HUDD'S HILL GARDENS / ROAD, BS5. *See Hudd's Vale Road.*

HUDD'S VALE ROAD, BS5. The Hudd family worked a quarry in this area in the nineteenth century.

HUGHENDEN ROAD, BS8. Hughenden House in Buckinghamshire was the residence of Benjamin Disraeli, Earl of Beaconsfield, and this would seem to have influenced the choice of name.

HUGHENDEN ROAD, BS7. Probably for the same reason as above.

HULBERT CLOSE, BS4. Named after Canon Norman Francis Hulbert, a much-loved vicar of St. Luke's church. He was vicar there from 1945 to 1955.

HULSE ROAD, BS4. Possibly named after a village in Cheshire. It means 'hollows'.

HUMBERSTAN WALK, BS11. Giles Humberstan received seventeen shillings for repairing the Alms House in Henbury in 1691.

HUMPHRY DAVY WAY, BS8. Humphry Davy (1778-1829) was born in Penzance and came to Bristol to study at Dr Beddoes' Pneumatic Institution in Dowry Square. Dr. Beddoes believed that the inhalation of gases could cure diseases, and he employed cows to breathe on consumptive patients to this effect. Davy was his assistant in many curious experiments, often at great (though probably unsuspected) danger to himself. He discovered the effects of nitrous oxide (laughing gas) in 1800 and in 1815 invented the safety lamp for miners that bears his name. He was the first professor of chemistry at the Royal Institute and was knighted in 1812. He became a baronet in 1820. Apart from his chemical researches, he was an enthusiastic angler and wrote *Salmonia, or Days of Fly Fishing* in his last years. He died in Geneva in May 1829.

HUNG ROAD, BS11. An ancient name for the navigation channel in the Avon at the first bend two miles from the mouth. The derivation is Middle English *honge*, floated.

HUNGERFORD CLOSE / CRESCENT / GARDENS / ROAD / WALK, BS4. During the fifteenth century Frideswide, daughter of Lord Hungerford, released the rights of Stockwood to Sir Richard Choke who owned Long Ashton and was Justice of Common Pleas from 1461 until his death in 1483. Walter, First Baron Hungerford, was a warrior and statesman who fought at Agincourt. He died in 1449. His grandson and great-grandson were both executed for treason. The Hungerfords, based at Farleigh Castle near Bradford-on-Avon were an unpleasant lot through the centuries, especially in their domestic relationships, with husbands and wives variously strangling, poisoning, disinheriting and imprisoning each other. Giles Hungerford may have led a more blameless life: when he died in August 1869 he was buried at Westbury, where a handsome marble monument was erected to his memory.

HUNTER'S WAY, BS12. Built on land that belonged to Conygres Farm. The last owner, Charles Bridgeman, was a devotee of hunting.

HUNTERS CLOSE / DRIVE / ROAD, BS15. There was a Hunter's Hall in the area at the end of the nineteenth century.

HUNTINGHAM ROAD, BS13. Field name from the Anglo-Saxon *ham*, home, therefore 'home of the hunters'. This field was on Earl Temple's estate at Bishopsworth.

HUNTS LANE, BS7. Built on the site of Hunt's builders' yard.

HURLE CRESCENT / ROAD, BS8. This was the name of a prominent local family. In 1688 Simon Hurle was an Alderman of the City and John Hurle was Master of the Merchant Venturers in 1849-50.

HURLINGHAM ROAD, BS6. The name of a park in London where hockey and polo are played, now best known for the pre-Wimbledon warm-up tournament, but the reason for this naming is not clear.

HURST ROAD / WALK, BS4. Hurst is a name for the deepest part of a wood and continues the St. Anne's wood theme.

HURSTON ROAD, BS4. Walter de Hurston held lands in Somerset in the fourteenth century.

HURSTWOOD ROAD, BS16. Thought to be a made-up name.

HUTTON CLOSE, BS9. Either after the famous cricketer Len Hutton (there is a Hammond Close nearby) or named after the village in Somerset, which would tie in with another of the roads on this estate. *See Beverley Close.*

HUYTON ROAD, BS5. A town in Lancashire, the first syllable of which means landing place. A number of towns have been used as street names in this area.

HYLAND GROVE, BS9. Probably a field name from the OE *heah* meaning lofty.

ISF ROAD, BS11. This lies within the Britannia Zinc works. The name refers to the Imperial Smelting Federation.

IDA ROAD, BS5. One of three adjacent roads using a personal name. They may have been members of the builder's family. Or perhaps there is a Gerrish family connection. *See Ivor Road and Herbert Street.*

IDDESLEIGH ROAD, BS6. After Sir Stafford Henry Northcote, Earl of Iddesleigh (1818-87). He was President of the Board of Trade 1866, Secretary for India 1867, Chancellor of the Exchequer 1874-80 and Foreign Secretary 1886-87. He died suddenly on the day he resigned this last position.

IDSTONE ROAD, BS16. Parish in Berkshire. Quite a number of place names have been used for the surrounding roads.

ILCHESTER CRESCENT / ROAD, BS13. A town in Somerset the name of which translates as 'Roman fort on the River Yeo (or Ivel)'. The town was formerly known as Ivelchester. There was a prison here, notorious for the ill-treatment of its inmates. Other roads nearby are called after towns in the West Country.

ILEX CLOSE, BS4. There are a few roads in the vicinity with names of plants and shrubs.

ILMINSTER AVENUE, BS4. Near Ilchester Road.

ILSYN GROVE, BS14. The name of a small wood in the Hundred of Keynsham, sometimes spelt Islings. It means 'where the elms grow'.

IMBER COURT CLOSE, BS14. There was a coal distributor, George Imber, operating in the Bedminster area early in the twentieth century. It was also the name of an abandoned village on Salisbury Plain whose residents were forced out of their homes so the land could be used as an army training site. A pilgrimage is made there each year. The latter explanation could tie in with the Viking invasion theory. As far as the geographical theme goes the derivation could be from the OE and Norwegian words *immer* and *ember* which could relate to a goose of this name sometimes called the Northern Diver. In this case perhaps this relates to livestock kept at the farm on the hill. *See Ravenhead Drive and Allanmead Road.*

IMPERIAL ROAD / WALK, BS4. Named after the nearby sports ground provided by the Imperial Tobacco Company.

IMPERIAL ROAD, BS6. There may be a royal connection here, as a nearby road used to be called Kings Parade.

INGLESIDE ROAD, BS15. Would seem to be a made-up name. Two authorities believe the first component to be a corruption of 'English' while another opts for 'fireplace'.

INGMIRE ROAD, BS5. Built on land owned by the Smyth family. They had a property in Westmorland called Ingmire Hall. Translated from the Middle English the name means 'swampy meadow'.

INKERMAN CLOSE, BS7. This Horfield Site was acquired from the War Department, so military names were favoured. The battle of Inkerman was one of the bloodiest of the Crimean War and was fought on 5 November 1854.

INNOX GARDENS, BS13. This was the name of one of the fields of Pigeon House Farm at Hartcliffe - derived from OE *innoke* and meaning 'land temporarily enclosed from fallow land and cultivated'.

INNS COURT AVENUE / DRIVE, BS4. The residence of Sir John Inyn once stood on this site and was used as a farmhouse until comparatively recent times. The ancient tower was saved by public demand in the 1930s and was restored. When the vicarage was built the tower was incorporated. There is a memorial to Sir John in St. Mary Redcliffe church.

INSTOW ROAD / WALK, BS4. In common with others in the locality, these roads are called after a town in Devon.

IPSWICH DRIVE, BS4. Probably continuing the theme of Cathedral cities. Although technically Ipswich is not a Cathedral city, possessing no cathedral, it is in the diocese of Bury St Edmunds which does have one.

IRBY ROAD, BS3. Emma Smyth, stepdaughter of Sir Greville, married the Hon. Gilbert Neville Irby, son of Baron Boston, in 1891. He later took the name of Smyth.

IRENA ROAD, BS16. One of three roads in the locality called after mystery ladies.

IRETON ROAD, BS3. Henry Ireton (1611-51) was quartered with Cromwell and his troops in Bedminster where they used the parish church as stabling. He married Cromwell's daughter. The name Ireton means 'home of the Irish'.

IRONCHURCH LANE, BS11. The first church in Avonmouth was, in fact, built from iron.

IRONMOULD LANE, BS4. Abraham Darby used the brass mills at Keynsham for experimenting with casting iron pots in sand moulds instead of the loam that had always been used in the past. Perhaps this lane led to the mills or perhaps the loam that had been formerly used was taken from this area.

IRVING CLOSE, BS16. Captain John Irving (1779-1865) was shipwrecked in the West Indies. He was washed up at Annaton Bay in Jamaica and built a Wesleyan chapel there to give thanks for his survival.

ISLAND GARDENS, BS16. This may seem like an island, tucked away from the motorway with fields behind.

ISLEYS COURT, BS15. This may well be from the same derivation as Ilsyn. Certainly elms were a feature of the scenery here at one time.

ISLINGTON ROAD, BS3. District of London, the first component being a personal name, Ilsyn. A number of streets in the locality have been given place names.

ISON HILL ROAD, BS11. In 1842 this was written as Hyson Hill. Before 1750 it was known as Pidley Hill.

IVOR ROAD, BS5. Possibly a member of the builder's family, or there may be a Gerrish family connection. *See Herbert Street.*

IVY LANE, BS16. Descriptive.

IVYWELL ROAD, BS9. Site of Ivywell House, home of the Budgett family.

JACK KNIGHT HOUSE, BS7. It was requested that the memory of this Bristol councillor be perpetuated by naming this complex after him.

JACOB STREET, BS2. From the nearby church of St. Philip and St. Jacob. Jacob is an abbreviation of Jacobus, the Latin form of James.

JACOB'S WELLS ROAD, BS8. Jacob's Wells was one of Bristol's most important springs, traditionally associated with Bristol's Jewish community, who had to live beyond the Bristol city walls, when they were expelled by Edward I in 1290. There used to be a Jewish cemetery on the slopes of Brandon Hill. The well was used for Jewish purification rites, according to Mosaic law. A ritual bath, or mikvah, was built in the twelfth century, to allow for total immersion, and still stands there today. This is the only medieval ritual bath to have been found in England. During the Middle Ages, the waters were used by the monks of St. Augustine's Abbey, then in 1373 the monks granted the right for the water to be used by the city of Bristol, on condition that it was piped by conduit to the city and docks. The water was also piped to the Abbey through the Dean and Chapter's Conduit. Gaunt's Pipe branched off to supply Gaunt's Hospital (which is now on the site of the Midland Bank, on the corner of Park Street). The waters attracted pilgrims throughout the Middle Ages, a tradition continuing to the eighteenth century, and its waters were even bottled and sold in famous Bristol Blue Glass bottles. In 1889 the well was used to supply public baths and wash houses. The purity of its water has led to recent attempts to revive its commercial fortunes, but all attempts to date have failed. Currently Jacob's Well cannot be visited although this may change in the near future.

JAMAICA STREET, BS2. This street was developed around 1750, a few years after Bristol privateers had captured several Spanish ships in West Indian waters, and this booty brought great prosperity to the plantation owners there. Perhaps one of the Bristol merchants who returned to his homeland used the fortune he had amassed to develop this street. The man who founded the Bristol Royal Infirmary, John Elbridge, hailed from Jamaica. The name Jamaica is a corruption of a West Indian word Xaymaco that means 'the country abounding in springs'.

JAMES CLOSE / ROAD, BS16. There is no obvious reason for the naming of these roads, possibly a family connection with the builder.

JAMES PLACE, BS8. Presumably a tribute to James I.

JAMES STREET, (2) BS2. There are two streets of this name, one in St. Werburgh's and one in St. Paul's. That sited off Mina Road is close to John Street, suggesting that the brothers James and John, disciples of Christ, were the inspiration. The road in St. Paul's is more likely to be the name of a person. It runs off White Street, which is also thought to be the builder's name, so perhaps there is a family connection.

JANE STREET, BS5. Named after a member of the large Gerrish family. *See Gerrish Avenue.*

JARVIS STREET, BS5. Perhaps the surname of the owner of the site, or its builder. It was also the surname of two sheriffs of Bristol in the early sixteenth century.

JASMINE GROVE, BS11. This has no clear link with any of the surrounding street names. Jasmine is a semi-tender climbing plant with sweet-smelling small white flowers. It flourishes in Bristol's mild and damp climate, so perhaps the plant used to grow here.

JASPER STREET, BS3. Another local road named after a gemstone. *See Beryl Road.*

JEAN ROAD, BS4. One of the daughters of Mr Griffee the builder.

JEFFERIES HILL BOTTOM, BS5. In old records this appears as Jeffery's Hill and it formed part of the city boundary in 1652. Perhaps the name came from the family who owned Jeffery House.

JEFFERY COURT, BS15. There was a Jeffery House at Warmley as far back as 1610. By 1670 the Jeffrey family possessed coal pits in Lord Stafford's liberty and was the first family to be involved mining in Warmley. A liberty was the right to dig for coal on a manorial estate.

JERSEY AVENUE, BS4. One of a group of streets named after Channel Islands.

JESSOP UNDERPASS / COURT, BS1. William Jessop was an engineer who submitted the original plan for the Floating Harbour. It was many years before an amended scheme was put into operation, as the merchants were afraid of losing their control of shipping.

JIM O'NEIL HOUSE, BS11. This honours the memory of an esteemed Bristol councillor.

JOCELYN ROAD, BS7. William Lee built these houses, and Jocelyn was one of his relatives by marriage.

JOCKEY LANE, BS5. There is no apparent reason for this unusual choice of street name, unless there was stabling here at one time. There were a number of horse dealers operating in this area.

JOHN CABOT COURT, BS1. John Cabot (1425-98) was an Italian navigator and cartographer who received letters-patent from King Henry VII for him and his three sons to take possession on behalf of England any 'new' lands they might discover. He set sail from Bristol in the *Matthew* in 1497 and sighted the coast of Newfoundland. He returned to Bristol with the news, and set off again in 1498 but never returned. His son Sebastiano was born in Bristol and probably accompanied his father on the first voyage. He acted as a cartographer of South America on behalf of the Spanish king, and later spied on the Spanish on behalf of Henry VIII. He became the first governor of the Merchant Venturers, accidentally finding sea routes to Russia, which soon opened up English sea and overland trade routes to Central Asia. Sebastian Cabot died in 1557.

JOHN CARR'S TERRACE, BS8. John Carr, who died in 1586, was a wealthy soap maker and the founder of Queen Elizabeth's Hospital. In his will he left certain of his properties for the purpose of providing shelter for Bristol's orphans and poor children. The school opened first at Gaunts Hospital in Unity Street, then moved to St. Bartholomew's Hospital in Christmas Street, finally being established in 1847 in its present setting on the slopes of Brandon Hill. It is believed John Carr is buried in the Lord Mayor's Chapel, but the tomb there is marked only with the initials J.C.

JOHN JAMES COURT, BS7. Named after the philanthropist John James, who was born in 1906 in Bedminster, the son of a docker. He served in the RAF as a radio operator which sparked his interest in opening a radio shop in civilian life. From his first shop in Kingswood he built a whole empire of radio and TV shops. After the tragic death of his daughter, Dawn, in a road accident, he set up a trust fund in her memory of 10 million pounds to benefit senior citizens by means of coach outings. He also donated vast amounts to hospitals.

JOHN STREET, BS1. Built c. 1750 and originally called St. John Street, owing to the proximity of St. John's Church which is built on the wall, with the street running alongside.

JOHN STREET, BS2. The connection would appear to be with the saint, as there is another street close by called James Street, and James and John were brothers.

JOHN WESLEY ROAD, BS5. In honour of the founder of Methodism, John Wesley (1703-91), who was associated particularly with this side of town, where he was an inspiration to the mining community, and had founded a medical dispensary for the poor.

JOHNNY BALL LANE, BS1. This was formerly known as Bartholomew's Lane. The name would seem to be a corruption of the name of John a Ball who owned the property adjoining the Franciscan Friary that stood in Lewins Mead. Some also suggest that he had some responsibility for the erection of Bristol Bridge.

JOHNSON DRIVE, BS15. This road was called after Joey Johnson, a milkman in the area many years ago. He left money to the church.

JOHNSONS LANE / ROAD, BS5. Once a market garden covered this land which belonged to the Johnson family. The 1903 directory lists a Frank Johnson living at The Limes, Whitehall, a house that still exists today.

JOY HILL, BS8. A lovely inspirational name, perhaps, but no other obvious connection.

JUBILEE CRESCENT, BS16 / ROAD, BS16. These celebrate George V's Silver Jubilee in 1936.

JUBILEE PLACE, BS1 / BS5 (2) / BS4. These roads all celebrate one of Queen Victoria's milestones - either her Golden Jubilee in 1887 or her Diamond Jubilee in 1897.

JUBILEE ROAD, BS2. The only Jubilee Road to celebrate fifty years of the reign of George III. This road appears in the directory for 1850.

JUBILEE WAY, BS11. On the Avonmouth trading estate, named after the Silver Jubilee of Queen Elizabeth II in 1977.

JULIAN CLOSE / ROAD (2) BS9. From the Via Julia, the Roman road which led from Bath. It passed through Bitton and reached Bristol by way of St. George and Baptist Mills, crossed Coldharbour Road and continued through Redland before coming out on the Downs near the reservoir.

JULIUS ROAD, BS7. This is the forename of J.H.E. Shadwell. The family were Lords of the Manor and patrons of the Living of Horfield. A memorial to John

Shadwell states 'he was Lord farmer of this manor for 66 years, it having been held by his family from the time of Henry VIII to his day, when it passed into the hands of the Bishop of Gloucester and Bristol.'

JUNCTION ROAD, BS4. Probably referring to the railway line which ran along this route and down the Avon Gorge. The road has now been built over and is the site of Sainsburys.

JUNIPER COURT, BS5. Another in the group of roads called after herbs.

JUPITER ROAD, BS12. There is a little knot of roads in this area inspired by figures from Roman mythology who gave their names to aircraft and engines. The Bristol Jupiter was a 9-cylinder radial engine used in the Bristol Bulldog fighter and the Handley Page HP42 airliner. It was exported and has been used on the Japanese Nakajima fighter and an Italian reconnaissance plane.

JUSTICE ROAD, BS16. A number of families of this name were living in the Fishponds and Stapleton areas pre-1914, so it is reasonably safe to assume that this was the owner of the land.

K

KEBLE AVENUE, BS13. The name was selected to commemorate the Rev. John Keble (1792-1866) of Bishopsworth church. He was the author of *The Early Church at Bishopsworth.*

KEEDWELL HOUSE, BS13. A gentleman of this name held land here at the time of the Dundry Enclosure Award of 1815.

THE KEEP, BS15. This used to be the local pound where stray animals were penned until the owners paid the necessary fine.

KEINTON WALK, BS10. Richard Keinton was Vicar of Henbury 1377-1405.

KELLAWAY AVENUE / CRESCENT, BS7. Harris's theory was that the name was originally Chaillouet and cites Philip de Chailewai being mentioned in the Gloucestershire Pipe Rolls of 1165, while another member of the family, also Philip, owned Kellaways, a manor in Wiltshire. In Roman times it meant a place to stay overnight, usually a cottage; this led him to suspect that this Kellaway may have marked the route of Roman legions journeying from East Bristol to Sea Mills. However, in the *Images of England,* a book covering this area and compiled by members of the Bishopston, Horfield and Ashley Down History Society, it is clearly stated that the road was opened in 1921 by Postmaster General F.G. Kellaway M.P. who was born nearby. He may have been a descendant of the old family.

KELSTON GARDENS, BS10. Among a group of roads similarly called after West Country locations.

KELSTON GROVE, BS15. There was a Kelston View nursery not far from here in the early years of the twentieth century.

KELSTON ROAD / WALK, BS16. Many roads in the area given English place names.

Kellaway Avenue in the 1920s

KEMBLE CLOSE, BS15 / GARDENS, BS11. Kemble was a Cotswold village listed in the Domesday Book as having 30 villagers and 15 cottages with 18 ploughs and 6 serfs.

KEMPTON CLOSE, BS16. One of a group of roads called after racecourses.

KENCOT WALK, BS13. Kencot was a hamlet in the parish of Long Ashton.

KENDAL ROAD, BS7. Place names seem a favourite choice for roads in this area. Kendal is in the Lake District.

KENDALL GARDENS / ROAD, BS16. A number of people of this name were trading in the district in the early part of the twentieth century.

KENDON DRIVE, BS10. This is apparently a made-up name. Perhaps it was an amalgam of two names, e.g. Kenneth and Donald.

KENILWORTH DRIVE, BS15. Among a group of roads called after famous castles.

KENILWORTH ROAD, BS6. Continuing the Walter Scott influence in the area. *Kenilworth* was one of Scott's later novels. Unwise investment in a printing scheme left him in financial difficulties, forcing him to write so prolifically.

KENMARE ROAD, BS4. Irish names have been given to the roads in this vicinity. *See Bantry Road.*

KENMORE CRESCENT / DRIVE, BS7. There is a village on Loch Tay of this name and as adjacent roads have Scottish connections it seems to be safe to conclude this is the inspiration.

KENN ROAD, BS5. Village near Clevedon, Somerset, named from the River Kenn. Perhaps the landowner or builder had links with that area.

KENNARD CLOSE / RISE / ROAD, BS15. Seems to be a made-up name - other roads nearby begin with Kenn.

KENNEL LODGE ROAD, BS3. From the house of the same name.

KENNETH ROAD, BS4. One of several roads in the area apparently called after someone with local connections.

KENNINGTON AVENUE, BS7. One of the roads round the County Ground with cricketing connections - this is named after Kennington Oval, London home ground of Surrey County Cricket Club.

KENNINGTON ROAD, BS16. A number of random place names used in this locality.

KENNION ROAD, BS5. This would appear to be a made-up name like the other Kenn roads in the area.

KENNMOOR CLOSE, BS15. This is an area of Clevedon but the connection with the area where this road stands is unknown.

KENSAL AVENUE / ROAD, BS3. There is a district of London called Kensal Rise so the hilly nature of this area might be the connection. The first syllable means king and the last syllable is from OE *salh*, 'willow'.

KENSINGTON PARK ROAD, BS4. From Kensington House, described as being 'the splendid mansion of Richard J. Poole King', a slave trader working out of West Africa. The company that he founded, R & W King, went out of business circa 1906. Apparently this was a very beautiful house 'on a rising slope of a park-like verdant lawn, surrounded by exotics and evergreens of the choicest selection, and is in the centre of a noble hedgerow plantation of luxuriant elm, beech and other timber trees'. It was demolished in 1973 to build the People's Dispensary for Sick Animals.

KENSINGTON PARK, BS5. Probably after the London district, in keeping with many other roads in the area.

KENSINGTON PLACE, BS8. Several roads in the locality named after palaces.

KENSINGTON ROAD, BS5. Near Battenburg Road so clearly a royal connection. *See Battenburg Road.*

KENSINGTON ROAD, BS16. No apparent reason for this choice of name unless it refers to a property which once stood here.

KENSINGTON ROAD, BS6. Probably from Baron Kensington.

KENT ROAD, BS7. Named after the county cricket club in accordance with other roads near the County Ground.

KENT STREET, BS3. Most probably named after the mother of Queen Victoria, who was Duchess of Kent.

KENTON MEWS, BS9. Named after a small town in Devon. Perhaps the builder had associations with the place.

KENTS GREEN, BS15. Perhaps named after some long-forgotten resident of the area.

KERRY ROAD, BS4. An Irish place name in keeping with surrounding roads. *See Bantry Road.*

KERSTEMAN ROAD, BS6. From Mervyn Kersteman King, member of a well-known Bristol family. He was a member of the City Council for Redcliffe ward 1874-79 and Justice of the Peace 1898. The reason for this road's choice of name was Mr King's long association with Redland High School. Kersteman was his mother's maiden name.

KESTREL CLOSE, BS12. All local roads are given the names of British birds.

KESWICK WALK, BS10. This name was chosen because it runs from Wigton Crescent and Keswick is located near Wigton.

KETCH ROAD, BS3. This choice of name is a complete mystery. A ketch is either a two-masted sailing vessel or a soubriquet for a hangman, neither of which seems a likely reason for thus naming this road, although many executions had taken place at Cumberland Road Gaol. One famous hangman with the name of Ketch was himself hanged after murdering a woman in London.

KEW WALK, BS4. Named after the builder, W.J. Kew.

KEWSTOKE ROAD, BS9. Village near Weston-super-Mare. It is thought that the first syllable refers to St. Kew, the Cornish saint who came here from Ireland circa 460 AD. This road lies in the part of Stoke Bishop known as Druid Stoke, which may be the reason for the choice of name.

KEYS AVENUE, BS7. Near to Manx Road and Douglas Road, so the name would seem to be a reference to the Parliament of the Isle of Man, the House of Keys.

KILBIRNIE ROAD, BS4. No apparent reason why this was named after a small town in Ayrshire.

KILBURN STREET, BS5. Following a trend in the area for naming after London districts. From OE *cylenburna*, stream by a kiln.

KILDARE ROAD, BS4. A theme of Irish place names runs through this development. *See Bantry Road.*

KILKENNY STREET, BS2. This road was either called after the county and town in Eire, the home of the powerful Butler family, or after one of two hamlets in Gloucestershire. This road has been in existence since at least 1794. St. Augustine's Abbey once held lands in Kilkenny but whether or not this has a bearing on the street name is hard to tell.

KILMERSDON ROAD, BS13. John Kilmersdon was Master of St. Catherine's Hospital, Bedminster from 1353-73.

KILMINSTER ROAD, BS11. A man called Kilminster owned the land on which these houses were built.

KILN CLOSE, BS15. So called because it was built on the site of a former brick works, possibly that of the Hollybrook Brick Company.

KILNHURST CLOSE, BS15. A house of this name once stood near here. The road was built on the site of Oliver Keeling's lime works.

KILVERT CLOSE, BS4. Rev. Francis Kilvert (1840-79) was born at Hardenhuish, near Chippenham, son of a rector. The diary he kept, which was edited by William Plomer and published 60 years after his death, gives a fascinating insight into country life in those times. He had relatives in Bristol and visited on numerous occasions.

KIMBERLEY AVENUE / CRESCENT / ROAD / CLOSE, BS16, ROAD, BS15. As this road was built at the time the Boer War was being fought it seems reasonable to suppose that the road was named after the great Kimberley diamond mine on the Cape of Good Hope in South Africa, where the greatest man-made hole in the world was created by tens of thousands of hopeful diggers after the discovery of the *Star of South Africa* diamond in 1869. In October 1899 the mine was besieged by Boers struggling to control this priceless asset. The seige was not relieved by

British troops until February 1900. The mine was then, and still is, run by the DeBeers company. Perhaps it is not too fanciful to speculate that the developer of these Bristol roads had the Kimberley mine to thank for his own fortune.

KING DICK'S LANE, BS5. An ancient right of way on land that was once Kingswood Forest. It was in existence in the reign of Richard 1, so it was in all likelihood named after him as he was a very popular monarch.

KING EDWARD CLOSE, BS14. After Edward III, whose charter in 1373 created Bristol as a city and county.

KING GEORGE V PLACE, BS1. Self-explanatory.

KING GEORGE'S ROAD, BS13. After George V. The road was developed between the wars.

KING JOHN'S ROAD, BS15. Kingswood Forest has always been associated with King John as he is credited with building its many hunting lodges, the last of which was still standing at the end of the nineteenth century.

KING ROAD, BS4. Named after Richard Jenkins Poole-King, merchant and mayor of Bristol from 1844-45. He lived at Kensington House from the 1840s until his death in 1874. His widow lived there until 1884.

KING ROAD AVENUE, BS11. King Road lies off the mouth of the Avon, nearby. A road in the nautical sense is a sheltered area where ships may lie at anchor.

KING SQUARE, BS2. Built c. 1737 and named in honour of George II, who was on the throne at that time.

KING SQUARE / STREET, BS11. After Edward VII, who opened Avonmouth Dock in 1908.

KING STREET, BS1. Named in honour of Charles II, being built in 1670 shortly after the Restoration. Location of the famous Theatre Royal and the Llandoger Trow.

KING STREET, BS5. The King is Edward VII and this street adjoins Queen Street and New Queen Street.

KING STREET, BS5. As this road was built during the reign of Queen Victoria the King in question must be the builder or landowner.

KING WILLIAM AVENUE, BS1. After William of Orange, who died in a riding accident in 1702. He was the son of William, Prince of Orange and Mary, daughter of Charles I.

KING WILLIAM STREET, BS3. After William IV (1765-1837), third son of George III. He reigned from 1830 until his death.

KING'S AVENUE / DRIVE, BS7. Built in the 1920s; the King would be George V (1865-1936).

KING'S HEAD LANE, BS13. There has been a hostelry of this name here since time immemorial. The King was probably Charles I, who lost his head in 1649.

KING'S PARADE AVENUE / MEWS, BS6. The section of Whiteladies Road adjacent to these developments was once known as King's Parade.

KING'S ROAD, BS4. Apparently named by the builder.

KING'S ROAD, BS8. In 1879 J. W. King, a builder and architect, opened his Royal Bazaar and Winter Gardens here, the gardens extending over 20,000 sq ft. It cost him £10,000 and the project failed. The premises were taken over by Knee Bros., the furniture removers. Shops now stand in front of it.

KINGFISHER DRIVE, BS16. All the road in this area are named after British birds

KINGS AVENUE / DRIVE / CHASE, BS15. A reminder of forest connections from long ago.

KINGS PARK AVENUE, BS2. Built on the site of the King George V playing fields.

KINGS WESTON AVENUE / LANE / ROAD. *See Kingsweston.*

KINGS WALK, BS3. This probably derives from King's Head Lane.

KINGSCOTE PARK, BS5. Named after a housing association involved with the development.

KINGSCOURT CLOSE, BS14. Royal forest connections recalled here, in common with other roads nearby. The king referred to may have been Henry III.

KINGSDOWN ROAD / PARK, BS2. Part of the Royal Downs extending from Bristol Castle. Kingsdown Parade was formerly called Montague Parade from the tavern of the same name, well known for duels and turtle soup. Live turtles were brought from the quay and kept until required.

KINGSFIELD LANE, BS15. From the farm of the same name.

KINGSHILL ROAD, BS4. It runs into Queenshill Road. There was a Kingshill Farm in the vicinity.

KINGSHOLM ROAD, BS10. The name of a suburb of Gloucester. Last syllable is OE *ham*, a river meadow, land in a bend or enclosure.

KINGSHOLME ROAD, BS15. Derivation is from OE *kyngeshamme* meaning 'water meadow on the king's estate', which would have been an accurate description of the place.

KINGSLAND CLOSE / ROAD, BS2. Literally the king's land. This land was attached to Bristol Castle.

KINGSLEIGH COURT / GARDENS / PARK, BS15. The word means, quite simply 'king's wood', from OE *leah*, wood.

KINGSLEY ROAD BS5, BS6. Both roads were named after Canon Charles Kingsley (1819-78) author of *Westward Ho!* and *The Water Babies.*

KINGSMEAD ROAD / WALK, BS5. An apt description, for it was once one of the King's meadows.

KINGSMILL, BS9. The theme of this development is mills.

KINGSTON CLOSE / DRIVE, BS16. Perhaps named after the town in Surrey, or after someone connected with the site.

KINGSTON ROAD, BS3. Possibly a place name, but more probably the name of the builder. There was a well-known builder and property owner called W.P. Kingston, who was listed in the 1903 directory as living and trading in Southville.

KINGSTREE STREET, BS3. The 1903 directory calls it 'King's Tree Street' so it refers perhaps to the oak tree in which Charles II hid to evade the Parliamentarian troops. Perhaps oak trees grew here once.

KINGSWAY AVENUE / CRESCENT / KINGSWAY, BS5. A made-up name referring to the fact this was once part of Kingswood Forest.

KINGSWEAR ROAD, BS3. Many roads names in the locality are associated with Devon.

KINGSWESTON, BS11. An ancient demesne held by the King in the thirteenth century. It has been recorded that as Maurice de Berkeley lay dying he gave by deed to the king Beverstone, Aylburton and Weston - hence King's Weston. The name means 'king's west farmstead'.

KINSALE ROAD / WALK, BS4. Irish seaport, another two streets following the Irish theme. *See Bantry Road*

KINVARA ROAD, BS4. Continuing the theme of naming the roads after Irish locations. *See Bantry Road.*

KIPLING ROAD, BS7. After the writer and poet, Rudyard Kipling, who was awarded the Nobel Prize for Literature in 1907.He was also the author of *If*, judged to be the nation's favourite poem in a BBC Radio survey in 2001. He was a cousin of the Prime Minister, Stanley Baldwin.

KIRKBY ROAD, BS11. John Kirkby was the first known Prebend of Lawrence Weston and Member of the Royal Council in 1276, being the Treasurer in 1284. He became the Bishop of Ely in 1286. Contemporary chroniclers described him unfavourably.

KIRKSTONE GARDENS, BS10. Named after a pass in the Lake District, in keeping with the theme of the other roads in the vicinity.

KIRTLINGTON ROAD, BS5. Village in Oxfordshire. The derivation is OE *tun*, or 'settlement', of Cyrtla's people. This road is sited on what was the Cottrell-Dormer estate and the family had strong connections with this part of Oxfordshire.

KITE HAY CLOSE, BS16. This sounds as if it is an old field name.

KNAPPS LANE, BS5. Probably a personal name. One authority suggests original as OE *cnæpp* meaning 'hilltop'.

KNIGHTON ROAD, BS10. The name of a number of towns throughout the British Isles but none that seems to have link with this development.

KNIGHTSTONE COURT / SQUARE, BS14 / PLACE, BS15. Named by the Knightstone Housing Association in the twentieth century.

KNOLE LANE, BS10. Place name and name of a mansion near Almondsbury. From OE *cnoll* meaning 'hilltop' or 'hillock'.

KNOLL HILL, BS9. Although the spelling is different, the derivation is as for Knole Lane.

KNOVILL CLOSE, BS11. Elizabeth, granddaughter of Robert de Gourney, married John de Badenham, who held the manors of Redwick and Northwick. These passed to John de Knovill in 1320.

KNOWLE ROAD, BS4. There is considerable speculation as to the origin of this name. Some give derivation as OE *cnoll*, 'knoll' or 'hillock'; while another authority says it was originally spelt Canola or Chenola, which others give Canole. Much of Knowle itself was developed between 1870 and 1914, but there was also considerable building activity between the two wars and after 1945.

KNOWSLEY ROAD, BS16. A town in Lancashire where can be found Knowsley Hall, seat of the Earls of Derby. The first syllable is a personal name. Several roads hereabouts are named after towns in the north.

KYLROSS AVENUE, BS14. Probably an invented name.

KYNGES MILL CLOSE, BS16. Named after an old mill in the area.

L

LABURNUM ROAD, BS15 / GROVE, BS16. A decorative name.

LACEY ROAD, BS14. Mrs Lacey (or Lacia) was a widow residing in Bedminster on 17 November 1670. She was granted exemption from Hearth Tax.

LACOCK DRIVE, BS15. All roads in this precinct are named after abbeys. Lacock Abbey in Wiltshire was founded for women in 1232 by Ela, Countess of Salisbury, in memory of her husband, William Longspree. She was its first Abbess in 1241 and the only female Sheriff that Wiltshire ever had. During the Middle Ages the Abbey was a flourishing place of education for girls, and a refuge for the sick and needy. It was suppressed during the Reformation, the Abbey torn down and the Great Hall re-built. It eventually became the home of William Henry Fox Talbot, the nineteenth century photographic pioneer, and is now in the ownership of the National Trust.

LADD CLOSE, BS15. After A. Ladd, Clerk to the School Board 1899. He lived at The Park, Kingswood.

LADIES MILE, BS8. A favourite path on the Downs along which the local society ladies used to ride their horses.

LADMAN GROVE / ROAD, BS14. John Ladman resided in Keynsham in 1674. He was exempt from Hearth Tax.

LADYSMITH ROAD, BS6. Named after a strategic gold and diamond mining town in Natal, South Africa, where twelve thousand British troops were besieged in 1899 by the Boers for four months, a struggle that marked the beginning of the Anglo-Boer War, during which thousands died on both sides from enteric fever as well as in battle. The place owes its name to the wife to Sir Henry George Wakelyn Smith (1787-1860), Governor of the Cape of Good Hope. Lady Smith was a Spanish girl called Juanita whom he had rescued during the Peninsular War. She was fourteen when they married.

LAKE ROAD, BS10. Named for the proximity to Henleaze Lake, formed from a flooded quarry and now a private swimming club.

LAKE VIEW ROAD, BS5. A reference to the lake in nearby St. George's Park.

LAKEMEAD GARDENS / GROVE, BS13. A field name of Whitemead Farm, Long Ashton Manor, shown on the 1794 Survey. First syllable from OE *lacu*, stream.

LAKESIDE, BS16. Near the site of the old Lido, and a favourite spot for bathing until the 1970s when it was filled in.

LAKEWOOD CRESCENT / ROAD, BS10. An invented name combining reference to the nearby lake and Badock's Wood - so called because it was given to Bristol Corporation by Sir Stanley Badock in the 1920s.

LAMB STREET, BS2. From the Lamb Inn, built in 1651 and demolished in 1905, and the scene of alleged poltergeist activities in the eighteenth century. During the Monmouth Rebellion six companies of horse were mustered at the Lamb Ground, Lawford's Gate.

LAMBERT PLACE, BS4. Constant Lambert (1905-51) was a composer of ballet scores and jazz-related works. He was born in London and studied under Vaughan Williams. Among his more famous compositions were the *Merchant Seaman* suite and the score for the 1948 version of *Anna Karenina* starring Vivien Leigh.

LAMBLEY ROAD, BS5. This development took place between 1900 and 1926, so there may be a connection with the local vicar, as the church owned the land that this road stands upon, as well as that of adjoining Glebe Road and Church Drive.

LAMBOURN COURT, BS3. Among other roads with a hill range theme. The Lambourn Hills are part of the Berkshire Downs and a favourite area for running race horses in training.

LAMBROOK ROAD, BS16. A village in Somerset. One authority suggests the meaning as being 'the boundary brook'.

LAMPETER ROAD, BS9. Lampeter was the home town of John Harford, M.P. *See Falcondale Road.*

LAMPTON AVENUE / GROVE, BS13. Lampton was a hamlet in the Hundred of Hartcliffe, a mile and a half from Long Ashton.

LANAWAY ROAD, BS16. The name of a man who lived in the area in the early nineteenth century. His residence was called the Hermitage and is described as being a homestead with a very pretty gabled roof. It had lawns and flower gardens, ornamental ponds and specimens of drooping and other trees in abundance. At the time there were only a few cottages and the occasional larger property in the area. The Hermitage was demolished many years ago and houses were built on the site. *See Hermitage Road.*

LANCASHIRE ROAD, BS7. One of the numerous roads hereabouts called after cricket clubs, owing to their proximity to the County Ground.

LANCASTER ROAD, BS2. After the Lancashire town whose name means 'fort on the River Lune'. A number of place names have been used in local roads, for no obvious reason.

LANCASTER STREET, BS5. Adjoining York Street, it would seem to have been named after the Royal House of Lancaster, opponent of the House of York during the Wars of the Roses (1455-85), Lancaster being represented by the red rose, York by the white. The wars ended at the Battle of Bosworth in 1485 when Henry VII defeated the Yorkist Richard III, and the two dynasties were finally united when Henry VII married Elizabeth of York in the same year.

LANSDOWN VIEW, BS15. Probably an accurate description of the view.

LANDSEER AVENUE, BS7. Sir Edwin Henry Landseer (1802-1873) was a very popular Victorian painter, famed for his dramatic studies of deer and dogs. He also designed the bronze lions at the foot of Nelson's Column in Trafalgar Square, erected in 1869. He was knighted in 1850.

LANERCOST ROAD, BS10. The name of a village near Carlisle, in keeping with the other street names used in the area.

LANESBOROUGH RISE, BS4. A house of this name was built to accommodate the Earl of Lanesborough while he was receiving treatment from Dr Fox at his Brislington asylum. The house was demolished in 1975 and is now the site of the Harlequins Rugby Club clubhouse.

LANGDALE ROAD, BS16. Named after a hill in the Lake District, as is the adjoining road.

LANGDOWN COURT, BS14. A field name taken from the 1843 Whitchurch tithe map.

LANGFIELD CLOSE, BS10. This was named after A. Levy-Langfield, a wealthy landowner in the Henbury area during the early twentieth century. He owned the Henbury Court Hotel with the Lennard family, and was an alderman from 1913-27. He served with distinction in the Bristol Docks Committee for many years and edited the Bristol Channel District Guide. He was also a major benefactor when the Bristol Royal Infirmary was being built.

LANGFORD ROAD, BS13. Among a number of streets called after West Country villages.

LANGFORD WAY, BS15. One of two roads called after Somerset villages, but no obvious reason for this choice.

LANGHAM ROAD, BS4. This is a fairly common place name, the derivation being 'long ham', *ham* meaning homestead or village.

LANGHILL AVENUE, BS4. One of the original roads built in the area, probably taken from a field name.

LANGLEY CRESCENT, BS3. A village in Gloucestershire whose name translates as 'long wood'. Perhaps the Smyths had connections with the place, as the crescent is built on their land at Ashton, and they also owned estates in Gloucestershire. However there seems to be no pattern to road names in this area, so it is hard to be certain.

LANGTON COURT ROAD, BS4. Langton Court was Brislington's second manor house. The oldest part of the manor, dating from 1590-1610, still remains, although the main part of the house was demolished for the building of the Langton Court Arms Pub in 1902. The Langton family (latterly the Gore-Langtons) were Lords of the Manor of Brislington from 1667, to the present day.

LANGTON PARK, BS4. After W.H. Gore-Langton, M.P. for Bristol 1852-65. He also served as Mayor in 1852 and was a member of the City Council and a J.P. He was a member of the well-known Somerset family of Earl Temple of Stowe and of Newton St. Loe near Bath.

LANGTON ROAD, BS4. The Langton family purchased the Manor of Brislington from Rowland Lacey of Oxford during the reign of Charles II.

LANGTON WAY, BS4. A de Warr married a Sackville and the family moved to Knole House. There was no male heir and the title passed to the Langton family in 1677. The Langtons were prominent civically, one being a Mayor, another a J.P. Langton was the name of the Manor at Brislington.

LANSDOWN CLOSE, BS15 / PLACE / ROAD, BS8 / ROAD, BS5 / ROAD, BS6 / TERRACE, BS7. All would seem to derive their name from the village near Bath, although perhaps the one in Redland may owe its nomenclature to the local Marquisate of Lansdowne, which produced several distinguished statesmen.

LANSDOWN VIEW BS15. Faces towards Lansdown in Bath.

LANSDOWNE, BS16. This road is sited near others named after stately homes so this may refer to the Marquisate of Lansdowne, a title borne by the Fitzmaurice family since 1784.

LAPHAMS COURT, BS15. William Lapham was a councillor and resident in Hanham in 1899.

LAPWING GARDENS, BS16. This continues the theme in the neighbourhood of calling roads after British birds. The name comes from OE *hleape*, leap and *wince,* waver, which describes its tumbling flight.

LARCH ROAD, BS16. Many local roads are named on an arboreal theme, perhaps in recognition of the flora here in times past.

LARCH WAY, BS12. Within a group of roads all named on a sylvan theme.

LARK'S FIELD, BS16. Quite possibly a field name.

LARKLEAZE ROAD, BS15. Almost certainly an old field name.

LASBURY GROVE, BS13. The name of someone who held land under the Dundry Enclosure award of 1815.

LATCHMOOR HOUSE, BS13. A name taken from the 1843 Bedminster tithe map.

LATIMER CLOSE, BS4. John Latimer (1824-1904) was a noted Bristol historian. He was editor of the *Bristol Mercury* for 25 years and compiler of the *Annals of Bristol* for the sixteenth, seventeenth, eighteenth and nineteenth centuries, every local historian's Bible. He came originally from Newcastle-upon-Tyne.

LATTON ROAD, BS7. A village in Wiltshire. One authority states the derivation to be 'homestead or enclosure where leeks are grown'. Among other Wiltshire street names in the area.

LAUNCESTON AVENUE, BS15. There was a Launceston farm in the area run by the Grindell family.

LAUNCESTON ROAD, BS16. Named after a town in Cornwall, the derivation being Old Cornish *lanscawett,* enclosure by an elder tree. A number of Cornish place names have been used in the area.

LAUREL STREET, BS15. There was a house near here called The Laurels owned by the Peacock family, boot manufacturers in 1899.

THE LAURELS, BS16. Perhaps built on the grounds of an old house where these bushes flourished.

LAURIE CRESCENT, BS9. Neither a place name nor a local surname, so there are no clues as to why this name was chosen.

LAURIE LEE COURT, BS15. Among other roads named after twentieth century writers. Laurie Lee (1914-97) was born and grew up in the village of Slad, near Stroud. He is world famous for his autobiographical memoir *Cider with Rosie,* which has sold over 6 million copies.

LAVERS CLOSE, BS15. Edgecombe Lavers was proprietor of the Golden Valley Coal Works, so it is possible that the Close was named after him.

LAVINGTON ROAD, BS5. Either a place name or a surname. The first component would appear to be a personal name, 'the village of Lafa's people'. There were people of that name prominent in business in Bristol during the late nineteenth century.

LAWFORDS GATE, BS2. Originally the East Gate into Bristol. In Saxon times it was Hanford's Gate. *Hlaf* (or *Laf*) was a loaf and Hlaford was the title given to a wealthy man able to supply many men with bread. In this case the Hlafords were the Lords of the Castle, a structure, probably wooden, forerunner of the Norman castle.

LAWFORD STREET, BS2. Leads off Lawford's Gate.

LAWN AVENUE / ROAD, BS16. The site of a house called The Lawns, although it was originally known as The Lawn. It was auctioned in June 1805 with stabling for horses listed amongst its assets.

THE LAWNS, BS11. The Lawns was the name of a large house in Shirehampton High Street.

LAWNWOOD ROAD, BS5. A house called Lawnwood stood nearby Tyndall Road until the 1950s.

LAWRENCE AVENUE, BS5. It is possible that this avenue was named after the eminent painter, Sir Thomas Lawrence (1769-1830), the son of a Bristol innkeeper, who was born at 6 Redcross Street, St. Jude's. Even at the age of five he was famous for his recitations and crayon portraits. He was a favourite portrait painter of George III and became President of the Royal Academy. The name may, however, merely have been that of the builder or someone who had connections with the site. There was a builder called John Lawrence living in Rosemary Street in 1872, which would be the right era. It has also been suggested that the connection may be St. Lawrence's church - the 'Leper church' of ancient times - which was situated about half a mile away. Many of these houses were owned by Mr. Littleton of Anstey & Littleton, as were those in Rene Road, so another possibility is that they were members of his family. This may account too for the naming of Eve Road. *See Anstey Street and Littleton Street.*

LAWRENCE GROVE, BS9. Perhaps a name linked with nearby Owen Grove, so possibly a forename of someone associated with the building of the street.

LAWRENCE HILL, BS5. The name was derived from the leper hospital that stood here for hundreds of years. When it was no longer required for its original use it became a manor house. The last vestiges could be seen as late as 1820. The church of St. Lawrence was built on the site in 1889, and demolished in the 1960s.

LAWRENCE WESTON ROAD, BS11. Lawrence Weston was once a village, so called because the land was owned by the Hospital of St. Lawrence during the reign of Edward III. Weston is West Farmstead, to the west of Henbury in which hundred it was situated.

LAXEY ROAD, BS7. Another local road named after a town in the Isle of Man. One can only suppose the builder had connections with the place.

LEA CROFT, BS13. This would seem to be an old field name denoting a small enclosure on meadowland.

LEAHOLME GARDENS, BS14. To judge by surrounding roads this must be an old field name.

LEAP VALE / VALLEY CRESCENT, BS16. The name comes from the Leap, a stream which flows through the area.

LEAR CLOSE, BS15. Named after Alfred Lear, a coal merchant and councillor, who was largely responsible for the building of the local Youth Centre.

LEDA AVENUE. BS14. There seems no obvious reason for this naming. Leda figured in a classical legend in which Zeus took the form of a swan to seduce her. She gave birth to two eggs: out of one hatched Helen of Troy, and out of the other, the twins Castor and Pollux.

LEDBURY ROAD, BS16. A market town in Hereford. The first syllable comes from the River Leddon or Liddon on which the place stands. Ledbury Road was previously Kendall (or Kendalls) Lane, possibly named after the developer. *See Lewington Road.*

LEE CLOSE, BS12. Perhaps this was one of the roads built by William Lee.

LEEMING WAY, BS11. Another of the ancient names used in this area where signs of occupation by the Romans have been discovered. This was called after Leeming Lane, part of Ermine Street in North Yorkshire. The name is derived from *lhe* - way and *maen* - stone.

LEES HILL / LANE, BS15. There were people of this name living in Warmley at the end of the nineteenth century, so perhaps they owned the land in both these locations.

LEICESTER SQUARE BS16. This appears to have been an old name for this area. There was once a boot factory here, so there may have been an industrial link with Leicester, which is well known for shoe and shoe machinery manufacture.

LEICESTER STREET, BS3. Many local streets here have been named after English towns.

LEICESTER WALK, BS4. Continuing the theme of naming roads after places with a religious connection. At Leicester can be founds the ruins of St. Mary's Abbey, where Cardinal Wolsey died.

LEIGH ROAD, BS8. A popular road name - the derivation is from OE *leah* meaning wood, woodland glade or clearing.

LEIGH STREET, BS3. This could be a surname of someone connected with the area, perhaps the person who owned the land where these houses were built.

LEIGHTON ROAD, BS3, BS4. Perhaps from Frederic, Baron Leighton of Stretton (1830-96), a painter and President of the Royal Academy. There was once a Leighton Villa that stood in Southville.

LEINSTER AVENUE, BS4. *See Bantry Road.*

LEMON LANE, BS2. Sited near Orange Street.

LENA AVENUE / STREET, BS5. Quite a few personal names are in use locally - perhaps this was a relative of the builder.

LENOVER GARDENS, BS13. A field name taken from Bedminster tithe map, 1843. Probably derived from Middle English *leyne*, an arable strip or layer, and OE *ofer*, a slope, hill or ridge.

LEONARD LANE, BS1. This used to be known as St. Leonard's Lane, after the nearby church. It was in a tavern here that Liverpool Nell was attacked in 1748. She was later found in the river, tied up in a sack. Jeremiah Hayes was hanged on Durdham Downs for her murder.

LEONARD ROAD, BS5. Believed to be another of the Gerrish family. *See Gerrish Avenue.*

LEONARDS AVENUE, BS5. This was the name of a family of market gardeners once resident in this locality.

LEOPOLD ROAD, BS6. This was the first name of the Duke of Albany, the youngest son of Queen Victoria. *See Albany Road.*

LESCREN WAY, BS11. The name of one of the partners in the company who developed the site.

LEWIN STREET, BS5. Several families bearing this name are listed in the local directory at the time the road was built, so this could be someone who had associations with the area.

LEWINGTON ROAD, BS16. Lewington Road is first shown with this name on maps from 1933. It was previously known as Maggs Lane and before then, Kendalls

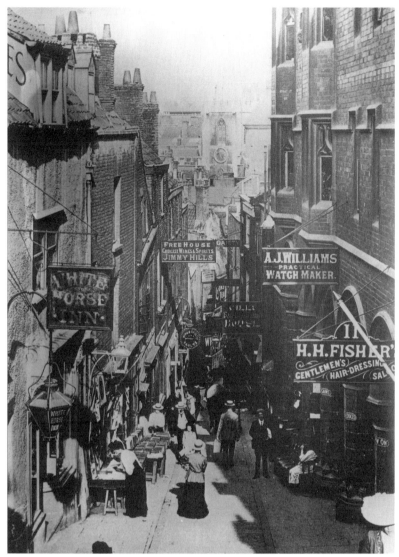

Lewins Mead

Lane. Who Lewington, Maggs or Kendall were, is not known. Possibly Kendall was the owner of the land on which the lane was developed. *See Ledbury Road.*

LEWINS MEAD, BS1. The meaning is 'the meadow of Leofwine', who was youngest brother of Sweyn, Earl of Bristol in 1049. His name derives from OE *loef*, beloved, pleasant and *wine* - friend, lord. In the 1300s it was known as Lowans Mead. In 1373 John Kyngton was ordered to pay to the Commonalty (an early form of local council) a sum for the maintenance of a latrine in Lewins Mead.

LEWIS CLOSE, BS15. Named after Edith Lewis, who died in 1988 aged 95. At the time she was the oldest resident in the parish.

LEWIS ROAD, BS3. There was a builder by this name erecting houses in this area at the time, so it seems probable that he built this road.

LEWIS STREET, BS2. Possibly a personal name as there is a Philip Street which runs parallel.

LEYLAND WALK, BS13. A field name from the Bishopsworth estate owned by Earl Temple. The first syllable is from the OE *leah* meaning wood, woodland glade or clearing.

LEYTON VILLAS, BS6. Named after a London suburb, so-called because of the River Lea flowing through it.

LICHFIELD ROAD, BS4. Another road named after a famous cathedral, which dates from 700 and is the burial place of St. Chad.

LILAC CLOSE. BS10. There is no obvious reason for the use of this popular garden shrub as a name for this street.

LILLIAN STREET, BS5. Another member of the Gerrish family. *See Gerrish Avenue.*

LILSTOCK AVENUE, BS7. The name of a hamlet in Somerset. One authority gives *stoc* as meaning monastery or 'meeting place of Lydia and his people', although another favours *Lulla* who, he says, could be the matron in the Glastonbury Charter referred to as a 'handmaid of the Lord'. The Charter was reputed to be a record made by St. Patrick describing how missionaries came to the country in 166 AD and proclaimed Christianity, cleansing the king and his people at the sacred font.

LILTON WALK, BS13. This is the name of a Somerset village.

LILYMEAD AVENUE, BS4. A field name: 'meadows where the lilies grow'.

LIME CLOSE, BS10. Chosen because of the open space to the south of the development.

LIME GROVE / ROAD, BS3. Perhaps these trees were planted here when Lime Road was built at the end of the nineteenth century.

LIME ROAD, BS15. Named for the calcium compound rather than the tree, as there were quarries nearby.

LIMERICK ROAD, BS6. The Earl of Limerick had close associations with this city.

THE LIMES, BS16. Among a group of roads named after trees.

LINCOLN STREET, BS5. The houses which stood here before the vast changes made to the area during the 1950s were built between 1865 and 1870, which suggests that the Lincoln might be Abraham Lincoln who was assassinated by John Wilkes Booth in 1865. This theory is borne out by the fact that there used to be a neighbouring road called Richmond Street. Richmond, Virginia, was the Head Quarters of the Confederacy during the American Civil War.

LINCOMBE AVENUE / ROAD, BS16. After the farm of that name.

LINDEN CLOSE, BS16. Probably descriptive. Many of these roads were planted with trees, Linden being the German name, as well as an English poetic name, for lime tree.

LINDEN CLOSE, BS14. Possibly a field name.

LINDEN ROAD, BS6. Again, possibly named after the German for lime tree.

LINDREA STREET, BS3. Lindreas were an old-established boot and shoe company with premises in Christmas Street that were demolished in 1970. There is no obvious connection with Bedminster but it is possible a member of the family owned the land where this short rank of houses was built.

LINDSAY ROAD, BS7. Uncertain: it could be a place name or a surname. The derivation of the first syllable is 'lime tree'.

LINGFIELD PARK, BS16. Among other local roads named after racecourses.

LINK LANE / ROAD (2), **BS12.** The Link Road was opened in 1964 to link Station Road with the main Gloucester Road after many, many years of debate on the subject. The second Link Road in BS12 lies within the B.Ae. security area.

LINNELL CLOSE, BS7. Named after John Linnell (1792-1882), a portrait and landscape painter, and lifelong friend of William Blake. He was never given any academic honours despite having many of his pictures accepted by both the Royal Institution and Royal Academy, and so declined their eventual offer of membership.

LINNET CLOSE, BS12. Amongst a group of roads called after birds.

LINTERN CRESCENT, BS15. In view of the number of local people who have been celebrated in road names locally, the origin of this may well have been Edward Lintern, a popular Methodist lay preacher who died in 1902 aged 51. 1500 men attended his funeral.

LINTHAM DRIVE, BS15. Another Methodist church connection. *See Cade Close.*

LISBURN ROAD, BS4. Among other roads named after locations in Ireland. *See Bantry Road.*

LITFIELD ROAD, BS8. Originally Litt Fields (lead fields). In 1574 two Mendip miners 'dug for lime and lead upon the Downs and, being stifled with smoke, died and were buried at Clifton Parish Church'.

LITTLE ANN STREET, BS2. The Ann in question is Queen Anne.

LITTLE BIRCH CROFT, BS14. Clearly an old field name.

LITTLE BISHOP STREET, BS2. Leads to Bishop Street.

LITTLE CAROLINE PLACE, BS8. Caroline was the wife of George II.

LITTLE DOWLES, BS15. A field name from the old tithe map.

LITTLE GEORGE STREET, BS2. Named in honour of George I.

LITTLE HEADLEY CLOSE, BS4. *See Headley Close.*

LITTLE KING STREET, BS1. Runs parallel to King Street.

LITTLE MEAD, BS11. A field name meaning small meadow.

LITTLE PARADISE, BS3. This was built on an orchard of this name.

LITTLE PAUL STREET, BS2. Leads to Paul Street.

LITTLESTOKE ROAD, BS9. Stoke means independent farmstead.

LITTLE WITHEY MEAD, BS9. Situated by Withey Mead.

LITTLETON COURT, BS12. All roads in this section are called after Gloucestershire villages.

LITTLETON ROAD, BS3 / STREET, BS5. Quite possibly after Anstey Littleton and Co., accountants who had a stake in a few developments throughout the city. *See Anstey Street.*

LITTLEWOOD CLOSE, BS4. Understood to be built on wooded land, part of the Lyons Court estate. Perhaps a field name.

LLEWELLYN COURT, BS9. Probably a Westbury College connection here as Llewllyn was the name of the Prince of Wales when Godfrey Gifford, Bishop of Worcester, founded the College. *See Gifford Road.*

LOCK GARDENS, BS13. People of this name were resident in the district in 1914, or it may be a reference to the lock gates by the Cumberland Basin, which would be visible from this vantage point.

LOCKEMOR ROAD, BS13. A place name in the manor of Bedminster in the fourteenth century. The first syllable is from the OE *loc*, fold. *Mor* is moor or grassland.

LOCKLEAZE ROAD, BS7. A field name. There existed, before development, Lockleaze, Hither Lockleaze, Further Lockleaze - to name but a few.

LODGE CAUSEWAY, BS16. Site of one of the ancient lodges built by King John on the highest land in Kingswood forest. It was known as Kingswood Lodge and later as Brain's Lodge when a colliery owner of that name lived there.

LODGE DRIVE / HILL / ROAD, BS16. From Lodge House, which used to stand near here and was once the property of the Dukes of Beaufort.

LODGE STREET, BS1. Originally Red Lodge Street, from the house which has a side entrance here and once had a garden which ran the whole length of the street. The Red Lodge in Lower Park Row is still visitable today, and its garden is maintained just as it would have been in the sixteenth century. During the nineteenth century the great Bristol philanthropist Mary Carpenter founded a school and home for street girls in the property, which dates from the sixteenth century and was built on the site of an ancient Carmelite Priory. *See Byron Street and Mary Carpenter Place.*

LODGE WALK, BS16. The lodge referred to here is that belonging to the mansion of Cleeve Hill.

LODGESIDE AVENUE / GARDENS, BS15. Built on the site of Kingswood Forest, near where one of the hunting lodges stood.

LODORE ROAD, BS16. Named after a place in the Lake District. Other streets nearby are also named after places in that locality. The name means 'the lower gap in the ridge between Watenlath and Borrowdale'. 'The Cataract of Lodore' was the title of one of Robert Southey's poems.

LODWAY ROAD, BS4. Named after a village in Somerset near Pill. The first syllable is probably from the OE *lad*, a watercourse.

LOGAN ROAD, BS7. Probably a surname. It has been suggested it was named after the Reverend J. Moffat Logan, Minister of the Old King Street Baptist church. For many years he held a very popular discussion group on Sunday afternoons in Montpelier, which may be considered near enough to justify the choice.

LOGUS COURT, BS15. This originates from an old field called Logus Conduit.

LOMBARD STREET, BS3. Probably after the name of the bank which was once prominent in the area. It has always been a name synonymous with banking since the Lombards set up as moneylenders in London in the twelfth century, after the expulsion of the Jews from England in 1291. The Lombards in turn were expelled from England by Elizabeth I.

LOMOND ROAD, BS7. Named after the famous Scottish loch north of Glasgow. A profusion of Scottish names exist in this small area.

LONDON ROAD, BS2. There is no apparent reason for this to be named after the capital city.

LONDON STREET, BS15. This was the beginning of the pre-motorway route to London.

LONG ACRES CLOSE, BS9. Clearly an old field name.

LONG BEACH ROAD, BS15. Another American-influenced naming to fit in with California Road. Coincidentally, there was an area here called Beach before the development took place. *See California Road.*

LONG CLOSE, BS16. A field name taken from the 1846 tithe map.

LONG CROSS, BS11. A field name, from the OE *lang* meaning long strip of land, length or long stretch.

LONG EATON DRIVE, BS14. Easton is a place name, the meaning of which is 'a farm by the river'. *See Allanmead Close.*

LONG HANDSTONES, BS15. An old field name shown on the tithe map.

LONG MEADOW, BS16. A descriptive field name from the past.

LONG ROAD, BS17. Descriptive.

LONG ROW, BS1. A very ancient street that existed as long ago as 1293 when Simon de Burton built his almshouses there. Reference was made to the street as early as 1250. From the OE *lang* and *raew* - a long row of houses.

LONGACRE ROAD, BS14. An old field name.

LONGDEN ROAD, BS16. Most probably an old field name meaning long valley.

LONGFIELD ROAD, BS7. Perhaps a place name though a field name seems more likely.

LONGFORD AVENUE, BS10. The last syllable could be the Welsh *fford* road. It is also an earldom created in 1758.

LONGLEAT CLOSE, BS9. There is no obvious reason why this has been named after the seat of the Marquis of Bath in Wiltshire.

LONGMEAD AVENUE, BS7. A field name, and it has also been suggested it is named after a stream which still flows beneath the houses.

LONGMEAD CROFT, BS13. Apparently a field name, meaning 'the dwelling in the small meadow'.

LONGMOOR ROAD, BS3. From the geography of the land before development took place.

LONGNEY PLACE, BS12. As are many of the local roads, this is named after a Gloucestershire village. Longney used to be famous for its August Feast.

LONGREACH GROVE, BS14. The name of an old property that stood in the Bath Road. It is also a field name so perhaps the name goes back a long way. The last syllable is from the OE *rac*, the reach of a river, reach being a continuous stretch.

LONGWAY AVENUE, BS14. A field name taken from the OE *lang*, long strip of land and *weg*, path or road.

LONGWELL HOUSE, BS15. Longwells was one of the Forest boundaries in 1652.

LONGWOOD, BS4. Self-explanatory field name.

LORAIN WALK, BS10. A field name, thought to be a corruption of Lords Rhine, rhine being a ditch.

LORTON ROAD, BS10. Named after a place in Cumbria, in keeping with other local names.

Children playing in a traffic-free Lower Ashley Road, early twentieth century

LOUISA STREET, BS2. It has been suggested that the road is called after the Lady of the Haystack, a mysterious woman who appeared at Flax Bourton in 1776 and slept in a haystack for four years. She then had the doubtful advantage of being befriended by Hannah More, who had her removed to a private asylum at Hanham. It was later rumoured she was an illegitimate daughter of the Emperor of Austria. She became totally insane and died in 1800.

LOUISE AVENUE, BS16. Possibly the wife or daughter of the builder.

LOVELL AVENUE, BS15. As this is situated near the Sir Bernard Lovell School it would seem to honour the astronomer Sir Bernard Lovell (1913-), who was born at Oldland Common and completed his PhD in physics at the University of Bristol. He was leader of the team that built the Jodrell Bank telescope in 1957, then the world's largest steerable radiotelescope, and was largely responsible for the building of the Hubble telescope.

LOVERINGE CLOSE, BS10. Sarah Loveringe was Matron of Henbury school in 1726.

LOVER'S WALK, BS6. A magnificent avenue of beeches flanking a path running alongside Redland Grove leading to Redland Road and the edge of Redland Court - now Redland High School for Girls - which was built by John Cossins in 1732. It is an obvious name for such a romantic walk, and the trees were protected from felling when the estate was developed when the Fry family bequeathed the area to the City Corporation in 1879. The second section of the Walk was saved when Mr G.O. Edwards, the heir to Redland Court, presented the rest of the walk to the Corporation in 1884.

LOWBOURNE, BS14. A field name.

LOWER ASHLEY ROAD. *See Ashley Road.*

LOWER CASTLE STREET. *See Castle Street.*

LOWER CHAPEL ROAD, BS15. Joins Chapel Road.

LOWER COLLEGE STREET. *See College Street.*

LOWER FALLOW CLOSE, BS14. A field on one of the farms that were demolished to make way for the new housing.

LOWER GAY STREET, BS2. The adjective 'lower' is hardly applicable now as Gay Street itself disappeared long ago, although there is a Gay Street in Bath. Gay Street was so named in honour of the poet and playwright John Gay (1685-1732), who was born in Barnstaple in North Devon. He was a close friend of Alexander Pope, and is best known as author of *The Beggar's Opera* and the pastoral poem *Acis and Galatea*, which was set to music by Handel.

LOWER GROVE ROAD, BS16. Runs off Grove Road.

LOWER HANHAM ROAD, BS15. *See Hanham Road.*

LOWER HIGH STREET. *See High Street.*

LOWER HOUSE CRESCENT, BS12. Named after a house of this name that was occupied by the Milletts and later the Barnsleys.

LOWER KNOLE LANE, BS10. Knole was an area of Brentry, this being the lower section.

LOWER LAMB STREET, BS8. Lamb Street itself has long since gone. Lower Lamb Street is probably named after a former ale house.

LOWER MAUDLIN STREET, BS2. *See Maudlin Street.*

LOWER PARK ROW, BS1. *See Park Row.*

LOWER REDLAND ROAD, BS6. *See Redland Road.*

LOWER SYDNEY STREET, BS3. *See Upper Sydney Street.*

LOWER STATION ROAD, BS16. (2). In both cases the station itself closed in the 1960s.

LOWER THIRLMERE ROAD, BS12. Off Thirlmere Road.

LOWLIS CLOSE, BS10. The origin of this name is in doubt. It could be the name of a resident in the area. A Peter Lowlis was Chaplain to William Canynge who, in his will dated 12 November 1474, describes himself as 'Clerk, Dean of the Collegiate church and College of Holy Trinity, Westbury on Trym by Bristol and lately a merchant of the Town of Bristol, aforesaid' Lowlis was bequeathed 'the best pair of vestments in velvet'.

LOWTHER ROAD, BS10. After Lowther Fell, following the theme of Lake District namings.

LOXTON SQUARE, BS14. Possibly named after the Keynsham family who ran a coal business in the area.

LUCAS CLOSE, BS4. Named after a former Captain and President of the Knowle Golf Club.

LUCCOMBE HILL, BS6. In 1872 there was a house in the neighbourhood called Luccombe House, which is named after a village in Somerset and a deep inlet on the Isle of Wight. The first syllable could be the personal name *Leifa*, or it may be from the OE *lufu*, love, which would have the charming meaning of 'a valley where courting took place'.

LUCKINGTON ROAD, BS7. A village in Wiltshire. It could also be derived from a personal noun Luca, though one authority prefers Loc, Locan or Lucan.

LUCKLEY AVENUE, BS13. A tenement or holding included in the Dundry Enclosure Award of 1815.

LUCKWELL ROAD, BS3. This was the site of St. Luke's Well, but it became known as the Luck Well when it became the custom to throw in coins, pins and thimbles and make a wish. It was situated some 20ft from Luckwell Lane in an alcove and was quite deep, deep enough, in fact, for a child once to fall in and drown. After this tragedy the well was covered and a pump installed. The well was finally closed in 1906. There is another legend explaining that the name related to the Roundheads. It is said that when they reached Bedminster in 1645 they plunged their helmets in the water and toasted each other with the words 'Here's luck!'

LUCKY LANE, BS3. This may be a corruption of Lokeing (or Locking) Lane as Lokeing Croft must have been very close to this site.

LUDLOW CLOSE, BS2. Named after a nineteenth century parochial benefactor.

LUDLOW CLOSE, BS15. Among other roads named after castles.

LUDLOW ROAD, BS7. After the Shropshire town of Ludlow in the English Marches, following a similar theme of names for the roads in this area.

LULLINGTON ROAD, BS4. A village near Frome and a place in Derbyshire. The derivation is the *tun*, or settlement, of Lulla and his people.

LULSGATE ROAD, BS3. This road leads to the village of Lulsgate.

LULWORTH CRESCENT, BS16. Amongst other roads called after seaside resorts, Lulworth Cove is in South Dorset.

LURGAN WALK, BS4. Another of the local streets named after Irish towns. *See Bantry Road.*

LUX FURLONG, BS9. This sounds like a field name. *Lux* is Latin for light. Perhaps it was a particularly sunny spot.

LUXTON STREET, BS5. Probably these houses were built by Mr Luxton, mason and builder of Little Victoria Street. His daughter, Daisy, was a well-respected dancing teacher for many years.

LYDDINGTON ROAD, BS7. Local streets are named after towns and villages; Lyddington is in Leicestershire.

LYDFORD WALK, BS3. A small town on the North Devon coast. Many West Country names have been chosen for roads in this area.

LYDIARD CROFT, BS15. There was once a Lyddiard Farm in the vicinity.

LYDNEY ROAD, BS10. Among other local roads called after villages in Gloucestershire.

LYDNEY ROAD, BS15. A number of Gloucestershire place names have been used for roads in this area. At the time of Domesday, Lydney was a Hundred owned by Earl William, who had his manor here.

LYDSTEP TERRACE, BS3. Named after a town on Carmarthen Bay.

LYNCH COURT, BS15. This is taken from the local field name Glass Lynches.

LYNCOMBE WALK, BS16. Among other local roads with rural-sounding names.

LYNDALE AVENUE, BS9. All roads in this development incorporate 'lyn' in their names.

LYNDALE ROAD, BS5. Possibly a made-up name.

LYNDE CLOSE, BS13. George Lynde was one of the commissioners appointed in the reign of Edward V1 to inquire into the state of the churches in the part of Somerset that included the Hundred of Hartcliffe.

LYNDHURST ROAD, BS9. Named after John Singleton Copley, Baron Lyndhurst (born Boston, USA 1772, died London 1863) who was the son of the famous painter, J.S. Copley. He served three terms as Lord Chancellor. *See Copley Gardens.*

LYNMOUTH ROAD, BS2. Named after the North Devon seaside town at the mouth of the River Lyn. Most of the roads in this area are called after locations in the British Isles.

LYNN ROAD, BS16. Lynn is a Welsh word meaning lake, and this road was not far from the lake at Duchess Gate.

LYNTON PLACE, BS5. Thought to be named after a member of the Gerrish family. *See Gerrish Avenue.*

LYNTON ROAD, BS 3. Either a surname, or possibly denoting a field.

LYNTON WAY, BS16. Built on or near land that once formed two closes called The Lintons. Elliot is of the opinion that it could derive from W. L. Linton, who had connections with the parish in 1823.

LYNTON, BS15. This may well have been an old field name although it is also a place name, in keeping with the naming of other nearby roads.

LYONS COURT ROAD, BS4. This was a manor to the west of Whitchurch that dated from the fourteenth century and was still standing in 1916. It was once a monastery or nunnery. The Lyons family lived here from the thirteenth century to the sixteenth.

LYPPIAT ROAD, BS5. Shown on maps dating 1600 as Lypp Gate. The old style G resembled a Y and it became Lypp Yate. In the early part of the twentieth century the Sweet family had a fruit and asparagus garden in the area known as Lippiatt Close and Sanyfield. The Saxon *Hlyp Geat* was a Leap Gate - an enclosure into which deer can leap but cannot escape.

LYPPINCOURT ROAD, BS10. Richard Lyppingcourt was a resident in Westbury parish in 1591.

LYSANDER ROAD, BS12. Among other roads named after aircraft and engines, although Lysanders were built at Yeovil. Initially the planes were used by the British Expeditionary Force in 1939 but were outclassed by the Luftwaffe and were subsequently employed carrying agents and supplies to the French Resistance groups. *See Pegasus Road.*

LYTCHET DRIVE, BS16. Dorset locations were the choice when it came to naming these roads.

LYTHAM HOUSE, BS4. This follows the trend for naming all local streets after golf courses.

LYTTON GROVE, BS7. After Edward George Earle Lytton Bulwer Lytton, First Baron Lytton (1803-73), politician, man of fashion and prolific novelist best known for *The Last Days of Pompeii* and *The Last of the Barons.*

LYVEDEN GARDENS, BS13. Roger Lyveden of Bristol purchased the Manor of Ashton Philips in the Hartcliffe hundred in 1421.

M

MACAULEY ROAD, BS7. Named after Thomas Babington Macaulay, first Baron Macaulay (1800-59). A historian and poet, he wrote a *History of England* covering the period from the accession of James II to the closing years of the reign of William III. His earlier years had been spent as the legal advisor to the Supreme Council of India and he wrote essays on Clive and Warren Hastings. He was raised to the peerage in 1857.

MACDONALD WALK, BS15. When this area was being developed, the senior partner of the new Orchard Medical Centre, Dr David Skelton, suggested it would be appropriate to name a road after Dr Macdonald of the practice.

MACEY'S ROAD, BS13. Macey's was one of the tenements or holdings included in the Dundry Enclosure Award 1815.

MACHIN CLOSE, BS10. Rev. William Machin was incumbent of Henbury church in 1541.

MACKIE AVENUE / GROVE / ROAD, BS12. After Rev. John Mackie and his son, also John.

MADDOCKE HOUSE, BS13. Ann Maddocke is recorded as living in the area in November 1672 when she was granted exemption from Hearth Tax.

MADELINE ROAD, BS16. This was the name of a relative of the builder.

MAESBURY, BS15. Among a group of roads named after hills. Maesbury lies north of Shepton Mallet. There is a hill fort on its summit; hence the name, which derives from the Welsh *maes*, 'field', and the OE *burh*, 'fortified place'. There was a halt on the now derelict Somerset and Dorset Railway named after it. A German bomber flew into the hill on the way to Liverpool in 1941.

MAESKNOLL ROAD, BS4. *Maes* is Welsh for 'plain' or 'open field'. The Maes Knoll Tump is on the Dundry Ridge, and was once part of the enormous Wansdyke defence system. From here there are spectacular views of the Chew Valley and Bristol.

MAGDALENE PLACE, BS2. From the original name of the nearby building which later came to be known as Hooke's Mill and was, for some years prior to its demolition, used as an orphanage for the Blue Maids, who were thus named because of the uniform they wore.

MAGGS LANE, BS5. Samuel Maggs once had a market garden here.

MAGGS CLOSE, BS10. The Chairman of Avondown Housing Association, also a Lord Mayor of Bristol 1982-83 was George Maggs.

MAGPIE BOTTOM LANE, BS5. This leads to Magpie Bottom. This may be taken to mean it was the habitat of these birds, although it was also a nickname for Anglican bishops.

MAGPIE BOTTOM LANE, BS15. This seems to be an old name for the area frequented by those birds famed in rhyme: 'one for sorrow, two for joy…' If you see a solitary magpie, according to folklore you must wish him good day and ask after his family to lift the curse. The Ugly House stood here, a name given by locals to what must have been a particularly hideous building, before it was demolished. Squatters used to live here in the woods during the lean years of the 1930s.

MAIDEN WAY, BS11. Another of the Roman-influenced names chosen as a reminder of the Roman occupation of the area. Maiden Castle, just outside Dorchester, was the chief stronghold of the Durotriges and was stormed by the 2nd Augustan Legion under Vespasian in AD44.

MAIDENHEAD ROAD, BS13. Maidenhead Inn and Green are mentioned in Dundry Enclosure Award 1815.

MAIDSTONE ROAD, BS3. A town in Kent. The name means maiden's stone. Nearly all roads running parallel here begin with M.

MAKIN CLOSE, BS15. No reason has been found for this name.

MALAGO ROAD / VALE EAST, BS3 / WALK, BS13. From the nearby brook. The origin, according to Harris, could be the Portuguese meaning 'I go ill' although Anton Bantock, the local historian, expresses the belief that it could derive from *melis*, mill and *agos*, place.

MALDOWERS LANE, BS5. Unknown origin although possibly the surname of someone connected with the development.

THE MALL, BS8. Named after the London street. The name comes from *mall* as in mallet used in the game of Pall Mall, or the alley or sheltered walk in which the game was played.

MALLARD CLOSE, BS5. Perhaps named after the bird, although more likely to be the name of someone who owned land here.

MALMAINS DRIVE, BS16. Malmains was the name of an old house that once stood on this site.

MALMESBURY CLOSE, BS6. Place name, believed to be derived from a personal name, Maildulf, a Scot, or Aldhelm, said to have once been a bishop of Malmesbury.

MALMESBURY CLOSE, BS15. Amongst other roads called after abbeys.

MALVERN COURT / ROAD, BS5. No nearby road gives any clue as to why this Worcestershire town was selected as a name for these roads.

MALVERN DRIVE, BS15. All roads in the development are called after ranges of hills.

MALVERN ROAD, BS4. Another road named after famous public schools.

MANCROFT AVENUE, BS11. Field name. *Croft* is OE for 'small enclosure' and *man* is most probably from OE *mæne*, 'common' or 'communal'.

MANGOTSFIELD ROAD, BS16. In the Domesday Book this area is referred to as Manegodesfielde, the derivation of which is in some doubt; but the one perhaps most favoured is *maen - coed - fille* which translates from the Welsh as 'place of stone in a wood on a hill', which is a fairly accurate description.

MANILLA ROAD, BS8. From Manilla Hall, described in Morgan's Guide of 1851 as 'an elegant family mansion, embosomed in limes and evergreens'. In the grounds stood an obelisk to the memory of William Pitt, Earl of Chatham, and a

cenotaph dedicated to the 'Warriors of the 79th Regiment' who defended Madras and fought in the battles at Wandewash, Arcot, Pondicherry, Manilla and the Philippine Islands. The memorials were erected there by Sir William Draper, who took part in the campaign and was in command at the capture of Manilla in 1762. The obelisk now stands on the Downs.

MANOR COURT DRIVE, BS7. A reference to the old manor of Horfield.

MANOR COURT, BS16. Presumably because it is quite close to Manor Road.

MANOR GROVE, BS15. Rodway is the manor on question. It seems the original owner in the thirteenth century was a man called Putot and his descendants were the Blounts. There was another house there before the present one was built c. 1257.

MANOR PARK, BS6. From Redland Manor House which was demolished in 1890. It was built by Francis Gleed in 1658 and occupied for many years by Charles Ludlow Walker, a sheriff and Mayor of Bristol in the first half of the nineteenth century.

MANOR PLACE, BS16. Built on part of the Manor estate in the 1960s. The Manor House itself is still standing in Beckspool Road.

MANOR ROAD, BS7. There is no evidence that a Manor House ever stood in Bishopston, but Horfield was a royal manor and there was a farm there called Manor Farm so perhaps the site of this road was once part of Horfield Manor.

MANOR ROAD, BS16. The Yalland family, many of whom are buried in St. Mary's churchyard, occupied the Manor House which stood here for many years. There are memorials to them in the church. The lodge belonging to the house still remains at the corner of Manor Road and College Road. This road was formerly known as Madhouse Lane because, it is rumoured, a man called Dr. Joseph Mason established a private asylum here in the eighteenth century.

MANOR ROAD, BS16. The manor here is Rodway House.

MANOR ROAD, BS13. This refers to Bishopsworth Manor. There is an ancient trackway nearby which runs between Manor Road and Vicarage Road, called Colliers Drum. It was so-named because of the sound of the miners' pit boots as they tramped to work from Bishopsworth to the pits of South Liberty.

MANSFIELD STREET, BS3. Town in Nottinghamshire, the name meaning 'open land by Mam Hill'. This street may, though, have been named after the builder, as one of that name is listed in the 1872 directory about the time the houses were erected.

MANSTON CLOSE, BS4. Named after a Dorset village, in keeping with the Sturminster Road theme.

MANWORTHY ROAD, BS4. This was a field name on the 1846 tithe map.

MANX ROAD, BS7. One of a number of roads locally with names associated with the Isle of Man.

MAPLE AVENUE, BS16. Built on land once known as The Thicket, hence the woodland names. *See Thicket Road.*

MAPLE CLOSE, BS14. Perhaps built on land where these trees grew.

MAPLE ROAD, BS4. Among other woodland names.

MAPLE ROAD, BS7. Many of the roads in the area have tree names.

MAPLELEAZE, BS4. Probably a field name. The last syllable is OE *læs* meaning 'pasture' or 'meadow' and has been commonly used all over the country but particularly in Gloucestershire.

MAPLE LEAF COURT, BS8. This was built on the site of the premises of Wessex Coaches. Formerly they had been known as Maple Leaf Coaches.

MAPLEMEADE, BS7. This sounds as if it might be a field name.

MAPLESTONE ROAD, BS14. A made-up name.

MARBECK ROAD, BS10. This could well be a field name, the interpretation being 'pool into which the stream flows'.

MARDALE CLOSE, BS10. Among place names, but this is not on any historical map. Perhaps it is a made-up name.

MARDON ROAD, BS4. The Langton estate passed into the hands of Hall Sinnot (a solicitor), Heber Mardon and a Mr Harris in the middle of the nineteenth century. Harris and Mardon sold out to Sinnot and started a printing works. Mardon's daughter married Sinnot's son, who owned most of the land in St. Anne's. He kept Birchwood Lodge and held hunting parties there.

MARDYKE FERRY ROAD, BS8. Site of the Mardyke ferry, ferrying workers across the river to the sand and gravel works. Mardyke was probably the name of the wharf.

MARFIELD WALK, BS13. A field name which means 'meadow where the pool is sited'.

MARGARET ROAD, BS13. It is thought this was named in honour of Princess Margaret.

MARGATE STREET, BS3. A Kent seaside resort, and one of a number of roads running off St. John's Lane beginning with M.

MARGUERITE ROAD, BS13. Possibly a family connection of the builder, W.J. Kew.

MARIGOLD WALK, BS3. After the flower, which was so named because of the resemblance of its petals to the rays of the halo around the head of the Virgin Mary, as depicted by religious artists.

MARINA GARDENS, BS16. Built on the site of the old Lido.

MARINERS DRIVE, BS9. The road was built on the site of the ancient pathway, Mariner's Path, which descends from the Downs to the old Roman port of Abona at Sea Mills.

MARION WAY, BS15. Marion is the wife of the builder, Cleo Rogers.

MARION WALK, BS5. It is assumed this was a relative of the builder of these houses.

MARISSAL CLOSE / ROAD, BS10. Nicholas Marissal was husband of Mary Marissal and brother-in-law to Mr Cossins. He died in London in 1739. His body was moved from Christchurch, Edmonton and re-interred in the Cossins family vault under the communion table at Redland Chapel in 1747. The connection with Henbury is not clear but may have to do with land ownership. *See Cossins Road.*

MARISTON WAY, BS15. The name of a ship which docked at Albany in Australia on 17 May 1905. *See Albany Way.*

MARK LANE, BS1. It is generally assumed that the name derives from the saint to whom the Lord Mayor's chapel is dedicated, but Harris suggests the origin might be the last syllable of Denmark Street, with which it runs parallel.

MARKET SQUARE, BS16. Perhaps so called as this development was designed almost as a separate town when building began in the 1920s.

MARKHAM CLOSE, BS11. A village in Nottinghamshire; the derivation of the first syllable is OE *mære*, 'boundary'.

MARKSBURY ROAD, BS3. Many Somerset villages have been used in naming streets in this locality.

MARLBOROUGH AVENUE / DRIVE, BS16. The Avenue in Fishponds is more likely to be named after the Wiltshire town, as other place names have been used in the locality, but in the case of Frenchay it may be after Marlborough House as stately homes seem to be a popular source for road naming.

MARLBOROUGH HILL / HILL PLACE, BS2. In general all streets with this name are dedicated to John Churchill, Duke of Marlborough, who distinguished himself at Blenheim, Oudenarde, Malplaquet and Ramillies. When he was still Captain John Churchill Marlborough, he played a vital part in quashing the Monmouth Rebellion in 1685 by holding Keynsham Bridge against the rebels. There is also, of course, a town of the same name in Wiltshire. The derivation, according to one scholar, is that the first syllable is a personal name, but another favours *marl* - a type of red clay soil.

MARLBOROUGH STREET, BS1, BS5. As BS2.

MARLEPIT GROVE, BS13. The name of a field at Lamington Farm in the Manor of Long Ashton in 1794. *Marle* is Middle English, meaning clay or sand and stone mixed.

MARLING ROAD, BS5. It is possible the road was named as a tribute to the Marling family, baronets of Stanley Park, Gloucestershire. Sir Percival Scrope Marling was awarded the Victoria Cross for his part in the Sudan campaign of 1884 when he was a lieutenant in the 16th Hussars. He later held the rank of Colonel.

MARLWOOD DRIVE, BS10. Marlwood Grange was a property that stood in the Henbury Hundred.

MARMADUKE STREET, BS3. There was a house of this name in Totterdown in the 1880s. In Victorian times the word was used as a byword for a fop or dandy. Amongst a host of other streets beginning with the initial M.

MARMION CRESCENT, BS10. The Marmions were an old Gloucestershire family. Philip owned land at Oldland and Henry was Mayor and Sheriff of Bristol in the sixteenth century.

MARNE CLOSE, BS14. John Marne is listed in Dwelly's Directory of Somerset as being resident in the Hundred of Keynsham in January 1670.

MARSH LANE, BS5, BS2 / ROAD BS2. So called because they lead to St. Philips Marsh.

MARSH LANE, BS3. Named because of the lane's proximity to Gores Marsh.

MARSH STREET, BS1. Thus called because of its proximity to the marsh that is now covered by Queen Square. Until 1247 this was owned by St. Augustine's Abbey but thereafter only the western portion known as Canon's Marsh was retained. The marsh was used as a public pleasure ground for many years but by the beginning of the seventeenth century Marsh Street was the centre of a densely populated area. It was in an alley off this street that the 1603 cholera epidemic began which caused the loss of 2600 lives. It was originally known as Skadpulle Street, meaning 'overflowing pool'.

MARSH STREET, BS11. Descriptive: the area was extremely marshy.

MARSHAM WAY, BS15. The contractors who developed this site chose the name - it is one they used wherever they built an estate.

MARSHFIELD ROAD, BS16. Among other place names, Marshfield being a village near Bath.

MARSHFIELD ROAD, BS16. The road to Marshfield.

MARSTON ROAD, BS4. Follows the pattern of Somerset place names in the area. The derivation is Anglo-Saxon *mære-stan*, 'boundary stone'.

MARTIN CLOSE, BS12. All roads in this area are called after birds; in this case probably the house martin.

MARTIN STREET, BS3. Either someone's forename or the surname of the builder. A Samuel Martin is listed in the 1872 directory as a carpenter and builder with premises in Frogmore Street and Orchard Street.

MARTIN'S CLOSE / ROAD, BS15. These did once lead to Martin's farm but the name could be even older, as a man called Martin was granted mining rights in the chase in the seventeenth century and Martin's House Hill was part of the boundary of the King's Chase as defined on 26 May 1632.

MARTINGALE ROAD, BS4. No obvious reason for this choice of name. A martingale can be either a strap running from a horse's girth to its bit or a stay beneath a jib boom. It was the *nom de plume* of a nineteenth century natural history writer and is also a betting system of doubling stakes. Harris states that the builder might have chosen the name as the whole venture was a bit of a gamble.

MARTOCK CRESCENT / ROAD, BS3. Sited among other roads with random place names.

MARWOOD ROAD, BS4. Named after a town in Devon. West Country towns figure strongly in surrounding roads.

MARY COURT, BS5. Built on demolished Mary Street, which in turn was named after one of the Gerrish family. *See Gerrish Avenue.*

MARY CARPENTER PLACE, BS2. Mary Carpenter (1807-77) was a remarkable Bristol benefactress, who tirelessly devoted her life to helping and educating orphaned and vagrant children, founding a 'ragged' school for boys and the Red Lodge school for girls. She was the daughter of Lant Carpenter, schoolmaster and Unitarian preacher. In her sixties she visited India on several occasions to set up similar ventures there, and became internationally famous, travelling the

world to lecture about the necessity of her work. She was admired by Queen Victoria, who invited her to tea at Buckingham Palace. Her plaque can be seen in Bristol Cathedral.

MARY STREET, BS5. Another member of the Gerrish family. *See Gerrish Avenue.*

MARYBUSH LANE, BS2. On the 1789 map of Bristol this street is listed as Mary Bush, which suggests it could have been called after a member of the Bush family who were prominent in the city from the seventeenth century. Another suggestion is that it is a corruption of Mary Bouchier who left lands and money to various Bristol parishes in 1680. The name began to be spelt as it is today some time between 1826 and 1850.

MARYGOLDLEAZE, BS15. As for most of the roads in this small area, an old field name has been used.

MASCOT ROAD, BS3. Mascot is the name of a suburb of Sydney, Australia, or the name might be used here as a symbol of good fortune.

MASEFIELD WAY, BS7. Among other roads called after poets. John Masefield (1878-1967) was Poet Laureate, and is perhaps best remembered for his poem 'Sea Fever'.

MASKELYNE AVENUE, BS7. Mervyn Herbert Nevil Storey-Maskelyne (1823-1911) was MP for Cricklade, Wilts, landowner and benefactor to the Parish of Horfield. He contributed to the enlargement of the church building in 1895. He was also the grandson of Nevil Maskeleyne, who was Astronomer Royal in 1765. The family estate was at Salthrop House, Wroughton, in Wiltshire.

MATCHELLS CLOSE, BS4. Called after a field on the 1848 tithe map which described the area as Matchell's Upper and Lower Ground.

MATERMAN ROAD, BS14. Joseph Materman lived in Brislington in 1674 and was exempt from paying Hearth Tax.

MATFORD CLOSE, BS10. Matford is a village in Devon.

MATTHEW'S ROAD, BS5. From the nearby church, consecrated in 1873.

MATTHEWS CLOSE, BS14. No reason for the naming of this road has so far been discovered.

MAUNSELL ROAD, BS11. Thomas Maunsell was a rate-payer in the tithing of Stoke Bishop in 1656, assessed at £8.

MAURICE ROAD, BS6. After Henry Maurice, Prince of Battenberg, who married Queen Victoria's daughter Beatrice. He died of a fever while on service in Africa.

MAWDELEY HOUSE, BS3. Named after a fifteenth century landowner in the area.

MAXSE ROAD, BS4. The owner of the land on which the houses were built was a Frederick August Maxse (1833-1900). He served as an Admiral in the Royal Navy and was a political writer. The family owned land in the vicinity for many years. A John Maxse occupied an elegant house opposite Arno's Vale in 1805.

MAY STREET, BS15. Origin unknown. It could be the flower or someone's name.

MAYBEC GARDENS, BS5. Maybec is a surname, so this perhaps was someone connected with the development.

MAYBOURNE, BS4. Almost certainly a field name, as all around here were market gardens and smallholdings.

MAYCLIFFE PARK, BS6. A made-up name.

MAYFIELD AVENUE / PARK, BS16. Self-explanatory.

MAYNARD CLOSE / ROAD, BS13. The name of a man who held land here in 1815.

MAYOR'S BUILDINGS, BS16. Robert Castle, Mayor of Bristol, lived in nearby Beechwood House. He died in office in 1802.

MAYTREE AVENUE / CLOSE, BS3. Self-explanatory.

MAYVILLE AVENUE, BS12. This sounds as though it might be a made-up name.

MAYWOOD AVENUE / CRESCENT / ROAD, BS16. Either an invented name or chosen because the developer had connections with Minnesota. Maywood is a township there as is another nearby road, Millward Grove.

MAZE STREET, BS5. Named after one of the directors of the Great Western Cotton Works. *See Aiken Street.*

MCADAM WAY, BS1. John Louden McAdam was director of Bristol Rail Road Company in 1815 and General Surveyor of Roads to the Bristol Turnpike Company. The road surfacing material he first employed is still known as 'macadam'. The use of this compound was pioneered in Bristol at the start of the Bath Road.

MCLAREN ROAD, BS11. In memory of Martin McLaren, M.P. for Bristol North West for many years.

MEAD CLOSE, BS11. Named after a man who was on the committee of the Broadcasting Employees Housing Association, the builders of the development.

MEAD RISE, BS1. Keeping to the theme of 'meads' in the area, *mead* meaning meadow.

MEAD STREET, BS1. As above.

THE MEAD, BS12 / MEADOW CLOSE, BS16 / MEADOW COURT DRIVE, BS15/ MEADOW GROVE, BS11 / MEADOW VALE, BS5 / MEADOWLAND, BS10 / THE MEADOWS, BS15 / THE MEADS, BS16 / MEADWAY, BS9 / MEADOW STREET, BS11. All of these are field names or adaptations of the same.

MEADOW STREET, BS2. There was once a farmhouse here surrounded by meadows on which Newfoundland Road was later built.

MEADOWSIDE DRIVE, BS14. Meadowside was the home address of the M.P. for South Bristol in 1926, Alexander Walkden.

MEADOWSWEET AVENUE, BS12. After the farm of that name.

MEARDON ROAD, BS14. James Meardon was a resident of the parish of Brislington in 1674.

MEDE CLOSE, BS1. The Mede family were merchants in the city in the fifteenth century. Sir Thomas Mede and his brother Philip are buried in St. Mary Redcliffe church. Sir Thomas was Bailiff of Bristol in 1438 and Sheriff in 1452; Philip was Bailiff in 1444, Sheriff in 1454 and Mayor in 1458, 1461 and 1468. He was also an M.P. in 1460.

MEDICAL AVENUE, BS1. This road contained Bristol's first School of Medicine.

MEERE BANK, BS11. This was an ancient embankment along a Roman road. The name derives from the OE *mære*, 'boundary'. It was probably the northern boundary of Shirehampton. There was a Meere Bank Rhine (ditch) in the area.

MEG THATCHERS CLOSE / GARDENS, BS5. It is not known who Meg Thatcher was but a Meg Thatcher's Green appears in the 1615 survey of Bristol.

MELBOURNE ROAD, BS7. Place name meaning 'millstream' or 'middle stream'. It has been suggested that the road was named after the builder, who made a fortune in the Australian Gold Rush of 1851, when rich deposits were found near Melbourne. The Melbourne Argus reported that "all the ruffians and rogues from Melbourne, and the scum of convicts from Van Diemen's Land" surged 10,000 strong to the gullies and outcrops of Geelong to seek their fortunes. The oldest, top part of the road was shown on the 1887 street map as St. Michael's Place, and the bottom part is marked as Muller Road, which was forty years before what is now known as Muller Road was built.

MELBURY ROAD, BS4. Place name. According to one authority it is from the OE and means 'multi-coloured hill'.

MELITA ROAD, BS7. It has been suggested that this road was named after a granddaughter of Queen Victoria.

MELLENT AVENUE, BS13. Robert of Mellent married Mabel, daughter of Robert Fitzhamon, who was granted the manor and hundred of Hartcliffe and Bedminster by William Rufus. He was created Earl of Gloucester in 1100 and died in 1147.

MELROSE AVENUE / PLACE, BS8. Place name immortalised by Walter Scott in his 'Lay of the Last Minstrel'.

MELTON CRESCENT, BS7. Place name. The derivation is either from the OE *mæle*, 'spotless' or perhaps from *mylen*, 'mill'.

MELVILLE ROAD, BS6. Another peerage name; this is after the first Viscount Melville, freeman of the city. The family name was Dundas.

MELVILLE TERRACE, BS3. Possibly a surname connected with the builder or landowner. There were six people of this name listed in the 1903 directory living in this area and in 1872 a John Melville owned a property in Somerset Square.

MEMORIAL CLOSE / ROAD, BS15. After Memorial Cottage, which still stands by the entrance to Hanham High School. A memorial plaque by the cottage honours John Chiddy, who died saving many lives when he removed a large rock from the path of an on-coming train. A nation-wide collection was made to build a cottage for his widow and her eight children. The cottage key was given to Mrs Chiddy on January 8th, 1878.

MENDIP CRESCENT, BS16. Perhaps a reference to the hilly terrain.

MENDIP ROAD, BS3. Several roads in this hilly part of Bedminster are named after ranges or individual hills. According to one expert the first syllable means 'hill' and the last syllable 'valley'.

MENDIP VIEW AVENUE, BS4. A wishful, rather than an accurate description of the road.

MERCER COURT, BS14. John Mercer rented the field adjacent to Bathridge Mead known as Westfield Paddock.

MERCHANT STREET, BS1. This road has been known by various names over the years. Once it was called Marshal Street and was the military road from the castle to Kingsdown where exercises and tourneys took place. It was also known as Mercate Street from the Latin *mercatus*, 'market'. The name Merchant Street would seem to date from the sixteenth century.

MERCHANTS COURT / ROAD, BS8. A section of Hotwells Road appears on Chilcott's 1853 map as Merchant's Parade, which may be the origin of this naming.

MERCHANTS QUAY, BS1. Formerly the point at which the merchants disembarked.

MERCHANTS ROAD, BS8. Built c. 1860 on land owned by the Society of Merchant Venturers.

MERCIA DRIVE, BS2. The kingdom of Mercia was incorporated with Wessex in 920. St. Werburgh was a princess of this kingdom, hence the choice of name. The boundary actually ran through Bristol, laying the foundations for the north-south divide which still exists today, even to the extent of which football team the residents support.

MEREDITH COURT, BS1. It seems likely this was named after J. Nelson Meredith, who was the City Architect instrumental in building the new, post-war Bristol. The City Engineer was similarly honoured. *See Bennett Way.*

MERFIELD ROAD, BS4. Most probably a field name. The first syllable is from OE *mære* meaning 'boundary'.

MERIDIAN PLACE / ROAD / VALE BS6, BS8. This name would seem to derive from one meaning of the word - 'culmination' or 'high point'. Apparently it is sometimes used in Scotland to denote a midday dram of spirits.

MERIET AVENUE, BS13. Sir John de Meriet was Lord of the Manor of Ashton, Long Ashton during the reign of Edward II.

MERIONETH STREET, BS3. Place name, among other streets beginning with the letter M.

MERITON STREET, BS2. It has been suggested that this name may have some connection with the nineteenth century clay pits near the site of the street.

MERLIN CLOSE, BS9. The merlin is the smallest of the British falcons and the road was almost certainly named thus because of its proximity to Falcondale Road.

MERLIN ROAD, BS12. Amidst other roads called after aeroplanes and engines. The Rolls-Royce Merlin powered some of the greatest British aircraft of the Second World War, including the Spitfire, Hurricane, Lancaster and Mosquito. It was fitted to the North American P51 Mustang and built under license by Packard in the USA. More locally, it was used in some models of the Bristol Beaufighter. This powerful engine was also used in motor torpedo boats.

MERRIMANS ROAD, BS11. There were people of this name living in Westbury at the time the road was built. It is possible they owned the land, or perhaps had some interest in the quarry sited there before development took place.

MERSTHAM ROAD, BS2. Place name derived from OE *mear*, 'marten' and *sæt*, 'ambush', thus 'a trap for martens in a meadow'.

MERTON ROAD, BS7. Place name. The first syllable means lake. A house in this road was once the home of Lord Nelson who was commemorated by a hospital in the same road, named in his honour.

MERVYN ROAD, BS7. The forename of Mr Stony-Maskeleyne (1823-1911) owner of much of the land in this area. He was a celebrated mineralogist, M.P. for Cricklade 1880-92 and Lord of the Manor of Horfield. *See Maskelyne Avnue.*

METFORD GROVE / PLACE / ROAD, BS6. Named after William Ellis Metford 1824–1899. He worked as an engineer on the construction of the railway between Bristol and Exeter Railway from 1841 to 1846. He then emigrated to work on the East India Railway, arriving in 1857 just as the Mutiny broke out. His health broke down and he and his wife returned to England in 1858. He devoted the rest of his life to perfecting the design of his Metford Rifle, which from 1871 to 1894 only four times failed to win the Duke of Cambridge's prize of the National Rife Association, and many features of which were incorporated in the British Army's standard issue Lee-Enfield .303 magazine rifle in 1883. All the bullets used in his match and military rifles were made in his house (Redland Villa) in Elm Lane. He died there in 1899 aged 75. His biographer concedes, 'though devoted chiefly to scientific pursuits, he was above all a God-fearing man'. Metford Road. Place and Grove appear to have been given their names in 1930 because of the ownership of the land by Baron Cottesloe, who was a keen rifleman and a 'disciple' of Metford.

MIDDLE AVENUE, BS1. Self-explanatory.

MIDDLE ROAD, BS15. This may have been named after the Middle Pit at the nearby colliery.

MIDDLEFORD HOUSE, BS13. The name of a field belonging to Down Farm in the Manor of Bedminster 1798.

MIDDLETON ROAD, BS11. Built on lands belonging to the Manor of Bishop's Stoke, which had passed into the ownership of Lord Middleton in 1721.

MIDLAND ROAD, BS2. The original name for this road was Whipping Cat Hill, which is thought to have been a corruption of the Whip and cat Inn. The road was re-named in this less exciting fashion when the Midland Railway built nearby St. Phillip's station, which opened on 2nd May 1870.

MIDLAND ROAD / TERRACE, BS16. These, too, were near the railway line, so almost certainly as BS2.

MILDRED STREET, BS5. Possibly another member of the Gerrish family. *See Gerrish Avenue.*

MILE WALK, BS14. A reference to the boundary laid down in Edward III's Charter of 1373.

MILES ROAD, BS8. This road was established in 1869 upon building land sold by the Merchant Venturers. It may commemorate Henry Cruger Miles, who was a Merchant Venturer nominee on the Downs Committee at that time.

MILFORD STREET, BS3. A place name meaning 'ford by the mill'.

MILL AVENUE, BS1. There were still flour and corn mills here as late as the 1920s.

MILL HOUSE, BS5. Built in 1976 on land where a rank of shops once stood. On the opposite side of the road were the mills that gave Baptist Mills their name. *See Baptist Street.*

MILL LANE, BS3. Self-explanatory.

MILL LANE, BS15. The path which would once have led to the mill.

MILL POOL COURT, BS10. A field name taken from the Westbury-on-Trym tithe map.

MILLARD CLOSE, BS10. Named after the chairman of the development association.

MILLBANK CLOSE, BS4. Near the river, so perhaps the site of a mill many years ago.

MILLBROOK AVENUE, BS4. This is another on the Channel Islands theme. Millbrook is on the outskirts of St. Helier, Jersey.

MILLERS DRIVE, BS15. Obvious association with the trade carried out here.

MILLFIELD DRIVE, BS15. Field name pertaining to land by the mill.

MILLGROUND ROAD, BS13. Self-explanatory field name in Bishport Manor in 1683.

MILLIMAN CLOSE, BS13. Tenement or holding listed in the Dundry Enclosure Award of 1815. Derivation is OE *mylen,* 'mill' and *mæne,* 'common' or 'communal'.

MILLMEAD HOUSE, BS13. A field name - meadow by the mill.

MILLPOND STREET, BS2. Presumably descriptive.

MILLWARD GROVE, BS16. *See Maywood.*

MILNER GREEN, BS15. A fairly recent naming, and possibly named after a G.P., Dr. Milner, who worked in this area.

MILNER ROAD, BS7. After Alfred, Viscount Milner (1854-1925), whose hasty decision to end discussions with the Boers precipitated the second Boer War in 1899. In spite of this he was greatly admired because of his belief in imperial unity.

MILSOM STREET, BS5. A.C. Milsom, Builders, had their premises in nearby Beaufort Street.

MILTON PARK, BS5. Named after John Milton (1608-74), a colossus among English poets, whose best-remembered work is *Paradise Lost.*

MILTON ROAD, BS7. This is probably someone connected with the land on which these houses were built. There were people of that name living and trading in the area in the 1930s.

MILTONS CLOSE, BS13. This was a private road mentioned in the Dundry Enclosure Award of 1815.

MILVERTON GARDENS, BS6. Named after a small town in Somerset, the meaning being 'homestead or village by the mill ford'.

MINA ROAD, BS2. Named after a hero of the Peninsular War, General Francesco Espozy Mina, leader of a highly successful expeditionary force against the French under Wellington. He lived from 1781 to 1836.

MINEHEAD ROAD, BS4. Sited among other roads with West Country names.

MINTO ROAD, BS2. Given the date this road was built, the inspiration for the naming must have come from the fourth Earl of Minto (1845-1914). He was Governor-General of Canada and Viceroy of India.

MINTON CLOSE, BS14. Following the theme of calling roads after potteries and china manufacturers. There was a Pottery Farm in the area before development was started.

MITCHELL COURT, BS1. Off Mitchell Lane.

MITCHELL LANE, BS1. This street was established here prior to 1670 and it must be supposed that Mitchell was a person who traded there, although it could have derived from OE *mycel*, 'great'.

MIVART STREET, BS5. This may be the surname of the landowner. One of that name was a trader plying between Britain and the Gold Coast in the nineteenth century and he has descendants living in the Bristol area, one of whom retains the name Mivart as one of his forenames.

MODECOMBE GROVE, BS10. Robert Modecombe was vicar of Henbury 1359-61.

MOGG STREET, BS2. After Richard Mogg Bryant, owner of the Mina Road brickworks.

MOLESWORTH CLOSE / DRIVE, BS13. Named after Rev. Walter Molesworth, Vicar of Bishopsworth 1868-1909. This was his only benefice after serving fourteen years as curate at Lincoln and Painswick, Gloucestershire. A clock was installed in the church tower in 1913 in his memory.

MONK ROAD / MONK'S PARK AVENUE, BS7. Named in honour of James Henry Monk, Bishop of Gloucester (1830) and Bristol. His palaces were at Gloucester and Stapleton.

MONKS AVENUE, BS15. Named after Alfred Monks and Sons, who were builders in New Queen Street, who were responsible for much of the development in this area.

MONKTON ROAD, BS15. The name of a town in Devon. It adjoins Launceston Road, Launceston being a town in Cornwall.

MONMOUTH ROAD, BS7. Among other roads called after places in the British Isles. No pattern emerges.

MONMOUTH STREET, BS3. Among a long line of streets with the initial M.

MONSDALE CLOSE / DRIVE, BS10. Richard Monsdale lived in the parish of Westbury-on-Trym in 1636. He married Lois Jones on 18 September 1636 in Westbury church.

MONTAGUE HILL / PLACE / STREET, BS2. Said to have formed part of the land owned by the Montacutes. In 1766 a bowling green attached to a house in the Barton had a frontage of 184 ft on Montague Street.

MONTGOMERY STREET, BS3. The first in a succession of streets beginning with the letter M.

MONTREAL AVENUE, BS7. These houses were built by Teddy Williams, who had worked as a construction engineer in Montreal. Interestingly, he worked from models made of matchsticks rather than conventional plans. *See Toronto Road.*

MONTROSE AVENUE, BS6. James Graham, First Marquis of Montrose, fought for the cause of Charles I in Scotland during the Civil War. His story formed the basis of Sir Walter Scott's *A Legend of Montrose*, and so he found his way here, continuing the Walter Scott theme.

MONTROSE PARK, BS4. The Lindsay family, later the Grahams, were the Dukes of Montrose, but it is not possible to establish a local connection.

MONTROSE DRIVE, BS15. Continuing the theme of golf courses in this development.

MONTROY CLOSE, BS9. Apparently an invented name.

MOON STREET, BS2. Perhaps after the Full Moon Inn, an ancient hostelry.

MOOR CROFT DRIVE, BS15. This was the name of a field on the Barr's Court estate.

MOOR GROVE, BS11. Moor Grove is a wood at Lawrence Weston, the name being derived from OE *mor,* 'marshland' and *graf,* 'grove' or 'copse'.

MOOREND GARDENS, BS11. Field name.

MOORHILL STREET, BS5. Thought to be a made-up name.

MOORLANDS ROAD, BS16. Probably a reference to the terrain.

MORAVIAN COURT / ROAD, BS15. After the chapel here, built by the Moravians who first came to the area in 1670, having been driven out of Bohemia by Hapsburg persecutions in 1722. They were influenced by the seventeenth century Pietist movement which stressed temperate living, good works and bible study. Most members today live in North America.

MORDEN WALK, BS14. A Dorset village, whose name was chosen to continue the theme begun with Sturminster Road.

MORETON CLOSE / STREET, BS2. This was the family name of the Earls of Ducie, who played an important role in Bristol's civic history. *See Ducie Road.*

MORGAN STREET, BS2. Named after one of the partners of Franklyn, Davey, Morgan and Co, a tobacco firm, who was also very active in civic affairs. This was one of three streets built in the 1870s on land belonging to St. Nicholas Vestry (purchased 1698). This area was known as 'The Forlorn Hope estate' after an old house which stood in the area.

MORLEY AVENUE / CLOSE / ROAD, BS16 / ROAD, BS3 / SQUARE, BS7/ STREET, BS2, BS5 / TERRACE, BS15. Almost certainly all these streets were named after Samuel Morley, who was a Liberal M.P. for Bristol on three occasions in the second half of the nineteenth century, and was a generous benefactor of religious causes in the city.

MORNINGTON ROAD, BS8. The Earl of Mornington (1735-81) was the father of the Duke of Wellington, famed for his part in the Peninsular Wars. Wellington Park is situated nearby. The Earl of Mornington was also the title of the eldest son of the Wellesley family, which owned large areas of land in Bristol.

MORPETH ROAD, BS4. Among other roads named after places famous for their castles. Morpeth Castle is in Northumberland.

MORRIS ROAD, BS7. Celebrating William Morris (1834-96), leading light of the Arts and Crafts Movement; artist, poet, writer and wallpaper designer.

MORSE ROAD, BS5. Named after Morse Goulter, who owned the land here and had the houses built.

MORTIMER ROAD, BS8. From Mortimer House, home of Thomas Tod Walton, Sheriff of Bristol 1872-74 and Postmaster 1842-71. He died on Christmas Day 1885. In later years John Carter, Councillor for Clifton Ward 1852-25, owned the house. Apparently it was a fine house surrounded by elms with a plantation and extensive gardens at the back.

MORTIMER ROAD, BS12. After the Mortimer brothers, who farmed 'The Brimbles', part of Walliscourt Farm.

MOUNT GARDENS / MOUNT HILL GARDENS / ROAD, BS15. A reference to nearby Hanham Mount, scene of many of the open-air services which made this area such a stronghold of Methodism.

MOUNT PLEASANT TERRACE, BS3. This was a popular choice of name at the time these houses were built.

MOW BARTON, BS13. A field in Lamington Farm, Manor of Long Ashton in 1749. Mow is from OE *mawe*, 'meadow' and barton from Anglo Saxon *bere*, 'barley' and *tun*, 'farm', 'enclosure'.

MOWBRAY ROAD, BS14. Robert de Mowbray was the nephew of Godfrey, Bishop of Bristol. He inherited vast estates from his uncle.

MOWCROFT ROAD, BS13. Edward Mowcroft was Master of St. Catherine's Hospital, Bedminster in 1572. Robert de Berkeley founded the hospital in 1190. It was not primarily a religious house but a hostel for poor travellers. The last vestiges were demolished in 1887.

MOXHAM DRIVE, BS13. The name of someone who held land here in 1815.

MUIRFIELD, BS15. Another in the golf course series of roads.

MULBERRY CLOSE / DRIVE, BS15. Near Holly Crescent so this may have been built on parkland.

MULBERRY WALK, BS9. Following the arboreal theme of this development.

MULLER AVENUE / ROAD, BS7. After the Bristol philanthropist George Muller, who founded an orphanage in Wilson Street, trusting to God that the money and buildings to do so would be made available to him, which they always were, from many public donations. The orphanage thrived and was later moved to Ashley Down as the numbers increased. He died in March 1898 aged 92. The Muller Foundation still survives today, and its headquarters is in Cotham Park.

MULREADY CLOSE, BS7. William Mulready (1786-1863), painter and book illustrator. He designed the first penny postage stamp issued by Rowland Hill in 1840.

MURFORD AVENUE / WALK, BS13. Henry Murford was churchwarden of Long Ashton in 1767. His name is inscribed upon one of the bells in the church tower, which were cast by T. Bilbie of Chew Stoke.

MURRAY STREET, BS3. This was a tobacco firm that was taken over by Imperial Tobacco.

MUSGROVE CLOSE, BS7. John Musgrove possessed the manor of Aylminton in the Henbury hundred in 1277.

MYRTLE DRIVE, BS11. After the shrub renowned for its fragrance.

MYRTLE ROAD, BS2. This may be named after a person, rather than the Mediterranean evergreen shrub with sweet-scented white flowers, which would have been a popular conservatory plant, and was invariably used in Victorian wedding bouquets. It was also a popular girls' name in the nineteenth century.

MYRTLE STREET, BS3. This is another case in which the naming is more likely to be after a person than the shrub.

NAGS HEAD HILL, BS5. The Nag's Head was a popular name for a public house and it seems likely this hill took its name from one such hostelry. Another suggestion made is that it was the practice for carters to take hold of their horses' heads to help them up steep slopes such as this, so the name may have originated from this custom.

NAILSEA CLOSE, BS13. Named after a Somerset village, as are the surrounding streets.

NAPIER COURT, BS1. *See Napier Road BS6.*

NAPIER MILES ROAD / NAPIER ROAD / SQUARE, BS11. This was named after the last owner of Kingsweston House. The original property on the site was erected in the Tudor period but a new house designed by Sir John Vanbrugh was built for Sir Edward Southwell in 1710. Local masons were employed. It ceased to be a family home in 1937.

NAPIER ROAD, BS5. It seems probable that the origin of this choice was Robert Cornelius Napier, Baron Napier of Magdala (1810-90) who was in command of the British forces in the Abyssinian War of 1868 and successfully captured the capital, Magdala, for which he won a peerage. He had a distinguished military career and was Commander-in-Chief in India in 1870 and Governor of Gibraltar in 1876.

NAPIER ROAD, BS6. This Napier is probably Colonel George Napier (1751-1804) father of three sons with spectacular military careers. The Colonel himself saw service in Minorca and in the Irish Rebellion of 1798. He married Lady Sarah Lennox and lived in Bristol for several years prior to his death. He is buried in the churchyard of Redland Green Chapel, where there is a tablet to his memory.

Narrow Lane, BS16. Presumably descriptive.

Narrow Plain, BS2. Opposite Broad Plain, now divided from it by Temple Way.

Narrow Quay, BS1. Narrow Quay runs from the Bridgehead to the Arnolfini, and is so called because of the narrow distance between the buildings and the River Floar, which extended to the end of Baldwin Street. The Quay itself extended to St. John's Bridge.

Narroways Road, BS2. From nearby Narroways Hill. The name Narroways may have its origin in the fact that access to the hill is by a path only a few feet wide, alongside St. Werburgh's church, leading to Mina Road. On a 1769 map it is shown as Nethways Hill. For many years after the murder of Ada James in 1913 the locals referred to it as Cut-throat Lane because Ada's fiancé, Ted Palmer, slashed her throat with a razor after a quarrel by the stile at the top of the hill. Incredibly she managed to make her way to the corner of Lynmouth Road where she was found, bleeding to death, by the local bobby. Ted Palmer, an amateur boxer from Montpelier, was hanged for the crime.

Naseby Walk, BS5. Naseby, Northamptonshire, was the scene of a decisive Civil War battle in June 1645, won by the Parliamentarians under Fairfax and Cromwell.

Nash Drive, BS7. After Paul Nash (1889-1946), a watercolourist of great individuality. He was an official war artist in both world wars, but very much on his own terms: *'Feeble, inarticulate will be my message, but it will have a bitter truth and may it burn their lousy souls.'*

Neath Road, BS5. A place name. According to one authority it means sanctuary or retreat. It could also be named after the vast ruined abbey at Neath in South Wales, founded in 1130 by Richard de Granville. 'Neglected Neath, once the ornament of a lovely vale, looms up through its dense vale of smoke like the skeleton of a stranded ship.' Its precinct had been turned into a copper smelting and casting workshop during the eighteenth and nineteenth centuries.

Nelson Road, BS16. Possibly from Nelson and Sons, who traded at the top of what was then a lane.

Nelson Street, BS1. Formerly known as Hallier's Lane and before then, in the Middle Ages, as Grope (Cunt) Lane, because its narrowness encouraged such liberties in some passers by. The City Council ordered its name be changed in honour of the great naval hero, Admiral Lord Horatio Nelson (1758-1805), who died fighting the French and Spanish fleets at the Battle of Trafalgar, where he had hoisted his famous flag signal: 'England expects every man will do his duty.' 'Thank God, I have done mine'.

Nelson Street, BS3. Named together with Hardy Road and Trafalgar Terrace.

Neston Walk, BS4. Prince Rupert was based at Easton Neston Manor near Towcester in Cheshire in November 1643 with fourteen regiments, before going on the offensive against the Cromwellian troops in Bristol.

Netham Road, BS5. Leading to the district known as Netham - a field name, Neth Ham. The last syllable means river meadow, land in a bed or enclosure and the first syllable could be from the OE *naet*, moist or wet, thus 'small settlement in a damp place'.

Nettlestone Close, BS10. Probably a former field name.

Nevalan Drive, BS5. This would seem to be an invented name - perhaps an amalgam of Neville and Alan, for example.

NEVIL ROAD, BS7. After Mervyn Nevil Herbert Story-Maskelyne, principal land-owner in this district during the late nineteenth and early twentieth century. *See Mervyn Road and Maskelyne Road.*

NEVILLE ROAD, BS15. Possibly named after Henry Neville (1620-94), the English political writer who clashed with Cromwell and was forced to retire from the council of state. He was a staunch republican and spent time in the Tower of London accused of treason in 1663. However, given the relatively recent construction of the road it is more likely to be named after a person known to the builder.

NEW BUILDINGS, BS16. So named when they were built at the end of the nineteenth century.

NEW BRUNSWICK AVENUE, BS5. Developed in the 1930s and the 'new' was probably to distinguish it from other Brunswicks in the city. Perhaps named after the Canadian province.

NEW CHARLOTTE STREET, BS3. Appropriately sited next to Regent Road. Queen Charlotte Sophia of Mecklenburg-Strelitz was the wife of George III and bore him fifteen children, nine of them sons, the eldest being the dissipated Prince Regent, later George IV.

NEW CHELTENHAM ROAD, BS15. There was a Cheltenham Road that ran parallel to Regent Street on the Soundwell side of the street in the early years of the twentieth century, so presumably when the estate was developed this became known as New Cheltenham Road.

NEW FOSSEWAY ROAD, BS14. Named after the Fosse Way, the Roman road that ran from Lincoln to Exeter. The older Fosseway ran near where the A367 from Bath to Radstock can now be found and on to Shepton Mallet.

NEW JOHN STREET, BS3. Called after a nearby church that was destroyed in a bombing raid during the Second World War.

NEW KINGSLEY ROAD, BS2. This was once called Upper Cheese Lane and was renamed when Kingsley flats were built. It may have been named after the Canon and writer Charles Kingsley (1819-75) who was born at Holme in Devon and went to school at Clifton. He is mostly remembered today as author of *The Water Babies* and *Westward Ho!*. An alternative possibility, however, is Sir Kingsley Wood, a Minister for Health who was also responsible for housing, during the 1930's.

NEW QUEEN STREET, BS3. Adjoins Princess Street.

NEW QUEEN STREET, BS15. There is already a Queen Street nearby.

NEW ROAD, BS12 (2). The New Road was built in 1899 to replace access to Stoke Gifford after the railway was built across the bridle path. The second New Road in BS12 lies within the B.Ae. security area.

NEW STREET, BS2. This is hardly an apt description now as the street dates from the eighteenth century or even earlier.

NEW STATION ROAD, BS16. Leads to Station Avenue, the approach to Fishponds station, which was closed in the 1960s.

NEW THOMAS STREET, BS2. Probably built after Thomas Street, off Temple Street, now known as St. Thomas Street.

NEW WALLS, BS3. A close of this name appears on a 1610 map.

Newfoundland Road & Thomas Street before the Second World War

NEW WALK, BS15. This used to be a pathway called Short's Lane. In the late 1930s this land, behind the Kleenezee factory, was sold and a house built. The war then intervened and then, in the 1950s, more houses began to appear along the old lane, now the New Walk.

NEWBRIDGE CLOSE / ROAD, BS4. This leads to the bridge that crosses the Feeder canal.

NEWBURY ROAD, BS7. A town in Berkshire. Among other streets given place names.

NEWCOMBE DRIVE, BS9. Named after a small hamlet near Brean, Somerset.

NEWCOMBE ROAD, BS9. A made-up name with the local emphasis on Combe, meaning a wooded valley.

NEWENT AVENUE, BS5. A Gloucestershire village. From the Anglo-Saxon *neowe*, new, and the ME *went* or *wendu*, way.

NEWFOUNDLAND ROAD / STREET / WAY, BS2. Millerd's map of 1673 shows this as Newfoundland Lane. The name may refer to reclaimed land along the edge of the river wheron these houses were built. When nearby Cabot Street was built, it may have been assumed that Newfoundland Road had been named after Cabot's discovery, and so the offshoot gained its name.

NEWGATE, BS1. This was the site of a gate built in 1305 to replace one in existence as part of the defensive wall. It was an entrance to both the city and the castle. A prison once stood nearby at Castle Mill Street and Narrow Wine Street.

NEWLAND DRIVE / ROAD / WALK, BS13. Built on a field at Pigeon House farm, Hartcliffe.

THE NEWLANDS, BS16. From the Georgian manor of that name, demolished in the 1970s for this development. The house was known as the Frenchay Coffee House and Frenchay Inn in the eighteenth century, and became The New Inn in 1872.

NEWLYN AVENUE, BS9. A place name after the Cornish fishing port, which one expert translates as 'Church of St. Newelina'. St. Newellina was the daughter of King Ussig who resisted marriage arrangements made for her and escaped to Brittany, legend says, sailing on a leaf. A local prince fell in love with her but she rejected him as well, whereupon he cut off her head. The legend continues that she simply picked up her head and walked away. When she paused to rest, three drops of blood fell to the ground, causing three fountains to spring up at a place subsequently called Trois Fontaines. Her grave is venerated at Ste. Noyale, near Vannes in Brittany.

NEWLYN WALK, BS4. This is not among other nearby roads called after towns, so perhaps this had particular associations for the builder.

NEWMARKET AVENUE, BS1. This was built on the site of the new market where butchers traded, on ground purchased by the executors of Robert Kitchen's will for use by butchers as a shambles and tenement. It was conveyed to the Bristol City Corporation in 1654.

NEWNHAM CLOSE / PLACE, BS4. Named after the village of Newnham-on-Severn, in Gloucestershire. The derivation is 'new homestead' or village.

NEWPORT STREET, BS3. Place name meaning new town, probably named after Newport in Gwent, across the Bristol Channel.

NEWQUAY ROAD, BS4. The road, in common with others close by, is called after a town in Cornwall. There is no clear reason for this naming.

NEWRY WALK, BS4. Named after the town of Newry in Northern Ireland, in keeping with the theme of Irish place names on the Knowle West estate.

NEWTON CLOSE / DRIVE / ROAD, BS15. Undoubtedly after the Newton family, who were one-time owners of Barrs Court.

NEWTON STREET, BS5. Perhaps a place name, although the Newton family of Barrs Court had long associations with the city. Several members of the family are buried in the Cathedral where there is a Newton Chapel. There was once a Newton House in the street.

NIBLETT CLOSE, BS15. Another of the Methodist church names. *See Cade Close.*

NIBLETT'S HILL, BS5. This must once have led to the dwelling of someone of this name.

NIBLEY ROAD, BS11. A Gloucestershire village. The first syllable is from the OE *hnybba*, point or tip. Many local roads are called after Gloucestershire towns.

NICHOLAS LANE, BS5. Possibly named after the builder or an associate.

NICHOLAS ROAD, BS5. This began life as St. Nicholas Road, and lost the Saint tag in the early years of the twentieth century. Probably built on church land, as St. Nicholas Vestry owned considerable estates in the area.

NICHOLETTS, BS15. This was the name of the manager of the local Stuckey's Bank in 1911, which is now demolished. He was a prominent figure in civic activities.

NIGEL PARK, BS11. This development took place in the 1950s, obviously on the site of an old quarry as the main through road is an old quarry road. There were Merrimans living in Westbury-on-Trym, who may have had an interest in the business or owned the land, and Nigel may be a family connection. *See Merrimans Road, BS11.*

NINE TREE HILL, BS2. Built on land commonly known as Nine Trees, because of the elms upon it. The trees were burnt down by 'mischievous boys' prior to 1853.It was also the burial place of Mother Pugsley in 1702, faithful all her life to her Royalist husband who had been killed sixty years before during the Civil War. *See Dove Street.*

NINTH AVENUE, BS7. Following the transatlantic influence that seems to exist in this part of the city.

NOBLE AVENUE, BS15. John Noble, a yeoman, gave evidence at a trial regarding the liberties in 1629. Many roads in the area are influenced by the history of the Forest of Kingswood.

NORFOLK AVENUE, BS2. A number of roads locally are royalty-orientated. The Dukes of Norfolk, family name Howard, were in many periods of history the power behind the throne. Catherine Howard, the fifth wife and ill-fated teenage bride of Henry VIII, was a niece of the Duke of Norfolk.

NORFOLK AVENUE, BS2 / BS6. Probably named in the early years of the nineteenth century after the Duke of Norfolk, known as 'the eccentric gastronome' and a popular figure on his visits to the city. There is a Surrey Street near to the one in BS2; the eldest son of the Dukes of Norfolk always bears the title Earl of Surrey.

NORFOLK PLACE, BS3. *See Norfolk Avenue.*

NORLAND ROAD, BS8. From Norland House, long since demolished. The name means northern land.

NORLEY ROAD, BS7. A made-up name devised by the builder, William Lee, from the name of his daughter, Nora.

NORMAN GROVE, BS15. Perhaps a reference to the Norman Conquest. William the Conqueror's troops also occupied Bristol Castle.

NORMAN ROAD, BS2. Almost certainly the builder's name. There was a builder called James Norman living in Montpelier at the time these houses were built.

NORMANBY ROAD, BS5. In some directories this has been mis-spelt as Normandy. Normanby is a town near Middlesborough in North Yorkshire. The most probable origin is George Augustus Constantine Phipps, 2nd Marquis of Normanby, who held many important posts including Governor of New Zealand, Queensland and Victoria, and it is possible that he visited Bristol.

NORMANTON ROAD, BS8. From the Earldom of Normanton, family name Agar. The third Earl (1818-96) was M.P. for Wilton, Wiltshire.

NORRISVILLE ROAD, BS6. An invented name - the builder's name was Norris and *ville* is French for town.

NORTH CROFT, BS15. In all likelihood a field name.

NORTH DEVON ROAD, BS16. Harris suggests that there is a Devon Road in Whitehall and that this road lying to the north was so-called for that reason but this seems to be stretching a point somewhat. It is more likely the developer had associations with that area of the West Country.

NORTH GREEN STREET, BS8. Situated next to South Green Street - from the OE *grene*, grassy spot, village green. Perhaps there was such a feature here at one time.

NORTH PARK, BS15 / ROAD / STREET, BS3 / ROAD, BS6 / STREET, BS1, BS2/BS15/ BS16. The lie of these roads is not always north/south, so the namings seem to have an unclear geographical significance, known only to the developers.

NORTH VIEW, BS6. Not a strictly accurate description as the view is rather more to the west.

NORTH VIEW, BS16. There is a corresponding South View nearby.

NORTHCOTE ROAD, BS8. From the house of the same name, described in Morgan's Guide of 1851: 'attached to this very beautiful mansion is a shrubbery and garden with pleasure grounds in front of meadowland'. It probably took its name from nearby Cote House.

NORTHCOTE ROAD / STREET, BS5. Both these roads, one at St. George, the other in Easton, were called after Stafford Henry Northcote, First Earl of Iddlesleigh (1818-87) who held many important positions in government including Foreign Secretary and Chancellor of the Exchequer. His connection with Bristol is unclear, although he was interested enough in seafaring to write *A Short Review of the History of the Navigation Laws* in 1849.

NORTHCOTE ROAD, BS16. There was a house of this name in the area at the end of the nineteenth century.

NORTHEND AVENUE / GARDENS /ROAD, BS15. A directional naming.

NORTHFIELD AVENUE, BS15. Almost certainly a field name.

NORTHFIELD HOUSE, BS3. A field name taken from the tithe map.

NORTHFIELD ROAD, BS5. An old field name.

NORTHLEACH WALK, BS11. All the rounds in this development are called after Cotswold villages and towns.

NORTHOVER ROAD, BS9. To judge by the naming of nearby roads, this is a made-up name.

NORTHUMBERLAND ROAD, BS6. This naming is in keeping with other local roads called after members of the peerage - in this case the Sixth Duke (1810-99), who was Lord Privy Seal - as the road was constructed at the turn of the twentieth century.

NORTHUMBRIA DRIVE, BS9. Northumbria is the ancient name for Northumberland and these houses were built on the Northumberland House estate.

NORTHVILLE ROAD, BS7. A made-up name, the area being in the north of Bristol with the French last syllable meaning 'town'.

NORTHWAY, BS12. A geographically accurate description.

NORTHWICK ROAD, BS7. Named after the Gloucestershire hamlet.

NORTHWOODS WALK, BS10. A field name.

NORTON CLOSE, BS15. Named after the village of Bishop's Norton in the Dudstone Hundred. Archbishop Thomas held this at the time of the Domesday Book when there were fifteen villagers, with fifteen ploughs and four serfs.

NORTON ROAD, BS4. An old local name. There was once a field called Norton Road Paddock, shown on the 1845 Whitchurch tithe map.

NORWICH DRIVE, BS4. All the roads in this group are called after towns famed for their cathedrals or abbeys.

NOTTINGHAM ROAD, BS7. One of the roads surrounding the Gloucestershire County Ground and called after county cricket teams.

NOTTINGHAM STREET, BS3. Named after a town like Bristol, that has connections with the tobacco industry, which was so prominent in this area at one time. Here in Bedminster was the factory of Henry Overton Wills, later under the administration of his two sons, which brought work and prosperity to the local people. Local businesses flourished and a position with the company was coveted. People were willing to travel any distance for a chance to work at Wills. Nottingham was the home town of John Player, who formed the Imperial Tobacco Company with W.D. and H.O. Wills around 1901.

NOVA SCOTIA PLACE, BS1. Built in the eighteenth century. The street's name honours the Treaty of Utrecht in 1713 when France ceded Nova Scotia as well as Newfoundland, Hudson's Bay Territory and Gibraltar to Britain. The hotel of the same name was not built until 1811.

NOVERS CRESCENT / HILL / LANE / PARK DRIVE / PARK ROAD / ROAD, BS4. These street names derive from the OE *ofer*, a slope, ridge or hill. This area used to be called the Nubbers by old-time residents.

NUGENT HILL, BS6. Nugent House once stood here, so-named in honour of Robert Nugent (1702-88) M.P. for Bristol and poet. He was a popular figure who tried to advance the interests of the poor in Bristol, and died a tremendously rich man due to his habit of marrying rich widows, with whom he lived in great disaffection. Walpole coined the phrase "to nugentise", meaning to attempt to enrich oneself through the same process. He was a great friend of Oliver Goldsmith and wrote odes for his friends, although some suspected him of paying minor poets to write them for him... His character was summed up by Glover as 'A jovial and voluptuous Irishman, who had left Popery for the Protestant religion, money and widows'. A suggestion has been made that it may have been named after Sir George Nugent, his son, father in law to Sir Thomas Francis Fremantle.

Beneath the back boundary wall dividing No. 10 Nugent Hill from 2 Clare Road is the tablet which marked Mother Pugsley's Well. It was first mentioned in AD 883, when it was Waldes Well, and marked the boundary of lands restored to the church under King Alfred. It was thought to have curative propertites, and was devoted to the Virgin Mary in the Middle Ages. The area was a pleasure garden in the seventeeth century, and after the death of Mother Pugsley *(see Dove Street)* there were plans to rail the spring and to provide bigger basins for the public. Nothing was done, and in 1939 the builder of Spring Villa at 10 Nugent Hill enclosed the spring for his personal use. Despite the protests, The Corporation decided it did not have funds to pursue the public's right of access. *See Fremantle Road / Square.*

NURSERY GARDENS, BS10. Presumably descriptive of the original purpose of this ground.

THE NURSERY, BS3. Self-explanatory, again once the site of gardens.

NUTFIELD GROVE, BS12. Almost certainly an old field name.

NUTGROVE AVENUE, BS3. Possibly the scene, long ago, of a rural idyll.

NUTHATCH DRIVE / GARDENS, BS16. Chosen in keeping with the other bird names used for local roads.

NYMPSFIELD, BS15. The name of a long barrow in Gloucestershire excavated in 1936 by Mrs Clifford on behalf of the Bristol and Gloucestershire Archaeological Society.

OAK LANE, BS5. Probably oaks did grow here before this area was developed as an industrial site.

OAK ROAD, BS7. Several local roads are called after trees.

OAK TREE CLOSE, BS15. A reminder of when this was all woodland.

OAKDALE AVENUE / CLOSE / COURT / ROAD, BS16. The rural aspects of the locality are emphasised here.

OAKDALE ROAD, BS4. A made-up name.

OAKDENE AVENUE, BS5. This was formerly Cemetery Road, as it led to Ridgeway Cemetery. The name was changed around the 1950s when additional houses were built, so Oakdene is probably an invention of the developer.

OAKENHILL WALK, BS4. Oakenhill Farm, which is still standing, together with three neighbouring Oakenhill cottages, was built in the sixteenth century and is one of the district's oldest farmhouses.

OAKFIELD GROVE / PLACE / ROAD, BS8. Oakfield House stood nearby at one time.

OAKFIELD ROAD, BS15. Several roads in the immediate vicinity have names which may date from the past, which would suggest that these houses stand on the site of a field where oaks grew.

OAKHANGER DRIVE, BS11. Field name meaning a field on the hillside from OE *hangra*,'wooded slope'. This term survives as dialect in the South Downs of Sussex and Hampshire.

OAKHILL AVENUE, BS15. There seems not to have been a house of this name so perhaps it is purely descriptive.

OAKHURST ROAD, BS9. An apparently made-up name.

OAKLAND ROAD, BS6. Thought to be an invented name.

OAKLAND ROAD, BS5. Aptly named, this road overlooks the park.

OAKLANDS CLOSE / ROAD, BS16. Called after a farm that was demolished in the 1960s.

OAKLANDS DRIVE, BS16. Descriptive of the former terrain.

OAKLANDS DRIVE, BS15 After a house of this name in Barry Road.

OAKLEIGH AVENUE, BS5. A made-up name.

OAKLEIGH GARDENS, BS15. Another road named after a now vanished house.

OAKLEY ROAD, BS7. Place name meaning 'the glade where the oaks grow'.

OAKMEAD PARK, BS4. Probably this was once a meadow where oaks flourished.

OAKRIDGE CLOSE, BS15. Descriptive of locale in times past.

OAKTREE COURT / GARDENS, BS13. Self-explanatory.

OAKWOOD AVENUE / OAKWOOD ROAD, BS9. Self-explanatory.

OATLANDS AVENUE, BS4. A field name taken from the 1840 tithe map.

OBERON AVENUE, BS5. There is no obvious reason why this road was called after the king of the fairies in Shakespeare's *A Midsummer Night's Dream*. There is a chance it may have been someone's forename.

OKEBOURNE CLOSE / ROAD, BS10. Henry William Okebourne was Dean of Westbury College in 1451.

OLD ASHLEY HILL, BS6. There is no proof that this is, in fact, older than Ashley Hill.

OLD BARROW HILL, BS11. A name that seems to imply an ancient settlement here.

OLD BREAD STREET, BS2. Developed at the same time as New Bread Street in the eighteenth century.

OLD FARM LANE, BS15. Clearly this was the entrance to a farm, long since vanished.

OLD GLOUCESTER ROAD BS16. This was the old route to Gloucester.

OLD KING STREET COURT, BS1. A reminder of Old King Street, which stood here before the new shopping centre was built in the 1950s. It is uncertain to which king it refers; either Charles II or one of the first three Georges may have been the choice.

OLD MARKET STREET, BS2. This has been known as the Old Market since Norman times as it was the site of a Saxon market. The kitchens of Bristol Castle were near this part of the moat and the buying and selling took place between the Castle and Lawfords Gate.

OLD PARK / OLD PARK HILL, BS2. On the 1673 map the site of this road is shown as Ye Little Park. On Donne's map of 1773 the district is shown as The Park.

OLD QUARRY RISE / ROAD, BS11. Self-explanatory. These roads were developed towards the end of the First World War for the use of employees of the Ministry of Munitions who were based at Avonmouth.

OLD SNEED AVENUE / PARK / ROAD. BS9. Named after the house of the same name built circa 1650. It is described in 1779: 'though seated on the agreeable eminence, is sheltered by hills on every side'. It had recently been repaired at that time and 'is now a cheerful and comfortable habitation'. The infamous Sir Ralph Sadlier owned Sneed Park, as opposed to the house. The word Sneed or Sneyd comes from OE *snæd*, 'detached piece of land'. *See Sadlier Close.*

OLDACRE ROAD, BS1. This would seem to be an old field name.

OLDBURY CHASE, BS15. The Chase would have extended to this point.

OLDBURY COURT DRIVE / ROAD, BS16. Named after the estate and old house, built before 1610, which once stood here. It was demolished in 1949. The name means old fortified place or fortified manor house or farmstead.

OLDFIELD PLACE, BS8. From Thomas Oldfield who, in 1720, leased land at Hotwells, including Dowry Square, to George and William Tully, who built houses there. He was in partnership with the former, the builder of Dowry Chapel, at one time.

Old Market in the early twentieth century

OLDMEAD WALK, BS13. A field name: the old meadow.

OLVESTON ROAD. BS7. A village near Thornbury. The first syllable is a personal name, the Anglo Saxon *Ælf* and the last syllable *tun*, 'village', 'farm' or 'enclosure'.

OLYMPUS ROAD, BS12. In the group of aircraft-related namings at Cribb's Causeway. The Bristol Siddeley Olympus turbojet engine was developed for the Vulcan bomber in 1955. It was subsequently used for the ill-fated TSR (tactical strike and reconnaissance) project and for Concorde. In its final version, with the addition of reheat, it was capable of producing almost twice as much power as the earlier type.

ORAM COURT, BS15. Named after Peggy Oram, the last person to operate the Hanham ferry.

ORANGE STREET, BS2. From William Henry Nassau, Prince of Orange, who married the Princess Royal of England in 1734. He visited Bristol the month prior to the wedding. He dined at the Merchants' Hall, was conducted to the Hotwells and Quay and was later treated to a sumptuous supper and ball. He slept at the house of Alderman John Day. There is a Lemon Street nearby and both roads were close to St. Clement's church that calls to mind the nursery rhyme 'Oranges and Lemons', but the rhyme refers of course to London churches, and St. Clement's church was not built until 1854. It was destroyed in an air raid.

ORCHARD AVENUE / LANE / STREET, BS1. Built on the site of an orchard belonging to the Carmelite priory. Part of the orchard was thought to have belonged to Gaunt's Hospital.

ORCHARD BOULEVARD, BS15. To judge by the names of the surrounding fields this was built on farmland. It was designated a boulevard in keeping with the other Americanised names adopted by the developers.

ORCHARD CLOSE, BS9. Built on the site of an orchard within the grounds of Bishop's Knoll.

ORCHARD COURT / ROAD / SQUARE, BS5. This area was renowned for its market gardens until housing development began in the second half of the nineteenth century.

ORCHARD CRESCENT, BS11. The names of many roads hereabouts suggest that there was a religious order housed here. This clearly was the site of its orchard.

ORCHARD DRIVE, BS4. Field names have been used for nearby roads, leading one to suppose this road was built on farmland.

ORCHARD GARDENS / ROAD / VALE / THE ORCHARDS, BS15. All situated on the hillside, most probably on ground used by the market gardeners.

ORCHARD ROAD, BS7. This would have referred to the orchard attached to either Seymour Villa or West Lodge, or else to the farm house which backs on to this road.

ORLAND WAY, BS15. The California link again here. *See California Road.*

ORLEBAR GARDENS, BS11. On the death of Sir Samuel Astry the estate, the manor of Bishop's Stoke and Henbury, was divided between his three surviving daughters one of whom, Diana, married Richard Orlebar of Hinwick in Bedfordshire.

ORMEROD ROAD, BS9. Perhaps named in honour of Dr H. L. Ormerod. He practiced in the area for many years and was Medical Officer of Health for the Henbury district of the Thornbury Union.

ORPEN GARDENS, BS7. Sir William Newnham Montague Orpen (1878-1931) was a portrait painter and official war artist in 1917-19.

ORWELL STREET, BS3. Although this is a place name, in this case the derivation would seem more likely to be a person's name, in keeping with other roads nearby. Perhaps it was the builder or the landowner.

OSBORNE AVENUE, BS7. The adjacent road is called after what was the parish church, St. Bartholomew's, so perhaps this was the name of one of its vicars.

OSBORNE ROAD, BS3. From Jeremiah Osborne, solicitor and owner of the land.

OSBORNE ROAD, BS8. Probably after Osborne House on the Isle of Wight, one of the homes of Queen Victoria and the place of her death in 1901.

OSBORNE TERRACE, BS3. Near Brighton Terrace so perhaps both called after royal holiday resorts.

OSBORNE VILLAS, BS2. Perhaps a person's name, as other surnames are in evidence locally. This may have been the landowner.

OSPREY COURT / ROAD, BS5. There seems no reason to call these developments after a rare bird.

OTTERFORD CLOSE, BS14. Continuing the theme of Somerset place names in the area.

OTTERY CLOSE, BS11. Ralph de Ottery, Prebend of Lawrence Weston in the fourteenth century. The chapel of Lawrence Weston was demolished before 1600.

OVERNDALE ROAD, BS16. From Overn House which once stood here.

OVERNHILL COURT / ROAD, BS16. From the house of the same name once occupied by the brother-in-law of the famous cricketer Dr. W. G. Grace.

OVERNHURST COURT, BS16. A combination, it would seem, of Overnhill and Hurstwood, which are nearby roads.

OVERTON ROAD, BS6. Perhaps the surname of the owner of this land.

OWEN GROVE, BS9. This may be a person's name, as there is a Lawrence Grove nearby.

OWEN STREET, BS5. Perhaps named after Robert Owen (1771-1858), the social reformer. He was born at Newtown in Wales and in 1794 purchased a cotton factory in New Lanark, Lanarkshire, where he employed no children under ten and established a ten-and-a-half hour working day for adults, which was unheard of at the time. He pioneered schools, and especially infant schools, for all children in the United Kingdom, and silenced many of his critics through his commercial success, although he also campaigned for trades unions to achieve better pay and conditions for workers. He was socially notorious for his publicly stated atheistic beliefs. Although he dreamed of community life where there no wages and no profits, his socialistic settlements in the United Kingdom and America were all unsuccessful, although the Co-operative movements he founded endure to this day.

OWLS HEAD ROAD, BS15. From the Owls Head Ground owned by Charles Bragge and leased to Thomas Britton and Partners, who were engaged in coal mining. There was an iron works here, too, in later years.

OXFORD PLACE, BS5. Perhaps named after the city. It joins up with Warwick Road.

OXFORD PLACE, BS8. Perhaps named after the Earl of Oxford, as the aristocracy are well represented in this area.

OXFORD STREET, BS2. It may be that this road is named after the city as place names have been used in surrounding streets.

OXFORD STREET, BS5. This Barton Hill street lies next to Cambridge Street.

OXFORD STREET, BS2. Probably after the Dukedom. Clarence Street lies nearby.

OXFORD STREET, BS3. This road runs off Cambridge Street.

OXLEAZE, BS13. Holding shown on Dundry Enclosure Award 1815. The name derives from OE *oxa*, 'ox' and *læse*, 'pasture'.

OXLEAZE LANE, BS13. This sounds as though it might have been pastureland on a farm that was once here.

OZLEWORTH, BS15. Ozleworth is in Gloucestershire, near Wotton-under-Edge. It is mentioned in the Domesday Book as being in the Hundred of Berkeley.

PADDOCK GREEN, BS4. It must be assumed that this was once a piece of farmland where the horses were kept.

PADMORE COURT, BS5. Named after a seventeenth century inventor who devised a pump for raising raise water from the river. This was first used at St. George by the Bristol Waterworks Company.

PADSTOW ROAD, BS4. Among other roads with West Country town names.

PAGE ROAD, BS16. After Alderman Page, who gave Page Park to the community.

PAGES MEAD, BS11. An old field name, 'Page's Meadow'.

PALMDALE CLOSE, BS15. This is a name chosen to continue the Californian theme triggered by the old pit.

PALMERS CLOSE, BS15. It is possible that this road was named after Alfred Palmer, who lived in Ashlands House on the Bath Road during the 1930s.

PALMERSTON ROAD, BS6. After Henry John Temple, third Viscount Palmerston (1784-1865), Foreign Secretary and later twice Prime Minister. He visited Bristol in 1865 to open an exhibition at the Drill Hall.

PALMERSTON STREET, BS3. *See Palmerston Road.*

PALMYRA ROAD, BS3. There is no apparent reason for this choice of name. The Syrian city of Palmyra, 'the city of the palm trees', said to have been founded by Solomon, is the site of magnificent Roman remains, including a colonnade nearly a mile long. There was a new vogue for re-discovering and appreciating such ruins by western archaeologists and travellers during the nineteenth century.

THE PARAGON, BS8. Described by Morgan in 1872 as 'a semi-circular range of handsome houses at the south-east end of Princess Buildings' from which one could view 'the most delightful scenery of Leigh Woods and the packets plying to and fro'. A packet was a steam ship which operated in the Bristol Channel. The houses were begun in 1807 and completed in 1814 and the selection of name is apt as it means 'model of perfection'.

THE PARADE, BS9. When this development was laid out in the 1920s many simple descriptive names were used for roads to suit the unfussy layout.

PARBROOK COURT, BS14. Continuing the local theme of Somerset village names.

PARFITT'S HILL, BS5. Presumably the name of the landowner. It is a fairly common surname in this part of the country.

PARK AVENUE, BS5. Adjoins St. George's Park. The park was laid out c. 1890.

PARK AVENUE, BS3. Adjacent to Victoria Park. The park was opened in 1891.

PARK CLOSE / CRESCENT / ROAD / WAY, BS15. Possibly named after a nearby farm, called Parkwall Farm.

Looking up Park Street towards the Wills Building, in the 1920s

PARK CLOSE / VIEW / ROAD / THE PARK / PARKLANDS, BS15. Named for their proximity to Kingswood Park.

PARK CRESCENT / THE PARK, BS16. The park referred to here is Frenchay Park.

PARK CRESCENT, BS5. This road is at the Whitehall end of St. George's Park, which was completed between 1895 and 1897. The land was purchased from the Ecclesiastical Commissioners and covered thirty-eight acres. The idea of a park in the area was first proposed by Handel Cossham, although he envisaged it as being on land near his Holly Lodge house.

PARK FARM COURT, BS15. The Haskins family ran Park Farm at the beginning of the twentieth century.

PARK GROVE, BS6, BS9. An offshoot of Henleaze Park Drive. The park here was a private estate attached to Henleaze House.

PARK HILL / ROAD, BS11. Adjacent to Shirehampton Park.

PARK LANE, BS2 / PLACE, BS8. These were part of the Little Park estate, which was owned by the Dunning family, who were Bristol merchants in the late seventeeth and early eighteenth centuries.

PARK PLACE, BS5. So named for its proximity to Stonebridge Park. It is also in the vicinity of Eastville Park, purchased by the Bristol Corporation in 1889 for £30,000.

PARK ROAD, BS16.(2) Of the two Park Roads in BS16, one is named for its proximity to Duchess Park, so named after the Dowager Duchess who occupied Stoke House. *See Countess Walk.* The other runs past Page Park, which was opened in 1910, a gift

to the community from Alderman Page, a well-respected benefactor. Before the park was built this was a field with a pond which had been enlarged into a lake.

PARK ROAD, BS12. Built on part of the Filton Park Estate.

PARK ROAD, BS3. There was a Park House in Beauley Road when these houses were built.

PARK ROW / STREET / AVENUE, BS1. The street was built through Bullocks Park, part of the Tyndalls Estate, during the Georgian period. Park Row used to be known as Griffin Lane.

PARK STREET / PARK VIEW TERRACE, BS5. Near to St. George's Park. *See Park Crescent.*

PARK STREET, BS4. The park here is that of Arnos Court. The only park near here now is the cemetery, but perhaps the land did belong to Arnos Court prior to the construction of these Totterdown streets.

PARK WOOD CLOSE, BS13. There was once a field near here called Park Ground.

PARKER STREET, BS3. Probably after the auctioneers and estate agents of that name.

PARKERS BARTON / CLOSE, BS5. Presumably after the owner of a farm here.

PARKFIELD AVENUE, BS5. Named after the old Parkfield Colliery, owned by the Bristol Colliery Co. Ltd., which closed in 1936.

PARKHURST AVENUE, BS16. The name of a forest on the Isle of Wight, mentioned in the Domesday Book. It is also the name of a prison on the island.

PARKLANDS ROAD, BS3. So named for its proximity to the Ashton Court estate of which it must, at one time, have formed part. For 400 years Ashton Court was home to the Smyth family. The house and land were acquired by the Bristol Corporation in 1960.

PARKSIDE GARDENS, BS5. The road adjoins playing fields.

PARKSTONE AVENUE, BS7. Named after a village near Poole, Dorset.

PARKWALL CRESCENT / ROAD, BS15. After the farm of this name which, in turn, was called after the wall around the park of Barrs Court estate.

PARLIAMENT STREET, BS4. It appears that this area figured prominently in the Civil War. Canon were unearthed there a couple of centuries later.

PARNELL ROAD, BS16. The road was built in 1912. At that time the Parnell family owned a foundry at the end of the road, and eleven years later Parnell Shopfitters, probably a branch of the same family, also moved here.

PARRY'S CLOSE / LANE, BS9. One source suggests that Parry's Lane was originally called Paddy's Well Lane, while Grundy states there was a Perry's Well nearby. Harris gives the origin as OE *pirige*, pear tree.

PARSLOW BARTON, BS5. From the farm owned or occupied by one called Parslow, a name still to be found in the area today.

PARSON STREET, BS3. A field name - the development was on a site called Parson's field.

PARSON'S PADDOCK, BS14. A field name appearing on the old tithe map of the area.

PARTITION STREET, BS1. So called because it divided Lower College Street from Thatched House Lane.

PARTNERS CLOSE, BS10. Named after company associations with developers.

PASSAGE LEAZE, BS11. This old street was truncated by the construction of the Portway just after the First World War. It contains the ancient inn called 'The Lamplighters'. The last word means pasture and the first refers to the passage or ferry to Pill. The name Lamplighters originates from one-time owner, Josiah Swetname of Small Street, who was contracted to light the lamps in several city parishes.

PASSAGE ROAD, BS10. The old road to Aust Passage, from which the ferry plied between Bristol and Wales from Roman times, until the building of the first Severn Bridge in the 1960s.

PASSAGE ROAD, BS2. The street was built at the same time as the construction of St. Philips Bridge in 1841, to replace the old ferry. The street provided a passage to the bridge.

PAUL STREET, BS2. This street was developed in the 1790s and may have been named after a local family of this name.

PAULTON DRIVE, BS7. Named after a village in Somerset. The first syllable could come from the Danish *pald* meaning a raised place, or else it is a personal noun Pauhild that was corrupted to Pauel and finally Paul.

PAULTOW ROAD, BS3. Seemingly a made-up name.

PAVEY CLOSE / ROAD, BS13. The Pavey family were well-known residents of the area many years ago.

PAWLETT ROAD / WALK, BS13. The Paulett or Poulett family owned Inns Court after the death of Sir John Inyn in 1439, and it was still in the possession of an Earl Poulett in 1791. Inns Court was purchased by Bristol Corporation in 1934, then demolished, and the site used to build the Knowle and Bedminster estates.

PAYBRIDGE ROAD, BS13. Paybridge Tyning was a field at Bishopsworth Farm as recorded in the 1802 survey. A tyning is an enclosure.

PAYNE DRIVE, BS5. After Charles Payne who was Mayor in 1834-35.

PEACHE ROAD, BS16. After the popular Rev. Albert Peache, who served as vicar of Mangotsfield from 1859 to 1875.

PEACOCK LANE, BS15. Peacock Bros. had a boot factory near here in the late nineteenth century.

PEARCES HILL, BS16. William and Henry Pearce owned Frenchay Mill from 1851 to 1871. This road leads from Beckspool Road to the mill.

PEARL STREET, BS3. Many streets in the vicinity are called after jewels. *See Beryl Road.*

PEARSALL ROAD, BS15. It was here that John Pearsall established a mill for rolling and splitting hoop iron in the eighteenth century. A descendent of the

family, R.L. Pearsall, was an eminent nineteenth century composer who was born in Clifton. He wrote madrigals and was a founder member of the Bristol Madrigal Society in 1837; it still exists today, although it has been re-named.

PEART CLOSE / DRIVE, BS13. The land on which these houses were built was once known as The Peart. This is a dialect word which means lively and in good spirits.

PEARTREE LANE, BS5. Given that this area abounded in market gardens until the first quarter of the twentieth century this would seem to be an appropriate name.

PEARTREE LANE, BS15. Built on land where Peartree Farm once stood.

PEEL STREET, BS2. Built pre-1850, the street almost certainly takes its name from the eminent statesman, Sir Robert Peel (1788-1850), who established the first police force. The nickname "bobby" for a policeman is taken from his first name. He was elected Prime Minister in 1841 on the understanding that he would preserve the system of Corn Law trade tariffs which were dear to his Tory supporters but were inhibiting trade and maintaining monopolies. Once elected he famously repealed them and replaced them with a system of income tax.

PEGASUS ROAD, BS12. Among a group of roads whose names relate to aircraft and aero engines. The Bristol Pegasus was a 9-cylinder radial engine powering such aircraft as the Short Sunderland, Fairey Swordfish, Bristol Blenheim, Vickers Wellington, the Polish PZL P37 and German Ju 86. The name was revived for the Bristol Siddeley Pegasus vector-thrust jet engine that powers the Harrier. Bristol Aeroplane Company's symbol was Pegasus, the mythical flying horse, and the theme was continued throughout their products.

PEMBERTON COURT, BS16. A man named Green built these houses, and Mrs Pemberton was his wife's cousin, who lived in Yatton.

PEMBERY ROAD, BS3. Named after Joseph Pembery, J.P. and Councillor for Bedminster West Ward 1894. He lived in the adjoining road, Ruby Street.

PEMBROKE GROVE / PLACE / ROAD / VALE / VILLAS, BS8 / AVENUE / ROAD, BS11 / ROAD, BS3 / ROAD, BS15 / STREET, BS2. All streets with this appellation are named in honour of the Earls of Pembroke, who held office in the city as Lord Lieutenants and High Stewards. During the sixteenth and seventeenth centuries. Pembroke Road in Clifton was formerly known as Gallows Acre Lane, scene of many an execution prior to the opening of the gaol in Cumberland Road, which was built in 1820 at a cost of £60,000.

PEN PARK ROAD, BS10. *Pen* is from OE meaning small enclosure. When the road was built there was in existence a Pen Park Farm at the northern end of which could be found the infamous Pen Park Hole, said to be at least 300 ft deep. This place achieved notoriety in March 1775 when the Rev. Thomas Newnham, a Minor Canon at the Cathedral, fell to his death while exploring the chasm.

PENARD WAY, BS15. Presumably named after East and West Penard in Somerset.

PENDENNIS AVENUE / ROAD. BS16. After Pendennis House, which once stood here.

PENDENNIS PARK, BS4. Probably named after Pendennis Castle in Cornwall. The meaning of the name is 'fort on the headland'.

PENDOCK CLOSE / ROAD, BS16. Jonathan Pendock held property for the Dibden Estate at Rodway Hill in 1788. He was churchwarden at Mangotsfield in 1805.

PENFIELD ROAD, BS2. Field name from OE *penn*, small enclosure or, more probably in view of surrounding terrain - Welsh *penn*, hill.

PENLEA COURT, BS11. There was a house called Penlea here in the 1880s.

PENN STREET, BS1. One of three streets in the Quakers Friars area commemorating William Penn, the English leader of the Quakers, and the only one remaining. The others were Callowhill Street (he married Hannah Callowhill) and Philadelphia Street. The capital of the state of Pennsylvania, North America, was founded by William Penn in 1681 and named in honour of his father. Penn was governor of Pennsylvania from 1682-84, after which he returned to England and became a supporter of the Catholic James II and worked for religious tolerance.

PENNARD COURT, BS14. Another in the series of Somerset village names.

PENNGROVE, BS15. This would seem to be a made-up name.

PENNINE ROAD, BS15. Among other roads named after ranges of hills.

PENNLEA, BS13. Perhaps an old field name.

PENNYROYAL GROVE, BS16. It was decided to call all roads here after wild flowers and herbs.

PENNYWELL ROAD, BS5. In the past this street was known as Pamwell and Paris Well, from the the Pamiwell or Pennywell spring, which rose near what is now the farm pub in St. Werburghs. The acknowledged source is that the Black Friars of the Dominican Priory obtained their water by means of a conduit from a well called Panewell (sometimes spelled Pamwell) by license of Henry III. This well was source of the Key pipe, the most important northern water conduit taking water to the harbourside and heart of the city. John Cabot is said to have taken water from this spring on his voyage of discovery to Newfoundland in 1497. A conduit house was built over the spring, and during times of military victories during Queen Anne's reign, its cistern was filled with wine. Half a kilometre to the south is the Boiling Well, another spring.

PENPOLE AVENUE / LANE / PLACE, BS11. The first syllable is of Celtic origin and means hill or hilltop. One authority believes the first syllable to come from the Welsh for head.

PENRITH GARDENS, BS10. Named, in accordance with other roads hereabouts, after places in the Lake District.

PENROSE, BS14. Perhaps after Bartholomew Penrose, who ran a shipbuilding business with his brother Thomas in Bristol. He emigrated to Philadelphia in 1700. Around 1706 he worked in partnership with William Penn and his son, building 'The Diligence'.

PENSFIELD PARK, BS10. Presumably a field name taking its first syllable from the nearby river.

PENSFORD COURT, BS14. This was a field name taken from the 1787 tithe map.

THE PENTAGON, BS9. Simply named, as this is a five-sided complex.

PENTIRE AVENUE, BS13. Called after Pentire Head in Cornwall. The name means the end of the land.

PERCIVAL ROAD, BS8. From the Right Reverend John Percival (1834-1918). He was the first headmaster of Clifton College public school from 1862-1879. Later he became President of Trinity College, Oxford and then Headmaster of Rugby School, where he had taught before coming to Bristol. From 1895-1917 he was Bishop of Hereford.

PERCY STREET, BS3. One of the roads built by Philip Percy Doveton Clarke. It was also the site of Percy Hall, a mansion sold by auction in 1865. *See Hall Street.*

PERROTT ROAD, BS15. Named after Dr. C.J. Perrott, Kingswood's Medical Officer of Health from 1894-1936. He was in partnership with Dr. Henry Grace. *See Grace Drive BS15.*

PERRY ROAD, BS2. Almost certainly named after John Perry, Councillor for District Ward 1855-73. He was Chairman of the Streets Committee when this road was opened in August 1868.

PERRY STREET, BS5. This, too, may have been named in honour of John Perry although it was quite a common name in the East Bristol area and may have been that of the owner of the land.

PERRYCROFT AVENUE / ROAD, BS13. A field at Brook Farm, Bishopsworth (Earl Temple's estate). From OE *pirige*, pear tree and *croft*, a small enclosure.

PERRYMANS CLOSE, BS16. Field name. The first component, perry, means pear.

PESLEY CLOSE, BS13. A field name shown at Bishopsworth Farm on the 1802 survey First syllable could be from OE *pise* or *poesu* meaning peas. Ley is from OE *leah* meaning wood, woodland, place or clearing.

PETER'S TERRACE, BS5. This road, built in the early years of the twentieth century, would probably have been named after the landowner.

PETERCOLE DRIVE, BS13. Thought to be a made-up name, perhaps from the name of the developer or landowner.

PETERSON SQUARE, BS13. The holder of land here in 1815.

PETERSWAY GARDENS, BS5. Perhaps someone with the surname Peters had some connection with the area.

PETHERBRIDGE WAY, BS5. Named in honour of the footballer George Petherbridge, who was present when the road was named. He scored more than 80 goals for Bristol Rovers during the 1950s and 1960s. He now lives in Street, Somerset.

PETHERTON CLOSE, BS15. Named after a location in Somerset.

PETHERTON GARDEN / ROAD, BS14. A place name, the derivation of which is 'place on the River Parrett', the name of which, in turn, according to one authority, comes from Pedrida, King of the West Saxons. Another theory is that the British name of the river was Perydon, celebrated by a seventeenth century Welsh bard in a poem. This meaning translates as 'a stream possessing some wonderful virtues, a divine river'. Again it is possible to link the name with the Viking invasion theme of local roads, as Cannington, where the Danes were defeated by Alfred's Army, was in the Hundred of North Petherton. However, being guided by the geography of the area, it could be translated as 'farm by the river'. *See Ravenhead Road.*

PETTICOAT LANE, BS1. Perhaps named for the same reason as the thoroughfare of market stalls selling clothing which once existed in London. Although the London lane is still referred to as Petticoat Lane, the Victorians preferred the more decorous name of Middlesex Street.

PETTIGROVE GARDENS / ROAD, BS15. In 1826 William Pettigrove was the rate collector for this area.

PEVENSEY WALK, BS4. The connection here is Norman castles - an extension of the Cowdray/Colchester theme. Pevensey is in Sussex and was the landing place of William the Conqueror.

PEVERELL CLOSE / DRIVE, BS10. Thomas Peverell, 16th Bishop of Worcester, came to Henbury in 1419. Prior to this appointment he was Bishop of Ossory and Llandaff and was active against the Lollards, the followers of John Wyclif, whose writings were declared heretical by Henry IV.

PHILADELPHIA COURT, BS1. After the street of the same name demolished in the 1950s. The connection is William Penn. *See Penn Street.*

PHILIP STREET, BS1. Adjacent to St. Philip's Bridge.

PHILIP STREET, BS3. Another of the tightly packed streets built by Philip Percy Doveton Clarke.

PHILIPPA CLOSE, BS14. Philippa was the wife of Edward III, who is celebrated in a nearby road.

PHIPPEN STREET, BS1. Named after Robert Phippen, Mayor of Bristol in 1840.

PHIPPS STREET, BS3. A surname, perhaps that of the builder. There was a joiner, James Phipps, listed in the 1872 directory as living in the district.

PHOENIX HOUSE, BS5. This was named after Phoenix Street, which was pulled down to make way for new housing in the 1960s. Phoenix Street obtained its name after the Phoenix Works cotton factory there.

PHOENIX GROVE, BS6. Named, as are the surrounding roads, after a sporting venue, in this case Phoenix Park, Dublin.

PICTON LANE / STREET, BS6. Named in honour of Waterloo hero, Lieutenant-General Sir Thomas Picton (1758-1815). It is believed he was wounded three days earlier in another battle but concealed it in order to lead his troops into battle. The earlier wound was only discovered after his death.

PIGEONHOUSE DRIVE, BS13. Named after Pigeonhouse Farm. The estate was built on the land belonging to the farm, the farmhouse itself was retained initially as a youth club, but was demolished in the 1930s.

PIGOTT AVENUE, BS13. One of the tenants of Sir John Smyth, Lord of the Manor of Bishport in 1683.

PILGRIMS WAY, BS11. Perhaps the connection here is the Quakers' burial ground at Lawrence Weston.

PILGRIMS WAY, BS16. Perhaps the link here is also the Quakers: this is near Quaker's Road.

PILGRIMS WHARF, BS4. The connection here is the pilgrimage, which took place annually to worship at the holy well of St. Anne's.

PILKINGTON CLOSE, BS12. After Councillor Harry Pilkington, a dignitary from the 1960s.

PILLINGERS ROAD, BS15. The Pillingers had a boot factory nearby in the late nineteenth century while another division of the family owned market gardens in the area.

PINE GROVE, BS7. All the roads in this development are named after trees.

PINE GROVE PLACE, BS7. Perhaps a description of the place before development.

PINE ROAD, BS10. Thought to be in keeping with the large expanse of open space to the south of this development.

PINE RIDGE CLOSE, BS9. Chosen by developers as being descriptive of the place.

PINECROFT, BS14. Thought to be a field name.

PINES ROAD, BS15. Named after the Pines Express which traveled through Bitton station on its way to Bournemouth.

PINEWOOD CLOSE, BS9. Descriptive.

PINEWOOD, BS15. Another reminder of the days of the King's forest.

PINHAY ROAD, BS13. Named after a Devon village.

PINKHAMS TWIST, BS14. Pinkham was a pilot who flew from the now defunct Whitchurch airport. He was a master of aerobatics and perfected what was known as 'Pinkham's Twist'.

PIPE LANE, BS1. In the thirteenth century the Carmelites installed a conduit to bring water from the Park Street side of Brandon Hill to their house in St. Augustine's Back through Frog Lane (now Frogmore Street) and along Pipe Lane.

PIPPIN COURT, BS15. There was an orchard here and all the roads have been named after different varieties of apple.

PITCH AND PAY LANE, BS9. A wooden stile at the end of the lane leading from Stoke Bishop to the Downs was the line of segregation between the plague-infested city and the countryside. The villagers brought produce to the stile and pitched it over to the townsfolk who threw back their coins in payment. The stile remained until the 1900s. However, this theory has recently been disputed, so we await further suggestions.

PITCH LANE, BS6. Perhaps so named because it runs by the school sports pitch.

PITCHCOMBE GARDENS, BS9. A name devised from Pitch and Pay and Coombe Dingle.

PITHAY COURT / THE PITHAY, BS1. Derived from *puit,* a French word for well, and *hae,* hedge or sunken enclosure. It was the site of an ancient and popular well of this name, also called the Wine Street conduit. The pithay led to the castle wall and in the tenth century was known as Aylward's street or the Aylward. Aylward, Governor of Bristol Castle, died in 980.

PITT ROAD, BS7. In all probability the name of the builder.

PITVILLE PLACE, BS6. Pittville is a district of Cheltenham. This tiny, hidden terrace of Georgian houses off Cotham Hill could also be named after William Pitt (1759-1806) the eminent British Prime Minister who was in power for twenty years from 1784-1805.

PLAYFORD GARDENS, BS11. After Mary Playford, recipient of poor relief in 1662 and buried in Westbury on 4 November, 1679. The inspiration for many roads in this area was the old *Westbury Poor Book*, edited by the Rev. H.J. Wilkins, from which names of recipients of relief were taken.

PLEASANT ROAD, BS16. Seemingly purely descriptive.

PLUMMERS HILL, BS5. Site of the house belonging to the Plummer family. There was also a withy (reed) bed called Plummers owned by a Henry Warner near here in the nineteenth century.

PLUMPTON COURT, BS16. Another in the series of roads called after racecourses.

POETS' CLOSE, BS5. Chosen because the site adjoins four cottages called after Tennyson, Coleridge, Burns and Byron.

POLLY BARNES CLOSE / HILL, BS15. This lady's history remains a mystery.

POLYGON ROAD / THE POLYGON, BS8. A reference to the design of the road, designed by Henry Brook and George Jones, and completed in May 1826.

POMPHRET GARDENS, BS14. *See Pomphret House.*

POMPHRET HOUSE, BS13. George Pomphret(t) resided in the parish of Bedminster and was granted exemption from Heath Tax in November 1670.

POMPHREY HILL, BS16. A farm of this name was once here and the whole area was known as Pomphrey.

PONSFORD ROAD, BS4. Possibly a surname.

PONTING CLOSE, BS5. Robert Ponting owned a great deal of land in the St. George area in the late eighteenth and early nineteenth centuries.

POOL ROAD, BS15. There was a Pool Farm at Wick.

POOLE STREET, BS11. After Frank Poole, a Shirehampton councillor and commercial reporter.

POPLAR AVENUE, BS9. So called because it leads off from Woodland Grove.

POPLAR CLOSE / ROAD, BS15. There was a farm of this name here. The land was used for this development.

POPLAR PLACE, BS16. This is near Ivy Lane and continues the woodland theme.

POPLAR ROAD, BS5. Perhaps such trees grew here before the development took place.

POPLAR ROAD, BS15. Built on land that was part of Poplar Farm.

POPLAR ROAD, BS3. Possibly a feature of the locale before development.

POPULAR TERRACE, BS15. Was this a mis-spelling of the tree species, or just a much sought-after place to live?

PORTBURY GROVE / WALK, BS11. Portbury can be seen from these roads.

PORTISHEAD WAY, BS3. The road to Portishead.

PORTLAND COURT / PLACE / SQUARE / STREET, BS1 / BS2. Almost certainly all these streets were named in honour of the Third Duke of Portland (1738-1809) who was Lord High Steward from 1786 until his death.

PORTLAND PLACE / STREET, BS16. There used to be a Portland Villa here.

PORTMEIRION CLOSE, BS14. Continuing the theme of famous potteries suggested by the Midlands-based developers of this site.

PORTVIEW ROAD, BS11. The residents here have a view of the docks.

PORTWALL LANE, BS1. The portwall was a defensive structure which was sited here. It had crenellated towers and two of its main gates were Temple and Redcliff. The fortification ran the length of Freshford Lane to Queen Square. It was removed in 1850.

PORTWAY, BS11. Constructed just after the First World War as a swift route for travel to the port of Avonmouth. It is a popular name for such a road throughout the country.

POUND DRIVE / LANE BS16. The site of this road was the original pound or pinfold for the detention of stray animals, whose owners had to pay a fine to redeem them. Three of the walls of the enclosure were standing as late as the 1930s.

POUND ROAD, BS15. The animal pound was sited here.

POUNTNEY DRIVE, BS5. John Decimus Pountney was Mayor of Bristol in 1847.

POW'S ROAD, BS15. Issac Pow had a bootmaking factory in Moravian Road. He was chairman of Kingswood UDC from 1901-1902. He also owned Pow's Orchard in Cock Road. His brother, William, founded Potters Wood Methodist Church, so the road may be named after either of the brothers.

POYNTZ COURT, BS15 / ROAD, BS4. Sir Anthony Poyntz was appointed Warden of Kingswood forest in 1529. The family lived at Iron Acton Court and were prominent in local and national affairs from the early fourteenth century for more than 350 years. Sir Anthony received his knighthood in 1513. He was a naval captain in the fleet which sailed against France and he attended Henry VIII at the Field of the Cloth of Gold. The last member of the family, Sir John, died in 1680 with no one to succeed him.

PRATTEN'S LANE, BS16. There were both a baker and bootmaker of this name here in the late nineteenth century.

PREDDY'S LANE, BS5. There are many families with this name in the area. This lane would have led to the dwelling of one such person.

PRESSMOOR DRIVE, BS15. This was a field name shown on an old tithe map.

PRESTON WALK, BS4. Preston was a village in the Longbridge Hundred mentioned in the Domesday Book.

PRESTWICK CLOSE, BS4. The name of a famous golf course, in keeping with its location near Knowle Golf Course.

PRETORIA ROAD, BS12. There is no known reason for the South African influence here.

PrincessVictoria Street, Clifton

PREWETT STREET, BS1. William Prewett was a man of considerable wealth and a draper by trade. He died in 1594 and left money for repairs to the highway between Redcliff and the Brightbow (Bedminster Bridge) and also to the road between Lawford's Gate and Don John's Cross (today's Church Road).

PRIDDY COURT / DRIVE, BS14. Priddy is a village high on the Mendips which hosts an annual sheep fair. Many West Country names have been used for the roads in the area.

PRIESTWOOD CLOSE, BS10. This was once woodland. Derived from OE *preost* meaning press or priest, so possibly the woodland belonged to an ecclesiastical order.

PRIMROSE CLOSE / LANE, BS5. A reminder of days when this was a country path.

PRIMROSE TERRACE, BS15. There was a Primrose Vein at the nearby Hanham Colliery. Might this be the reason for the naming?

PRINCE STREET, BS1. Laid out in 1700, this was named in honour of Prince George of Denmark, the consort of Queen Anne.

PRINCES' BUILDINGS, BS8. The site was owned by the Bristol Merchant Venturers, and was conveyed for building in 1789, but building of this elegant row overlooking the Avon Gorge was delayed by the financial collapse of 1793 and was not completed until about 1800. It was originally known as Prince of Wales Crescent, and appears thus on the 1805 map. The spelling suggests that more than one son of George III was being honoured.

PRINCE'S PLACE, BS7. As this runs parallel to Denmark Place, the prince in question must be the future Edward VII, who married Princess Alexandra of Denmark.

PRINCES COURT, BS15. As other roads near this one have forest connections this may refer to the princes and kings who often hunted in this area.

PRINCES' LANE, BS8. This was not shown in the Bristol directories until the 1930s, and was never shown as inhabited by any directory (which currently go to 1973). The top half of Princess Victoria Street used to be known as Prince's Place, and as Prince's Buildings is also nearby the name may derive from both of these sources.

PRINCESS GARDENS, BS16. Among a group of roads which have been given female titles of nobility - the connection being nearby Duchess's Park.

PRINCESS ROW / STREET, BS2. Situated near King Square which was named after George II, so this clearly honours one of his daughters.

PRINCESS STREET, BS3. Built circa 1840, it is probably named in honour of Queen Victoria's first child, Victoria (Vicky) born on 21 November 1840.

PRINCESS ROYAL GARDENS, BS5. Nearby is Albert Street and this continues the theme of Queen Victoria's immediate family. *See Princess Street, BS3.*

PRINCESS VICTORIA STREET, BS8. Named after Princess Alexandrina Victoria who ascended the British throne in 1837 as Queen Victoria.

PRIORY AVENUE / COURT / ROAD / DENE / GARDENS, BS9. A house called The Priory once stood here.

PRIORY COURT, BS15. This land was once owned by Lacock Abbey.

PRIORY GARDENS / ROAD, BS11. A Priory House once stood near here.

PRIORY ROAD, BS8. The grounds of the ancient Priory of St. James would have extended as far as the site of this road.

PRIORY ROAD, BS4. Prior's Wood house stood in nearby Talbot Lane.

PRITCHARD STREET, BS2. This could be named after the owner of the land, as there are two businesses listed locally at the time the development took place. There was also a William Pritchard, Warden of the St. Stephen's Ringers, who died in 1837 and who may have held the land.

PROBYN CLOSE, BS16. After Edward Probyn, Lord of the Manor in the late eighteenth century.

PROCTOR CLOSE, BS4. Built on a former cricket ground and named after Mike Proctor, who was Gloucestershire captain during the 1977-78 season.

PROSPECT AVENUE / CRESCENT, BS5. This might be a name taken from one of the old veins in the local pit.

PROSPECT PLACE, BS5. Prospect House formerly stood on this site.

PROSPECT PLACE, BS2. Descriptive of the view from the road.

PROVIDENCE PLACE / STREET, BS3. There is an area of this name above the Long Ashton road after which this street may have been named.

PRUDHAM STREET, BS5. There is no obvious reason for this name.

PULLIN COURT, BS15. Named after an Oldland man who ran a cycle shop here. The premises are now used as a chip shop.

PUMP LANE, BS1. There was a spring in Pump Lane piped via a conduit from the spring's source in Knowle. The spring had been a gift from Lord Robert of Berkeley to William, the Chaplain of Redcliffe, in 1190. At the time the Spring was known as "Rudge Well" (Ridge Well) and was intended for the joint use of the parishioners and brethren of Redcliffe and the Hospital of St John the Baptist.

PURCELL WALK, BS4. After Henry Purcell (1658-95) who was one of the greatest English composers and a master of the Baroque. He was organist at Westminster Abbey and wrote a great deal of sacred music, as well as chamber music and the opera *Dido and Aeneas.* He collaborated closely with the poet John Dryden, who wrote an ode on his death:

ON THE DEATH OF MR. PURCELL.
The heavenly choir, who heard his notes from high,
Let down the scale of music from the sky;
They handed him along,
And all the way he taught, and all the way they sung.

PURDEY ROAD, BS16. Named after Victory Purdey, the Methodist preacher, nicknamed "The Walking Bible" because he had read it so often he was able to quote chapter and verse for any question. He died, aged 75, in July 1822, and is buried at Stapleton, having composed 1,853 hymns, preached 2,882 sermons and travelled 22,896 miles, mostly on foot.

PURDOWN ROAD, BS7. After the nearby hills.

PURTON CLOSE, BS15. Another Domesday Book link here. Purton was in Earl Williams's holding. It was in the Hundred of Bledisloe.

PURTON ROAD, BS7. A place name, the derivation being *pera*, OE for pear tree, and Celtic *dun,* hill.

PUXLEY CLOSE, BS14. Deborah Puxley was resident in the parish of Bedminster in 1674 and was exempt from Hearth Tax.

PYECROFT AVENUE, BS9. It has been suggested that Roger Clark of the famous Bristol pie company may have been influencial in this road naming as the family owned property in the area. If so it would seem to be a play on words relating to his trade.

PYLLE HILL CRESCENT, BS3. This section of Totterdown was known as Pylle Hill.

PYNNE CLOSE / ROAD, BS14. Joel Pynne was a resident of Bedminster in 1674 and was exempt from Hearth tax.

PYRACANTHA WALK, BS14. Among other roads named after shrubs.

THE QUADRANT (WEST AND EAST), BS16. A description of the layout of these roads.

QUAKER'S CLOSE / ROAD, BS16. There was a Quaker burial ground here for four centuries from 1657 until it was sold for development in 1961.

QUAKERS' FRIARS, BS1. The Dominican Friary was built here in 1229, but it was held after 1609 by the Society of Friends, or Quakers, who built their meeting house here in 1669.

QUANTOCK COURT, BS15. This development has hill ranges as its theme.

QUANTOCK ROAD, BS3. Many rather steep roads in the area are called after ranges of hills.

QUARRINGTON ROAD, BS7. First syllable derives from OE *cweorn*, meaning 'hand mill'. In 1923 the Rev. John Quarrington is named as being one of the commoners and leasees of the Parish of Horfield.

QUARRY LANE, BS11. Not surprisingly, the site of an old quarry.

QUARRY ROAD, BS16. There were six quarries in the vicinity at one time.

QUARRY ROAD, BS15. There were several quarries in the area.

QUARRY STEPS, BS8. There is clear evidence here of quarrying carried out in former times.

QUARRY WAY, BS8. Quarrying was carried out here many years ago.

QUAY STREET, BS1. The Bristol quay once stretched as far as this. In Norman times this was the Old Jewry area. Today its development has been a subject of great controversy. The City Council consulted widely as to whether the Quay should be restored to the city centre, so that once more ships could dock outside the Hippodrome. Despite widespread approval for such a picturesque scheme it was finally abandoned for cited reasons of expense. The old harbour remained covered over, but, as a regretful gesture of recognition of Bristol's glorious seafaring past, sixty-nine little fountains now spurt fitfully in the place where once sailing ships rode at anchor.

QUAYSIDE, BS4. The development is next to the river.

QUEEN ANN ROAD, BS5. Site of a Queen Anne style house. It was believed the Queen actually stayed here and was entertained by Sir Thomas Day at his town residence, the Great House on Bristol Bridge, at a cost of £22.19s, later reclaimed from the corporation, although there is a school of thought that the present Rhubarb Tavern was Sir Thomas's house. This street used to be known as Pottery Lane.

QUEEN CHARLOTTE STREET, BS1. This was originally known as Back Street Lane and was renamed in honour of George III's wife.

QUEEN STREET, BS1. Built on the site of a Bristol castle gate leading to the King's Orchard but named after Queen Catherine of Braganza (1638-1705), wife of Charles II. She was reputedly haughty and mean, but kind to Charles' many bastard children.

QUEEN SQUARE / SQUARE AVENUE, BS1. Built in the reign of Queen Anne, who visited Bristol on her way to Bath, where she was taking the waters to relieve her gout.

QUEEN STREET, BS5, BS2, BS11, BS15 / SQUARE, BS11. Built late nineteenth century and named after Queen Victoria.

QUEEN VICTORIA ROAD, BS6 / STREET, BS2. Self-explanatory.

QUEEN'S AVENUE, BS8. No reason for the naming of this road so far has been discovered.

QUEEN'S DRIVE, BS7. Near King's Drive. Built c. 1925 when George V and Queen Mary visited Bristol.

QUEEN'S PARADE, BS1. Developed 1786. The queen in question is Charlotte Sophia, wife of George III.

QUEEN'S ROAD, BS13. Takes its name from the Queen's Head pub that stood there before the road was developed between the wars.

QUEEN'S ROAD, BS5. Developed after 1914-18 war, so the queen must be Mary (1867-1953), wife of George V.

QUEEN'S ROAD, BS7. Built in the last quarter of the nineteenth century, so the queen it honours is Victoria.

QUEEN'S ROAD, BS8, BS15. Probably named after Queen Victoria.

QUEENS' DRIVE, BS15. As for BS8.

QUEENSDOWN GARDENS, BS4. Queensdown is a place name in Kent.

QUEENS ROAD, BS4. Although mainly developed in the 1930s it owes its name to Queen Victoria, since nearby Jubilee Road celebrates her sixty years on the throne.

QUEENSDALE CRESCENT, BS4. From the demolished farm of this name.

QUEENSHILL ROAD, BS4. A made-up name.

QUEENSHOLM AVENUE / CLOSE / DRIVE, BS16. So called because it is near Sandringham Avenue, Sandringham being a royal residence.

QUICKTHORN CLOSE, BS14. A few roads locally are called after prickly shrubs. The description has nothing to do with speed; quickthorn gets its name from the OE *cwic* meaning 'living'. Anglo-Saxon farmers would use 'dead' hedges of stakes and woven hazel as a temporary boundary, and plant seedlings of hawthorn to create a more permanent quick, or living, hedge.

QUILTER GROVE, BS4. This honours Roger Quilter (1877-1953) who was born in Brighton. He wrote an opera called *Julia* but is best known, perhaps, for his *Children's Overture.*

R

RACKHAM CLOSE, BS7. Arthur Rackham (1867-1939) was a highly influential illustrator, chiefly of children's books, whose designs fall somewhere between the height of Edwardian Gothic style and Art Nouveau.

RACKHAY, BS1. An old trade connection. Cloth was stretched or bleached at a place called Rackhithe, by the river, hithe meaning a landing place. The name changed to Rackhay. Bristol Red used to be a well-known cloth. The dye was obtained from a flower, *lychnis chalcedonica*, known as the 'Bristol flower'.

RADLEY ROAD, BS16. From the town in Berkshire. The prefix means 'red' and the suffix OE *leah*, wood.

RADNOR ROAD, BS7, BS9. Possibly from the Earls of Radnor, who had associations with Bristol. The Henleaze Radnor Road is in a small knot of Welsh place names.

RAEBURN ROAD, BS5. Presumably after Sir Henry Raeburn, the Scottish portrait painter (1756-1823).

RAGLAN LANE, BS5 / RAGLAN PLACE / ROAD, BS7. After the popular and seasoned campaigner, Field Marshal Lord Raglan (1788-1855), son of the fifth Duke of Beaufort (family name - Somerset). He fought in the Peninsular Wars, lost an arm at Waterloo and commanded the British troops in the Crimea, where he died of cholera. He is buried in the family vault in the church at Badminton.

RAILWAY TERRACE, BS16. Near what used to be Staple Hill station. The adjoining trackbed is now part of the Bristol to Bath cycle track.

RALEIGH ROAD, BS3. Named after Sir Walter Raleigh. Several other local streets bear the names of famous Elizabethans, but this one is particularly appropriate since it was Raleigh who first imported tobacco to England and this area was, for many years, the centre of cigarette production.

RALPH ROAD, BS7. The name of the builder who developed much of this area between the wars.

RAMSEY ROAD, BS7. Named after a resort on the Isle of Man, which is in line with the Manx theme in the locality.

RANDALL CLOSE, BS15. Perhaps after Alfred Randall, J.P. and councillor in 1920, or else after Mrs Sarah Goldney Randall, whose family also owned property at Warmley.

RANDALL ROAD, BS8. Mrs Sarah Goldney Randall was the owner of this site. She was the daughter of Gabriel Goldney of Goldney House.

RANDOLPH AVENUE / CLOSE, BS13. John Randolph was master of St. Catherine's Hospital, Bedminster, from April 1332 to October 1338.

RANGERS WALK, BS15. A reference to the Forest of Kingswood. In ancient times each forest ranger had his designated patrol.

RANNOCH ROAD, BS7. One of a number of roads in the area named by the builder's Scottish foreman.

RAPHAEL COURT, BS1. Named after a typeface, as are other courts in this development. *See Berlington Court.*

RAVENDALE DRIVE, BS15. A Californian location. *See California Road.*

RAVENGLASS CRESCENT, BS10. Continuing the Lake District theme here. Ravenglass is on the Cumbrian coast from where the Ravenglass and Eskdale light railway runs up into the mountains.

RAVENHEAD DRIVE, BS14. As this road is near Appledore Close, the connection might be the defeat of the Danes in 878 at Kynwith Castle near Appledore, Kent where the Danish standard, the Magical Raven, was captured.

RAVENHILL AVENUE / ROAD, BS3. From Raven's Well, the subterranean source of the spring which supplied the Temple pump. It was the property of John Gourney, Lord of Knowle, who, in 1368, granted the inhabitants the right of conduiting the water by pipes near a Friary which stood by Temple Gate.

Redcliffe Hill, looking towards St. Mary Redcliffe c.1910

RAVENS WOOD, BS15. Another of the American-influenced names. *See California Road.*

RAVENSCOURT ROAD, BS12. No reason for the naming of this road so far has been discovered.

RAVENSWOOD ROAD, BS6. Another Sir Walter Scott association here; Ravenswood being the surname of two characters in *The Bride of Lammermoor.*

RAYLEIGH ROAD, BS3. Named after a village in Essex, meaning meadow, or 'where rye is grown'. Rayleigh is also a baronetcy but one which has no obvious connections with Bristol.

RAYMEND ROAD / WALK, BS3. Seemingly a made-up name.

RAYMILL, BS4. The name of a house in Lacock, Wiltshire, once home of Mrs Keppel, a mistress of Edward VII. The reason for this naming however, is unclear.

RAYNES ROAD, BS3. From Rayne's or Rayen's Cross, a hamlet once existent in Long Ashton.

RECTORY LANE, BS12. Built near the church.

REDCATCH ROAD, BS4. Before the houses were built here the area used to be known as 'The Red Catch', 'catch' being land that had been seized. The 80 acre Catch House Farm also stood on the site.

REDCLIFF BACKS / HILL / MEAD LANE / PARADE / STREET / WAY, BS1. Named after the district of Redcliffe. A decision was taken in 1969 by the council to drop the final e, but this has been generally ignored. The district is called Redcliffe, while other spellings vary.

REDCROSS LANE / STREET, BS2. There is some doubt regarding the interpretation of this derivation. It does indeed indicate the sometime presence of a cross but is 'red' a corruption of 'rood' (from OE *rod* - cross)? The Knights Templar wore a red cross on their left shoulder, and indeed the flag of St. George itself is a red cross on a white ground.

REDDING ROAD, BS5. Probably a surname and possibly that of an Edwin Redding who was a maltster in nearby Stapleton Road. It is likely that he owned the land where the houses were built

THE REDDINGS, BS15. Thought to be a field name.

REDFIELD ROAD, BS12. Presumably taken from the colour of the earth of the farmlands which were here once.

REDFORD CRESCENT / WALK, BS13. Field name shown as on the land of Bishopsworth Farm in 1802 survey.

REDHILL CLOSE / DRIVE, BS5. Probably named after the village in Somerset.

RED HOUSE LANE, BS9. From the farm of that name which once stood nearby. It was, at one time, occupied by Jacob Sturge, a member of the well-known family of surveyors and estate agents.

REDLAND COURT ROAD / GROVE / GREEN ROAD / HILL / PARK / ROAD / TERRACE, BS6. There are many views on the origin of the name 'Redland'. Evans says that in the eleventh century it was known as Rudeland whereas Smith, picking up on references to the area in 1208 as 'Thryddeland', suggests that it refers to the practice under Roman law where a man's property was divided on his death into three parts - one for his wife, one for his children and one for free disposal. However, whilst there are several similar variations on the name over the years, it also appears simultaneously as Redeloade and Redelyngton. Ekwall is of the opinion that it means 'cleared land' from the OE *rudding.*

REDSHELF WALK, BS10. Adam Redshelf was Dean of Westbury College from 1488 to 1497.

REDWICK CLOSE, BS11. Redwick was a hamlet in the hundred of Henbury. The name meant a dairy farm among the reeds.

REDWOOD CLOSE, BS15. No known reason for this naming.

REED COURT, BS15. This was the name of one of the forest rangers whose walk was from Stapleton to Conham.

REEDLEY ROAD, BS9. Apparently a field name meaning the reedy meadow, wood or clearing.

REEDLING CLOSE, BS16. One of a number of local roads named after British birds.

REGENCY DRIVE, BS4. The naming of this street is still a mystery.

REGENT STREET, BS8. Constructed in the first quarter of the nineteenth century. The Regent is the future George IV.

REGENT STREET, BS15. One of the roads built by Daniel Flook, the Kingswood industrialist whose aim was to provide decent housing for working-class people. He called the roads he built by rather grandiose names.

REMENHAM DRIVE / PARK, BS9. Place name which refers to a homestead or village by the bank.

RENE ROAD, BS5. One of many Christian names used for streets in the area. *See Lawrence Avenue.*

REPTON ROAD, BS4. One of a number of roads in the locality called after public schools.

RETORT ROAD, BS11. One of many street names which refer to local industry. This is part of the Britannia Zinc complex.

REYNOLDS WALK, BS7. Perhaps after the portrait painter Sir Joshua, or more likely, Richard Reynolds the Quaker philanthropist, an iron merchant born in Corn Street in 1735. He amassed a huge fortune and gave away at least £200,000 in his lifetime.

RICHESON WALK / CLOSE, BS10. Thomas Richeson was one of the collectors of the Poor Rate in Westbury-on-Trym in 1675. He married Mary Beavan in Westbury church on 7 April 1636.

RICHMOND AVENUE / ROAD, BS6, DALE / HILL AVENUE / HILL / PARK ROAD / HILL, BS8. It seems certain that all these roads, built prior to 1850, are named in honour of Charles Lennox, fourth Duke of Richmond (1764-1819), who fought at Waterloo and reached the rank of General.

RICHMOND ROAD, BS5. Another road which was almost certainly named after the Fourth Duke, hero of Waterloo.

RICHMOND ROAD, BS16. A number of royal names chosen for roads in the area.

RICHMOND STREET, BS3. The naming of this street is still a mystery.

RICHMOND TERRACE, BS8. Named after the third Duke of Richmond and Gordon (1735/1795), distinguished general and statesman who was a member of Pitt's cabinet in 1783. The proximity of Gordon Road nearby seems to confirm this.

RICHMOND TERRACE, BS11. No clear reason for this naming although there are a Queen Street and King Street nearby, so perhaps a Royal connection.

RICHMOND MEWS, BS8. Built on the site of Richmond Garage (Pembroke Grove).

THE RIDE, BS15. This name has obvious connections with the Forest of Kingswood.

THE RIDGE, BS11. Descriptive of the terrain.

RIDGEHILL, BS9. Descriptive of the location.

RIDGEMEADE, BS14. This would appear to be a field name.

RIDGEWAY COURT, GARDENS, LANE, BS14. There was an old track across here called the Ridgeway.

RIDGEWAY COURT, THE RIDGEWAY, BS10. It has been suggested that these roads were laid on the line of the old Ridgeway. *See BS16.*

RIDGEWAY PARADE, BS5. Named for its proximity to Ridgeway Cemetery.

RIDGEWAY ROAD, BS16. The Ridge (or Rudge) was an old track. Ridgeway House appears on an old Kingswood Forest map of 1610. This street was once known as Crooked Lane and was a part of Fishponds Road.

RIDINGLEAZE, BS11. Field name. 'Riding' means a clearing and 'leaze' is pasture land.

THE RIDINGS, BS13. This used to be a popular spot for horse riding before the houses were built.

RINGWOOD CRESCENT, BS10. Town and village names were a popular choice when naming the roads in this area. Ringwood is a town in the New Forest.

RIPLEY ROAD, BS5. There seems to be no particular reason for calling this road after a Derbyshire town.

RIPON COURT, BS16. One of a number of roads called after abbeys.

RIPON ROAD, BS4. All the surrounding streets are named after cities with famous abbeys or cathedrals.

RISDALE ROAD, BS3. Either a made-up name or that of the builder or owner of the land. The road was developed between the wars.

RIVER STREET, BS2. Before the Frome was culverted it used to flow down the middle of this road.

RIVER VIEW, BS16. Commands a view of the Frome.

RIVERLAND DRIVE, BS13. A field shown on the 1683 survey as in the Manor of Bishport.

RIVERLEAZE, BS9. This would, indeed, once have been a meadow overlooking the river.

RIVERSIDE CLOSE, BS11. Name chosen because of proximity to River Avon.

RIVERSIDE MEWS, BS4. Self-explanatory.

RIVERSIDE COTTAGES / WAY, BS15. Descriptive of the locality.

RIVERWOOD ROAD, BS16. This road was built in 1958-9 on land that had formerly been part of the estate of Riverwood House. Prior to the early 1950's, Riverwood House had been called Frenchay Grove. The house still stands, and a letterbox in its walls is still labelled 'Grove House'.

RIVIERA CRESCENT, BS16. These houses were built in 1935 on land owned by the Rivers sisters, who were unmarried all their lives and died within a short time of each other.

ROAD TWO, BS11. A typical Avonmouth-style no-frills naming.

ROBERT STREET, BS5. Apparently some connection of the builder's.

ROBERT STREET, BS5. The Robert in question is unknown.

ROBERTSON ROAD, BS5. Samuel Robertson of Pennywell Road built these houses.

ROBIN CLOSE, BS14. Many local streets were given bird names but this was also named in honour of the Bristol City Football Club (known as the Robins) on attaining a place in the First division.

ROBINIA WALK, BS14. There is no obvious reason why this road has been called after a tree.

ROBINSON DRIVE, BS5. Elisha Smith Robinson was a leading figure in civic affairs during the second half of the nineteenth century, being a member of the City Council, Mayor, J.P. and Member of Parliament. He was a founder of the well-known printing firm of ES & A Robinson, and was a keen cricket fan and a philanthropist, as were his two sons.

ROCHESTER ROAD, BS4. Among a host of roads named after cities which have Norman castle ruins and famous churches.

ROCK CLOSE and THE ROCK, BS4. This was the oldest inhabited part of Brislington dating back to medieval times. It is reputed that there was a quarry here, the stone from which was used to build St. Mary's church, Redcliff.

ROCKLAND GROVE / ROAD, BS16. Probably a field name.

ROCKLEAZE / ROCKLEAZE AVENUE / ROAD, BS9. This was an old field name literally meaning stony field.

ROCKSIDE AVENUE / GARDENS, BS16. A made-up name.

ROCKSIDE DRIVE, BS9. Believed to be a made-up name.

ROCKSTOWES WAY, BS10. The name of a property which once stood on this land.

ROCKWELL AVENUE, BS11. The name was selected by the developers, which indicates that it had some special meaning for them.

RODBOROUGH WAY, BS15. Named after a Gloucestershire village, as have been other roads nearby.

RODBOURNE ROAD, BS10. Rodbourne Farm was in the Hundred of Henbury Derived from OE *rod,* rood of land and *bourne,* reedy stream.

RODFORDS MEAD, BS14. Field name taken from the 1845 tithe map.

RODMEAD WALK, BS13. *Rod* is OE for a rood of land. This was a field in the Manor of Bishport in 1683.

RODNEY AVENUE / ROAD, BS5. After the Lord Rodney pub, which in turn was named after the famous admiral. *See Rodney Place BS8.*

RODNEY CRESCENT, BS12. After Rodney Farm which once covered this ground.

RODNEY PLACE, BS8. After George Brydges Rodney, First Baron and the admiral who defeated the French under De Grasse off Martinique in 1782. He visited Bristol in 1782 when he received the Freedom of the City. This road was built within two years of his visit.

RODNEY WALK, BS5. This may have been someone connected with the builder or landowner.

RODWAY HILL / ROAD / VIEW, B15. Near Rodway manor and common.

RODWAY ROAD, BS12. The naming of this street is still a mystery.

ROEGATE DRIVE, BS4. Presumably named for the same reason as Royate Hill.

ROGERS CLOSE, BS15. Named after a good-natured and well-liked boy called Roger Jefferies who died as a result of an accident.

ROKEBY AVENUE, BS6.

> *'I read you, by your bugle horn,*
> *And by your palfrey good,*
> *I read you for a ranger sworn*
> *To keep the king's greenwood.'*

Walter Scott, *Rokeby*

Another road with Sir Walter Scott connections. *Rokeby,* an extended poem, was unsuccessful; it went on far too long, in the manner indicated here.

ROMAN ROAD / WAY, BS8, BS9. A reminder of the Roman occupation of this area.

ROMAN WALK, BS4. Chosen by Brislington Conservation and Amenity Society, the name refers to the site of a Roman villa which was discovered when nearby Winchester Road was being built in 1899. The villa dated from around 270-300 AD and was thought to be at the centre of a large estate destroyed by fire in 367 AD.

ROMAN ROAD, BS5. The road was built in the 1870s-80s and, when the water mains were being laid, labourers unearthed a large number of unused Roman coins dated 336 AD.

ROMNEY AVENUE, BS7. George Romney (1734-1802) was mainly a portraitist, although one of his most famous works, 'The Death of General Wolfe', is actually a subject painting.

RONALD ROAD, BS16. There is no clue as to who Ronald might be.

RONAYNE WALK, BS16. James Ronayne lived at Downend House towards the end of the nineteenth century, a residence which dated from the early eighteenth century and was once home to Dr. H.M. Grace, father of the famous W.G.

ROOKERY ROAD, BS4. No known reason for the naming unless there were elms standing there where rooks nested. The road was developed circa 1911.

ROOKERY WAY, BS14. Named after the nearby Rookery Farm which once thrived in this area.

ROSEACRE, BS10. Thought to be a field name.

ROSE GREEN CLOSE / ROAD, BS5. This was a very ancient way marked on the 1610 map of Kingswood Forest. Ekwall suggests it is from the Old Norse *hrossa*, horse or it could be from a personal name such as Rowe or, indeed, Rose.

ROSE MEAD, BS7. Name taken from the Horfield tithe map.

ROSE ROAD, BS5. In all likelihood the builder's wife or daughter.

ROSE STREET, BS1. A very old street. This used to adjoin the Great Gardens, so perhaps that was the origin of the name, unless it was called after a long-forgotten inn.

ROSE WALK, BS16. Mainly tree names here as an echo of past scenes when the area was known as the Thicket.

ROSEBAY MEAD, BS16. Chosen in keeping with other botanical names in the development.

ROSEBERRY PARK / ROAD, BS5. Most probably named after the Earl of Rosebery, though misspelt. He held many high offices and was an MP. The Earl was made a freeman of the city in 1894, when he unveiled a statue to Edmund Burke.

ROSEBERY AVENUE, BS2. As above.

ROSEDALE ROAD, BS16. *See Rose Walk.*

ROSELARGE GARDENS, BS10. Mistress Rose Large has an effigy in Westbury church which states that having lived virtuously 80 years she departed most virtuously to God on 29 August 1610. She was the daughter of William Cock of Hampshire and lived at Stoke Bishop.

ROSEMARY LANE, BS5. All the roads here bear the names of herbs.

ROSEMONT TERRACE, BS8. Derivation doubtful. This was a popular name for houses, so perhaps there was one of that name nearby.

ROSERY CLOSE, BS9. There may have been a rose-growing nursery here at some time or other.

THE ROSERY, BS16. Among a group of other rose names here.

ROSEVEAR, BS5. A rocky island in the Scilly Isles, site of a ruined lighthouse. *Rose* is Celtic for high wasteland and *vear* means big.

ROSEVILLE AVENUE, BS15. Another Californian place name. *See California Road.*

ROSLING ROAD, BS7. From the owners of the site who occupied Berry Lane Farm for many years.

ROSLYN ROAD, BS6. Another road with a Sir Walter Scott connection. It is the name of a village and chapel immortalised in his metrical romance, *The Lay of the Last Minstrel.*

ROSSALL ROAD, BS4. In common with other local streets, this is named after a public school.

ROSSITER'S LANE, BS5. A well-known local family name indicating that this was almost certainly a lane which led to the dwelling of a person of that name.

ROUNDMOOR GARDENS, BS14. The naming of this street is still a mystery.

ROUSHAM ROAD, BS5. Named after a village in Oxfordshire whose church holds many memorials to the Dormer family. As the Cottrell-Dormer family owned much of the land in this area, the reason for the naming becomes apparent.

ROWACRES, BS14. An old field name.

ROWAN CLOSE, BS16. All sylvan names here to mark the area's arboreal history. *See Rose Walk.*

ROWAN WAY, BS15. This area borders on Hencliffe Wood and many roads have been given appropriately sylvan names.

THE ROWANS, BS16. Tree names have been chosen for much of the development, thus emphasising the rural location.

ROWBERROW, BS14. Named after a Somerset village.

ROWLAND AVENUE, BS16. A Christian name or surname of someone whose story has been lost in the mists of time.

ROWLANDSON GARDENS, BS7. Thomas Rowlandson (1756-1827) was an artist and caricaturist whose work became extremely popular with the public, and presented a valuable chronicle of contemporary England. In his later years he chiefly illustrated books, such William Combe's *Three Tours of Doctor Syntax*, the *English Dance of Death* and the *Military Adventures of Johnny Newcombe*.

ROWLEY STREET, BS3. Thomas Rowley was a bailiff during the time Canynge was mayor in the mid-fifteenth century. This was also the name Chatterton adopted when he attempted to pass off his poems as archive material.

ROWNHAM CLOSE / COURT / MEAD / HILL, BS3. This is thought to be a descriptive entry from years ago meaning a weedy or stubbly enclosure.

ROY KING GARDENS, BS15. A tribute to a late and much-respected councillor.

ROYAL ALBERT ROAD, BS6. The road was developed many years after the death of the Prince Consort of Queen Victoria, so it is more likely to have been named after either the warship of that name (launched by the Queen in 1854) or Albert Prince of Wales, who later became Edward VII.

ROYAL CLOSE, BS11. No reason has been discovered for the naming of this road.

ROYAL FORT ROAD, BS2. Converted from the shell of an old windmill, the fort grew out of a small redoubt built as part of the city's defences in the Civil War. It was extended to form the Royal Fort and the Headquarters of Prince Rupert. The fort was demolished by Cromwell after the Civil War. In 1760 Royal Fort House was built for Thomas Tyndall, a merchant. Roman coins dated 338-40AD have also been found on the site.

ROYAL PARK, BS8. Sited near Victoria Square, so the association is clear.

ROYAL PROMENADE, BS8. A regal name for an impressive road.

ROYAL YORK CRESCENT, BS8. The Royal York celebrated here was Frederick Augustus, Duke of York, second son of George III (1763-1827). The crescent was designed by William Paty and built in the grounds of Clifton Manor House. It was begun in 1750 but not completed until 1820 as the builders went bankrupt during the financial crisis of 1793, which interrupted building all over the city.

ROYATE HILL, BS5. In the mid to late ninth century this was known as Roeyate Lane because the Roe Gate was situated here, one of the entrances to the Kingswood Forest in the 1600s. A roe is a small deer.

ROYCROFT ROAD, BS12. Named after Lieutenant Commander Richard Roycroft MBE, J.P., local councillor and Chairman of the Naming of Roads Committee. This road was named after him only months before he died in 1946.

ROYSTON WALK, BS10. Perhaps after the town in Hertfordshire, as other random place names are used in the area.

ROZEL ROAD, BS7. Place name of a parish and headland in Jersey.

RUBY STREET, BS3. Another of the jewel names chosen for streets in the district.

RUDGEWOOD CLOSE, BS13. Wooded area formerly in the Dundry area ('rudge' being a variant on 'ridge').

RUDHALL GREEN, BS7. John Rudhall recast the No. 1 bell of Horfield church in 1807. He was a descendant of Abraham Rudhall, who established a bell foundry in Gloucester in 1684. The firm cast many bells for West Country churches and in 1774 it was said that the family had produced 3594 bells up to Lady Day that year.

RUDTHORPE ROAD, BS7. Apparently a made-up name.

RUGBY ROAD, BS4. Another in the series of streets named after public schools.

RUNNYMEAD AVENUE, BS4. Runnymead was the site of the signing of the Magna Carta by King John in 1215. The prefix is from the OE *run*, council and *ieg*, island, suggesting an ancient meeting-place.

RUNNYMEDE, BS15. This name has obvious forest and King John connections.

RUNSWICK ROAD, BS4. Perhaps after the village in Yorkshire. The first syllable means 'secret meeting place' or council, and the second means village.

RUPERT STREET, BS1. Named in honour of Prince Rupert, who was Governor of Bristol Castle during the Civil War.

RUSHY, BS15. Linking past with present, this was an old field name.

RUSKIN GROVE, BS7.

> *"There is hardly anything in the world that someone cannot make a little worse, and sell a little cheaper, and the people who consider price alone are that person's lawful prey."*

Probably named after John Ruskin (1819-1900), the eminent Victorian writer, critic and art historian. He published an impressive defence of Turner, an appreciation of the religious painters of Florence and Venice and the English Pre-Raphaelite school in his five volume series, *Modern Painters* (1843-60). He was elected Slade Professor of Fine Art at Oxford four times, and also found time to initiate better housing schemes in Mary-le-bone, London, promote educational and social schemes for the working people in the Lake District and the North, founded several museums, including the St. George Ruskin Museum in Sheffield, set up art classes for the poor and encouraged home industries, such as spinning and linen making. A year before his death he was honoured by Oxford University when Ruskin College was founded to enable artists and artisans from all backgrounds to study at the university.

RUSS STREET, BS2. This street was developed in the third quarter of the nineteenth century which probably takes its name from a local family. The 1850 Bristol directory lists one person of this name - a blacksmith of Frogmore Street.

RUSSELL GREEN / ROAD, BS6. The origin, judging by the connection with neighbouring streets, is Lord Russell of Killowen (1832-1900) who was a Lord Chief Justice. He was one of the earliest life peers.

RUSSELL ROAD, BS16. Named either after the builder or after Earl Russell who served three terms as Prime Minister in the 1800s. *See Russell Town Avenue.*

RUSSELL TOWN AVENUE, BS5. East Bristol was a Radical stronghold in the 1850s. Lord John Russell spent two days in Bristol in 1854 for the opening of the Bristol Athenaeum Club in Corn Street (later known as the Bristol Club). He was Prime Minister in 1846 and 1865.

RUTHERFORD CLOSE, BS15. Another Californian town. *See California Road.*

RUTHVEN ROAD, BS4. Among a number of roads called after locations of historic castles. Ruthven in Scotland had medieval origins, but was refortified by the Hanoverians for a garrison as part of their policy of suppressing the Jacobites.

RUTLAND AVENUE, BS7. Most of the neighbouring roads are called after locations in the United Kingdom.

RYDE ROAD, BS4. Seaside resort on the Isle of Wight. The word means 'small stream'.

RYE CLOSE, BS13. A field name in Ridings Farm in the Manor of Long Ashton recorded on surveys of 1780 and 1794. From the OE *Ryge* - rye.

RYLAND PLACE, BS2. This is named after the eighteenth century Baptist Preacher John Collett Ryland. His son Dr. John Ryland and grandson Jonathan Ryland continued his strong Baptist tradition and were held in high esteem.

RYLESTONE GROVE, BS9. Village in Yorkshire, and also public gardens at Shanklin, Isle of Wight. It means the town or homestead by the brook.

RYSDALE ROAD, BS9. A made-up name.

SABRINA WAY, BS9.

> *There is a gentle Nymph not far from hence,*
> *That with moist curb sways the smooth Severn stream;*
> *Sabrina is her name, a virgin pure....*

John Milton, *Comus*

This is the Latin name for the River Severn, after the legendary goddess of the river celebrated in John Milton's poem.

SADLIER CLOSE, BS11. Sir Ralph Sadlier (1507-87) was granted the manor of Bishop's Stoke and Henbury in Saltmarsh by Edward VI. One writer refers to him as a notorious grabber of church lands. He was Chief Falconer to Queen Elizabeth I. He was a man of eminence, serving as a diplomat under three monarchs: Henry VIII, Edward VI and Elizabeth I. He negotiated the peace treaty with Scotland in 1567 and was guardian to Mary Queen of Scots and envoy for James VI of Scotland, afterwards James I of England. At his death he was said to be owner of 23 manors, several parsonages and great parcels of land in Gloucestershire, Warwickshire, Worcestershire and Herefordshire.

SAFFRON CLOSE, BS5. Built on the site of Saffron Street, so called because saffron was produced here when the area formed part of the grounds of Whitehall House. Saffron is derived from the stigmas of *Crocus sativus,* naturalised in Britain and bearing purple flowers in autumn. It has been grown in Kashmir and India and used as an ingredient in cooking for over a thousand years, and was introduced to England in the sixteenth century by Thomas Smith, Secretary of State to Edward VI.

ST. AGNES AVENUE / WALK, BS4. Named after the Anglican convent in Redcatch Road.

ST. AIDAN'S CLOSE / WALK, BS5. From the nearby church built in 1894. St. Aidan came from Connaught and was taught by St. David in Pembrokeshire. Among the miracles he was reputed to have performed was the saving of a stag from the hunt by rendering it invisible.

ST. ALBAN'S ROAD, BS6. From the church of that name built in 1894. St. Alban was bishop of Malmesbury.

ST. ALDWYN'S CLOSE, BS7. Most probably named after Sir Michael Hicks-Beach, first Earl St. Aldwyn (1837-1915) M.P. for Bristol West in which this road is situated. He served two terms as Chancellor of the Exchequer and was Leader of the Opposition 1885-86. He was made a Freeman of the City in 1906. He was nicknamed Black Michael because of his heavy beard.

ST. ANDREWS ROAD, BS11. From the church of that name built in 1893.

ST. ANDREWS ROAD, BS6. The church of St. Andrews was built in 1845 and stood here until its demolition in 1970.

ST. ANDREWS, BS15. All the roads in this development are named after famous golf courses.

ST. ANNE'S CLOSE / DRIVE, BS15. The parish church of Oldland is dedicated to St. Anne and was built in 1830 on the site of an old chapel. St. Anne was the mother of the Virgin Mary.

ST. ANNE'S ROAD / PARK ROAD / TERRACE, BS4. In St. Anne's Park, a track known as the Pilgrim's path leads to the holy waters of St. Anne's Well and the chapel of St. Anne's, founded by John de la Warre in c. 1276, was built next to it. It became a shrine visited by many distinguished visitors praying to conceive children, the third most important place of medieval pilgrimage in the country. One visitor was the Queen of Henry VII, Elizabeth of York, who offered 2s 6d to help her conceive a son and eleven months later gave birth to Prince Arthur.

Bristol sailors would also visit the chapel before setting out to sea, as St. Anne was patron saint of harbours and sailors. Local people believed it would cure scurvy and rheumatism. Henry's son, Henry VIII, destroyed the chapel, under the Dissolution of the Monasteries Act in 1538, although fragments remained until the late nineteenth century, when they were removed by a landowner who wanted to discourage the public from visiting the well. After a legal battle the lower part of St. Anne's valley passed into public ownership, after the jury accepted the extraordinary testimony of a witness who claimed that the water of St. Anne's Well had cured a cataract in his eye. A modern church of the same dedication was built just prior to the First World War. In 1924 the annual St. Anne's day pilgrimage to the well was restored, when the well is blessed.

ST. ANNE'S ROAD, BS5. It has been suggested that it was so named because St. Anne's, Brislington can be seen from this high spot.

ST. AUBIN'S AVENUE, BS4. This follows the Channel Islands theme of the roads in this area. St. Aubin's Bay lies to the west of St. Helier, Jersey. St. Aubin was Bishop of Angers and shares St. David's feast day, 1 March.

ST. AUGUSTINE'S PARADE / PLACE, BS7. This may be named for the church erected c. 1200, rebuilt in 1480 and eventually demolished in 1969 after suffering bomb damage during the Second World War, or alternatively after the Cathedral, previously the Abbey church, of St. Augustine's of the Black Canons, on College Green.

ST. BARNABAS CLOSE, BS4. Built near the church of the same name. St. Barnabas was an associate of Paul, John and Mark. He was stoned to death in 61AD in Salamis, Greece.

ST. BARTHOLOMEW'S ROAD, BS1. The name comes from the church erected here in 1894 to replace the one that had stood at the bottom of Union Street since 1860. It was demolished to build Fry's offices, which are now the site of the Odeon cinema. Fry's donated funds for a new church to be built in St. Andrews.

ST. BEDE'S ROAD, BS16. A temporary church of this name was built here but is no longer used as such, as the parish is now united with St. John's.

ST. BERNARD'S ROAD, BS11. The name is from the Roman Catholic church built here in 1902 as a memorial to Bishop Brownlow, Bishop of Clifton 1893-1902. St. Bernard, 'Apostle of the Alps' (923-1008), is the patron saint of skiers. He was archdeacon of Aosta, Italy, and founded hospices in the Alps, run by monks who trained the famous St. Bernard dogs to search for travellers lost in the snows. Today he has two alpine passes named after him.

ST. BRELADES GROVE, BS4. Another Channel Islands location in keeping with other nearby roads. St. Brelade is adjacent to St. Aubin in Jersey.

ST. BRENDAN'S WAY, BS11. Perhaps this saint was chosen for his seafaring connection. He was born in Tralee, Ireland, in the sixth century, and spent seven years sailing his sealskin curragh round the Atlantic in search of the Isles of the Blessed. He may have found America on his travels. It has been said he spent some time in Bristol and built a cell on Brandon Hill.

ST. CATHERINE'S PLACE, BS3. Named after the hospital which stood here many years ago.

ST. DAVID'S AVENUE, BS15. Named after the builder's son, David Bees.

ST. DAVID'S CRESCENT, BS4. Continuing the religious and historic theme by naming this crescent after a city with an historic cathedral, this time St. David's in Pembrokeshire, Wales.

ST. DUNSTAN'S ROAD, BS3. From the church of the same name built circa 1920. Dunstan (c.909-988) was born in Baltonsborough, Somerset and became Abbot of Glastonbury Abbey. He was a harpist and worked in precious metals, and introduced the Benedictine Rule into monasteries in England.

ST. EDWARD'S ROAD, BS3. Named, for no apparent reason, after one of the two saints of this name, either Edward, King of the English, murdered at Corfe Castle in 978, or Edward the Confessor who died in 1066.

ST. EDYTH'S ROAD, BS9. St. Edyth was the daughter of King Edgar who died in 975 AD. She built a church at Wilton (the ancient capital of Wiltshire) and died in 984 AD.

ST. FAGAN'S COURT, BS15. A Civil War connection here. St. Fagan's, near Cardiff, was the scene of a battle in which the Royalists were defeated. Fagan was the first Archbishop of Caerleon in 177AD.

ST. FRANCIS ROAD, BS3. Named after the nearby church. The original building was bombed and a replacement now occupies the site.

ST. GABRIEL'S ROAD, BS5. After the church which once stood in this road. It was built in 1870 and demolished in the 1970s.

ST. GEORGE'S ROAD, BS1. Perhaps named after the church in Great George Street, now a prestigious concert hall.

ST. GREGORY'S ROAD / WALK, BS7. Named after the nearby church. St. Gregory (c.540-604) left his office as praetor of Rome to distribute his wealth to the poor and live in a monastery in Rome. Seeing some slave children for sale, he asked who they were and was told 'Angles' (Anglo-Saxons). He famously replied, 'Not Angles but angels', and thereafter devoted his life to the conversion of England to Christianity. He became pope and systemized the sacred chants of the Christian litany.

ST. HELEN'S WALK, BS5. Place name of a town in Lancashire. A number of streets in the locality have been named, apparently randomly, after towns in the British Isles.

ST. HELENA ROAD, BS6. Named after the island in the Atlantic where Napoleon Bonaparte spent his final years in captivity. It was also used for Boer prisoners during the Boer War, and this seems to be the reason for the choice of name as there is a Ladysmith Road adjoining.

ST. HELENS DRIVE, BS15. Perhaps a colliery connection here, as St. Helens, Lancashire, was a predominantly mining town.

ST. HELIER AVENUE, BS4. Continuing the theme in this locality for Channel Island names. St. Helier is the main town and port of Jersey.

ST. HILARY CLOSE, BS9. A place name after St. Hilary, Bishop of Limomum in Gaul, who died circa 367 AD. He gave his name to the Hilary Law sittings which begin on his feast day, 11 January. The religious theme is echoed in nearby St. Laud Close.

St. Michael's Hill

ST. IVEL WAY, BS15. A distribution depot for this product range, part of the Unigate group, was built here when out-of-town trading estates were becoming increasingly favoured. The building is now used by Wincanton Transport.

ST. JAMES BARTON, BS2. Built on the site of the barton, or farm, of the Priory of St. James. This, the first Bristol monastery, was founded in 1129.

ST. JAMES'S PLACE / STREET, BS16. After the nearby church which was called after the priory of that name in Bristol, which owned all this land.

ST. JOHN'S BRIDGE / STEEP, BS1. Leads to St. John on the Wall, the ancient church built into the city wall.

ST. JOHN'S CRESCENT / LANE / ROAD / STREET / TERRACE, BS3. There was a church of this name in the district for many centuries. One was erected here during the reign of Charles II to replace the one burnt down by Prince Rupert's men. The last church to bear the name was bombed during the Second World War.

ST. JOHN'S ROAD, BS8. From the church dedicated to St. John the Evangelist, built in 1841. This St. John is the brother of James, one of Christ's disciples.

ST. JOSEPH'S ROAD, BS10. Named after the husband of the Blessed Virgin Mary.

ST. LAUD CLOSE, BS11. The Bishop of St. Laud held land here at the time the Domesday Book was compiled. He held the land from Earl Herald. There was also an Eldred Close here at one time. Eldred held the land from the Earl after the death of Bishop Laud. *See Herald Close.*

ST. LEONARDS ROAD, BS5, BS7. Named after the church of St. Leonard built in 1901.

ST. LUCIA CLOSE / CRESCENT, BS7. The largest of the Windward Islands, discovered in 1502. They came under British rule in 1803.

ST. LUKE STREET, BS5. From the church of the same name built in 1843 when the area began to develop after the Great Western Cotton factory opened.

ST. LUKE'S CRESCENT / ROAD, BS3. From St. Luke's church, built 1859. The first vicar, Dr. D.A. Doudney (1811-94) was there until his death. He was a noted author of religious works and a caring man who established a soup kitchen in what was a poor parish.

ST. LUKE'S GARDENS, BS4. Built in the grounds of St. Luke's vicarage.

ST. MARGARET'S DRIVE, BS9. This was the site of St. Margaret's School, demolished in the 1960s. The girls wore an enviably attractive uniform of red and white with a daisy emblem on their blazers.

ST. MARK'S GROVE / ROAD / TERRACE, BS5. From the now deconsecrated church of that name, consecrated May 1848. The first vicar, the Reverend J. R. Woodford, later became Bishop of Ely. He wrote several hymns still sung in Anglican churches today.

ST. MARTIN'S CLOSE / GARDENS / ROAD / WALK, BS4. From the nearby church built in 1901. St. Martin is the patron saint of innkeepers and drunkards, this being because his feast day is 11 November coinciding with the Roman Feast of Bacchus.

ST. MARY'S ROAD / WALK, BS11. After the church built in 1827. Within the church are stained glass windows in memory of members of the Miles family of Kingsweston House.

ST. MATTHEW'S ROAD, BS6. The church of St. Matthew was erected in 1835 on part of Mother Pugsley's field. John Bangley, a merchant from Lewin's Mead, donated much of the money needed for building the church. Mother Pugsley was the widow of a soldier who died in the Civil War after they had been married only a brief while. She remained devoted to his memory throughout a long life and was buried in her wedding gown. In her field was a well reputed to have healing properties. *See Springhill.*

ST. MATTHIAS PARK, BS2. Named after the church which used to stand here and was destroyed in the Blitz.

ST. MICHAEL'S HILL / PARK / COURT, BS2. From the church of St. Michael the Archangel on the Mount Without, which was built on the foundations of an earlier church in 1777. The original church was in existence as early as 1174 and its tower and some memorials still remain. 'Without' meant outside the city walls.

ST. NICHOLAS PARK, BS5. It is possible the site formed part of the estate of St. Nicholas Vestry.

ST. NICHOLAS' ROAD, BS2. Developed circa 1870 on land owned by St. Nicholas Vestry, it was known as the Forlorn Hope Estate from a building of that name nearby.

ST. NICHOLAS ROAD, BS14. From the parish church dedicated to St. Nicholas of Myra, patron saint of maidens, children and sailors. The church dates from Norman times.

Bristol Bridge, near St. Nicholas Street

ST. NICHOLAS STREET, BS1. From the church next to Bristol Bridge. All but the crypt and tower were destroyed in the Blitz and it is now used as the city's tourist Information Office.

ST. OSWALD'S COURT / ROAD, BS6. St. Oswald was Bishop of Worcester from 961 to 992 and, as such, was associated with the building of Westbury College. In nearby St. Alban's church is a chapel dedicated to this saint, and this may have influenced the choice of name here.

ST. PAUL STREET, BS2. From the church designed by Daniel Hague in 1794, '...perhaps with some help or interference by the Vicar. ... (the tower's) details and those of the church are of a happily uninformed Gothic...' Nikolaus Pevsner, *The Buildings of England - North Somerset and Bristol.* Apparently its ornate tower was also much criticised at the time of building.

ST. PAUL'S ROAD, BS8. From the church of that name, now the University church, which was consecrated in 1854 but almost totally destroyed by fire in 1867 and rebuilt.

ST. PETER'S RISE / WALK, BS13. The name of the local parish church, which dates from 1846.

ST. PHILIPS CAUSEWAY, BS2. Named by readers as the result of a Bristol Evening Post competition after the old Bristol district that the Causeway runs through.

ST. PHILIPS ROAD, BS2. From the church of St. Philip and St. Jacob, always familiarly known as 'Pip'n'Jay', which may date back to the Norman period.

ST. PIERRE DRIVE, BS15. Another road named after a golf course, this one near Chepstow.

ST. RONAN'S AVENUE, BS6. Another road whose name is influenced by the works of Sir Walter Scott, in this case *St. Ronan's Well*, published in 1824.

ST. SILAS STREET, BS2. From the church originally constructed in 1867. By 1872 the sponginess of the soil on which it stood had caused so much damage to the building that a complete reconstruction was necessary and the new church opened in August 1873. It was destroyed in the air raids of 1940-41.

ST. STEPHEN'S AVENUE / STREET, BS1. From the church of this name which dates from the early thirteenth century. The street used to be called Fisher Lane, a reference to the fish market held here.

ST. STEPHEN'S CLOSE / ROAD, BS16. From the nearby church dedicated to the first Christian martyr.

ST. THOMAS STREET, BS1. The original church for which the street is named dated from c. 1300. All but the tower was taken down in 1789 and a new church built which opened in 1793.

ST. VINCENT'S HILL, BS6 / ROAD, BS8. Not after the obvious source, the famous St. Vincent's Rocks in the Avon Gorge, but after Admiral John Jervis, created Earl of St. Vincent after his defeat of the Spanish and French fleets, at Cape St. Vincent in 1797. He famously said when asked if the French invasion was likely "I do not say they cannot come, my lords. I only say they cannot come by sea."

ST. WERBURGH'S PARK / ROAD, BS2. After the local church, now no longer used for worship. St. Werburgh lived in the sixth century. She was a Mercian princess who took the veil, and is the patron saint of pregnant women. *See the District entry in the Introduction.*

ST. WHYTES ROAD, BS4. An ancient British saint. She was a hermit and had her cell at Felton, the old name for Whitchurch. The name Felton is derived from 'Filwood Chase'.

SALCOMBE ROAD, BS4. There is a group of streets here named after seaside resorts.

SALISBURY AVENUE, BS15 / BS4. Ela, Countess of Salisbury, founded Lacock Abbey, which had close associations with these areas.

SALISBURY ROAD, BS6. After Robert Cecil, Third Marquis of Salisbury (1830-1903). He was Prime Minister twice.

SALISBURY STREET, BS5. Not named in honour of Lord Salisbury, apparently although it is not known who this Salisbury might have been. It may have been the owner of the land.

SALISBURY GARDENS / ROAD, BS16. Quite a few roads in the locality are called after aristocratic families.

SALLYBARN CLOSE, BS15. A figure representing Ceres, the Roman goddess of the harvest, was erected on a barn in 1839 by John Couch's men who were paid at the rate of 7s per man and 1s per boy. Thought to be a relic from Keynsham Abbey, the figure became known locally as Sally.

SALLYSMEAD CLOSE, BS13. This is a field name. It was part of Bishopsworth farm in the late eighteenth century. The first component could be from the OE *salh* or *salig*, willow.

SALTHROP ROAD, BS7. This is a Wiltshire place derived from OE *sealthearpe* which one authority describes as being an apparatus for sifting salt. This is, in addition, another road with a Maskelyne connection, as Salthrop House, Wroughton, Wiltshire, was the Maskelyne family estate. *See Maskelyne Avenue.*

SALTMARSH DRIVE, BS11. Saltmarsh is mentioned in the Domesday Book. The name refers to the various parts of the salt marshes along the Severn from Berkeley to Avonmouth, more particularly to the northern stretch of these marshes between Redwick and Henbury. It was often flooded by the sea, as in 1607 when it was reported that 'the salt marsh was overflowed with sea water'.

SAMPSONS ROAD, BS13. A private road named in the Dundry Enclosure Award of 1815 which would have led to the house inhabited by someone by this name.

SAMUEL STREET, BS5. Samuel was the second son of George and Elizabeth Gerrish. Their home, Cambridge House, faced onto this street. It was demolished in the 1960s. *See Gerrish Avenue.*

SAMUEL WHITE ROAD, BS15. Named after a local industrialist who gave generously to church funds and good causes.

SAMUEL WRIGHT CLOSE, BS15. Named after the Clerk of Works, Warmley District Council in the 1960s and 70s.

SANCTUARY GARDENS, BS9. So named because of its proximity to Church Road and St. Mary's church suggested something with an ecclesiastical flavour.

SAND HILL, BS4. The majority of streets have the first syllable 'sand' in this area from nearby Sandy Park.

SANDBACH ROAD, BS4. As Sand Hill. The last syllable here means 'stream'. Sandbach is a town in Cheshire.

SANDBED ROAD, BS2. Probably a reference to the soil of the site.

SANDBURROWS ROAD / WALK BS13. Field name taken from the 1780 survey, part of Home Farm, Long Ashton Manor. The first syllable is obvious but last part is obscure. It could be from the OE *burh*, fortification or encampment, or ME *borowe*, burrow.

SANDCROFT, BS14. Field name meaning 'an enclosure with sandy soil'.

SANDFORD ROAD, BS8. Possibly named after John Sandford, Sheriff of the city 1687-88. Records also mention Robert Sandford who died in the mid-seventeenth century and left £100 to the poor of Redcliff.

SANDGATE ROAD, BS4. Another road with a sand theme. The last syllable, 'gate', means 'an opening to the shore'.

SANDHOLM ROAD, BS4. Last syllable 'holm' is a small island or a patch of dry land in a fen.

SANDHOLME CLOSE, BS16. Seemingly a name made up from Sandringham and Queensholme.

SANDHURST ROAD, BS4. The sand first syllable again, 'hurst' is a wood.

SANDLING AVENUE, BS7. A small village near Maidstone. The last syllable is from OE *hlinc* - hill.

SANDOWN CLOSE, BS16. Among a group of roads called after golf courses.

SANDOWN ROAD, BS4. Another case where sand has been used as a first syllable, 'down' is a hill.

SANDOWN ROAD, BS12. Near Ventnor Road, this refers to the town on the Isle of Wight.

SANDRINGHAM AVENUE / PARK, BS16. In 1935 a builder called Albert Smith lived in Badminton Road in a house called Sandringham and it seems highly likely he was responsible for this development.

SANDRINGHAM ROAD, BS4. Another road deriving its name from Sandy Road.

SANDRINGHAM ROAD, BS15. Among other roads called after royal residences, perhaps so named due to the proximity of Willsbridge 'castle'.

SANDWICH ROAD, BS4. One more in the Sand series: 'wich' means market town.

SANDY LANE, BS5. This may have been an accurate description many years ago.

SANDY PARK ROAD, BS4. An obvious reference to the quality of the soil. This was built over an ancient Brislington pathway, formerly known as Sandy Lane.

SANDYLEAZE, BS9. An old field name meaning sandy pasture.

SARAH STREET, BS5. Given the location, it is possible that this road was called after Miss Herapath. *See Glendare Street.*

SARGENT STREET, BS3. This began life in 1850 as Sergeant Street but the spelling changed by 1972. It seems likely that the owner of the land was a William Sergeant, a wholesale boot and shoe maker living near the New Cut.

SARUM CRESCENT, BS10. Sarum is the old name for Salisbury. Two other Wiltshire place names have been used for nearby streets. Old Sarum began as a hill fort in the Iron Age and was subsequently fortified by the Romans and the Normans. Eventually it lost favour to Salisbury (new Sarum) and had dwindled to the status of a Rotten Borough by the time the 1832 Reform Acts were passed, consisting of three houses and fifteen people. The term Rotten Borough referred to a constituency that scarcely existed although the M.P. could still claim his salary and expenses.

SASSOON COURT, BS15. All roads locally called after writers. Siegfried Sassoon (1886-1967) was a poet. His best-known work is the *Memoirs of a Foxhunting Man.*

SATCHFIELD CLOSE / CRESCENT, BS10. Arthur Satchfield lived in Westbury Parish in 1666.

SATES WAY, BS9. Named after one the directors of the development company, Ladbrokes Homes Limited.

SAUNDERS ROAD, BS16. No clue as to who Saunders was but perhaps the name of someone who lived or traded here long ago.

SAUNTON WALK, BS4. Named after a Devon village. Nearby roads follow this trend.

SAVILLE GATE CLOSE. BS9. This was intended to be known as Saville Grove but was called Saville Gate while under construction and the residents requested it be renamed Saville Gate Close. It is near Saville Road.

SAVILLE PLACE, BS8. Building was begun here in 1790 but was not completed until the beginning of the nineteenth century owing to financial problems. The Saville is almost certainly Sir George who was made a Freeman of the Merchant Venturers in 1766. He was M.P. for Yorkshire and a politician of some merit.

SAVILLE ROAD, BS9. Probably named for the same reason as Saville Place.

SAVOY ROAD, BS4. This was named after the cabbage variety as the road was built on the site of a former market garden.

SAY WALK, BS15. Named after a past vicar of St. Barnabas church.

SAXON ROAD, BS2. There is a Mercia Road in the area and Mercia was one of the kingdoms of the Saxon Heptarchy.

SCANDRETT CLOSE, BS10. The name of a prominent Quaker family. The Quaker burial ground was at Lawrence Weston.

SCHOOL CLOSE, BS14. Adjoins a local school.

SCHOOL LANE, BS16. The Stapleton National Mixed School stood here until the 1950s.

SCHOOL ROAD, BS4. From St. Luke's School, built in 1822 on three separate sites and brought together under one roof in 1859. The building was destroyed in the 1942 blitz.

SCHOOL ROAD, BS4. Self-explanatory.

SCHOOL WALK, BS5. Built on the site of Rose Green School.

SCHOOL ROAD, BS15. There is a school close by. There are two School Roads in BS15.

SCOTT COURT, BS15. Amidst other roads named after literary figures. This celebrates the work of Sir Walter Scott (1771-1832), famed for his Scottish novels.

SCOTT WALK, BS15. This was the surname of a one-time vicar of St. Barnabas, Warmley.

SCOTT LAWRENCE COURT, BS16. The name of a landowner taken from an old tithe map.

SEA MILLS LANE, BS9. The name is derived from 'saye', the type of cloth made in the mills in this area, a mixture of wool and silk. Saye comes from the Latin word *sagum* meaning a military cloak.

SEAGRY CLOSE, BS10. This is a place in Wiltshire. The meaning has been given as 'sedge brook' from the OE *seeg-rin*. There are a number of roads called after towns in the vicinity but no particular theme emerges.

SEARLE COURT AVENUE, BS4. Searle would seem to have been the builder. The court is from nearby Langton Court.

SEATON ROAD, BS5. A Devon place name which means 'village on the sea'. One in a series of roads called after seaside resorts.

SEAWALLS / SEAWALLS ROAD, BS9. After a number of fatalities on the Downs at Black Rock Quarry John Wallis built a wall there in 1746. It was known as Wallis's Wall, but the name was later changed to Sea Walls.

SECOND WAY, BS11. Another strictly practical choice of name.

SEDDON ROAD, BS2. Perhaps named after the Prime Minister of New Zealand, Robert Seddon (1845-1906). He visited Britain several times and supported the British in their battle against the Boers.

SEDGEFIELD GARDENS, BS16. Another in the group of roads called after race courses.

SEFTON PARK ROAD, BS7. A district of Liverpool. There is no obvious reason for this choice of name.

SELBORNE ROAD, BS7. Place name derived from OE *sealh*, sallow and *burna*, a stream. Most of the adjoining streets are called after places in the British Isles. Gilbert White, whose home it was, wrote *The Natural History and Antiquities of Selborne* in 1789.

SELBROOKE CRESCENT, BS16. According to Emlyn Jones, author of *Our Parish*, Margaret, widow of Edmund Blount of the Manor of Rodway, who died in 1381, married, as her second husband, a man by the name of Selbrooke.

SELBY ROAD, BS5. Town in Yorkshire. Many random place names used in the area.

SELDEN ROAD, BS14. Mrs Joanne Selden, a widow, was living in the tithing and parish of Keynsham on 9 January 1670, and was exempted from Hearth Tax.

SELKIRK ROAD, BS15. After the mariner Alexander Selkirk who was abandoned on the uninhabited island of Juan Fernandez in 1704 and rescued two years later. Alleged to have met Daniel Defoe in Bristol's Llandoger Trow Inn, who was inspired to write up his story as *Robinson Crusoe*.

SELLEY WALK, BS13. Selleys Mead was a field on Bishopsworth Farm according to the 1798 survey. It may be a personal name or else derived from the OE *salh* or *salig*, willow.

SELWORTHY ROAD, BS4. Place name which means 'enclosure by the sallow copse'. There are other place names among adjoining streets but the selection is apparently random.

SELWORTHY, BS15. In keeping with other local roads, this is named after a village in Somerset.

SENECA PLACE / STREET, BS5. No apparent reason for this choice of name, which recalls the Roman philosopher and writer, or a tribe of native Americans.

SEVENTH AVENUE, BS7. Another in the series in this area which aped the American style.

SEVERN ROAD (2) / WAY, BS11. Self-explanatory.

SEVIER STREET, BS2. Perhaps the name of the builder, as there is one listed in the street directory when this road was developed in the last quarter of the nineteenth century.

SEYMOUR AVENUE / ROAD, BS7. Built late nineteenth century. The name is probably that of the landowner or builder.

SEYMOUR ROAD, BS5. Built in the early nineteenth century, so it was perhaps named after the Dukes of Somerset, as this was their family name.

SEYMOUR ROAD, BS16. Either after Baron Thomas Seymour of Sudeley Castle, whose family had strong links with this area, or Sir Seymour Williams, a local solicitor.

SHADWELL ROAD, BS7. From the Shadwell family, who were Lords of the Manor of Horfield. There is a plaque to John Shadwell and his wife in Horfield church. When he died in 1849 the lands passed to the Bishop of Gloucester and Bristol. Until that time it had been farmed by the Shadwell family since the days of Henry VIII.

SHAFTESBURY AVENUE / TERRACE, BS6. From Anthony Ashley Cooper, Third Earl of Shaftesbury (1801-85) M.P. and social reformer. The road was built at about the time of his death.

SHAKESPEARE AVENUE, BS7. In keeping with the theme of naming roads in the area after famous literary figures.

SHALDON ROAD, BS7. Shaldons was the name given to the vast expanse of land part of which was used for building when the Lockleaze estate was developed in the 1950s.

SHAMROCK ROAD, BS5. No apparent reason for this choice of name unless, of course, the builder was an Irishman.

SHANKLIN DRIVE, BS12. There are other roads in the vicinity with holiday postcard names, all from the Isle of Wight, Dorset or Devon.

SHAPCOTT CLOSE, BS4. Probably a field name derived from OE *sceap*, sheep and *cot*, cottage, hut, shelter or shed

SHAPLANDS, BS9. Almost certainly a field name denoting an area where sheep grazed.

SHARLAND CLOSE, BS13. Named after Ray Sharland, a community activist who worked enthusiastically to improve living conditions for local residents from the 1950s to the 1990s. He founded the original Hartcliffe Community Centre, and was one of the founders of the community farm.

SHAW CLOSE, BS5. John George Shaw was Mayor of Bristol in 1853-54.

SHEENE LANE, BS3. Sheene House once stood in East Street. The word means shelter.

SHEEPS CROFT, BS13. A field name in the Manor of Bishport mentioned in the 1683 survey. Derivation is from OE *sceap*, sheep, croft being a small enclosure.

SHEEPWOOD CLOSE / ROAD, BS10. A field name mentioned in the 1839 Henbury tithe award.

SHELDARE BARTON, BS5. This would appear to be land on which, at some time, a man called Sheldare had a farm.

SHELDRAKE DRIVE, BS16. The theme of all the surrounding roads is British birds.

SHELLARD ROAD, BS12. This was the name of a family who once owned Filton House.

SHELLARDS ROAD, BS15. Daniel Shellard lived at Chestnut House in 1899.

SHELLEY CLOSE, BS5. Perhaps after the poet, although there seems no particular reason for this choice.

SHELLEY WAY, BS12. Another in the group of roads named after poets. Percy Bysshe Shelley (1792-1822) was a prolific writer. He is perhaps best known today for his *Ode to a Skylark* and *Ode to the West Wind.* His wife, Mary, was the author of *Frankenstein.* Shelley was drowned at la Spezia off the coast of Italy, and is buried in the Protestant cemetery in Rome.

SHEPHERDS CLOSE, BS16. There used to be a coal mine here owned by people of this name.

SHEPPARD ROAD, BS16. Alderman Frank Sheppard (1863-1956) served the City almost continuously between 1893 and 1956. A universally loved and respected man, he served as Lord Mayor, J.P. and Member of the Housing Committee.

SHEPTON WALK, BS3. Probably takes its name from Shepton Mallet, as many Somerset names have been used for roads in the area.

SHERBOURNE CLOSE, BS15. A man of this name, although spelt without the u, was manager of nearby Parkfield Colliery. It may, of course, be called after the Dorset town of Sherbourne.

SHERBOURNE STREET, BS5. Place name (without the u). It is derived from the Anglo Saxon *scir* and *burna* - a bright, clear brook. A high proportion of the roads in the area are called after British towns.

SHERIDAN ROAD, BS7. Richard Brinsley Sheridan (1751-1816) was both a dramatist and M.P. for Stafford, Westminster and Ilchester. His plays, notably *A School for Scandal* and *The Rivals*, are still performed regularly.

SHERIDAN WAY, BS15. Another Californian place name. *See California Road*

SHERRIN WAY, BS13. Taken from Sherrins Mead, a field on Bishopsworth Farm shown on the 1802 survey. Sherrin is most probably a personal name.

SHERSTON CLOSE, BS16. There is no obvious reason for this choice of name as the road which runs parallel is named after a Scottish location. Perhaps there is some connection with the Vassals estate.

SHERSTON ROAD, BS7. Called after a small town in Wiltshire, as is a road nearby.

SHERWELL ROAD, BS4. This road was named after David Cox Sherwell, Parish Councillor and Superintendent of Brislington Wesleyan Methodist Chapel in Brislington Square. He lived at Hill Cottage on Brislington Hill from 1884 until his sudden death in 1924.

SHERWOOD ROAD, BS15. Perhaps so-called because of the forest connection, there being once an ancient forest in Kingswood of which a few traces still remain today.

SHETLAND ROAD, BS10. Among other place names but no other Scottish ones.

SHIELDS AVENUE, BS12. After the well-known family who ran the laundry in Filton for many years.

SHILTON CLOSE, BS15. No apparent reason has been discovered so far for the naming of this road.

SHIMSEY CLOSE, BS16. Field name taken from 1846 tithe map.

SHIP LANE, BS1. An appropriate name as it is near the New Cut. It is thought there was an inn of that name here at one time.

SHIPHAM CLOSE, BS14. Named after a Somerset village, as are other roads in the vicinity.

SHIPLEY ROAD, BS9. The owner of this land was Arthur Shipley, a locally well-known antiquarian.

SHIRE GARDENS, BS11. Named after the nearby village of Shire Hunt.

SHIREHAMPTON ROAD, BS11. A Saxon composite for a place cut off from the surrounding district, from *shire*, shorn, *ham*, home, and *ton*, town.

SHORT STREET, BS2. Self-explanatory.

SHORTLANDS ROAD, BS11. A field name.

SHORTWOOD ROAD / WALK, BS13. Shortwood Common is mentioned in the Dundry Enclosure Award of 1815.

SHORTWOOD VIEW, BS15. Named after a hamlet between Siston and Mangotsfield.

SHOWERING ROAD, BS14. Richard Showering was a resident of Brislington in January 1670 and was granted exemption from Hearth Tax.

SHRUBBERY COTTAGES, BS6. Built in the grounds of what was a house called The Shrubbery, which stood in four and a half acres and was advertised for sale in 1866.

SHRUBBERY ROAD, BS16. After Shrubbery House which still stands here.

SHUTER ROAD, BS13. Shuters Wood was on land belonging to the Hall family.

SIDCOT, BS4. Called after a Somerset village, home to a famous Quaker school.

SIDELAND CLOSE, BS14. A field name taken from the 1846 Whitchurch tithe map.

SIDELANDS ROAD, BS16. Sideland was the name of the field in which Lincombe Barn, now the Downend Folk House, stands.

SIDMOUTH GARDENS / ROAD, BS3. Continuing the theme of Devon names used locally.

SIGNAL ROAD, BS16 The railway station was once sited near here.

SILBURY ROAD, BS3. From the ancient Silbury Hill in Wiltshire, the tallest artificial mound in Europe. It was once thought to be a burial mound but when it was excavated no traces of interments were found, so its purpose is obscure. It lies close to the avenue of stones which run from West Kennet Long Barrow to the Avebury Ring. The first syllable means 'seat' or 'station'. Appropriately it links up with Avebury Road.

SILCOX ROAD, BS13. Silcox's was a holding mentioned in the 1815 Dundry Enclosure Award and was probably a personal name.

SILKLANDS GROVE, BS9. Field name taken from 1844 Westbury tithe map.

SILVER STREET, BS1. Although this was the street's original name it was changed at one point to St. James' Back. The name was reinstated in 1875. In the fifteenth

century it was mainly garden ground belonging to 'the few houses of the opulent who were located in the neighbourhood'. William of Worcester was born here in 1415. The original Silver Street led from Lower Maudlin Street to the Horsefair. There are several theories as to the derivation of the name. One expert thinks it could have been where the silversmiths had their premises, another suggestion is that it is a Viking name such as Selvar or Silva, while yet another idea is that it is a Saxon corruption of the Latin *silva* meaning a wood, so with *strata* meaning road it would translate as 'the road leading to the wood'. William Silver, a man of some substance, lived in St. James in the fifteenth century so perhaps the street owes its name to him. A suggestion has also been made that prostitutes used to ply their trade here and demanded silver coins for their services.

SILVERHILL ROAD, BS10. This owes its name to a local landmark.

SILVERTHORNE LANE / WHARF, BS2. This was the name of the owner of the site. The 1863 directory lists a William Silverthorne who was a boot and shoe manufacturer at Kingswood, but whether this is the same man is not known.

SILVERTON COURT, BS4. All the roads in this section have been given the names of West Country locations.

SION HILL / PLACE / LANE, BS8. Named after the famous Sion spring, the pump room of which was in the building later to become the St. Vincent Rocks Hotel.

SION ROAD, BS3. From the Hebron Methodist church erected here in 1854.

SIR JOHN'S LANE, BS5. Called after Sir John Smyth, whose family owned Heath House to which this lane leads. Sir John was Knight of the Shire in the first parliament of James I.

SIXTH AVENUE, BS7. Another road named after the United States fashion.

SKIPPON COURT, BS15. Philip Skippon was Governor of Bristol Castle in the seventeenth century.

SLOAN STREET, BS5. This may have some connection with Burges and Sloan, solicitors.

SLYMBRIDGE AVENUE, BS10. Named after Robert Slymbridge, Dean of Westbury College in 1474.

SMALL LANE / STREET, BS1. One of the five main streets in the medieval city Perhaps the one of least importance (therefore 'small') as the others (Corn, Broad, High and Wine) led to the High Cross. Evans suggests the origin might be Francis Sammaricus who was Warden of Bristol in the tenth century.

SMEATON ROAD, BS1/ BS3. Smeaton was the architect who was called in to advise on modifications to the Pump Room, at the Hot Wells. He produced a proposal for a dry dock in 1764.

SMITHMEAD, BS13. From the OE *smic,* smith or blacksmith. The holding is referred to in the Dundry Enclosure Award of 1815.

SMOKE LANE, BS11. Clearly a reference to the industrial aspect of the area.

SMYTH ROAD, BS3. After the famous family who owned Ashton Court from the sixteenth century. They were originally merchants living in Small Street and at that time the name was spelt Smith.

SMYTHE CROFT, BS14. Possibly a connection with the famous land-owning family, despite the difference in spelling.

SMYTHS CLOSE, BS11. The famous Ashton Court family owned land at Avonmouth.

SNOWBERRY WALK, BS5. Part of an immediate post Second World War development of pre-fabricated houses, all roads on the development being given names of shrubs.

SNOWDON CLOSE / ROAD, BS16. An old field name which appears on the Kingswood Enclosure awards 1778-89.

SOMERDALE AVENUE. BS4. The name given to the Fry's factory at Keynsham, based on the example of other confectionery manufacturers like Rowntrees, Terrys and Cadburys with their worker-friendly manufacturing complexes. Prior to the move to Keynsham Fry's works were in the centre of town. The final demolition of the famous Fry's chimney took place as recently as the 1960s.

SOMERMEAD, BS3. Field name, first consonant OE *sumor, meaning* 'a hayfield used in the summer months'.

SOMERSET ROAD, BS4. Developed in the second half of the nineteenth century. Probably named after the county as other place names appear in surrounding streets.

SOMERSET SQUARE / STREET, BS1. Developed in the middle of the eighteenth century. Probably named after the Dukes of Somerset.

SOMERSET STREET, BS2. Again the origin would seem to be the Dukedom of Somerset or Lord Raglan, who was originally Lord Fitzroy Somerset. The land was originally owned by the Priory of St. James and the area was known as Prior's Hill until the end of the seventeenth century. A defensive Fort with thirteen cannon (twice as many as the Brandon Hill or Royal Forts) stood here, with defences running down to Hillgrove Street, diagonally across Kingsdown Parade through Colston's Mount to Royal Fort. It was the centre of fierce fighting during the Civil War, and the key to a long line of defences running from Stokes Croft to the River Avon. General Fairfax had his headquarters on nearby Ashley Hill in 1645 and decided against a siege and in favour of storming the fort. On 10th September that year most of the defending royalists were massacred, and the Fort, along with Bristol Castle and the city's other defences, were demolished at the end of the war.

SOMERSET TERRACE, BS3. Developed in the first half of the nineteenth century and probably called after the nearby county.

SOMERTON CLOSE, BS15. A few roads in this small area bear the names of Somerset towns and villages. The Westons once owned this land. Perhaps they held estates in Somerset, too.

SOMERTON ROAD, BS7. This could be a place name, meaning summer town, or the surname of someone connected with the development, as it is a not uncommon local name.

SOMMERVILLE ROAD, BS6. Perhaps after William Sommerville, who was a J.P. at the beginning of the twentieth century.

SOUNDWELL ROAD, BS15 / BS16. The derivation seems to be OE *sund*, meaning healthy, therefore 'a spring with beneficial properties'. *See Districts section in the introduction.*

SOUTH CROFT, BS9. Field name, a croft being a small enclosure.

SOUTH DENE, BS9. Made-up name. The last syllable is OE *denu*, valley.

SOUTH GREEN STREET, BS8. In the early part of the nineteenth century this was known as Green Street, with parklands dividing it from Albemarle Row. By 1872 it had become South Green Street and North Green Street, a section on either side of Hope Chapel Hill.

SOUTH GROVE, BS6. Self-explanatory. Grove is from the OE *graf*, copse.

SOUTH HAYES, BS5. This name derives from OE *haeg* and means enclosure in the south.

SOUTH LIBERTY LANE, BS3. Site of the old Ashton Vale Iron Company's colliery of this name. Once Lords of the Manor claimed liberty (or Manorial right) to dig for coal on their land.

SOUTH ROAD / STREET, BS3. Self-explanatory.

SOUTH ROAD / TERRACE, BS6. Certainly not directionally correct. Perhaps a surname? It is not unknown in this context in Bristol.

SOUTH ROAD, BS15. This bisects West Street.

SOUTH VIEW, BS16. This runs parallel to North View.

SOUTHDOWN ROAD, BS9. A hamlet in Dorset. No obvious reason for this choice.

SOUTHERNHAY AVENUE / CRESCENT / SOUTHERNHAY, BS8. Either a place name (district of Exeter) or a field name, the last syllable being OE *haeg*, enclosure or fenced-in section of forest, thus translating as 'the south enclosure'.

SOUTHERNHAY ROAD, BS16. A field name is likely in this case as the cottages here are probably some of the oldest in the area.

SOUTHEY AVENUE / COURT, BS15. After the poet Robert Southey. *See Southey Street.*

SOUTHEY STREET, BS2. Named after the poet, Robert Southey, who was born in Wine Street in 1774. He gave lectures in Bristol to fund his dream of emigrating to America and founding a communistic settlement, and was supported by the Bristol printer Cottle, who published his verses. The dream never came to fruition. He was appointed Poet Laureate in 1813 and was awarded a pension of £300 by Peel's government, by which he supported not only his own family but that of Coleridges as well. He and Samuel Taylor Coleridge had married sisters, both in St. Mary Redcliffe church. He died in 1843. His most enduring works are not so much his poems - he wrote a series of poetic epics, including *Joan of Arc, Madoc and Roderick,* 'from which the dust is rarely blown' *(Nelson's Encyclopedia, 1913)* - as his biographies of Nelson, Wesley and Cowper.

SOUTHFIELD AVENUE, BS15. Field name.

SOUTHFIELD COURT / PLACE / ROAD, BS6 / BS9. In all cases this is a field name.

SOUTHLEIGH ROAD, BS8. Perhaps after the Devonshire village or maybe a field name meaning south wood or clearing. However, as it is to the south of Leigh Road this may be the simple answer.

SOUTHMEAD ROAD, BS10. From Southmead House, described by Morgan in 1851 as 'surrounded by fine pasture and arable land'. The whole area once belonged to the long defunct Nunnery of St. Mary Magdalene.

SOUTHOVER CLOSE, BS9. Improvised name. Various streets nearby have names with Northover, Eastover, Westover.

SOUTHSEA ROAD, BS12. Other streets nearby are called after places in the Lake District so this choice of a south coast resort is puzzling.

SOUTHSIDE CLOSE, BS9. Invented name. It adjoins Southwood Road.

SOUTHVILLE ROAD, BS3. An invented name. *Ville* is French for town. *See Eastville.*

SOUTHWAY DRIVE, BS15. Named after the local historian and writer Matthew Southway, who died shortly before this development was completed.

SOUTHWELL STREET, BS2. Built circa 1760 this street is called after Edward Southwell, M.P. for Bristol 1739-54. He lived at Kingsweston House, which had been rebuilt by his father. He seems to have been an extremely wealthy man.

SOUTHWOOD AVENUE / DRIVE, BS9. There appears to have been a wood of this name here many years ago.

SOVEREIGN GARDENS, BS9. The name of the developers who built these houses.

SPALDING CLOSE, BS5. After the town in Lincolnshire, but the reason for this choice is unknown.

SPAR ROAD, BS11. Another industrially influenced name used in the area.

SPARTLEY DRIVE / WALK, BS13. Field name. Lamington Farm, Long Ashton Manor, is shown on the survey of 1794. The derivation is doubtful, however. It could be from the OE *spear*, rafter or shaft. Ley is from OE *leah*, woodland, glade.

SPEEDWELL AVENUE / ROAD, BS5. *See Districts section in the introduction.*

SPINNEY CROFT, BS13. Almost certainly a field name.

SPIRES VIEW, BS16. The spire in view would be that of Stapleton Parish church.

SPRING GARDENS, BS4. This adjoins Springleaze. It is possible there was a spring here at one time.

SPRING HILL, BS2. A spring did exist here once. One historian associates it with Mother Pugsley's well in a field in Ninetree Hill, in an area which was a public park until the mid nineteenth century. People suffering from eye diseases had visited the spring since medieval times. Mother Pugsley was the beautiful, grief-stricken widow of a young Royalist officer who had been killed by enemy cannon immediately after the wedding, while defending Prior's Hill Fort. His wife buried him by the ancient well on land which he owned below the fort, and took up residence by the well, dressed in mourning and rejecting all suitors. She dispensed wise advice from those taking the waters there, which by now was supposed to be doubly beneficial through the addition of 'the maiden widow's tears'. When she died in 1702 aged 80 the well and the field were

known by her name. However, it was enclosed in the garden of Spring Villa by 1861. *See St. Matthews Road, Dove Street. and Fremantle Road*

SPRING HILL, BS15. Almost certainly after a spring on this hillside.

SPRING STREET / STREET PLACE, BS3. There was at one time a spring here. An advertisement in the *Bristol Times and Mirror* in April 1865 invites tenders for 'laying down iron pipes from the end of Spring Street, Bedminster, to their Reservoir at Lower Knowle' as a replacement for the existing lead pipes.

SPRINGFIELD AVENUE, BS7. There were certainly both springs and fields on this stretch of hillside at the beginning of the nineteenth century.

SPRINGFIELD AVENUE / LAWNS, BS11. A field name.

SPRINGFIELD AVENUE / CLOSE / ROAD, BS16. Named because of the Leap Stream, which flows nearby.

SPRINGFIELD GROVE, BS6. From the house of that name, long since demolished. It is described by Morgan in 1851 as being 'the first mansion to the right of the road leading from Durdham Down to Henleaze, the seat of Mrs F Savage'.

SPRINGFIELD, BS6. In 1872 there was a Springfield House in Cotham New Road and Springfield Villas at Cotham Brow and Sydenham Hill, so any of these might be the origin of the street name.

SPRINGFIELDS, BS12. Built on the site of a house of that name, the residence of the local doctor.

SPRINGLEAZE, BS4. *See Spring Gardens.*

SPRINGLEAZE, BS16. Once a meadow near the stream.

SPRINGVILLE CLOSE, BS15. The Californian connection again. *See California Road.*

SPRUCE WAY, BS12. Amongst a cluster of tree names.

THE SQUARE, BS4. Shops and houses are positioned on all four sides.

THE SQUARE, BS16. Descriptive of the geography of the place.

SQUIRES COURT, BS15. Named after a portion of land on the Barrs Court estate.

STACKPOOL ROAD, BS3. Origin unknown; perhaps it was the surname of someone connected with the development.

STADIUM ROAD, BS7. Adjoins other roads called after famous sporting venues.

STAFFORD ROAD, BS2 / STREET, BS3. In both cases a place name from OE *staek*, staff and ford. Edmunds suggests a pole stuck in the water to indicate where it is fordable. It is possible, of course, that it is a surname but in both instances there are nearby streets also called after towns and counties. In the case of the BS2 road, another connection could be Hooke's Mills which once stood nearby. Sir Humphrey Stafford of Hooke was a constable of Bristol Castle.

STAFFORDS COURT, BS15. The Sir Humphrey Stafford connection could well apply here as in Stafford Road, bearing in mind the close links in ancient times between the Castle and the Forest.

STAINER CLOSE, BS4. This continues the British composers theme. Sir John Stainer (1840-1901) was Professor of Music at Oxford and wrote the oratorio *The Crucifixion,* immensely popular in its day.

STANBRIDGE CLOSE / ROAD, BS16. A Stanbridge House once stood nearby.

STANBURY AVENUE / ROAD, BS16. Place name meaning 'stone fort'. No clear reason for this choice; perhaps it was of significance to the developer.

STANDFAST ROAD, BS10. Walter Standfast was Mayor of Bristol in 1591-92. He was a member of a well-known local family prominent in the sixteenth and seventeenth centuries. Richard Standfast was rector of Christ Church for 51 years but was deprived of his living because of his adherence to the Royalist cause. He died 24 August 1684 aged 78.

STANDISH CLOSE, BS10. Lady Standish lived in Westbury Parish and was buried in the church there on 13 September 1649.

STANDON WAY, BS10. This was an old village name which had the meaning 'stony hill'.

STANE WAY, BS11. The connection here is the Romans. Stane Street was a causeway which ran through Sussex and Hampshire.

STANFIELD CLOSE, BS7. Clarkson Stanfield (1793-1867) was a marine and landscape painter. His son George Clarkson (1828-78) was also a painter.

STANFORD PLACE, BS4. The composer Sir Charles Villiers Stanford was born in Dublin in 1852. He died in 1924. His most famous work is the opera *Seamus O'Brien.*

STANHOPE STREET, BS2. The name chosen for this street, built around 1830, probably pays tribute to the Third Earl Stanhope who was a politician, inventor and author.

STANHOPE ROAD, BS15. Placed among roads with names of royal residences so this choice is a little puzzling.

STANLEY AVENUE, BS7 / HILL, BS4 / CHASE / PARK, BS5 / ROAD BS6/ STREET / TERRACE, BS3. It is supposed that all streets with this appellation are named in honour of the Earls of Derby, as this is their family name. Many of them held high ministerial posts in the government and abroad.

STANLEY AVENUE / CRESCENT, BS12. After a farm of that name demolished in the 1940s.

STANLEY GARDENS / PARK ROAD / ROAD, BS15. Probably all named after Stanley Farm.

STANSHAW CLOSE / ROAD, BS16. The Stanshaw family levied fines in Stourden (near Winterbourne) and were a well-known family in South Gloucestershire during the reigns of Henry IV and Edward IV.

STANTON CLOSE, BS15. Hugh de Stanton was godfather to Edmund, son and heir to Hugh le Blount.

STANTON ROAD, BS10. George Stanton was the village policeman in 1902.

STAPLEGROVE CRESCENT, BS5. The name of a village near Taunton. The derivative is OE *stapol*, post or pillar, thus the grove where such items can be obtained. Perhaps such a place existed here once.

STAPLE HILL ROAD, BS16. Derivation as above, though Smith says it may be a standing stone. It was first recorded by this name in maps of 1900, and was previously known as Turnpike Road, or High Road, being one of the main routes out of Bristol towards Mangotsfield. This road was also informally known as Pin Factory Lane, for here stood the Charleton Pin Works owned by Thomas Rawbone. It later became the Eclipse Ladder Factory, and is now the Eclipse Business Park.

STAPLETON CLOSE / ROAD, BS16 / BS5. Another name derived from OE *stapol*, post or pillar. It has been suggested that the village grew around a collapsed Roman building. This was previously the route from Bristol to Gloucester and was called Gloucester Road until the 1800s.

STAR LANE, BS16. From the ancient hostelry nearby.

STATION AVENUE, BS16. This is not very close to the old station so the choice of name here is puzzling.

STATION CLOSE / ROAD, BS15. Near to where Warmley station used to be.

STATION LANE / ROAD, BS7. The approach to the former Ashley Hill station.

STATION ROAD, BS16. At Fishponds station you would catch the train which took you through Staple Hill, Mangotsfield and Warmley.

STATION ROAD, BS10. Self-explanatory.

STATION ROAD, BS6. Montpelier - one station that survived Dr Beeching's reign of terror when he savagely cut back Britain's railway network in the 1960s.

STATION ROAD, BS4. Pathway to another station lost forever.

STATION ROAD, BS11. Fortunately Shirehampton station is still in use.

STATION ROAD, BS15 / 16. Two more defunct stations remembered here, Staple Hill and Mangotsfield.

STAUNTON LANE, BS4. From Staunton Manor, long since demolished.

STAVELEY CRESCENT, BS10. This is another road with a Lake District name. Staveley is a town near Windermere.

STAVERTON WAY, BS15. Believed to have been built by Staverton contractors.

STAVORDALE GROVE, BS14. Village near Wincanton notable for its Priory of Black Canons, founded in the thirteenth century. The name means either 'stony ford in the valley' or the first component may be from OE *staefer*, stake.

STEEL COURT, BS15. Charles Steel was Senior Surgeon at the Bristol Royal Infirmary, but there is no obvious reason for the naming of this road.

STELLA GROVE, BS3. This road was developed between the wars. The name is possibly a female relative of the builder.

STEPHEN STREET, BS5. Almost certainly a member of the Gerrish family. *See Gerrish Avenue.*

STEPHENS DRIVE, BS15. Named after the man who founded the Stephens Ink Company. He lived at Willsbridge Castle.

STEPNEY ROAD / WALK, BS5. Probably after the London district, although it could be a surname. The meaning is 'Stybba's landing place'.

THE STEPPING STONES, BS4. This must surely be an old name for a marshy piece of land by the river.

STERNCOURT ROAD, BS16. Named after a large house in Winterbourne belonging to the Stern family. *See also Stourden Close.*

STEVENS CRESCENT, BS3. There is a Henry Stevens listed in the 1872 directory and as the adjoining street is called Henry Street perhaps he was the owner of the land.

STIBBS COURT, BS15. Joseph Stibbs owned a chemical plant at Oldland during the late nineteenth and early twentieth century, and John Stibbs was a pit owner.

STIBBS HILL, BS5. A past landowner's name.

STILE ACRES, BS11. An old field name from OE *stigel*,stile.

STILLHOUSE LANE, BS3. This led to the old brewery.

STILLINGFLEET ROAD, BS13. The Reverend Robert Stillingfleet was Prebendary of Durham and Master of Sherborne Hospital near Durham. He died on 3 August 1759 aged 53 and was buried at Long Ashton. He was grandson to Edward Stillingfleet, Bishop of Worcester, who also achieved fame as a writer.

STILLMAN CLOSE, BS13. Stillmans was a field name at Crox Bottom Farm, Novers, formerly owned by the Ashton Court Estate. The derivation is probably from the OE *stigel*, stile.

STIRLING ROAD, BS4. All roads near the Black Castle, part of the Arnos Court estate, bear the names of famous castles.

STOCKTON CLOSE, BS14. Stockton is a village in Wiltshire but no obvious link with this area.

STOCKTON CLOSE, BS15. Following the California theme this is a location in that state. *See California Road.*

STOCKWELL AVENUE / CLOSE / DRIVE / GLEN, BS16. A Mr. H. Andrews ran Stockwell Hill Farm in the early years of the twentieth century. It derives from a field name; Stockways Hill is shown on a map of 1697.

STOCKWOOD CRESCENT, BS4 / LANE, BS14 / ROAD, BS4. There are two possibilities as to the origin of the name Stockwood. The first syllable could be either OE *stoc*, place or secondary settlement, or *stocc* meaning tree-trunk or log or something made out of logs, with *wudu* meaning wood or woodland.

STOKE HAMLET / HILL / LANE, BS9. Stoke means 'dependent farmstead' and is used a great deal in this area.

STOKE LANE, BS16. After the nearby Stoke House once owned by the Dukes of Beaufort.

STOKE PADDOCK ROAD, BS9. From the OE *pearroc*, an enclosed piece of land, usually pasture, with adjoining stables, from which we obtain paddock. Stoke refers to the local village.

STOKE PARK ROAD / STOKE PARK ROAD SOUTH / STOKE ROAD, BS9. Continuing the Stoke theme.

STOKE VIEW ROAD, BS16. From here the view is of Stoke House, built on the site of an earlier residence by Lord Botetourt circa 1770. This was one of the titles of the Dukes of Beaufort.

STOKE VIEW, BS12. Most probably from nearby Stoke Brook.

STOKELEIGH WALK, BS9. An amalgam of Stoke and leigh, meadowland.

STOKES CROFT, BS2. The croft or enclosure of John Stoke, who lived in Redcliff Street and was married three times. He was Mayor in 1364, 1366 and 1379, and is buried in the chapel of the Blessed Mary in the parish of St. Thomas. His enclosure was previously the croft of Berewyke of Redelond (Redland).

STOKES COURT, BS15. Thomas Stokes leased land at Yew Tree Farm, Downend, in 1738.

STONEBERRY ROAD, BS14. Researches have not yet unearthed a historical connection with this name.

STONEBRIDGE PARK, BS5. This was probably a reference to the small bridge which connected with Clay Bottom.

STONECHAT GARDENS, BS16. British birds are the theme on this estate.

STONEHILL, BS15. This was the general name for a small area here prior to development.

STONELEIGH CRESCENT / ROAD / WALK, BS4. A place name, the meaning is 'stone or rock in the woodland clearing'. No obvious reason for the choice of name.

STORES ROAD, BS11. Another one of the choices of industrial names for many Avonmouth roads.

STOTHARD ROAD, BS7. Thomas Stothard (1755-1834) was a painter and illustrator.

STOTTBURY ROAD, BS7. It is a mystery why this road has been so named.

STOULTON GROVE, BS10. One of the livings appropriated by John Carpenter, Bishop of Worcester, towards the support of Westbury College, for which he worked so hard. He died in 1476.

STOURDEN CLOSE, BS16. This was the name of an ancient Manor House in the parish of Winterbourne occupied by the Sturden family. One, Hugo de Sturden, was commonly known as Hickery Stern or Hicken Stern, the hero of Pearsall's song 'Oh, who will o'er the Downs so free'. He was reputed to be a highwayman. He died circa 1340 and is buried in Winterbourne church.

STOURTON DRIVE, BS15. After Abbot John Stourton of Keynsham, who had to relinquish the abbey to the Crown in the reign of Henry VIII.

STOW HOUSE, BS11. This naming follows the Cotswold villages theme.

STOWICK CRESCENT, BS11. Stowick was a farm in the Hundred of Henbury. Stow is Anglo-Saxon for site or inhabited place and the last syllable *wick* or *wic* means a village or collection of houses. *See Wescott Crescent.*

STRADBROOK AVENUE, BS5. From the Strad Brook Bridge shown on the 1610 map of Kingswood Forest.

STRADLING ROAD, BS11. John Stradling with his wife Joan held part of the Manor of Aust, which was formerly a tithing of Henbury. The family lived at the Manor House, Dauntsey, Wilts, in the sixteenth and seventeenth centuries.

STRAIGHT STREET, BS2. Self-explanatory.

STRAITS PARADE, BS16. Until the 1930s this stretch of road was known as The Straits and many still refer to it as that today. Legend had it that George III was riding in a carriage with the Duke of Beaufort along this road which was, at that time, a narrow road, full of twists and turns. The king was so exasperated at being jolted so that he bellowed at the Duke "Make this road straight and I'll make you a present of the land of either side of it". The Duke carried out the necessary work and claimed his prize. The road was known as the Straits from that time hence.

STRATFORD CLOSE, BS14. The name of a village near Tewkesbury. Many links existed between Bristol and Tewkesbury in medieval times.

STRATHMORE ROAD, BS7. Either a place name or in honour of the Earls of Strathmore of Glamis Castle. Queen Elizabeth the Queen Mother is a member of this family, whose name is Bowes-Lyon.

STRATTON STREET, BS2. This was originally part of Pritchard Street and was renamed sometime in the first half of the nineteenth century. It would seem to be after the Stratton in Stratton, Hughes and Co., Ironfounders and manufacturers of carts, wheels, wagons and agricultural equipment, who had premises in Water Street, Meadow Street and Clarke Street, all of which adjoined Stratton Street.

STRAWBRIDGE ROAD, BS5. Thought to be named after the coal merchant, Cyril Strawbridge, who had yards at both Lawrence Hill and Horfield in the 1920s.

STREAM CLOSE, BS10. Not surprisingly, close to a stream.

STREAM SIDE, BS16. Descriptive.

THE STREAM, BS16. Close to the water.

STRETFORD AVENUE / ROAD, BS5. The name of a Manchester suburb. Lancashire places have been favoured in this area as suitable names for roads near the park for some reason unknown.

STROUD ROAD, BS12. Among other town names, seemingly randomly selected although Gloucestershire locations do appear to be most favoured.

STROUD ROAD, BS11. All the roads in this district are named after Cotswold towns and villages.

STUART STREET, BS5. Possibly a member of the Gerrish family. *See Gerrish Avenue.*

STURDEN LANE, BS16 / ROAD, BS3. The Smyth family owned the Manor of Sturdon (or Stourden) at Winterbourne as well as Ashton Court. *See Stourden Close.*

STURMINSTER CLOSE / ROAD, BS14. The name of a town in Dorset, meaning 'church or minster on the river Stour'.

SULLIVAN CLOSE, BS4. After composer Sir Arthur Sullivan (1842-1900) resoundingly popular even today for his collaboration with W S Gilbert in producing the Savoy light operas.

SUMMER STREET, BS3. This was the name of the builder responsible for developing this road.

SUMMERHAYES, BS15. Named after Miss Summerhayes, the dispenser for Dr Aubrey of Bitton.

SUMMERHILL ROAD / TERRACE, BS5. From the old name Summer Hill, which was a grassy eminence before this development took place.

SUMMERLEAZE, BS16. Possibly a field name.

SUMMERS ROAD, BS2. Development took place in the first half of the nineteenth century. Summers may have been the owner of the land.

SUNDERLAND PLACE, BS8. Probably from the Duke of Sunderland, George Granville Leveson-Gower (1758-1833). A house of that name once stood here, which served as a school at one time. The name means separate land, land apart from the main estate or private land.

SUNNINGDALE DRIVE, BS15. Another road in the golf course sequence.

SUNNINGDALE, BS8. A place in Berkshire. No apparent reason for this choice.

SUNNY BANK / WALK, BS16. Apparently descriptive.

SUNNYBANK, BS16. A house of this name stood in Westerleigh Road.

SUNNYDENE, BS4. Made-up name.

SUNNYHILL DRIVE, BS11. There was an old street near here called Sunny Hill, so almost certainly the name derives from that.

SUNNYSIDE, BS9. An optimistic name for houses built by W.E. George of the brewing dynasty for various members of his staff c. 1906.

SUNNYVALE DRIVE, BS15. It is thought this was chosen for its cheery note.

SUNRIDGE BS16. A hilltop which catches the sun.

SUNRISE GROVE, BS4. Clearly this faces east.

SURREY ROAD, BS7. Following the theme of naming all streets round here after county cricket clubs as they surround the County Ground.

SURREY STREET, BS2. The street was built in the latter part of the eighteenth century and was named after the Duke of Surrey, who took a great deal of interest in West Country affairs and was three times Mayor of Gloucester. The name Surrey is a corruption of the Anglo-Saxon *Suth-ray*, 'south of the river'.

SUSSEX PLACE, BS2. This may have been named after the dukedom or after the Duke of Sussex pub, which, although it probably did not pre-date the street, may have been built over an earlier hostelry of the same name. Many local roads also honour branches of the aristocracy.

SUSSEX STREET, BS2. The street was developed in the first quarter of the nineteenth century. The Duke of Sussex, Augustus Frederick (1773-1843) visited Bristol with his brother the Prince of Wales in 1808 and received the Freedom of the City.

SUTHERLAND AVENUE, BS16. Named after the Duke of Sutherland, of the Leveson-Gower family, who owned the land upon which this road was built.

SUTTON AVENUE, BS4. Part of the 1924 development by the Sutton Dwellings Trust which provided the city with nearly 200 houses and flats for working-class people at cheap rents. W. R. Sutton, who ran a carrier firm, left nearly a million pounds for this purpose.

SWAINSWICK, BS14. A village near Bath. The owners of the land here may have had links with Bath.

SWAISH DRIVE, BS15. This was named after John Swaish, a businessman and magistrate in the early part of the twentieth century, who owned pawnbrokers' shops on this side of the city.

SWALLOW DRIVE, BS12. Birds' names have been used for all the roads around here.

SWANE ROAD, BS14. Widow Swane was resident in the parish of Keynsham in 1674 and was exempt from Hearth Tax.

SWANMOOR CRESCENT, BS10. Swanmoor is a rhine (ditch) in the Henbury area.

SWEETS CLOSE / ROAD, BS15. Most likely named after the family of market gardeners who traded on this side of town.

SWISS DRIVE / ROAD, BS3. There is no obvious reason for this choice of name.

SYCAMORE CLOSE, BS5 / DRIVE, BS12. In both cases there are surrounding roads also named after trees.

SYCAMORE CLOSE, BS15. A road among other with a sylvan influence, the reason for this naming may be a local Wesleyan connection, as John Wesley was described as preaching 'under the sycamore at Kingswood'.

SYDENHAM HILL / LANE / ROAD, BS6. The Sydenham Trust owned all this land, according to Latimer. There were at least three eminent gentlemen of that name, and these streets could be named after a shipbuilder and president of the Colston Society in 1749.

SYDENHAM ROAD, BS4. There are several villages of that name and it is also a London district. The first syllable may be a personal name, Cippa, although it could be from the OE *sid*, large, spacious, long.

SYDENHAM WAY, BS15. Land near here was known as Sydenham's Meadow. Monmouth's army camped here two days before its defeat at the Battle of Sedgemoor (1685).

SYDNEY ROW, BS1. As this road was developed c.1800 it seems that the Sydney in question is Thomas Townsend, Viscount Sydney (1733-1800). He was Home Secretary 1783-89. Sydney, Australia, was named after him.

SYLVAN WAY, BS11. Purely descriptive.

SYLVIA AVENUE, BS3. The Smyths of Ashton Court owned this land, and this avenue was named after a daughter of the family.

SYMES AVENUE, BS13. Almost certainly named after Robert Henry Symes, who served the city as four times as Mayor of Bristol and twice as Lord Mayor between 1893 and 1903.

SYMINGTON ROAD, BS16. Name of two locations in Scotland. No obvious reason for this choice.

SYSTON WAY, BS16. From the ancient Manor of this name.

TABERNACLE ROAD, BS15. After the Whitefield Tabernacle, built in 1930, which benefited considerably from the patronage of wealthy families such as the Budgetts.

TACKLEY ROAD, BS5. A village in Oxfordshire. The name was chosen because the Dormer family who together with the Cottrells owned all this land, originated from Oxfordshire.

TAILOR'S COURT, BS1. From the hall of the Fraternity of Tailors, an ancient guild founded in the reign of Edward II. By the early nineteenth century there was but one member, Isaac Amos, who appointed himself master each year and drew expenses for attendances at meetings, taking office, acting as auditor, etc. He died in 1824.

TALBOT AVENUE, BS5. Among a small group of roads named after Victorian notables. W.H. Fox Talbot (1800-1877) was a pioneer in photography.

TALBOT ROAD, BS4. Named after the ancient inn of the same name, favoured by the Talbot family, Earls of Shrewsbury. A Talbot was a large hunting dog now extinct.

TALGARTH ROAD, BS7. A village in the Black Mountains, Powys. The name derives from the Welsh *tal*, end or front; and *garth*, headland. Many random place names have been used in this area.

TALLIS GROVE, BS4. After Thomas Tallis (1513-85), composer of church music, including the famous Tallis Canon, and organist at the Chapel Royal. This street is one of many in the area dedicated to British composers.

TAMAR ROAD, BS2. Perhaps the proximity of the Feeder Canal inspired this choice of name, although the beautiful river which separates Devon from Cornwall bears little resemblance to the waterway here.

TANKARD'S CLOSE, BS1. Tankard's Close is a corruption of an old field name, *Tinker's Close*, which had formerly been known as *Broome Hay*. The Close was named Tinkard's Close, and the name finally changed to Tankard's Close.

TANNER CLOSE, BS15. Named after a well-known local family. There were three brothers' Tom, Albert and Arthur, all prominent in the community.

TANNERS COURT, BS16. After a solicitor called William Tanner who used to live at Frenchay Park (now Frenchay Hospital). One of his clients, Mrs Rooke, left him the house in her will and he lived there until his death in 1887.

TANORTH CLOSE, ROAD, BS14. Field name taken from the 1845 tithe map.

THE TANYARD, BS15. There used indeed to be a tanning yard here run by the Williams family. They appear in the 1899 directory.

TAPSTERS, BS15. An old field name providing an obscure reminder of links with the past.

TARNOCK AVENUE, BS14. An old field name taken from the 1845 tithe map.

TAUNTON WALK, BS7. Many place names are used for roads in this area.

TAVERNER CLOSE, BS4. Continuing the composers theme, this is named after John Taverner (1490-1545) remembered for his choral music and festal masses.

TAVISTOCK ROAD / WALK, BS4. Most of the streets in the vicinity have the names of West Country towns.

TAYLOR CLOSE, BS15. This would seem to be named after Robert Taylor, who owned a boot factory in the vicinity in the late nineteenth and early twentieth centuries.

TAYLOR GARDENS, BS13. Taylor's Ground was one of the fields at Pigeon House Farm, Hartcliffe. Taylor was most probably the occupier of the land.

TAYMAN CLOSE, BS7. A name probably chosen by the builder.

TAYNTON CLOSE, BS15. A Forest of Dean village. The name chimes in with the adjacent Verwood (New Forest) and Oakhill (Mendips), which is not in a forest but sounds as if it should be.

TEEWELL AVENUE / CLOSE / HILL, BS16. This was originally known as Tea Well Hill. There were a number of wells in the area but this is certainly a curious name for one.

TEIGNMOUTH ROAD, BS4. Another road in the West Country towns pattern.

TELEPHONE AVENUE, BS1. The site of the first telephone exchange in Bristol.

TELFORD WALK, BS5. Steel houses of the Telford type were erected in this cul-de-sac. The Telford after whom they are called is presumably Thomas Telford (1757-1834), the civil engineer whose design for the Clifton Suspension Bridge was not accepted. His work can be admired in the shape of the Iron Bridge in Shropshire.

TEMPLE BACK / GATE / STREET / WAY, BS1. All roads here refer to the Knights Templar. Temple church (the one with the famous leaning tower just off Victoria Street) is the key to this pattern of names. This was also where the Temple Pipe conduit emerged in a fountain head. A statue of Neptune was erected over it. Money for the upkeep of the pipes was collected during the rowdy annual Temple Fair, but it was suppressed in 1835 due to unmanageable crowd behaviour, and gradually the pipe and fountain fell into disrepair until the arrival of the railway. The water was then used exclusively by the GWR at Temple Meads station, but now runs to waste. The statue of Neptune was removed to the dockside, near the Watershed.

TEMPLELAND ROAD, BS13. Field name in Bishport Manor taken from the 1683 survey. The temple in question was a house of the Knights Templar - members of a religious and military order founded in Jerusalem in 1118 to protect the pilgrim roads to the holy places. The organisation spread rapidly throughout the Western Christian world and acquired great wealth. It was dissolved in 1312.

TENBY STREET, BS5. A Pembrokeshire resort. From the Welsh name Dinbych; *dinas*, fort; *bach*, small. And this is, appropriately enough, a small street.

TENNESSEE GROVE, BS6. Perhaps a play on words as there was a Tennis Road here formerly and there are tennis courts nearby.

TENNIS ROAD, BS4. There were tennis courts here before the site was developed in the 1930s.

TENNIS COURT ROAD, BS15. Perhaps, in times long past, the site of a tennis court in the grounds of one of the larger houses. There is also a very old inn of the same name facing the beginning of the road.

TENNYSON ROAD, BS7.

> *'…thro' mountain clefts the dale*
> *Was seen far inland, and the yellow down*
> *Border'd with palm, and many a winding vale*
> *And meadow, set with slender galingale…'*
>
> Alfred, Lord Tennyson, *The Lotus Eaters*

…but that was before the developers reached Horfield. Tennyson (1809-92) was Poet Laureate. His close friend, Arthur Hallam, lived at Clevedon, and his untimely death inspired Tennyson's great poetic work *In Memoriam*.

TENTH AVENUE, BS7. Another of the district's Americanisms.

TERRELL GARDENS, BS5. There may be some connection here with the local rope manufacturing family of this name, who may have owned this land.

TERRELL STREET, BS1. Originally known as Redcoat Lane, the street became Terril Street in the mid-1800s before settling down as Terrell Street around 1872. It has been suggested the origin was the Terrell family, who were prominent in civic circles, or Edward Terrill, who helped found Broadmead Baptist chapel.

TETBURY ROAD, BS5. Near Avening Road so perhaps the builder had connections with Gloucestershire.

TEWKESBURY ROAD, BS2. From the town in Gloucestershire, whose name derives from the personal name Teodoc and *burh*, a fortified place. There may be a connection here with Humphrey Stafford of Hooke, appointed Constable of Bristol Castle by Edward IV after the decisive battle of Tewkesbury. *See Stafford Road.*

TEWTHER ROAD, BS13. Matthew Smyth of Ashton Court, who died in 1583, married Jane, daughter and co-heir of Thomas Tewther of Ludlow in Shropshire.

TEYFANT ROAD / WALK, BS13. John Teyfant held a moiety, which was a half portion, of the Manor of Ashton Philips in Hartcliffe in the fourteenth century.

THACKERAY WALK, BS7. William Makepeace Thackeray (1811-63) was author of *Vanity Fair*, *The Virginians* and many other well-loved works.

THANET ROAD, BS3. Place name which is believed to mean "bright island" or "fire island", i.e. one with a beacon or lighthouse.

THERE AND BACK AGAIN LANE, BS8. This part of Park Street suffered in the Blitz, and was sensitively rebuilt in the New Brutalist manner, employing a great deal of concrete. The general consensus of opinion seems to be that this is a light-hearted name for this short cul-de-sac.

THERESA AVENUE, BS7. Theresa was the wife of Mervyn Herbert Nevil Story-Maskelyne. *See Maskelyne Avenue.*

THICKET AVENUE / ROAD, BS16. The road was first constructed by the Kingswood Enclosure Commissioners in 1780 and the name is descriptive of the terrain as it was when building began. The land actually belonged to the family of the Dukes of Beaufort and was always known as The Thicket.

THIERY ROAD, BS3. Named after a French friend of the builder, whom he met during the First World War. Is it possibly a commemoration of a dead soldier?

THINGWALL PARK, BS16. According to Isaac Taylor, this Norse name means 'assembly field' where the battle colony exercised their accustomed privilege of local government, but it is unclear why this road was so called. Professor Wyld believes the name to come from 'the well of Thengil' (a Norse name). Thingwall is also a location in merseyside, as is Huyton Avenue, which runs off Thingwall Park, but no Liverpool connection has yet been established with this part of Fishponds.

THIRD AVENUE, BS7. Continuing the American-style namings.

THIRD WAY, BS11. A further example of the business-like nomenclature employed by the street naming department locally.

THIRLMERE COURT, BS15. Among a group of roads called after famous British lakes.

THIRLMERE ROAD, BS12. All the roads in this area are called after locations in the Lake District.

THISTLE STREET, BS3. A cul-de-sac leading off The Nursery, this would seem to be an old field name.

THOMAS LANE / STREET, BS1. From the nearby church dedicated to St. Thomas-à-Becket.

THOMAS STREET, BS5. Named after another member of the Gerrish family.

THOMAS STREET, BS2. It would appear this street was named after the philan-thropist, George Thomas, who died in 1869. He lived at Eagle House, Brislington and amassed a fortune in the grocery business. He left £13,000 to charitable causes in his will.

THOMPSON ROAD, BS14. Ferdinando Thompson resided in the tithing of Keynsham in January 1670 and was exempt from Hearth Tax.

THOMSON ROAD, BS5. Quite a number of people with this surname were living in the locale when development took place towards the end of the nineteenth century, so the reference here could be to either the landowner or the builder.

THORNDALE, BS8. Perhaps a made-up name or a place name. The meaning is 'thorn tree valley'.

THORNLEIGH ROAD, BS7. This used to be known as Rowley Road after a field name, and was later renamed after the Thornleigh Park Estate.

THORNMEAD GROVE, BS10. Field name; OE *porn*, thorn and *mæd*, meadow.

THORNYCROFT CLOSE, BS7. Sir William Hamo Thornycroft (1850-1925) was a sculptor. One of his works is the statue of King Alfred at Winchester.

THREE QUEENS LANE, BS1.

> *'Come, all sad and solemn shows,*
> *That are quick-eyed Pleasure's foes!*
> *We convent naught else but woes.'*

William Shakespeare (or John Fletcher), *Dirge of the Three Queens*

There was an ancient inn which once stood here. It is an unusual name for an inn as opposed to Three Kings (the three wise men) which was relatively popular and there was one of this name in nearby Thomas Street. It has been suggested that the naming of the Three Queens was a jesting reference to the wives of the Three Kings. It may relate to the legend of the three queens who were supposed to have borne away the body of the dying King Arthur. This street used to be known as Ivy Lane prior to 1670.

THREE WELLS ROAD, BS13. A field name, Bishopsworth Farm, taken from the survey of 1802.

THRISSELL STREET, BS5. In the 1700s this was known as the Ropewalk in the days when Stapleton Road was called Gloucester Road. Here Edward Thrissell, a ropemaker, built a factory which remained on this spot for 200 years. The site is now a business park.

THROGMORTON ROAD, BS4. Sir Nicholas and Sir Baynham Throgmorton (or Throckmorton) were Rangers for Kingswood Forest in the seventeenth century. Sir Baynham succeeded to the post in 1678 but does not seem to have met with great success, as on one occasion, he was driven out with his staff by the cottages. There are effigies of Sir Baynham Senior and Lady Throgmorton in the Lord Mayor's Chapel. Sir Nicholas was a distinguished Royalist during the Civil War but died in great poverty in 1664 as a result of his endeavours to prosecute his claims to Kingswood Forest and Filwood Chase.

THURLESTONE, BS14. The home village, in Devon, of Samuel Shirley, a Bristol magistrate in the 1930s.

THURLOW ROAD, BS5. Either a place name (Essex) or after Edward, first Baron Thurlow (1730-1806) who served as Lord Chancellor 1778-92.

THURSTON'S BARTON, BS5. From Thomas Thurston, who purchased the site from the Eyetone family in the early part of the nineteenth century and built cottages there. Barton comes from OE *bære*, barley and *tun*, enclosure. The latter originally referred to a threshing floor, but later came to mean a farmyard.

TIBBERTON, BS15. Shown in the Domesday Book as being five hides in the hundred of Botloe in Gloucestershire. Wulfhelm held it from King Edward. It contained ten villagers and eight smallholders with eight ploughs and four slaves. All nearby roads are given the name of Gloucestershire villages.

TIBBOTT ROAD / WALK, BS14. John Tibbott was a resident of Keynsham in 1674 and was granted exemption from Hearth Tax.

TICHBORNE ROAD, BS5. About the time this street was built in the 1870s, the famous Tichborne trial was making headlines. This was centred on Arthur Orton, a butcher's son from Wapping, who laid claim to the baronetcy of Tichborne in Hampshire. He was sentenced to six years imprisonment for perjury.

TIDE GROVE, BS11. Field name, that of a pasture in Saltmarsh held by Nicholas Cotrith in 1275.

TIFFANY COURT, BS1. Named after a typeface, as are other courts in theCaxton Gate development. *See Berlington Court and Franklin Court.*

TILLING ROAD / WALK, BS7.

> *'Now, what sort of night, sir, eh?*
> *Did you take the mixture, pray?*
> *Iodine and anodyne,*
> *Ipecacuanha wine,*
> *And the draught and pills at nine?'*
>
> Stanley Hutton, from *Bristol and its Famous Associations*

Albert Edward Tilling (1864-1920) was a Bristol author who wrote *Bristol and its Famous Associations* and *Bristol and Bath* under the pseudonym of Stanley Hutton. He was also a poet and contributor to both local and national press. He was appointed Assistant City Librarian in 1919, having begun his career in this field at St. Phillips Library in 1879.

TIMBER DENE, BS16. A purely descriptive name, as the road looks over the forested banks of the river Frome.

TIMBERSCOMBE WALK, BS14. The name of a village near Minehead, but this choice does not seem to fit in with any pattern set by the surrounding roads, so perhaps there is another explanation.

TIMSBURY ROAD / WALK, BS3. Among other roads named after Somerset villages.

TINDELL COURT, BS15. No reason for the naming has been discovered so far.

TINTERN AVENUE, BS5. From the site of a ruined Cistercian abbey in the Wye Valley, Monmouthshire, the subject of the well-known poem by William Wordsworth. From the welsh *tyn* (*tyddyn*) farm, *dwr,* water.

TINTERN CLOSE, BS15. Among a cluster of roads all called after abbeys.

TIPPETTS ROAD, BS15. The original meetings of the Moravians were held in the house of Mr Tippetts. They began in 1737. *See Cennick Avenue.*

TIVERTON WALK, BS16. One of a host of place names used for the roads in this area.

TORONTO ROAD, BS7. Another road named by the builder, Teddy Williams, on his return from Canada. *See Montreal Avenue.*

TORMARTON CRESCENT, BS10. Richard Tormarton was Vicar of Westbury in 1361.

TORPOINT ROAD, BS3. This continues the use of names of Devon towns in the area.

TORRANCE CLOSE, BS15. The Torrance family were owners of the Phoenix Iron Works at Bitton.

TORRINGTON AVENUE, BS4. Among other roads which have been given West Country place names.

TORTWORTH ROAD, BS7. A village in Gloucestershire where members of the Throckmorton family lived who were wardens of the Kingswood Forest from the twelfth to seventeenth centuries. The derivation is 'Torhta's enclosure'. It was also the name of the house at Falfield where the Earl of Ducie resided.

TOTSHILL DRIVE / GROVE, BS13. Totshill Common was included in the Dundry Enclosure Award of 1815. The name is derived from OE *tot*, look-out and *hyll*, hill.

TOWER HILL / LANE / STREET, BS2. One of the towers of the old castle was sited here.

TOWER LANE / ROAD, BS15. Site of a large windmill used for grinding corn. Its tower gained it the name of the Round House. Tower Road adjoins Castle Street, the site of a mock castle. *See Castle Road, BS15.*

TOWNSEND CLOSE / ROAD, BS14. Farden Townsend was resident in the tithing of Keynsham in 1674 and was exempt from Hearth Tax.

TRACY WALK, BS14. After Sir John Tracy who, in 1364, was one of three officials appointed to investigate the theft of timber from the Chase.

TRAFALGAR TERRACE, BS3. On 21 October 1805, off Cape Trafalgar, Cadiz, a Royal Naval fleet under Nelson met and defeated the numerically superior combined naval forces of France and Spain, decisively conferring upon Britain the mastery of the seas. It is surprising that such a battle only gets one road named after it. The word Trafalgar means 'promontory of the cove'.

TRALEE WALK BS4. All the roads round here are endowed with Irish names.

TRAMWAY ROAD, BS4. This road used to lead to the old tram works.

TRANMERE AVENUE / GROVE, BS10. A mercifully brief foray into the honouring of football teams. The road connects with Charlton Road. The teams being Tranmere Rovers and Charlton Athletic.

TRATMAN WALK, BS10. Thomas Tratman held land in the area in 1596 including the Manor of Southmead and Durdham Down.

TRAVERS CLOSE, BS4. Another in the British composers group of roads. John Travers (1703-58) wrote religious and organ music.

TREDEGAR ROAD, BS16. Either the town in Blaenau Gwent, or Geoffrey Morgan, First Viscount Tredegar (1831-1913), who fought in the Crimean War. He was the last survivor of the Charge of the Light Brigade, famously commemorated in a poem by Tennyson. *See Somerset Street.*

TREEFIELD PLACE, BS2. Probably a made-up name, though quite possibly before development there would have been a field with trees here.

TREGARTH ROAD, BS3. A village near Bangor, Gwynedd. Place name with the meaning *tref,* town and *garth,* hill or field. It alliterates neatly with the adjacent Trevanna Road, whose connections with this part of Bristol are equally obscure.

TRELAWNEY ROAD, BS6 / AVENUE, BS5 / PARK, BS4.

> *'And have they fixed the where and when?*
> *And shall Trelawney die?*
> *Here's twenty thousand Cornish men*
> *Will know the reason why!'*

> R.S. Hawker, *Song of the Western Men*

Probably all these roads are named after Jonathan Trelawny, Bishop of Bristol from 1685-1689, who was imprisoned for sedition but later acquitted. He forced his beautiful daughter Rebecca into a loveless marriage to a man hideously scarred from smallpox. The bishop died in 1721.

TRENCHARD STREET, BS1. Originally called Trencher Street because in 1239 it was a guard for the trench in the marsh of St. Augustine. An alternative suggeston has been made that John Whitson, ship owner and financial backer of Martin Pring's sailing expedition to America did, in 1630, start life as an apprentice to a Mr Trenchard, wine cooper and ship owner. On Trenchard's death John Whitson inherited the business and also his widow!

TRENDLEWOOD PARK, BS16. Probably a name-up name. It was formerly a wooded area.

TRENTHAM CLOSE, BS2. The site of one of St. Werburgh's convents. *See Hanbury Close.*

TREVANNA ROAD, BS3. There is a Trevanna Cross near Helston in Cornwall.

TREVELYAN WALK, BS10. Walter Trevelyan (1763-1830) was Vicar of Henbury and Rector of Nettlecombe in Somerset. He was a keen naturalist.

TREVERDOWE, BS10. William Treverdowe was Prebend of Westbury 1424.

TREVETHIN COURT, BS15. No reason has been discovered yet for the naming of this street.

TREVISA GROVE, BS10. John de Trevisa was Canon of Westbury College 1387-1412. He was a Fellow of Exeter and Queens College, Oxford, but he was expelled in 1379. He was also Vicar of Berkeley and an author and translator from the Latin. He is reputed to have translated the first book printed by Wynken de Worde in the fifteenth century. He lived from 1326 until 1412.

TREWINT GARDENS, BS4. Place name: Trewint is a village on the edge of Bodmin Moor where John Wesley had a cottage.

TRIANGLE SOUTH / WEST, BS8. These roads form two sides of a triangle whose third side is Queen's Road.

TRIDENT CLOSE, BS16. Named after the de Havilland / Hawker Siddeley Trident airliner. It was the first three-engined jet, and had the first automatic landing system, but was otherwise undistinguished.

TRIN MILLS, BS1. *Trin* is an old term for tree. The name was used because the site was at one time occupied by a millpond surrounded by trees. The road was variously known as Trine, Trene and Trenelly. Mentioned as early as 1247.

TRINITY ROAD / STREET / WALK, BS2. All named for the now redundant church, which was consecrated on 23 September 1829.

TROON DRIVE, BS15. Among a host of roads named after golf courses.

TROOPERS HILL ROAD, BS5. Once known as Harris's Hill, it was renamed after a battle between the Royalists and the Roundheads in 1643. It was once nicknamed Donkey Island.

TROWBRIDGE ROAD / WALK, BS10. All roads in the locality are named after West Country towns.

TRURO ROAD, BS3. The Cornish town. As is often the case, to find the meaning of a Cornish name, look to the Welsh. Here you will find *tref*, town; and *rhiw*, hillside.

There are a large number of roads locally which have been given place names.

TRYM CROSS ROAD, BS9. *See Trym Road.*

TRYM ROAD / SIDE, BS9. The river Trym flows at the back of these houses. Trym is from OE *trymme* or *trum*, firm and strong.

TRYMLEAZE, BS9. Again named after the river.

TRYMWOOD CLOSE, BS10. Also named after the nearby river (though actually, the Hazel Brook which flows through Henbury is considerably closer!).

TUCKER STREET, BS2. The name was originally Towker or Touker. Temple was that part of the city where cloth was manufactured. Tucker Street housed the tuckers or fullers. The Toukes were clothiers of Normandy.

TUCKETT LANE, BS16. Named after Frank and Alice Tuckett, who lived at the Old House and were great benefactors, giving to Frenchay village a large piece of land between Beckspool Road and Cleeve Road and the Frome. Frank died in 1913, Alice in 1928.

TUDOR CLOSE, BS15. This may have been the surname of someone who owned the land here.

TUDOR ROAD, BS5. Probably after the royal dynasty, there is a York Road nearby.

TUDOR ROAD, BS2. A not uncommon surname, so perhaps someone connected with the development of this road.

TUDOR ROAD, BS15. This was the name of the builder responsible for these houses.

TUFFLEY ROAD, BS10. A place in Gloucestershire. It originates from the Anglo-Saxon personal name Tuffa. Baddeley gives it as 'Tuffa's pasture' while Smith opts for 'glade or clearing'. Sited amongst streets which have also been given place names.

TUGELA ROAD, BS3. This is a river in Natal, scene of a Boer War battle. It was a British victory, though at the cost of 2259 killed, wounded or missing, against Boer casualties of just 232.

TUNSTALL CLOSE, BS9. From the OE *tun*, farm; *stow*, place.

TURLEY ROAD, BS5. This is thought to be the name of the landowner.

TURNBERRY WALK, BS4. Named after a famous golf course, as are all the roads surrounding Knowle Golf Club.

TURNBERRY, BS15. Another road on the golf course theme.

TURNBRIDGE ROAD, BS10. Mrs Turnbridge paid Poor Rate to Westbury in 1684. She was assessed at 2s.8d in the pound.

TURNER GARDENS, BS7. Joseph Mallord William Turner (1775-1851) was England's earliest landscape painter in the impressionist style. Probably his most famous work is *The Fighting Temeraire*, painted in 1839. He also worked locally, portraying the Avon Gorge at Hotwells. The French Impressionists drew their inspiration from his dramatic use of light.

TURNERS COURT, BS15. Henry Turner was a churchwarden in 1894 and held the post as overseer for Mangotsfield Parish Council.

TURTLEGATE AVENUE / WALK, BS13. Turtle Gate was a field name in the Manor of Bishport shown on the 1683 survey. The derivation is uncertain but could be from OE *tot-hyll* meaning look-out hill. It might, alternatively, be a reference to the turtle doves which were kept in every manor and grange.

TURVILLE DRIVE, BS7. Perhaps after Acton Turville in Wiltshire. The name means dry field.

TWEENY LANE, BS15. This name suggests a lane which runs between two properties. It may have run between the buildings of Allens' farm in this area.

TWENTY ACRES ROAD, BS10. Almost certainly an old field name.

TWICKENHAM ROAD, BS7. Quite a few local streets are named after famous sporting venues.

TWO ACRES ROAD, BS14. A field name taken from the 1845 tithe map.

TWO MILE COURT / TWO MILE HILL ROAD, BS5. Two Mile Hill is actually three miles from the city centre, and is certainly not two miles long!

THE TWYNINGS, BS15. An ancient field name.

TYLER CLOSE, BS15. No reason has been discovered so far for this naming.

TYLER STREET, BS2. Built on the site of Tyler's Fields.

TYLER'S LANE, BS16. In 1849 Mr. Tyler was appointed Relieving Officer to the parish when a strong endeavour was made to improve sanitation in the area and avoid the ravages of the cholera epidemic.

TYNDALE AVENUE, BS16. After William Tyndale, translator of the Bible, who was thought to have been born in Slimbridge, Gloucestershire. In 1524 he visited Martin Luther in Wittenberg, and began printing his translation of the New Testament in English in Cologne. Before he could finish work on his Old Testament in Antwerp he was accused of heresy by the Catholic authorities and was burnt at the stake for heresy in Vilvorde, now in Belgium, in 1536.

TYNDALE ROAD, BS15. Presumably as for BS16.

TYNDALL AVENUE / ROAD, BS5. After Tyndall House which stood here. The building was demolished in the 1960s.

TYNDALL PARK / MEWS / ROAD, BS8. The Tyndall family were prominent in civic life in Bristol and owned, in the eighteenth century, the house and land where these roads were later built. Tyndall was immensely influential in the development of Bristol University between the wars. It is thought there may have been some family connection with William Tyndale.

TYNE ROAD, BS7 / STREET, BS2. Tyne Road has been so-named for centuries. It runs along part of a medieval trackway, known as St. Augustine's Track. This ran from St. Augustine's Abbey to South Wales, via Hatfield Road, Cotham Brow,. Tyne Path, Tyne Road, Broadway Road Wentworth Road and Beauchamp Road across to Quabb farm on Horfield Common. The Quabbs were fishponds which belonged to the Abbey. The route continued from Hatfield Parish Church to Aust, and from there the traveller would have taken the ferry to South Wales.

TYNE STREET, BS2. Tyne Street in St. Werburgh's did not connect with Tyne Road on the St. Augustine's Track, so this naming is probably after the River Tyne which rises in Northumberland and flows via Newcastle into the North Sea.

TYNING CLOSE, BS4. There was a Tyning Farm situated near here.

TYNING ROAD, BS3. Field name from the Anglo-Saxon *tynan*, enclosing. The OE word *tyning* had the same meaning. There was also a Saxon word *tine* which meant to trim a hedge or could also mean the enclosing hedging or fencing.

TYNTE AVENUE, BS13. The Tynte family were prominent in the area for at least two centuries as landowners and Members of Parliament. They lived at the Manor House at Chelvey in this hundred. The founder of the family is said to have distinguished himself at the siege of Ascalon under Richard the Lionheart. It has been suggested the name comes from the Latin *tinctus* - tincture.

TYNTSFIELD ROAD, BS13. This was the name of the house of George Abraham Gibbs, M.P. for Bristol West in 1926.

TYRONE WALK, BS4. Another road in the Irish theme group.

ULLSWATER CLOSE, BS15. All roads in this group were named after places in the Lake District.

UNION STREET, BS2. This is so called simply because it connects Oxford Street with Barton Road.

UNION STREET, BS1. This road linked Dolphin Street with the Horsefair.

UNITY STREET, BS1. Unity Street commemorated the reconciliation of the Prince of Wales and George II in 1742, after years of estrangement.

UNITY STREET, BS2. This road is perhaps named for the same reason as the one in BS1 as it was built in the same era.

UNIVERSITY CLOSE / ROAD / WALK, BS8. Located near the University of Bristol.

ULLSWATER ROAD, BS1. Many of the roads in this area, being near Henleaze, were named after locations in the Lake District.

UPHILL ROAD, BS7. Uphill is the name of a village near Weston-super-Mare. The derivation is from the OE '*uppan pylle*', place above the pill or creek.

UPJOHN CRESCENT, BS13. An Upjohn held land here at the time of the Dundry Enclosure Award of 1815.

UPLANDS ROAD, BS16. A descriptive field name.

UPPER BELGRAVE ROAD, BS8. *See Belgrave Road.*

UPPER BELMONT ROAD, BS6. *See Belmont Road.*

UPPER BERKELEY PLACE, BS8. *See Berkeley Place.*

UPPER BYRON PLACE, BS8. *See Byron Place.*

UPPER CHELTENHAM PLACE, BS6. Takes its name from nearby Cheltenham Road.

UPPER CHURCH LANE, BS2. The church here is St. Michael's.

UPPER CRANBROOK ROAD, BS6. *See Cranbrook Road.*

UPPER MAUDLIN STREET, BS2. The name comes from the nunnery of St. Mary Magdalene which stood at the foot of St. Michael's Hill. There is some dispute as to who was responsible for the foundation of the nunnery. Some say it was Ella, who died in 920 and was the first Lord of Bristol Castle. Another school of thought suggests it may be named after Eva, wife of Robert Fitzhardinge, who founded St. Augustine's Priory in 1140. It was an extensive site, Southmead Manor also being owned by this priory.

UPPER PERRY HILL, BS3. This is, in fact, the only Perry Hill now in existence in this area. Perry may well have been the surname of someone connected with the land on which building took place, perhaps the owner.

UPPER SANDHURST ROAD, BS4. *See Sandhurst Road.*

UPPER STATION ROAD, BS16.

UPPER SYDNEY STREET, BS3. There is quite a distance between this and Lower Sydney Street. It may have been named after Thomas Townshend, First Viscount Sydney, the Colonial Secretary (1733-1800), after whom the city of Sydney in Australia is named. Less exotically, there was also a Sydney Pit in the close vicinity so this may have been the origin.

UPPER WELLS STREET, BS1. There is but a fragment left of this street the name of which indicates the source of a water supply in olden times.

UPPER YORK STREET, BS2. This street was built in 1766 and was named in honour of George III's brother Edward Augustus, Duke of York and Albany (1739-67).

UPTON ROAD, BS3. Upton was the original name of Sir J. R. Greville Smyth who took the latter name when he inherited the estate. He owned vast stretches of land to the south of the city.

URFORDS DRIVE, BS16. Erfords Lane was part of the boundary of Kingswood Chase as recorded on 26 May 1652. The E seems to have changed to a U over the years.

VALE LANE, BS3. This is descriptive of its location.

VALE STREET, BS4. The connection here is Arnos Vale.

VALENTINE CLOSE, BS14. Valentine was the sister of the developer, Leonard Nidditch. *See Gilda Close.*

VALERIAN CLOSE, BS11. Continuing the Roman theme in this area, this road was named after the Emperor Valerian (c.190-266 AD) who died in Persia as a prisoner of the king, Shapur, whom he underestimated to his cost when he marched against him. He spent a miserable captivity acting as a mounting step for Shapur's horse. After his death his skin was stuffed with straw and put on display in a temple.

VALLEY GARDENS, BS16. This is named for its proximity to Leap Valley.

VALLEY ROAD, BS3. The valley of what was once called the Warm Lee.

VALLEY ROAD, BS16. Descriptive.

VALMA ROCKS, BS15. This is, apparently, an old name for the area so rocky that all the houses there are on different levels. Who or what Valma was has yet to be discovered.

VASSALL COURT / ROAD, BS16. The Vassall family lived at Oldbury Court, which was designed by Humphry Repton, for over 100 years. The Vassall family sold it in 1938, and the house was demolished c. 1960.

VAUGHAN CLOSE, BS10. This was the name of a very well-known Bristol family who held high office in civic affairs from the fifteenth to the seventeenth centuries.

VENTNOR AVENUE, BS5. Ventnor is a seaside resort on the Isle of Wight. '*Venta*' means bright and shining.

VERA ROAD, BS16. Perhaps this was the name of the wife or daughter of the builder?

VERNON STREET, BS4. Vernon Street was built some time between 1870 -1880 and may, perhaps, be named after Admiral Edward Vernon (1664-1757), who earned the nickname Old Grog from his habit of wearing a waterproof boat cloak made of grogram. He led a punitive expedition to the West Indies in the 'War of Jenkins' Ear' in 1739 and captured Porto Bello. He was concerned for the welfare of his men, which was unusual in that day and age. He introduced the mixture of rum, water and lime juice to his men, - as an early preventative against scurvy, and this drink became known as grog. On the other hand, it may merely have been named by the builder.

VERRIER ROAD, BS5. A G. Verrier was a well-known St. George personage being a councillor for Easton ward in 1897 and a J.P. in 1898. He owned the land on which this street was built.

VERWOOD DRIVE, BS15. Sited near Bitton station, this road is said to be named after a famous steam engine, the Pines Express, which travelled through Verwood en route to Bournemouth. Verwood also used to be the venue for a traction engine fair. *See Pines Road.*

VICARAGE COURT, BS15. This is near the church so presumably it was the location of the vicarage. This was formerly known as Ragged Lane, and George Manning's market garden was to be found nearby.

VICARAGE ROAD, BS5. Two vicarages were located in Whitehall Road: that of St. Matthew's, Redfield, and St. Gabriel's, Easton.

VICARAGE ROAD, BS3. This was the site of St. John's vicarage, demolished in 1901.

VICARAGE ROAD, BS13. This one is named after the vicarage of St. Peter's.

VICARAGE ROAD, BS9. The vicarage here is that belonging to St. Mary's church.

VICAR'S CLOSE, BS16. Developed on land owned by the church, this cul-de-sac houses the modern vicarage of St. Mary's, the original one having been demolished in the 1960s.

VICTOR ROAD, BS3. There is no known reason for this choice but, with Albert Street nearby, it was probably named after Albert Victor (1864-92), eldest son of Edward VII.

VICTOR STREET, BS5. There are three choices for the origin of this name. It could be Prince Albert Victor, Duke of Clarence and Avondale, who was made a freeman of the city in 1888, or John Victor, Minister of Unity Chapel in Midland Road, or merely the forename of someone connected with the development.

VICTORIA AVENUE, ETC. All these roads and places are named in honour of Queen Victoria. Victoria Square in Clifton used to be known as Ferney Close.

VIGOR ROAD, BS13. A person of this name held land here at the time of the Dundry Enclosure Award, 1815.

VILLIERS ROAD, BS5. The most probable origin of the choice of name for this road is Edward Villiers, who was General Manager and Chief Superintendent of Clifton Zoological Gardens, although he does not appear to have any connection with this part of the city. The other candidate may be George Villiers, Second Duke of Buckingham, during the reign of Charles II. By marrying Thomas Fairfax's daughter he was able to reclaim his estates seized by parliament during the Civil War.

VIMPANY CLOSE, BS10. The name is derived from Vimpenny's Common in the Hundred of Henbury. It has been suggested that it was a nickname, 'winpenny' denoting a profitable piece of land, but Vimpany is a local family name which appears in the Westbury church registers for 1571-1602, and there is a memorial to someone of that name in Redland church.

VINCENT CLOSE, BS11. This road is named after St. Vincent, who was martyred at Valencia in 305 AD. There was once a chapel dedicated to this saint at the highest point of St. Vincent's Rocks overlooking the Avon Gorge, near Clifton Suspension Bridge. It was 27ft long and 9ft broad and was still standing in 1480.

VINING WALK, BS5. This is named after John Vining, Mayor of Bristol 1855 -56.

VINTERY LEES, BS9. Name taken from the 1823 field survey for this district.

VIVIAN STREET, BS3. This street was either named after the diplomat Sir Hussey Crespigny Vivian (1834-93), the 3rd Baron Vivian, or after a person connected with the development of the site. The road was built towards the end of the nineteenth century.

VOWELL CLOSE, BS13. This was the name of a tenant of Sir John Smyth, as shown on the 1683 survey.

VYVYAN ROAD / TERRACE, BS8. These roads are named for Sir Richard Rawlinson Vyvyan, MP for Bristol in 1832-37. The road was developed in 1847-48.

WADE STREET, BS2. Nathaniel Wade, in a vain attempt to save his own life, betrayed all his companions in Monmouth's rebel army at Judge Jeffreys' notorious trial. The bridge he and Abraham Hook built near here to facilitate the estate they owned was, for many years, known as Traitor's Bridge. After it was rebuilt in 1798 it was known as Froom Bridge. Wade's final resting place was the Red Cross Street burial ground. He was the grandson of John Wade, Mayor of Bristol in 1576.

WADES ROAD, BS12. There was a Wade's Farm here at one time.

WADHAM DRIVE, BS16. John Wadham was Lord of the Manor of Frenchay in 1818.

WAINBROOK DRIVE, BS5. The Wainbrook was a stream in the Whitehall area. W.T. Sanigar wrote in his book *St. George's in the East*: 'In olden times, flushed by sportsmen from the reeds and rushes along the banks of the Wainbrook, snipe whirred into the air and flew zig-zag over the fields hidden now by houses.'

WAKEFORD ROAD, BS16. No reason has been found for the naming of this road.

WALDEGRAVE HOUSE, BS13. Richard Waldegrave was Master of St. Catherine's Hospital from May 1523to April 1543. Unusually for this post, he was a layman.

WALKER CLOSE, BS5. This is named after Charles Ludlow Walker, Mayor of Bristol in 1834-35.

WALKER CLOSE, BS16. Frederick Walker was the owner of Black Horse farm, late nineteenth/early twentieth century.

WALKER STREET, BS2. This street was built in the 1790s and may have been named after the landowner. It is tempting to suggest another possibility, that it was later renamed after the mayor of Bristol from 1834-1835, Charles Ludlow Walker.

WALLINGFORD ROAD, BS4. There is a little bunch of roads here all named after famous castles. Wallingford is in Berkshire and was home at one time to the Black Prince. Cromwell destroyed it.

WALLISCOTE AVENUE / ROAD, BS9. Perhaps the connection here is the road of the same name in Weston-super-Mare which was built many years prior to this one. There is a village called Wallerscote, the meaning being 'salt-boiler's cottage'.

WALLSCOURT ROAD, BS12. This road was built on fields which belonged to Wallscourt Farm. The development here took place in the 1940s.

WALNUT CLOSE / CRESCENT / LANE, BS15. Walnut trees grew near all these sites at one time.

WALNUT WALK, BS13. Perhaps this is named after Walnut Farm, East Dundry.

WALSH AVENUE, BS14. This was the name of the people who formerly farmed the land.

WALSINGHAM ROAD, BS6. Walsingham, in Norfolk, is the site of a ruined abbey. The connection here may be that there was once a religious house at the foot of Ashley Hill. The building of the abbey resulted from a dream experienced by Richeldis de Faverches in which the Virgin Mary instructed him to build a replica of the Holy House of the Annunciation. The shrine to Our Lady of Walsingham still survives. It has been stated that this road was named after Sir Francis Walsingham (1532-90), Elizabeth I's Secretary of State and former English ambassador to Paris. He was the key advisor who furthered Elizabeth's cause against Mary, Queen of Scots and gathered the evidence that led to her execution. Elizabeth did not really trust him and he ended his life in poverty.

WALTER STREET, BS3. This road may be named after Joseph Walter, the local maritime artist.

WALTON AVENUE, BS4. All roads in this group are named after famous abbeys and cathedrals. King Harold was buried at Walton, or Waltham, Abbey.

WALTON CLOSE, BS15. Possibly there is a railway connection here.

WALTON ROAD, BS11. The Walton here is Walton-in-Gordano near Pill.

WALTON RISE, BS9. This is a well-known Bristol family, one of whom was Postmaster in the mid-nineteenth century.

WALTON STREET, BS5. There was a Sheriff of Bristol of this name although in this case it might well be the name of the person who owned the land.

WALWYN GARDENS, BS13. Hugh Brook, Lord of the Manor of Ashton Philips in the Hundred of Hartcliffe, had four daughters and co-heiresses, one of whom, Elizabeth, married Giles Walwyn of Hereford. She became possessed of a part of the Manor but sold it to Jane Smyth, widow of Matthew, in 1593.

WANSCOW WALK, BS9. In 1913 Henleaze Park, a mansion and estate consisting of 46 acres was offered for sale by William Cowlin and Sons. In the grounds were two lodges, a pagoda, extensive stabling and a lofty coach house with garaging for three motor cars. In 1915 44 acres were sold but the property was withdrawn as it did not reach the reserve price of £12,750. Eventually Messrs. Cowlin and Wansborough were involved in developing the land. Wanscow was a corruption of the two names.

WANSDYKE CLOSE, BS14. This road is named after the Saxon earthwork cutting through Somerset. The Wansdyke was an earthwork of the Dark Ages, cutting north and south across the West of England and reaching Bristol at its northern

extremity. The first syllable is a personal name: Woden, the Saxon god. Some say it was built by the Britons in the same period as they won a victory over the Saxons and halted their progress westwards. Legend has it that King Arthur was responsible for the victory but there has emerged no proof of these claims. The road that was here before development began was called Wansdyke. *See Maesknoll Road.*

WAPPING ROAD, BS1. Presumably this road is named after the parish of London which is also a dockland district. The derivation is from the OE *'wapol'*, meaning spring or pool.

WARDEN ROAD, BS3. Either this is a place name, the derivation being the OE *'weard dun'*, watch hill, or there is an ecclesiastical connection since there is a Dean Lane adjacent.

WARDOUR ROAD, BS4. This is another road called after a castle. Wardour Castle is at Tisbury in Wiltshire and was under siege for five days during the Civil War. Realising her untenable position, Lady Arundel negotiated an honourable surrender but she was executed along with the entire garrison. It is said that her ghost still haunts the ruins.

WARMAN CLOSE / ROAD, BS14. Mrs Warman, a widow, resided at Keynsham in 1674. She was exempt from Hearth Tax.

WARMINGTON ROAD, BS4. This was the name of the builder responsible for these houses in the 1930s.

WARMINSTER ROAD, BS2. The name is taken from the town of this name in Wiltshire. The meaning is minster or church on the River Were.

WARNER CLOSE, BS15. This is another road in the Methodist church and school group. *See Cade Close.*

THE WARNS, BS15. This is an old field name, probably a corruption of 'warrens'.

WARREN GARDENS / ROAD, BS14. John Warren lived in Bedminster in July 1674. He was exempt from Hearth Tax.

WARRINGTON ROAD, BS4. This is a place name of a town in Lancashire, and also a hamlet in Somerset. It is thought the first component is a personal name, Werenc.

WARWICK AVENUE / ROAD, BS5. The manor of Barton Regis belonged to Anne, Countess of Warwick, who granted it to Henry III in 1487.

WARWICK CLOSE, BS15. This is another of the group of roads called after castles.

WARWICK ROAD, BS6. The reference here is almost certainly the Earldom of Warwick, whose family name was Greville. The fifth Earl was MP for Somerset East from 1879-85. The derivation may be from *'wering'*, the OE for weir or dam, or the first syllable could be 'Waer's people'. Another theory is that the word could be from the Anglo-Saxon 'waerwic', meaning garrison.

WASHINGPOOL LANE, BS11. This place, one of the dykes by the Severn, was probably used to dip sheep. There was a Washing Pool farm in the area.

WASHINGTON AVENUE, BS5. Colonel Washington, an ancestor of the American president of the same name, is best known for an incident which occurred in Bristol during the Civil War. He was astute enough to notice a weak spot in the Roundhead defences between Brandon Hill fort and the Royal Fort near where

Park Row joins Park Street. There is a plaque there commemorating the fact. He took some troops under the Roundhead guns which left the spot uncovered, and so entered the city, which eventually surrendered. For years afterwards the site was known as Washington's Breach.

WATCHILL AVENUE / CLOSE, BS13. This is a field name of a meadow at Home Farm in the Manor of Long Ashton in the late eighteenth century. The name means 'lookout' or 'watch hill'.

WATER LANE, BS1. This name was clearly chosen because of its proximity to the river.

WATER LANE, BS3. Self-explanatory.

WATER LANE, BS4. A descriptive name.

WATER LANE, BS15. Near the river.

WATER'S LANE, BS9. This used to be known as Betty Waters' Lane. Many years ago an old woman living in a cottage here sold water that was reputed to cure all ills.

WATERBRIDGE ROAD, BS13. This was a field name shown on the survey of 1683 as belonging to Bishport Manor.

WATERCRESS ROAD, BS2. The name comes from the ancient farmhouse here. A small tributary of the Frome rises nearby and, in the nineteenth century, there were watercress beds here. The area now houses the St. Werburgh's City Farm and the Ashley Down allotments.

WATERDALE CLOSE / GARDENS, BS9. Waterdale was a house last occupied by the Griffey family. Its grounds contained two pools, which were fed by a stream flowing from Manor farm.It was demolished to make way for Southmead Fire Station.

WATERFORD ROAD, BS9. A preference shown for naming roads after Welsh and Irish counties in this area is apparent.

WATERLOO PLACE / ROAD, BS2 / STREET BS2 / BS8. These are all named after the famous battle of 1815.

WATERS ROAD, BS15. Probably someone's name, as there is no river or stream nearby.

WATHEN ROAD, BS6. This is named after Sir Charles Wathen, a distinguished civic figure in Bristol during the nineteenth century. He served two terms as Mayor and was knighted on New Year's Day 1889. His home was in St. Andrews. He died on St. Valentine's Day 1893.

WATKINS YARD, BS9. Apparently this road is named after Edward Watkins, who is listed in the 1863 directory as a grocer and baker.

WATLING WAY, BS11. Some suggest that the Bristol Rovers player Josser Watling gave his name to this road, but it is more probable that the naming follows the theme of names in this area relating to the time of the Roman invasion in Britain. Watling Street ran from Dover through London to Wroxeter, Shropshire.

WATSON AVENUE, BS4. Most of the roads developed by the Sutton Trust have been given names of those associated with this Trust.

WATSON'S ROAD, BS15. Abraham Watson was a haulier in Willsbridge in 1914.

WAVERLEY ROAD, BS6. Once again we find the influence of Sir Walter Scott's works. *Waverley* was his first novel, published in 1814. It was based on the Jacobite uprising of 1745.

WAVERLEY ROAD, BS11. Possibly as for BS6.

WAVERLEY STREET, BS2. There were once two other nearby streets named on a Scottish theme so perhaps the builder had connections with that part of the British Isles.

WEARE COURT, BS1. There was once a Weare Street the other side of the river near Bath Bridge called after either George Weare, a Mayor during the late eighteenth century and holder of other high offices, or William Weare, a benefactor to the city who gave large amounts of money for road improvements in the city.

WEBB STREET, BS5. It has been suggested that this street was named after Captain Matthew Webb, the first man to swim the English Channel, but a more likely explanation is that it honours Robert Henry Webb who represented the District ward on the City Council, a ward that included this portion of Bristol. He died in 1875 and the street was built around that time.

WEDGEWOOD ROAD, BS16. Josiah and John Wedgwood, sons of the famous potter, lived in Bristol for some time during the late eighteenth century. The road name is mis-spelt.

WEDGWOOD CLOSE, BS14. This road is named after the famous pottery as the developers were a Midlands-based firm, although the influence may also be the former Pottery Farm that stood in the area.

WEDMORE CLOSE, BS15. Quite a few names of Somerset villages are used in roads in this small area, but the significance of this usage has not become apparent.

WEDMORE VALE, BS3. This is another road called after a West Country village.

WEEDON CLOSE, BS2. This road, part of a development from the 1970s, runs off Mercia Drive. Weedon is a small town near Aylesbury, where St. Werburgh presided over a convent. Weedon lay in her father's kingdom of Mercia. It was also the site of one of her miracles, when a flock of geese were banished for destroying crops. It is said that no goose has ever dared set foot in Weedon since...

WEIGHT ROAD, BS5. This name is taken from Robert Inkerman Weight, who owned the site which he had purchased from the executors of 'Gentleman' William Stone who died in 1898. Weight unsuccessfully contested the Council seat of St. George in 1897.

WELLHOUSE CLOSE, BS9. This road was developed on the grounds of Well House.

WELLGARTH ROAD / WALK, BS4. This is believed to be a field name from the OE *'waella'*, well or stream, and *'geard'*, yard or garden.

WELLINGTON AVENUE / LANE, BS6. These honour the First Duke of Wellington (1769-1852), who was granted the freedom of the city on a visit here in 1832. Wellington's title came from his family name of Wellesley, and he was created the First Duke of Wellington in 1814 after his campaigns in the Peninsular

War. He gave his name to wellington boots because of the distinctive riding boots which he wore.

WELLINGTON CRESCENT / DRIVE / HILL, BS7 / WALK, BS10. These are named after the Wellington Hotel, which in turn was named after the famous Duke.

WELLINGTON MEWS, BS11. This naming would be taken from the Somerset town, to judge by the surrounding roads.

WELLINGTON PARK, BS8. This was another street named after the Duke who had a distinguished military career commanding troops in the Peninsular War and the culminating Battle of Waterloo. He was Prime Minister in 1828-30, and in 1834. He died in 1852, aged 83, and is buried in St. Paul's Cathedral.

WELLINGTON ROAD, BS2. This is another road almost certainly named after the Duke.

WELLINGTON ROAD, BS16. More likely to be called after the Somerset town than the Duke as the trend in this area is to employ place names.

WELLS CLOSE, BS14. This Close was built by two brothers, Alfred John Wells and herbert William Wells, who traded as Wells Brothers in Overndale Road, Fishponds. Their solicitor arranged for their name to be perpetuated in this way.

WELLS ROAD, BS3 / BS14. Literally the road leading to the Cathedral City of Wells.

WELLS STREET, BS3. This is next to Bath Street, so probably named after the city of Wells in Somerset.

WELSFORD AVENUE / ROAD, BS16. This is probably named after the owner of the land. There were several people with this surname living in the general locality at the time these roads were built.

WELSH BACK, BS1. This is so named because Welsh products arriving in Bristol by ship were sold in a building on Welsh Back known as the Goose Market. It was demolished in 1854. Regarding the word 'back', some say it is from the Saxon *'bak'*, meaning river, while others insist that it is merely saying that the street is at the back of the river. The Llandoger Trow inn in nearby King Street emphasises the Welsh connection, a trow being a flat-bottomed boat common then in the Bristol Channel. Llandogo is a village on the Welsh bank of the Wye above Chepstow.

WELTON WALK, BS15. Welton is a village between Radstock and Midsomer Norton. Many Somerset names have been used in this locality, because the Duke of Beaufort, whose family name is Somerset, owned the land.

WENMORE CLOSE, BS16. No reason for this naming has been discovered to date.

WENTFORTH DRIVE, BS16. There may be a colliery connection judging from the names of streets nearby, but the exact origin is unknown.

WENTWORTH ROAD, BS7. As this road adjoins Berkeley Road it seems probable that the origin of this name is the castle in Yorkshire. The word means 'inhabited in winter'. It must be said, however, that a Wentworth Villa is shown as standing in Berkeley Road in 1872, so it is possible that this is the source.

WENTWORTH, BS15. This is another of the group of roads named after golf courses.

WESCOTT CRESCENT, BS11 This was known as Stowick Crescent until a few years ago, when it was renamed in honour of the late Ray Wescott of the Blaise Residents Association, who had worked tirelessly on behalf of the Association. It was through his efforts that the new Community Centre was built.

WESLEY AVENUE / CLOSE / HILL, BS15. It is safe to assume that all local roads with this appellation are named after John Wesley (1703-91), the founder of Methodism. It is likely that most of these streets are built on sites where he once preached.

WESLEY LANE, BS15. This used to be known as 'the little lane' before the Wesleyan Chapel was built at the Tower Road end in 1833.

WESLEY PLACE, BS8. The Durdham Downs Adult Sunday School was held in a room here.

WESLEY ROAD, BS7 / STREET, BS3. Both of these are near Wesleyan chapels.

WESSEX AVENUE, BS7. This is of course the ancient name of the kingdom of the West Saxons comprising Hampshire, Berkshire, Wiltshire, Somerset, Dorset and Devon.

WEST BROADWAY, BS7. The name comes from Broadway Farm, which once stood near this spot.

WEST COOMBE, BS9. This is possibly an old field name.

WEST CROFT, BS9. This is also thought to be a field name from the OE *croft*, meaning small enclosure.

WEST DENE, BS9. This is an invented name. *Dene* is from the OE, meaning valley.

WEST END, BS3. It is possible that this place had a connection with the colliery, perhaps the name of a vein.

WEST GROVE, BS6. This is a made-up name. There is an East Grove, too.

WEST MALL, BS8. Self-explanatory. A mall is a shaded avenue.

WEST PARADE, BS9. Simplicity was the keynote when these Sea Mills roads were laid out and named in the 1920s.

WESTPARK ROAD, BS16. This is to be found to the west of Page Park.

WEST PARK, BS8. This road was built on the west side of Tyndall's Park c. 1830. The Tyndall family continued to live in the house for many years afterwards.

WEST PRIORY CLOSE, BS9. This runs off Priory Court Road.

WEST ROCKE AVENUE, BS9. It is possible that this was the old name for the ground where these houses were built.

WEST SHRUBBERY, BS6. This was built in the grounds of The Shrubbery. *See Shrubbery Cottages.*

WEST STREET, BS3. Self-explanatory.

WEST STREET, BS2. Self-explanatory. It is a very ancient highway mentioned in a lease of the leper hospital of St. Lawrence, dated 1496.

WEST STREET, BS15. (2) Self-explanatory.

The Grove pub in West Grove, c. 1950

WEST TOWN AVENUE / GROVE / LANE / PARK / ROAD, BS4. This was one of Brislington's oldest inhabitated areas. The farm was demolished in 1953 so that the schools could be built on the land but West Town House, dating from around.1600, still stands in West Town Park.

WEST VIEW ROAD, BS8. This is presumably descriptive.

WEST WAY, BS10. Self-explanatory.

WESTACRE CLOSE, BS10. Presumably this would have been a field name.

WESTBOURNE ROAD, BS5. This is the name of a town in Sussex and a district of Bournemouth. It means 'place to the west of the stream'. There are a number of seaside resort names in the area.

WESTBOURNE GROVE, BS3. This is probably named for the same reason as BS5.

WESTBOURNE PLACE, BS8. Possibly named after an old field name.

WESTBOURNE TERRACE, BS16. Again, possibly an old field name.

WESTBROOK ROAD, BS4. Perhaps this is called after the Flax Bourton home of Capt. Herbert Neville-Ralph, who was a magistrate for Somerset.

WESTBROOKE COURT, BS8. Possibly an old field name.

WESTBURY COURT ROAD, BS9. There was a farm here called Westbury Court Farm in the late nineteenth century.

WESTBURY COURT / HILL / LANE / PARK / ROAD, BS9. *See Westbury Court Road, above.*

WESTCOURT DRIVE, BS15. This was built on land once part of Westcourt Farm.

WESTERING CLOSE, BS16. A poetic phraseology is employed here. The name can be either an adjective, 'lying to the west', or a noun, 'west wind'.

WESTERLEIGH CLOSE / ROAD, BS16. The name comes from the nearby village to which this roads leads.

WESTERN DRIVE, BS14. Self-explanatory.

WESTERN ROAD, BS7. Self-explanatory.

WESTFIELD CLOSE, BS15. This was common land at the time of the Enclosures in 1827.

WESTFIELD PARK, BS6. This was built on the western part of Tyndalls Park.

WESTFIELD PLACE, BS8. Perhaps this is an old field name.

WESTFIELD ROAD, BS9. This is almost certainly a field name.

WESTLAND AVENUE, BS15. Among other field names, so presumably this was too.

WESTLEIGH PARK, BS14. This is a place name in Devon. The last syllable is from the OE '*leah*', woodland or glade.

WESTLEIGH ROAD, BS10. Perhaps this is an old field name.

WESTMEAD ROAD, BS5. This is a field name: the west meadow.

WESTMINSTER ROAD, BS5. This is taken from the name of a hundred in Gloucestershire at a time when counties were divided into one hundred parishes.

WESTMORLAND ROAD, BS6. The name comes from the Earldom created in 1624. The family name is Fane. Sir Francis Fane had interests in the Henbury area; he died in 1689. One member of the family built Redland Manor House c. 1734. The name means 'Land belonging to the people of the West moors'.

WESTON AVENUE, BS5. In all probability this is named after the now demolished Weston Street which was so called in honour of Sir Joseph Lodge Weston, Liberal MP for Bristol East from 1890-1895. He was Chairman of the Great Western Cotton factory and one of the founders of the Bristol Wagon Works Company.

WESTON CLOSE, BS9. This is a place name of obvious derivation.

WESTON CRESCENT, BS7. This crescent was built in the 1930s upon land farmed by the Weston family.

WESTONS WAY, BS15. The family of that name were once Lords of the Manor of Gees Moor.

WESTOVER CLOSE / DRIVE / GARDENS / RISE / ROAD, BS9. A made-up name.

WESTWARD ROAD, BS13. Self-explanatory.

WESTWOOD CRESCENT / ROAD, BS4. Perhaps this is named after the village in Wiltshire, or else it is a made-up name from West Wood.

WETHERBY COURT, BS16. This is another of the roads named after racecourses.

WETHERALL PLACE, BS8. Sir Charles Wetherall, Chief Templar, was buried at Temple church in 1846.

WEXFORD ROAD, BS4. This is another in the series of roads named after locations in Ireland. *See Bantry Road.*

WEYMOUTH ROAD, BS4. Another in the group of West Country place names.

WHARF ROAD, BS16. This name comes from the coal wharfs sited here when the railway was in use.

WHARNECLIFFE CLOSE / GARDENS, BS14. Perhaps this naming is a tribute to the First Baron Wharncliffe (James Archibald Stuart Mortley-McKenzie), who accompanied the Prince Consort when he launched the *Great Britain* in 1843.

WHATLEY ROAD, BS8. The owner of the site, John Henry Shore, lived at Whatley House, Whatley, near Frome in Somerset. The meaning of the word is 'Walter's lea'.

WHINCHAT GARDENS, BS16. All the roads here given bird names in keeping with the rural environment. The whinchat favours heaths and commons.

WHIPPINGTON COURT, BS1. Whippington was a hamlet on land owned by the Bishopric of Hereford at the time of the Domesday Book. There was a fishery there.

WHITBY ROAD, BS4. This is named after the seaport in Yorkshire famous for its ancient abbey, and starting-off point for the voyages of Captain Cook to the south seas in 1768. The meaning is 'white village or town'.

WHITCHURCH LANE / ROAD, BS14. The first syllable comes from St. Whyte, an ancient female saint, who had her cell (she was an anchorite or hermit) in this area.

WHITE LODGE ROAD, BS16. It is thought a house of this name once stood near here.

WHITE STREET, BS2. This is probably the builder of these houses, as there is a White listed as a builder in the 1872 directory.

WHITE TREE ROAD, BS9. This is built on the site of the famous landmark tree.

WHITECROFT WAY, BS15. This would seem to be a field name.

WHITECROSS AVENUE, BS14. This name comes from Whitecross Court, a farm that used to occupy land nearby.

WHITEFIELD AVENUE / CLOSE, BS15. This is named after George Whitefield (1714-70), the famous Methodist preacher who was born in Gloucester. He was appointed chaplain for the Countess of Huntingdon in Wales, who built and endowed many chapels for him and his Calvanistic Methodist followers. He played a central part in the nineteenth century American religious revival, the 'Great Awakening'.

WHITEFIELD AVENUE / ROAD, BS5. This is named in honour of Alderman William Whitefield, a much-respected miners' leader and member of the City Council who died in 1925. The proximity of the road to the old Speedwell Pit may have prompted the choice of name.

WHITEHALL AVENUE / GARDENS / ROAD, BS5. There once stood a house here where pauper girls were employed spinning wool. They had been transferred here from a house adjoining Bridewell in the city which was called Whitehall House. This may have been the same place as the White Hall, referred to by Sanigar that stood near the northern end of Lyppiatt and Chalks Road This house was subsequently used as a poorhouse and later as an asylum for the insane.

WHITEHOUSE LANE / PLACE / STREET, BS3. This comes from the White House which stood here in the eighteenth century. There was also a Whitehouse Farm at Bishopsworth.

WHITELADIES ROAD, BS8. According to Arrowsmith (*see bibliography*) there was a thatched pub here shown on 1804 maps, which was known as the 'White Ladies'. There was also a stile of the same name which may be where White Ladies gate is today. Whiteladies Road was built on a field called Smock Acre. Due to the juxtaposition of Whiteladies Road and Blackboy Hill, rumours have abounded over the years linking the area with the slave trade, but there is no connection at all. *See Blackboy Hill.*

WHITELEAZE, BS10. This is a field name meaning 'white pasture of the meadow'.

WHITES HILL, BS5. This is presumably the name of someone who once lived or traded here. There was a Whiteshill Farm here in the nineteenth century.

WHITEWAY CLOSE / MEWS / ROAD, BS5. In 1803 this was shown on the map as White Way.

WHITEWAY COURT, BS4. It would appear this name has some connection with St. Anne's Well and the pilgrimages that were made to the thirteenth century chapel there by women praying to be able to conceive a child, but no-one can establish why this was so called. It could have been the name of the field in which the well was situated.

WHITEWOOD ROAD, BS5. This possibly derives from Whitwood corn mill on the river Frome, near Snuff Mills. It was owned by a John Whitewood in 1609. The mill was still operational in the first decade of the twentieth century.

WHITING ROAD, BS13. This is the name of a tenant of Sir John Smyth recorded in the 1683 survey of the Manor of Bishport.

WHITLAND AVENUE / ROAD, BS13. Maurice de Berkeley, Lord of the Manor of Bedminster, gave a house and lands in Bedminster to the Monastery of Whitland in Brecon for the sake of his soul and that of his wife Isobel in the thirty-first year of the reign of Henry III (1247). His uncle Robert de Berkeley founded a hospital for a master or warden and several poor people in Bedminster in honour of St. Catherine.

WHITMEAD GARDENS, BS13. This is a field name.

WHITMORE AVENUE, BS4. James I granted Anne Whitmore the Manor and Hundred of Keynsham on 6 March 1613.

WHITSON STREET, BS2. There is some doubt as to whether this is named after the seventeenth century benefactor, John Whitson. The street is marked as Whitson Court on old maps prior to Whitson's time, and it has been suggested that it was so named because the St. James Fair was held here at Whitsuntide.

WHITTINGTON ROAD, BS16. The Whittingtons were a prominent local family from the seventeenth century onwards and many are buried at Bitton church. It has been suggested that there was a family connection with Richard Whittington, thrice Mayor of London, who came from Hamswell, Cold Ashton, just a few miles from Bristol.

WHITTOCK ROAD / SQUARE, BS14. John Whittock lived in Bedminster in January 1670. He was granted exemption from the Hearth Tax.

WHITTUCKS CLOSE / ROAD, BS15. This refers to Samuel Whittucks who lived in Hanham Hall in the late eighteenth century. He bought the Newton Liberty, which were the mining rights to this area, from Charles Bragge in 1790.

WHITWELL ROAD, BS14. There are villages throughout the British Isles with this name. The first syllable means 'white'.

WHYTES CLOSE, BS9. This is apparently a surname, perhaps that of the builder or landowner.

WICK CRESCENT / ROAD, BS4. This is the site of Wick House. It was previously called Newyeke at the time when Roger le Warre (who died in 1320) endowed land and a house for a priest at the rear of Wick House.

THE WICKETS, BS12. This is another old field name.

THE WICKETS, BS15. These houses were built on an old cricket pitch.

WICKHAM COURT / GLEN / HILL / VIEW, BS16. The name comes from the ancient Wickham Court, believed to be the headquarters of the Roundheads during the English Civil War. It may have been the home of John Wickham, Mayor in 1462.

WICKLOW ROAD, BS4. Another in the series of Irish names so popular in this vicinity.

WICKWAR ROAD, BS15. This is named after the village in South Gloucestershire described in the Domesday Book as being four hides in the Hundred of Bagstone.

WIDCOMBE CLOSE, BS5 / WIDCOMBE, BS14. Widcombe is the name of a village near Bath.

WIGTON CRESCENT, BS10. This is named after the town in Cumbria, following the theme of surrounding roads.

WILBYE GROVE, BS4. This was named after John Wilbye (1574-1638). He spent his life in the service of Sir Thomas Kytson and other members of the same family. He was a composer of madrigals.

WILCOX CLOSE, BS15. This may be named after the Wilcox Chapel which was in Bibury Abbey at one time.

WILDCROFT HOUSE / ROAD, BS9. Perhaps this is a field name.

WILDER STREET, BS2. The land here was owned by a Peter Wilder and developed in the first half of the eighteenth century. In 1793 some cottages were built here and called Balloon Court to celebrate the first balloon flight by the Montgolfier brothers.

WILLADA CLOSE, BS3. This name seems to be an amalgam of William and Ada - perhaps the builder and his wife? There is a town of this name in Washington State, USA.

The Grosvenor pub in Wilder Street, c. 1950

WILLIAM MASON CLOSE, BS5. William Mason was a gifted teacher of Economics at Bristol University and head of a house for men at the Settlement. He was killed in action during the First World War.

WILLIAM STREET, BS2. Perhaps this is the forename of someone connected to the builder or the landowner.

WILLIAM STREET, BS2. This street is named after William IV (1765-1837). He was the third son of King George III, and was nicknamed 'the sailor king'.

WILLIAM STREET, BS3. These houses were built by William H. Green.

WILLIAM STREET, BS5. Possibly another of the Gerrish family. *See Gerrish Avenue.*

WILLIAM STREET, BS16. Who this William was is unknown.

WILLIAMS CLOSE, BS15. The Williams family were market gardeners at Upton Cheney and Bitton.

WILLIAMSON ROAD, BS2. This is probably the surname of the owner of the land, or it may have been the builder of these houses.

WILLINTON ROAD, BS4. Sir Ralph de Willington (sometimes spelt Wilinton) was Warden of Kingswood Forest in the thirteenth century. He was appointed Governor of Bristol Castle in 1223. He died in 1237.

WILLIS ROAD, BS15. There are two possibilities here: this was either named after the magistrate Captain Horace Willis, or after the local councillor Henry Ambrose Willis.

WILLMENT WAY, BS11. This is named after one of the directors of the development company.

WILLMOTT CLOSE, BS14. Named after Cllr. Roy Willmott, a Bedminster butcher.

WILLOUGHBY CLOSE, BS13. This road is thought to be named for the Willoughby family who hailed from Lincolnshire but had strong connections with the West of England.

WILLOUGHBY ROAD, BS7. This was named after Harry Willoughby Beloe, who was President of the Bristol Rugby Football Club.

WILLOW CLOSE, BS15. This road name probably continues the trees theme, although Poplar Road was called after a defunct farm.

WILLOW CLOSE, BS12. All the roads in this little pocket are named after trees.

WILLOW GROVE, BS16. This is another of the roads named after trees in the area once called The Thicket. *See Thicket Road.*

WILLOW ROAD, BS15. The majority of the roads in this district of Hanham have names to do with trees.

WILLOWFIELD, BS13. This name was requested by the residents of the complex in keeping with other sylvan names nearby.

THE WILLOWS, BS16. All roads in this group are called after trees.

WILLS DRIVE, BS5. Sir Frank Wills was Lord Mayor of Bristol in 1911. Another famous Wills was Charles, who was Sheriff of Bristol in 1898.

WILLSBRIDGE HILL, BS15. This leads to the village of that name.

WILLWAY STREET, BS2 / BS3. There were two major firms of this name in the Bristol area - the dyers and cleaners and an engineering firm. Harris feels the latter is the one to which the Bedminster street and the one in St. Philip's owe their name.

WILMOT COURT, BS15. This was the name of the people who lived at Hawthorne House in 1899.

WILSHIRE AVENUE, BS15. This avenue was named after Fred Wilshire, who began his life as a tea boy on the Great Western Railway but was persuaded to take up a singing career on account of his outstanding voice. Although successful he was then advised to follow a more stable career, so be became a barrister and ended his career as a judge. He is a relative of the well-known local writer, Lewis Wilshire.

WILSON PLACE / STREET, BS2. Developed in the latter part of the eighteenth century these appear to be named after Christopher Wilson, Bishop of Bristol from 1783-92. He presented a chalice to nearby St. Paul's church. He died in 1792.

WILTON COURT, BS10. This is called after a Wiltshire village, as are other roads in the area.

WILTSHIRE PLACE, BS15. Cannock Avenue is in this area. John Cannock had a large following in Wiltshire.

WIMBLEDON ROAD, BS7. This is another famous stadium name in keeping with adjoining roads.

WIMBORNE ROAD, BS3. Many local roads have been given place names in the West of England.

WINASH CLOSE, BS4. Named after an old house built on this land in around 1750 and demolished around 1960. The Winash family were landowners in Brislington from the eighteenth century until 1908.

WINCHCOMBE GROVE, BS11. This is one among a large group of roads named after Cotswold villages.

WINCHESTER AVENUE / ROAD, BS4. This follows the pattern hereabouts of naming roads after public schools.

WINCROFT, BS15. Probably a field name.

WINDCLIFF CRESCENT, BS11. This is a field name taken from the enclosure awards. There is a Wynd Cliff above the Wye to the north of Chepstow, a precipice and viewpoint.

WINDERMERE ROAD, BS12. All roads nearby are named after lakes.

WINDERMERE ROAD, BS15. Locations in the Lake District is the theme for this group of roads. The sheltered accommodation here also bears the name.

WINDMILL CLOSE / HILL, BS3. Prior to development there was a windmill on the crown of the hill.

WINDMILL LANE, BS11. This is not far from the site of an old windmill.

WINDSOR AVENUE, BS5. There was a builder in Bristol of this name at the time these houses were built. Alternatively, people of that name lived in the area and may have owned the land.

WINDSOR COURT / PLACE / TERRACE, BS8. All these Clifton roads are named because they stand high above the city in a similar manner to Windsor Castle, according to Harris. The Terrace with its magnificent view of the Avon, Bristol and the hills beyond, is today one of the landmark sights of the city. It was formerly known as Watts' Folly because the enterprise bankrupted the builder, William Watts. This was the same man who invented the shot tower method of producing lead shot.

WINDSOR COURT / PLACE, BS16. Royal residences and associations are favoured in this locality.

WINDSOR GROVE, BS5. This is another among roads in the area with royal associations. Brighton Road, which lies nearby, was a favourite resort of the Prince Regent, later George IV.

WINDSOR ROAD, BS6. Many roads in this area have royal connections in their names.

WINDSOR TERRACE, BS3. These houses were begun in 1868 and finally completed in 1881. This was the year of a Royal visit by Albert, Duke of Edinburgh, son of Queen Victoria. As he was born in Windsor Castle on 6 August 1844 this may have been the reason for the naming of this terrace.

WINE STREET, BS1. Originally this was known as Winch Street. It is said that a pillory worked by a winch was sited at the east end of this street. A 'wynch' was also used for winding up the castle drawbridge nearby.

Wine Street c. 1920s

WINEBERRY CLOSE, BS5. Varieties of berries were the choice for naming roads in this area. The wineberry is also known as the whinberry and whortleberry and is West Country dialect for redcurrant or gooseberry.

WINFORD GROVE, BS13. Many roads round here have been named after Somerset towns and villages.

WINGFIELD ROAD, BS3. This is the name of three villages in the British Isles. The first syllable means meadow, pasture or grazing ground.

WINKWORTH PLACE, BS2. This is named after two sisters Catherine and Susanna, local philanthropists. Catherine (1827-78) was a governor of Red Maids School and a promoter of Clifton High School for Girls. Susanna (1820-84) was one of the first people to take an interest in the housing problems of Bristol, especially in the tenements of Hotwells, the poor area of Clifton. Decent housing for the poor was built at Jacobs Wells Industrial Buildings, on her initiative, revolutionary for the time with their built-in comforts of gas and running water, and she took responsibility for their management. Between them the sisters made a considerable impact on improvements in education and social conditions for the poor of Bristol.

WINSFORD STREET, BS5. This is a place name - a village in Somerset. One authority gives the first syllable as the personal name, Wine.

WINSHAM CLOSE, BS14. As with other roads locally, this is named after a Somerset village.

WINSLEY ROAD, BS6. This is another village in Somerset. The meaning is 'Wine's Lea or pasture'.

WINTERSTOKE CLOSE / ROAD, BS3. Winterstoke was the name of one of the ancient Somerset hundreds (church parishes). Sir William Henry Wills was created Lord Winterstoke in 1906. He donated a large sum towards the building of the art gallery and the University. *See Wills Drive.*

WINTON STREET, BS4. Walter de Winton was Mayor of Bristol in 1224.

WITCH HAZEL ROAD, BS13. This name is listed as a holding in the Dundry Enclosure Award of 1815. Witch is probably from the OE '*wic*' meaning a dwelling used for a specific purpose, such as a dairy farm. Legend has it that the twigs of the witch hazel, or wych hazel, are capable of divining the presence of gold and silver.

WITCHELL ROAD, BS5. Named after Albert William Witchell Goulter, civil engineer and surveyor. He may have been a descent of Thomas Witchell, Lord of the manor of Kingswood in 1712.

WITHERLIES ROAD, BS16. The owners of a mill which once stood on the river Frome to the south of this development in the 1830s were called Wytherlies.

WITHEY CLOSE EAST / WEST, BS9. This is thought to be an old field name.

WITHINGTON CLOSE, BS15. There is a village in Gloucestershire of this name, but the significance is unclear.

WITHLEIGH ROAD, BS4. The name relates to a village in Devon. The first syllable means willow.

WITHYPOOL GARDENS, BS14. This is named after a Somerset village the meaning of which is willow pool.

WITHYWOOD GARDENS / ROAD, BS13. Withywood was a farm, the subject of a compulsory purchase order when the housing development was planned. The name is derived from the OE '*wioig*', willow, hence it means the 'willow wood'.

WOBURN CLOSE, BS15. This is sited among other roads all named after abbeys.

WOBURN ROAD, BS5. The name relates to the famous abbey in Bedfordshire, seat of the Dukes of Bedford, and comes from the OE *woburna*, 'crooked winding stream'. The Cottrell-Dormer family connection exists here as with other locations used for roads in the area.

WOLFERTON ROAD, BS6. The name comes from the village in Norfolk. The first syllable is a personal noun.

WOLFRIDGE GARDENS, BS10. This was a wood in the Henbury Hundred. The OE meaning is 'a ridge haunted by a wolf'.

WOLSELEY ROAD, BS6. This road is named after Garnet Joseph, Field Marshal the Viscount Wolseley (1833-1913). He fought in numerous campaigns including the Crimea, the Indian Mutiny, the Zulu War, Egypt and the Nile expedition.

WOOD END WALK, BS9. This name taken from the Westbury tithe map.

WOOD ROAD, BS15. There is probably a forest connection here.

WOOD STREET, BS5. This may well be the name of the builder, as there was a James Wood who had a building business. He was listed in the 1872 directory as living at Argyle House, Stanley Street, off Stapleton Road.

WOODBINE ROAD, BS5. This name comes from Woodbine Cottage where the Davis family lived. One of the clan was Richard Hart Davis, M.P. for Bristol in 1812-31.

WOODBOROUGH STREET, BS5. This is a place name meaning 'fort built of wood' or 'fort in a wood'. Originally this was called Woodborough Road.

WOODBRIDGE ROAD, BS4. Apparently this is named after a small town in Suffolk. It means 'wooden bridge'.

WOODBURY LANE, BS6. No reason for this naming has been discovered.

WOODCHESTER ROAD, BS10. This is the name of a place in Gloucestershire where Roman remains were found. The name means Roman fort in a wood or built of wood; 'chester' comes from the Latin *castra,* a camp.

WOODCHESTER, BS15. In all probability this was named for the same reason as BS10.

WOODCOTE ROAD / WALK, BS16. This is named in keeping with the thicket theme. *See Thicket Road.*

WOODCROFT AVENUE, BS5 / CLOSE / ROAD, BS4. This is a field name from the OE *wudu,* 'wood', and *croft* 'a small enclosure'.

WOODEND, BS15. Self-explanatory.

WOODFIELD ROAD, BS6. The name is taken from the villa of that name mentioned in Morgan's Guide as 'near Messrs. Garraway's nurseries'.

WOODGROVE ROAD, BS11. This is thought to be a field name.

WOODHALL CLOSE, BS16. This is named after B. W. Woodhall, the councillor for Downend Ward, Mangotsfield Urban District Council, in 1939.

WOODHOUSE GROVE, BS7. This grove was built in the 1960s on the land of the Rectory orchard, which had been sold in order to restore the Rectory to its original 1822 dimensions. It may have been named after the County Camp Site at Almondsbury which is used by the Scouts.

WOODINGTON COURT, BS15. Woodingtons were boot manufacturers who had their premises in Hillside Road, at the junction with Kenn Road.

WOODLAND AVENUE, BS15. Self-explanatory.

WOODLAND GROVE, BS9. This was named in keeping with the general sylvan theme.

WOODLAND ROAD / TERRACE, BS6. These roads were developed in the third quarter of the nineteenth century in Tyndall's Park on the wooded section of the estate.

WOODLAND WAY, BS16. This is a reference to the original topography.

WOODLAND TERRACE, BS15. Descriptive.

WOODLANDS / WOODLANDS RISE, BS16. Self-explanatory.

WOODLEAZE, BS15. This is an old field name, apparently.

WOODLEIGH GARDENS, BS14. This is named after the village in Devon, the name meaning woodland glade.

WOODMANCOTE ROAD, BS7. Named after the village near Dursley, Gloucestershire. It means 'woodman's cottage'. Bristol Corporation owned the Manor of Woodmancote.

WOODMARSH CLOSE, BS14. This is almost certainly a field name.

WOODMEAD GARDENS, BS13. Woodmead is a holding included in the Dundry Enclosure Award of 1815.

THE WOODNOOK, BS12. Situated in Wigton Crescent, this is called after a location in the Wigton area.

WOODSIDE GROVE, BS10. This is near Moorgrove Wood.

WOODSIDE ROAD, BS4. The road is situated beside St. Anne's Wood.

WOODSIDE, BS9. This is a perfect description of the location.

WOODSTOCK AVENUE / ROAD, BS6. This is another road on the Sir Walter Scott theme. This was the title of a novel he had published in 1826, the subject matter being Charles II's escape after the Battle of Worcester in 1651.

WOODSTOCK CLOSE / ROAD, BS5. This area was known as Woodstock in years gone by.

WOODVIEW CLOSE, BS11. Descriptive.

WOODWARD DRIVE, BS15. The Woodward family purchased the Weston estate in 1794.

WOODWELL ROAD, BS11. This is named after Woodwell Lake, on the eastern banks of the Avon and mentioned in documents dating back to 1373.

WOODYLEAZE DRIVE, BS15. This is an old field name.

WOOLCOT STREET, BS6. This is the only street in Redland, and adjoining it in lower Redland Road is a little row of Woolcot Cottages. According to the 1910 OS map, Woolcott Park was the name of the area centred around Chandos Road. Latimer states that in 1857 'in one somewhat extensive estate styled Woolcott Park a great number of houses were built'.

WOOLLEY ROAD, BS14. Mrs Alice Woolley was resident in Whitchurch in August 1674. She was exempt from paying the Hearth Tax.

WOOTTON CRESCENT / PARK / ROAD, BS4. This is a place name, the first syllable originating from the OE '*wudu*', meaning wood.

WORCESTER CLOSE, BS16. This street is built on land once owned by the Dukes of Beaufort. The elder son always took the title of Earl of Worcester. *See Fitzroy Road.*

WORCESTER CRESCENT / TERRACE, BS8 / ROAD, BS8, BS15. This name is taken from the Marquis of Worcester, heir to the Duke of Beaufort - probably Henry Somerset, the 8th Duke, who succeeded to the title in 1854. He was M.P. for East Gloucestershire from 1846-53.

WORDSWORTH ROAD, BS7. William Wordsworth (1770-1850) is one of England's most famous poets. He lived in Somerset and Bristol for part of his life and was a lifelong friend of Samuel Taylor Coleridge and Robert Southey. John Cottle of Bristol published their *Lyrical Ballads. See Tintern Avenue.*

WORKSHOP ROAD, BS11. This is another of Avonmouth's famous industrial namings. This is part of the Britannia Zinc Works.

WORLD'S END LANE, BS18. This derives its name from World's End House, reputedly the oldest inhabited domestic house in Bristol.

WORRALL ROAD, BS8. Almost certainly named after Samuel Worrall III, who died in 1873. It was his enclosure of a part of what had been traditionally part of the Downs in the 1850s which provoked the City and Merchant Venturers to obtain the 1861 Act preserving Clifton and Durdham Downs as an open space to be enjoyed in perpetuity by the people of Bristol. Originally only the western part of Anglesey Place was known as Worrall's Road. In the 1870s the Worrall family sold the land upon which the surrounding roads, including Hughenden Road and Beaconsfield Road, were built.

WORSLEY STREET, BS5. This was named after the Manager of the Netham Chemical Co, Philip John Worsley, who is listed in the 1863 directory. He was a member of and benefactor to Bethesda church, in Church Road, BS5.

WORTH CLOSE, BS15. This may be named after John Worth, who for many years was a Captain in the Gloucestershire Volunteer Artillery.

WORTHING ROAD, BS12. Many place names have been used for roads in the area.

WORTHY ROAD, BS11. There is a family of this name in the area but the road was not named after them, so the origin is a mystery.

WRAXALL GROVE, BS3. This is amongst other roads called after Somerset villages.

WRAXHALL ROAD, BS15. A very old road. Its course was altered by the building of the ring road. It was built on a field of this name which was part of the Barrs Court Estate.

WREN DRIVE, BS16. This is one of the roads in Stapleton named after birds.

WRENBERT ROAD, BS15. Herbert Wren was the proprietor of the Cinematograph Theatre (later the Regal Cinema) in the early years of the twentieth century.

WRINGTON CRESCENT, BS3. All roads here are named after Somerset villages.

WROUGHTON DRIVE, BS13. John Choke, son and heir of Sir Richard Choke, married Elizabeth, daughter of Sir John Wroughton. Sir Richard bought Long Ashton in 1454. He subsequently became Judge and Justice of the Court of Common Pleas. He died c. 1483.

WYATT AVENUE / CLOSE, BS13. Edwin Wyatt was a member of Bishopsworth church choir for 88 years. He died in 1946 at the age of 97. He was working as a solicitor's clerk until a couple of days before his death.

WYCHWOOD, BS15. The Wychwood is an ancient woodland in West Oxfordshire. This leads off Elm Road and runs parallel to High Elm so clearly wych elms grew here once.

WYCK BECK ROAD, BS10. This is a field name. *Wyck* is a dairy farm and *beck* means brook, hence it means 'dairy farm by the brook'.

WYCLIFFE ROAD, BS9. John Wycliffe was first prebend of Aust in the College of Westbury. A prebend took a share in the revenues of the collegiate church.

WYCOMBE GROVE, BS4. This is named after the town in Buckinghamshire. The first syllable is OE *'wic'*, a dwelling, building used for a specific purpose, or hamlet.

WYE CROFT CLOSE, BS10. This is named after a house which once stood in the area.

WYEDALE AVENUE, BS9. This is a made-up name.

WYKIS COURT, BS15. The Wykis family held Oldland Manor in the late fifteenth century.

WYMBUSH CRESCENT / GARDENS, BS13. Richard Wymbush, by marrying Jane, daughter of Roger Lyveden in the fifteenth century, became possessed of a moiety (or half) of the Manor of Ashton Philips in the Hundred of Hartcliffe.

WYNDHAM CRESCENT, BS4. Anne Wyndham married Thomas Bridges, Sheriff of Gloucester, who was granted the Manor of Keynsham by Edward VI in 1552.

THE WYNSTONES, BS15. This was an old field name when all this was farmland.

YELVERTON ROAD, BS4. The name is derived from Elleford, a village on the verge of Rodborough Down in Devon, which in turn takes its name from the eighteenth century Elford family. Local dialect turned Elleford to Yelverton.

YEOMANS CLOSE, BS11. this is named after Sir Robert Yeomans, whose sister married Alderman William Cann, a former owner of the tithing of Stoke Bishop.

YEOMANSIDE CLOSE, BS14. No reason has been discovered for this naming.

YEW TREE COURT, BS13. A farm of this name used to stand on the site in the nineteenth century.

YEW TREE DRIVE, BS15. This road is among others with tree names.

YEWCROFT CLOSE, BS14. A made-up name.

YORK AVENUE, BS7 / GARDENS, BS8 / PLACE, BS8, BS1 / ROAD, BS3, BS5, BS6 / STREET, BS2, BS5, BS8. All the city streets of this name celebrate the various Dukes of York over the last two centuries.

YORK CLOSE, BS16. This is named after the racecourse, as are all the roads in this area.

YORK ROAD, BS15. There are other roads nearby with place names.

Z

ZED ALLEY, BS1. This is so named because of the zig-zag structure of the steps.

ZETLAND ROAD, BS6. This was built during the lifetime of the First Marquis of Zetland (created in 1892). He was Lord-in-Waiting to Queen Victoria. The family name is Dundas.

ZINC ROAD, BS11. This is another of Avonmouth's famous industrial namings. It lies in the Britannia Zinc works complex.

Bibliography

Abstract of Bristol Historical Statistics, Political Representation 1700-1997. Compiled by Spencer Jordan, Keith Renney and Matthew Woollard. *UWE Publication 1998.*

Anglo-Saxon England by Sir Frank Stenton. *Oxford University Press 1943. Repr. 1971.*

Arrowsmith's Directory of Bristol 1884 and 1906.Bishopston, Horfield and Ashley Down. Local History Society. *Tempus Publishing, Stroud 1997.*

Brislington Bulletins by D.P. Lindegaard. *Self-publication, Bristol 1992.*

Bristol and How It Grew by Dorothy Brown *Bristol Visual and Environmental Group, 1981.*

Bristol Before the Camera by Redcliffe Press in Association with Bristol Museum and Art Gallery, 2001

Bristol in the 18th Century. Edited by Patrick McGrath. *David and Charles, London 1972.*

Bristol Past and Present by Nicholls Taylor. *J.W.Arrowsmith, Bristol 1881.Bristol Times. Bristol Evening Post.*

The Brittons of Kingswood Chase by G. Britton Spilsbury. *Self-publication, Bristol 1985.*

Bygone Brislington by Jonathan Rowe and Diddie Williams. *Self-publication 1985.*

The City and County of Bristol by Brian Little. *S.R. Publishers, Bristol 1967.*

Collieries of Kingswood and South Gloucestershire by John Cornwell. *D.Brown, Bristol*

Cotham Walks by Stephen Jones, *Redland and Cotham Amenities Society, 1980.*

The Domesday Book (Gloucestershire) edited and translated by John S Moore. *Phillimore, Chichester 1982.*

English Place Names by Kenneth Cameron. *B.T.Batsford, London. 1961.*

Essays in Bristol and Gloucestershire History edited by Patrick McGrath and John Cannon. *Bristol and Gloucestershire Archaeological Society, 1976.*

Filton, Gloucestershire by W. L. Harris. *Privately published, 1995.*

Go Home and do the Washing! by Laura Brierley and Helen Reid. *Broadcast Books, 2000.*

Forest Heritage compiled by the Kingswood and District History Society.

Hanham Our Home (1920-1940) Hanham Local History Society. Privately printed.1983.

A Guide to Old English by Bruce Mitchell. *Blackwell Oxford 1965.*

The History of Bristol by John Evans. *Privately printed. Bristol 1824.*

A History of the Bristol Royal Infirmary by A. Munro Smith. *Arrowsmith, Bristol 1917.*

A History of Clifton by Donald Jones *Phillimore & Co Ltd 1992.*

The History of England by G. M. Trevelyan. *Longmans Green and Co. 1933.*

The History of Kingswood Forest by A. Braine. *Published 1891.*

Holy Wells of Bath and Bristol Region by Phil Quinn *Longaston Press Herefordshire 1999.*

Kelly's Directories of Bristol - various.

Kingswood Heritage Trail, Kingswood Borough Council.

Landmarks of Old Fishponds by Peter Brown.

Latimer's Annals of Bristol: Nineteenth Century, pub.1887, Eighteenth Century, pub.1893, Seventeenth Century, pub. 1900.

Life as it Was in Cadbury Heath and Warmley (3 vols) Cadbury Heath History Group.

Life in Siston and Warmley 1894-1994, edited by Alan Bryant and Tony Fry. *Siston Parish Council Centenary Committee 1994.*

An Oldland Boy Looks Back by David Noble. *Filmed by 1st Take Videos of Yate 1997.*

Our Parish - Mangotsfield by Rev. A.E.Jones. *Published 1899.*

Picture Past by David G. Elliot. *Self-publication, Bristol 1988.*

Place Names of Somerset by James Hill

Roman Britain by Peter Salway. *Oxford University Press 1981.*

St George, Redfield and Whitehall compiled by Andy Jones, David Stephenson, David Cheesley and Jill Willmott. *Tempus Publishing, Stroud 2001.*

Secret Underground Bristol by Sally Watson, *Broadcast Books 2002.*

Signposts to the Past by Margaret Gelling. *J.M. Dent London 1978.*

Sketchley's Bristol Directory of 1775 - *Kingsmead Reprints, Bath 1971.*

Sneyd Park by Michael Morgan. *Self-publication, Bristol 1987.*

A Social History of England by Asa Briggs. *Weidenfeld and Nicolson, London 1984.*

The Taxpayers of Medieval Gloucestershire by Peter Franklin *Alan Sutton Publishing Ltd, Stroud 1953.*

Through the Years by Paul and Jill Willmott. *Privately printed.*

www.districtweb.co.uk (local history information for Oldland, Cadbury Heath, Warmley, Bitton, Longwell Green)

Other books by Broadcast Books

Where Kingcups Grew
A Westcountry Childhood
Lewis Wilshire

One of the leading chroniclers of the West Country through many books, newspaper articles and broadcasts on BBC Radio Bristol and Somerset Sound, Lewis Wilshire's graceful and intelligent writings have charmed his readers for well over half a century. *Where Kingcups Grew* is the author's personal selection of stories about his childhood, largely spent with his beloved Gran and Granfer in their Soundwell cottage - at that time well beyond the outskirts of Bristol. Detailed here are eccentric relations and childhood companions, in a now-lost landscape of Methodism and hardship, amid the stone-walled meadows where kingcups once grew.

Hardback, £10.95, cassette £4.95.

Secret Underground Bristol
Sally Watson

Plunge into the secret world beneath your feet ... down mysterious tunnels and hidden waterways, through eerie caves and glittering grottoes, forgotten mines and nuclear bunkers. Discover an ancient castle moat, undreamt-of by the crowds on the pavements above, and a monstrous cavern beneath a pretty public park. Find out where the Crown Jewels were hidden from Hitler, and how a canny clergyman guarded his love-nest with access tunnels too narrow for his portly wife to negotiate.

Secret Underground Bristol - the most popular book ever written about the City - is back in response to public demand. This beautiful new edition has been substantially extended to take in exciting underground features beyond the City boundaries. Full of colour and highly entertaining, it is packed with the latest information, fascinating photographs and vivid maps.

Paperback, £14.95

Go Home and do the Washing!
Three centuries of Pioneering Bristol Women
by Lorna Brierley and Helen Reid

"The educated woman is the hinge on which society turns" said Hannah More, explaining her drive to educate the poverty-stricken girls and women of Bristol. This fascinating book traces the lives and works of over fifty pioneering women over the last 300 years, who lived and worked to help improve or entertain the lives of their fellow Bristolians: here are doctors, educators, reformers, philanthropists, suffragettes, writers, singers and artists, many of them given their just recognition at last after a century or more of obscurity.
Paperback, £9.95

Available from good local bookshops. In case of difficulty, please contact Catherine Mason on 0117 9732010, or visit www.broadcastbooks.co.uk
Broadcast Books also publishes a range of pet titles, for details see the publisher.